Practical C Programming

Practical C Programming
Third Edition

Steve Oualline

O'REILLY®

Beijing · Cambridge · Farnham · Köln · Paris · Sebastopol · Taipei · Tokyo

Practical C Programming, Third Edition
by Steve Oualline

Published by O'Reilly & Associates, Inc., 101 Morris Street, Sebastopol, CA 95472.

Editor, First and Second Editions: Tim O'Reilly

Editor, Third Edition: Andy Oram

Production Editor: Nicole Gipson Arigo

Printing History:

July 1991:	First Edition.
August 1992:	Minor corrections.
January 1993:	Second Edition. Bugs fixed; programs all now conform to ANSI C.
June 1993:	Minor corrections.
August 1997:	Third Edition.

ISBN: 1-56592-306-5   [11/01]
[M]

Table of Contents

Preface

This book is devoted to practical C programming. C is currently the premier language for software developers. That's because it's widely distributed and standard. Newer languages are available, such as C++, but these are still evolving. C is still the language of choice for robust, portable programming.

This book emphasizes the skills you will need to do real-world programming. It teaches you not only the mechanics of the C language, but the entire life cycle of a C program as well (including the program's conception, design, code, methods, debugging, release, documentation, maintenance, and revision).

Good style is emphasized. To create a good program you must do more than just type in code. It is an art in which writing and programming skills blend themselves together to form a masterpiece. True art can be created. A well-written program not only functions correctly, but is simple and easy to understand. Comments allow the programmer to include descriptive text inside the program. When clearly written, a commented program is highly prized.

A program should be as simple as possible. A programmer should avoid clever tricks. This book stresses simple, practical rules. For example, there are 15 operator precedence rules in C. These can be simplified into two rules:

1. Multiply and divide come before add and subtract.

2. Put parentheses around everything else.

Consider two programs. One was written by a clever programmer using all the tricks. The program contains no comments, but it works. The other program is well commented and nicely structured, but it doesn't work. Which program is more useful? In the long run, the broken one. It can be fixed. Although the clever program works now, sooner or later all programs have to be modified. The worst thing that you will ever have to do is to modify a cleverly written program.

This handbook is written for people with no previous programming experience or programmers who already know C and want to improve their style and reliability. You should have access to a computer and know how to use the basic functions such as a text editor and the filesystem.

Specific instructions are given for producing and running programs using the UNIX operating system with a generic *cc* compiler or the Free Software Foundation's *gcc* compiler. For MS-DOS/Windows users, instructions are included for Borland C++, Turbo C++, and Microsoft Visual C++. (These compilers compile both C and C++ code.) The book also gives examples of using the programming utility *make* for automated program production.

How This Book is Organized

You must crawl before you walk. In Part I, *Basics*, we teach you how to crawl. These chapters enable you to write very simple programs. We start with the mechanics of programming and programming style. Next, you learn how to use variables and very simple decision and control statements. In Chapter 7, *Programming Process*, we take you on a complete tour of the software life cycle to show you how real programs are created.

Part II, *Simple Programming*, describes all of the other simple statements and operators that are used in programming. You'll also learn how to organize these statements into simple functions.

In Part III, *Advanced Programming Concepts*, we take our basic declarations and statements and learn how they can be used in the construction of advanced types such as structures, unions, and classes. We'll also introduce the concept of pointers. Finally, a number of miscellaneous features are described Part IV, *Other Language Features*.

Chapter by Chapter

Chapter 1, *What Is C?*, gives a brief description of the C language and its use. This chapter includes some background on the history of the language.

Chapter 2, *Basics of Program Writing*, explains the basic programming process and gives you enough information to write a very simple program.

Chapter 3, *Style*, discusses programming style. Commenting a program is covered, as well as writing clear and simple code.

Chapter 4, *Basic Declarations and Expressions,* introduces you to simple C statements. Basic variables and the assignment statement are covered in detail, along with arithmetic operators +, -, *, /, and %.

Chapter 5, *Arrays, Qualifiers, and Reading Numbers,* covers arrays and more complex variables. Shorthand operators such as ++ and %= are also described.

Chapter 6, *Decision and Control Statements,* explains simple decision statements including **if, else,** and **for.** A discussion of == versus = is presented.

Chapter 7, *Programming Process,* takes you through all the necessary steps to create a simple program from specification through release. Structured programming, fast prototyping, and debugging are also discussed.

Chapter 8, *More Control Statements,* describes additional control statements. Included are **while, break,** and **continue.** The **switch** statement is discussed in detail.

Chapter 9, *Variable Scope and Functions,* introduces local variables, functions, and parameters.

Chapter 10, *C Preprocessor,* describes the C preprocessor, which gives the programmer tremendous flexibility in writing code. The chapter also provides the programmer with a tremendous number of ways to mess up. Simple rules that help keep the preprocessor from becoming a problem are described.

Chapter 11, *Bit Operations,* discusses the logical C operators that work on bits.

Chapter 12, *Advanced Types,* explains structures and other advanced types. The **sizeof** operator and the **enum** type are included.

Chapter 13, *Simple Pointers,* introduces C pointer variables and shows some of their uses.

Chapter 14, *File Input/Output,* describes both buffered and unbuffered input/output. ASCII and binary files are discussed, and you are shown how to construct a simple file.

Chapter 15, *Debugging and Optimization,* describes how to debug a program, as well as how to use an interactive debugger. You are shown not only how to debug a program, but also how to write a program so that it is easy to debug. This chapter also describes many optimization techniques for making your program run faster and more efficiently.

Chapter 16, *Floating Point,* uses a simple decimal floating-point format to introduce you to the problems inherent in floating point, such as roundoff error, precision loss, overflow, and underflow.

Chapter 17, *Advanced Pointers,* describes advanced uses of pointers for constructing dynamic structures such as linked lists and trees.

Chapter 18, *Modular Programming,* shows how to split a program into several files and use modular programming techniques. The *make* utility is explained in more detail.

Chapter 19, *Ancient Compilers,* describes the old, pre-ANSI C language and associated compilers. Although such compilers are rare today, a lot of code was written for them and there are still a large number of programs out there that use the old syntax.

Chapter 20, *Portability Problems,* describes the problems that can occur when you *port* a program (move it from one machine to another).

Chapter 21, *C's Dustier Corners,* describes the **do/while** statement, the , operator, and the ? and : operators.

Chapter 22, *Putting It All Together,* details the steps necessary to take a complex program from conception to completion. Information-hiding and modular programming techniques are emphasized.

Chapter 23, *Programming Adages,* lists some programming adages that will help you construct good C programs.

Appendix A, *ASCII Table,* lists the octal, hexadecimal, and decimal representations of the ASCII character set that is now in almost universal use.

Appendix B, *Ranges and Parameter Passing Conversions,* lists the limits you can expect to come up against in handling numbers with various sizes of memory allocation.

Appendix C, *Operator Precedence Rules,* lists those impossible-to-remember rules, to help you when you encounter code written by rude people who didn't use enough parentheses.

Appendix D, *A Program to Compute a Sine Using a Power Series,* illustrates the manipulation of floating-point (real) numbers, which did not receive complete attention in the rest of the book.

The *Glossary* defines many of the technical terms used throughout the book.

Computer languages are best learned by writing and debugging programs. Sweating over a broken program at 2:00 in the morning only to find you typed "=" where you should have typed "==" is a very effective learning experience. There are many programming examples used throughout this book. Some examples don't work as expected and are posed as questions for the reader to solve. You are encouraged to enter each into your computer, run the program, and debug it. These exercises will introduce you to common errors in short programs so that you will know how to spot and correct them in larger programs of your own. You will find answers to questions at the end of each chapter. Also, at the end of many chapters, you will find a section called "Programming Exercises." These sections contain exercises that might be used in a programming class to test your knowledge of C programming.

Notes on the Third Edition

The C language has evolved since the first edition of *Practical C Programming* was published. Back then, ANSI compilers were rare and compilers that accepted the K&R syntax were common. Now the reverse is true.

The third edition reflects the industry shift to ANSI compilers. All programs and examples have been updated to conform to the ANSI standard. In fact, the older K&R syntax is discussed only in Chapter 19.

Other changes/additions to the book include:

* Additional instructions for more compilers including a generic UNIX compiler, the Free Software Foundations *gcc* compilers, Borland C++, Turbo C++, and Microsoft Visual C++.

* A completely rewritten Chapter 22. This chapter now uses a statistics program that should be more relevant to a larger number of readers.

Finally, I am a practical person. I tend to believe that if you know what I mean and I know what I mean, then the language has served its purpose. Throughout this book, I use the word "he" to denote a programmer. A few people in the "Politically Correct" crowd have labeled this practice as sexist. They also have labeled some passages in the book as being violent or racist.

Please note that when I use "he," I refer to a programmer, with no regard to gender. Secondly, when I suggest that some bad programmers should be shot, I do not speak literally.

My style has always been to communicate things clearly, concisely, and with a bit of humor. I regret any offense that this might cause anyone.

Font Conventions

The following conventions are used in this book:

Italic

is used for directories and filenames, and to emphasize new terms and concepts when they are introduced. Italic is also used to highlight comments in examples.

Bold

is used for C keywords.

`Constant Width`

is used in text for programs and the elements of a program and in examples to show the contents of files or the output from commands. A reference in text to a word or item used in an example or code fragment is also shown in constant-width font.

`Constant Bold`

is used in examples to show commands or other text that should be typed literally by the user. (For example, **`rm foo`** instructs you to type "rm foo" exactly as it appears in the text or example.)

`Constant Italic`

is used in examples to show variables for which a context-specific substitution should be made. (The variable *`filename`*, for example, would be replaced by some actual filename.)

" "

are used to identify system messages or code fragments in explanatory text.

%

is the UNIX shell prompt.

[]

surround optional values in a description of program syntax. (The brackets themselves should never be typed.)

. . .

stands for text (usually computer output) that's been omitted for clarity or to save space.

The notation CTRL–X or ^X indicates use of *control* characters. The notation instructs you to hold down the "control" key while typing the character "x". We denote other keys similarly (e.g., **RETURN** indicates a carriage return).

All examples of command lines are followed by a **RETURN** unless otherwise indicated.

Obtaining Source Code

The exercises in this book are available electronically by FTP and FTPMAIL. Use FTP if you are directly on the Internet. Use FTPMAIL if you are not on the Internet but can send and receive electronic mail to Internet sites. (This includes CompuServe users.)

FTP

If you have an Internet connection (permanent or dialup), the easiest way to use FTP is via your web browser or favorite FTP client. To get the examples, simply point your browser to:

ftp://ftp.oreilly.com/published/oreilly/nutshell/practical_c3/examples.tar.gz

If you don't have a web browser, you can use the command-line FTP client included with Windows NT (or Windows 95). If you are on a PC, you can get *examples.zip* instead of *examples.tar.gz*.

```
% ftp ftp.oreilly.com
Connected to ftp.oreilly.com.
220 ftp.oreilly.com FTP server (Version 6.34 Thu Oct 22 14:32:01 EDT 1992)
ready.
Name (ftp.oreilly.com:username): anonymous
331 Guest login ok, send e-mail address as password.
Password: username@hostname            Use your username and host here
230 Guest login ok, access restrictions apply.
ftp> cd /published/oreilly/nutshell/practical_c3
250 CWD command successful.
ftp> binary
200 Type set to I.
ftp> get examples.tar.gz
200 PORT command successful.
150 Opening BINARY mode data connection for examples.tar.gz (xxxx bytes).
226 Transfer complete. local: exercises remote: exercises
xxxx bytes received in xxx seconds (xxx Kbytes/s)
ftp> quit
221 Goodbye.
%
```

FTPMAIL

FTPMAIL is a mail server available to anyone who can send electronic mail to, and receive electronic mail from, Internet sites. Any company or service provider that allows email connections to the Internet can access FTPMAIL.

You send mail to *ftpmail@online.oreilly.com*. In the message body, give the FTP commands you want to run. The server will run anonymous FTP for you, and mail the files back to you. To get a complete help file, send a message with no subject and the single word "help" in the body. The following is an example mail message that gets the examples. This command sends you a listing of the files in the selected directory and the requested example files. The listing is useful if you are interested in a later version of the examples. If you are on a PC, you can get *examples.zip* instead of *examples.tar.gz*.

```
Subject:
reply-to username@hostname        (Message Body) Where you want files mailed
open
```

```
cd /published/oreilly/nutshell/practical_c3
dir
mode binary
uuencode
get examples.tar.gz
quit
.
```

A signature at the end of the message is acceptable as long as it appears after "quit."

Comments and Questions

We have tested and verified all of the information in this book to the best of our ability, but you may find that features have changed (or even that we have made mistakes!). Please let us know about any errors you find, as well as your suggestions for future editions, by writing to:

O'Reilly & Associates, Inc.
101 Morris Street
Sebastopol, CA 95472
1-800-998-9938 (in US or Canada)
1-707-829-0515 (international/local)
1-707-829-0104 (FAX)

You can also send us messages electronically. To be put on the mailing list or request a catalog, send email to:

info@oreilly.com (via the Internet)

To ask technical questions or comment on the book, send email to:

bookquestions@oreilly.com (via the Internet)

We have a web site for the book, where we'll list examples, errata, and any plans for future editions. You can access this page at:

http://www.oreilly.com/catalog/pcp3/

For more information about this book and others, see the O'Reilly web site:

http://www.oreilly.com

Acknowledgments

I wish to thank my father for his help in editing and Arthur Marquez for his aid in formatting this book.

I am grateful to all the gang at the Writers' Haven and Bookstore, Pearl, Alex, and Clyde, for their continued support. Thanks to Peg Kovar for help in editing. Special thanks to Dale Dougherty for ripping apart my book and forcing me to put it together right. My thanks also go to the production group of O'Reilly & Associates—especially Rosanne Wagger and Mike Sierra—for putting the finishing touches on this book. Finally, Jean Graham deserves a special credit for putting up with my writing all these years.

Acknowledgments to the Third Edition

Special thanks to Andy Oram, the technical editor. Thanks also to the production staff at O'Reilly & Associates. Nicole Gipson Arigo was the project manager. Claire-marie Fisher O'Leary and Sheryl Avruch performed quality control checks. Mike Sierra worked with the tools to create the book. Chris Reilley and Robert Romano fine-tuned the figures. Nancy Priest designed the interior book layout, and Edie Freedman designed the front cover. Production assistance, typesetting, and indexing provided by Benchmark Productions, Inc.

I

Basics

This part of the book teaches you the basic constructs of the C language. When you're finished, you'll be able to write well-designed and well-thought-out C programs. Style is emphasized early so that you can immediately start writing programs using a good programming style. Although you'll be limited to small programs throughout this part, they'll be well-written ones.

- Chapter 1, *What Is C?*, gives a brief description of the C language and its use. This chapter includes some background on the history of the language.

- Chapter 2, *Basics of Program Writing*, explains the basic programming process and gives you enough information to write a very simple program.

- Chapter 3, *Style*, discusses programming style. Commenting a program is covered, as well as writing clear and simple code.

- Chapter 4, *Basic Declarations and Expressions*, introduces you to simple C statements. Basic variables and the assignment statement are covered in detail, along with arithmetic operators +, -, *, /, and %.

- Chapter 5, *Arrays, Qualifiers, and Reading Numbers*, covers arrays and more complex variables. Shorthand operators such as ++ and %= are also described.

- Chapter 6, *Decision and Control Statements*, explains simple decision statements including **if**, **else**, and **for**. A discussion of == versus = is presented.

- Chapter 7, *Programming Process*, takes you through all the necessary steps to create a simple program from specification through release. Structured programming, fast prototyping, and debugging are also discussed.

1

What Is C?

Profanity is the one language that all programmers understand.

—Anon.

The ability to organize and process information is the key to success in the modern age. Computers are designed to handle and process large amounts of information quickly and efficiently, but they can't do anything until someone tells them what to do.

That's where C comes in. C is a programming language that allows a software engineer to efficiently communicate with a computer.

C is a highly flexible and adaptable language. Since its creation in 1970, it's been used for a wide variety of programs including firmware for micro-controllers, operating systems, applications, and graphics programming.

C is one of the most most widely used languages in the world and is fairly stable. An improved C language called C++ has been invented, but it is still in development, and its definition is still being worked on. C++, originally known as C with Classes, adds a number of new features to the C language, the most important of which is the class. Classes facilitate code reuse through object-oriented design (OOD).

Which is better, C or C++? The answer depends on who you talk to. C++ does great things for you behind your back, such as automatically calling constructors and destructors for variables. This processing makes some types of programming easy, but it makes static checking of programs difficult, and you need to be able to tell exactly what your program is doing if you are working on embedded control applications. So some people consider C++ the better language because it does things automatically and C doesn't. Other people consider C better for precisely the same reason.

Also, C++ is a relatively new language that's still changing. Much more C code exists than C++ code, and that C code will need to be maintained and upgraded. So C will be with us for a long time to come.

How Programming Works

Communicating with computers is not easy. They require instructions that are exact and detailed. It would be nice if we could write programs in English. Then we could tell the computer, "Add up all my checks and deposits, then tell me the total," and the machine would balance our checkbook.

But English is a lousy language when it comes to writing exact instructions. The language is full of ambiguity and imprecision. Grace Hopper, the grand old lady of computing, once commented on the instructions she found on a bottle of shampoo:

Wash
Rinse
Repeat

She tried to follow the directions, but she ran out of shampoo. (Wash-Rinse-Repeat. Wash-Rinse-Repeat. Wash-Rinse-Repeat...)

Of course, we can try to write in precise English. We'd have to be careful and make sure to spell everything out and be sure to include instructions for every contingency. But if we worked really hard, we could write precise English instructions.

It turns out that there is a group of people who spend their time trying to write precise English. They're called the government, and the documents they write are called government regulations. Unfortunately, in their effort to make the regulations precise, the government has made them almost unreadable. If you've ever read the instruction book that comes with your tax forms, you know what precise English can be like.

Still, even with all the extra verbiage that the government puts in, problems can occur. A few years ago California passed a law requiring all motorcycle riders to wear a helmet. Shortly after this law went into effect, a cop stopped a guy for not wearing one. The man suggested the policeman take a closer look at the law.

The law had two requirements: 1) that motorcycle riders have an approved crash helmet and 2) that it be firmly strapped on. The cop couldn't give the motorcyclist a ticket because he did have a helmet firmly strapped on—to his knee.

So English, with all its problems, is out. Now, how do we communicate with a computer?

The first computers cost millions of dollars, while at the same time a good programmer cost about $15,000 a year. Programmers were forced to program in a language in which all the instructions were reduced to a series of numbers, called *machine language*. This language could be directly input into the computer. A typical machine-language program looks like:

```
1010 1111
0011 0111
0111 0110
.. and so on for several hundred instructions
```

While machines "think" in numbers, people don't. To program these ancient machines, software engineers would write their programs using a simple language in which each word in the language stood for a single instruction. This language was called *assembly language* because the programmers had to hand translate, or assemble, each line into machine code.

A typical program might look like:

```
Program      Translation
MOV A,47 1  010 1111
ADD A,B      0011 0111
HALT         0111 0110
.. and so on for several hundred instructions
```

This process is illustrated by Figure 1-1.

Figure 1-1: Assembling a program

Translation was a difficult, tedious, and exacting task. One software engineer decided that this was a perfect job for a computer, so he wrote a program called an assembler that would do the job automatically.

He showed his new creation to his boss and was immediately chewed out: "How dare you even think of using such an expensive machine for a mere 'clerical' task." Given the cost of an hour of computer time versus the cost of an hour of programmer time, this attitude was not unreasonable.

Fortunately, as time passed the cost of programmers went up and the cost of computers went down. So letting the programmers write programs in assembly language and then using a program called an assembler to translate them into machine language became very cost effective.

Assembly language organized programs in a way that was easy for the programmers to understand. However, the program was more difficult for the machine to use. The program had to be translated before the machine could execute it. This method was the start of a trend. Programming languages became more and more convenient for the programmer to use, and started requiring more and more computer time for translation into something useful.

Over the years, a series of *higher-level* languages have been devised. These languages attempt to let the programmer write in a medium that is easy for him to understand, and that is also precise and simple enough for the computer to understand.

Early high-level languages were designed to handle specific types of applications. FORTRAN was designed for number crunching, COBOL was for writing business reports, and PASCAL was for student use. (Many of these languages have far outgrown their initial uses. Nicklaus Wirth has been rumored to have said, "If I had known that PASCAL was going to be so successful, I would have been more careful in its design.")

Brief History of C

In 1970 a programmer, Dennis Ritchie, created a new language called C. (The name came about because it superceded the old programming language he was using: B.) C was designed with one goal in mind: writing operating systems. The language was extremely simple and flexible, and soon was used for many different types of programs. It quickly became one of the most popular programming languages in the world.

C's popularity was due to two major factors. The first was that the language didn't get in the way of the programmer. He could do just about anything by using the proper C construct. (As we will see, this flexibility is also a drawback, as it allows the program to do things that the programmer never intended.)

The second reason that C is popular is that a portable C compiler was widely available. Consequently, people could attach a C compiler for their machine easily and with little expense.

In 1980, Bjarne Stroustrup started working on a new language, called "C with Classes." This language improved on C by adding a number of new features. This new language was improved and augmented, and finally became C++.

One of the newest languages, Java, is based on C++. Java was designed to be "C++ with the bugs fixed." At the time of this writing, Java has limited use despite being heavily marketed by Sun Microsystems and others.

How C Works

C is designed as a bridge between the programmer and the raw computer. The idea is to let the programmer organize a program in a way that he can easily understand. The compiler then translates the language into something that the machine can use.

Computer programs consist of two main parts: data and instructions. The computer imposes little or no organization on these two parts. After all, computers are designed to be as general as possible. The programmer should impose his organization on the computer, not the other way around.

The data in a computer is stored as a series of bytes. C organizes those bytes into useful data. Data declarations are used by the programmer to describe the information he is working with. For example:

```
int total;    /* Total number accounts */
```

tells C that we want to use a section of the computer's memory to store an integer named `total`. We let the compiler decide what particular bytes of memory to use; that decision is a minor bookkeeping detail that we don't want to worry about.

Our variable `total` is a simple variable. It can hold only one integer and describe only one total. A series of integers can be organized into an array as follows:

```
int balance[100];    /* Balance (in cents) for all 100 accounts */
```

Again, C will handle the details of imposing that organization on the computer's memory. Finally, there are more complex data types. For example, a rectangle might have a width, a height, a color, and a fill pattern. C lets us organize these four items into one group called a *structure*.

```
struct rectangle {
    int width;        /* Width of rectangle in pixels */
    int height;       /* Height of rectangle in pixels */
    color_type color; /* Color of the rectangle */
    fill_type fill;   /* Fill pattern */
};
```

The point is that structures allow the programmer to arrange the data to suit his needs no matter how simple or complex that data is. Translation of this data description into something the computer can use is the job of the compiler, not the programmer.

But data is only one part of a program. We also need instructions. As far as the computer is concerned, it knows nothing about the layout of the instructions. It knows what it's doing for the current instruction and where to get the next one, but nothing more.

C is a high-level language. It lets us write a high-level statement like:

```
area = (base * height) / 2.0;  /* Compute area of triangle */
```

The compiler will translate this statment into a series of cryptic low-level machine instructions. This sort of statement is called an *assignment statement*. It is used to compute and store the value of an arithmetic expression.

We can also use *control statements* to control the order of processing. Statements like the **if** and **switch** statements enable the computer to make simple decisions. Statements can be repeated over and over again by using looping statements such as **while** and **for**.

Groups of statements can be wrapped to form functions. Thus, we only have to write a general-purpose function to draw a rectangle once, and then we can reuse it whenever we want to draw a new rectangle.

C provides the program with a rich set of *standard functions* that perform common functions such as searching, sorting, input, and output.

A set of related functions can be grouped together in a single source file. Many source files can be compiled and linked together to form a program.

One of the major goals of the C language is to organize instructions into reusable components. After all, you can write programs much faster if you can "borrow" most of your code from somewhere else. Groups of reusable functions can be combined into a library. In this manner, when you need, for example, a sort routine, you can grab the standard function **qsort** from the library and link it into your program.

The data declarations, structures and control statements, and other C language elements, are not for the computer's benefit. The computer can't tell the difference between a million random bytes and a real program. All the C language elements are designed to allow the programmer to express and organize his ideas clearly in a manner tailored to him, not to the computer.

Organization is the key to writing good programs. For example, in this book you know that the Table of Contents is in the front and the Index is in the back. We use this structure because books are organized that way. Organization makes this book easier to use.

The C language lets you organize your programs using a simple yet powerful syntax. This book goes beyond the C syntax and teaches you style rules that enable you to make highly readable and reliable programs. By combining a powerful syntax with good programming style, you can create powerful programs that perform complex and wonderful operations, yet are also organized in a way that makes them easy for you to understand when change time comes around.

How to Learn C

There is only one way to learn how to program and that is to write programs. You'll learn a lot more by writing and *debugging* programs than you ever will by reading this book. This book contains many programming exercises. You should try to do as many of them as possible. When you do the exercises, keep good programming style in mind. Always comment your programs, even if you're only doing the exercises for yourself. Commenting helps you organize your thoughts and keeps you in practice when you go into the real world.

Don't let yourself be seduced by the idea that "I'm only writing these programs for myself, so I don't need to comment them." First of all, code that looks obvious to a programmer as he writes it is often confusing and cryptic when he revisits it a week later. Writing comments also helps you to get organized before you write the actual code. (If you can write out an idea in English, you're halfway to writing it in C.)

Finally, programs tend to be around far longer than expected. I once wrote a program that was designed to work only on the computer at Caltech. The program was highly system-dependent. Because I was the only one who would ever use it, the program would print the following message if you got the command line wrong:

```
?LSTUIT User is a twit
```

A few years later, I was a student at Syracuse University, and the Secretary at the School of Computer Science needed a program that was similar to my Caltech listing program. So I adapted my program for her use. Unfortunately, I forgot about the error message.

Imagine how horrified I was when I came into the Computer Science office and was accosted by the Chief Secretary. This lady had so much power that she could make the Dean cringe. She looked at me and said, "User is a twit, huh!" Luckily she had a sense of humor, or I wouldn't be here today.

Sprinkled throughout this book are many broken programs. Spend the time to figure out why they don't work. Often, the problem is very subtle, such as a misplaced semicolon or the use of = instead of ==. These programs let you learn how to spot mistakes in a small program. Then, when you make similar mistakes in a big program, and you *will* make mistakes, you will be trained to spot them.

2

Basics of Program Writing

The first and most important thing of all, at least for writers today, is to strip language clean, to lay it bare down to the bone.

—Ernest Hemingway

Programs start as a set of instructions written by a human being. Before they can be used by the computer, they must undergo several transformations. In this chapter, we'll learn how to enter a program, transform it into something the machine can use, and run it. Detailed steps are provided for the most popular UNIX and DOS/Windows compilers.

Programs from Conception to Execution

C programs are written in a high-level language using letters, numbers, and the other symbols you find on a computer keyboard. Computers actually execute a very low-level language called *machine code* (a series of numbers). So, before a program level can be used, it must undergo several transformations.

Programs start out as an idea in a programmer's head. He uses a text editor to write his thoughts into a file called a *source file*, containing *source code*. This file is transformed by the *compiler* into an *object file*. Next, a program called the *linker* takes the object file, combines it with predefined routines from a *standard library*, and produces an *executable program* (a set of machine-language instructions). In the following sections, we'll see how these various forms of the program work together to produce the final program.

Figure 2-1 shows the steps that must be taken to transform a program written in a high-level language into a executable program.

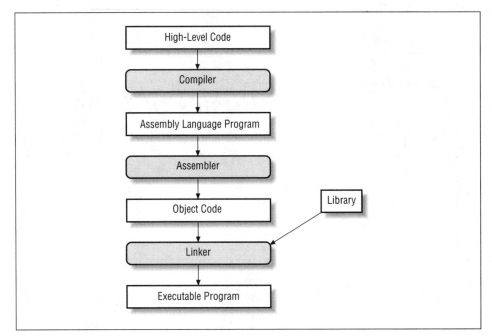

Figure 2-1: Transformation of a high-level language into a program

Wrappers

Fortunately you don't have to run the compiler, assembler, and linker individually. Most C compilers use "wrapper" programs that determine which tools need to be run and then run them.

Some programming systems go even further and provide the developer with an Integrated Development Environment (IDE). The IDE contains an editor, compiler, linker, project manager, debugger, and more in one convenient package. Both Borland and Microsoft provide IDEs with their compilers.

Creating a Real Program

Before we can actually start creating our own programs, we need to know how to use the basic programming tools. In this section, we will take you step by step through the process of entering, compiling, and running a simple program.

We will describe how to use two different types of compilers. The first type is the standalone or command-line compiler. This type of compiler is operated in a batch mode from the command line. In other words, you type in a command, and the compiler turns your source code into an executable program.

The other type of compiler is contained in an IDE. The IDE contains an editor, compiler, project manager, and debugger in one package.

Most UNIX systems use command-line compilers. There are a few IDE compilers available for UNIX, but they are rare. On the other hand, almost every compiler for MS-DOS/Windows contains an IDE. For the command-line die-hards, these compilers do contain a command-line compiler as well.

Creating a Program Using a Command-Line Compiler

In this section, we'll go through the step-by-step process needed to create a program using a command-line compiler. Instructions are provided for a generic UNIX compiler (cc), the Free Software Foundation's gcc compiler, Turbo C++, Borland C++, and Microsoft Visual C++.*

However, if you are using a Borland or Microsoft compiler, you might want to skip ahead to the section on using the IDE.

Step 1. Create a Place for Your Program

You can more easily manage things if you create a separate directory for each program that you're working on. In this case, we'll create a directory called *hello* to hold our *hello* program.

On UNIX type:

```
% mkdir hello
% cd hello
```

On MS-DOS type:

```
C:> MKDIR HELLO
C:> CD HELLO
```

Step 2. Create the Program

A program starts out as a text file. Example 2-1 shows our program in source form.

Example 2-1: hello/hello.c

```
[File: hello/hello.c]
#include <stdio.h>
```

---

* Turbo C++, Borland C++, and Microsoft Visual C++ are all C++ compilers that can also compile C code.

Example 2-1: hello/hello.c (continued)

```
int main()
{
    printf("Hello World\n");
    return (0);
}
```

Use your favorite text editor to enter the program. Your file should be named *hello.c*.

WARNING   MS-DOS/Windows users should *not* use a word processor such as MS-Word or WordPerfect to write their programs. Word processors add formatting codes to files, which confuse the compiler. You must use a text editor such as the MS-DOS "EDIT" program that is capable of editing ASCII files.

Step 3. Run the Compiler

The compiler takes the source file you've just made and converts it into an executable program. Each compiler has a different command line. The commands for the most popular compilers are listed below.

UNIX cc compiler (generic UNIX)

Most UNIX-based compilers follow the same generic standard. The C compiler is named *cc*, and to compile our `hello` program we need the following command:

```
% cc -g -ohello hello.c
```

The -g option enables debugging. (The compiler adds extra information to the program to make the program easier to debug.) The switch -ohello tells the compiler that the program is to be called `hello`, and the final `hello.c` is the name of the source file. See your compiler manual for details on all the possible options. There are several different C compilers for UNIX, so your command line may be slightly different.

Free Software Foundation's gcc compiler

The Free Software Foundation, the GNU people, publish a number of high-quality programs. (See the Glossary entry for information on how to get their software.) Among their offerings is a C compiler called *gcc*.

To compile a program using the `gcc` compiler use the following command line:

```
% gcc -g -Wall -ohello hello.c
```

The additional switch -Wall turns on the warnings.

The GNU compiler contains several extensions to the basic C language. If you want to turn these features *off,* use the following command line:

```
% gcc -g -Wall -ansi -pedantic -ohello hello.c
```

The switch -ansi turns off features of GNU C that are incompatible with ANSI C. The -pedantic switch causes the compiler to issue a warning for any non-ANSI feature it encounters.

Borland's Turbo C++ under MS-DOS

Borland International makes a low-cost MS-DOS C++ compiler called Turbo C++. This compiler will compile both C and C++ code. We will describe only how to compile C code. Turbo C++ is ideal for learning. The command line for Turbo C++ is:

```
C:> tcc -ml -v -N -w -ehello hello.c
```

The -ml tells Turbo C++ to use the large-memory model. (The PC has a large number of different memory models. Only expert PC programmers need to know the difference between the various models. For now, just use the large model until you know more.)

The -v switch tells Turbo C++ to put debugging information in the program. Warnings are turned on by -w; stack checking is turned on by -N. Finally -ehello tells Turbo C++ to create a program named HELLO with hello.c being the name of the source file. See the Turbo C++ reference manual for a complete list of options.

Windows Programming

You may wonder why we describe MS-DOS programming when Windows is widely used. We do so because programming in Windows is much more complex than programming in MS-DOS.

For example, to print the message "Hello World" in MS-DOS, you merely print the message.

In Windows, you must create a window, create a function to handle the messages from that window, select a font, select a place to put the font, and output the message.

You must learn to walk before you can run. Therefore, we limit you to the MS-DOS or Easy-Win (Simplified Windows) programs in this book.

Borland C++ under MS-DOS and Windows

In addition to Turbo C++, Borland International also makes a full-featured, professional compiler for MS-DOS/Windows called Borland C++. Its command line is:

```
C:> bcc -ml -v -N -P -w -ehello hello.c
```

The command-line options are the same for both Turbo C++ and Borland C++.

Microsoft Visual C++

Microsoft Visual C++ is another C++/C compiler for MS-DOS/Windows. To compile, use the following command line:

```
C:> cl /AL /Zi /W1 hello.c
```

The `/AL` option tells the program to use the large memory model. Debugging is turned on with the `/Zi` option and warnings with the `/W1` option.

Step 4. Execute the Program

To run the program (on UNIX or MS-DOS/Windows) type:

```
% hello
```

and the message:

```
Hello World
```

will appear on the screen.

Creating a Program Using an Integrated Development Environment

Integrated Development Environments (IDEs) provide a one-stop shop for programming. They take a compiler, editor, and debugger and wrap them into one neat package for the program.

Step 1. Create a Place for Your Program

You can more easily manage things if you create a separate directory for each program that you're working on. In this case, we'll create a directory called HELLO to hold our *hello* program.

On MS-DOS type:

```
C:> MKDIR HELLO
C:> CD HELLO
```

Step 2. Enter, Compile, and Run Your Program Using the IDE

Each IDE is a little different, so we've included separate instructions for each one.

Turbo C++

1. Start the Turbo C++ IDE with the command:

   C:> **TC**

2. Select the *Window|Close All* menu item to clear the desktop of any old windows. We'll want to start clean. The screen should look like Figure 2-2.

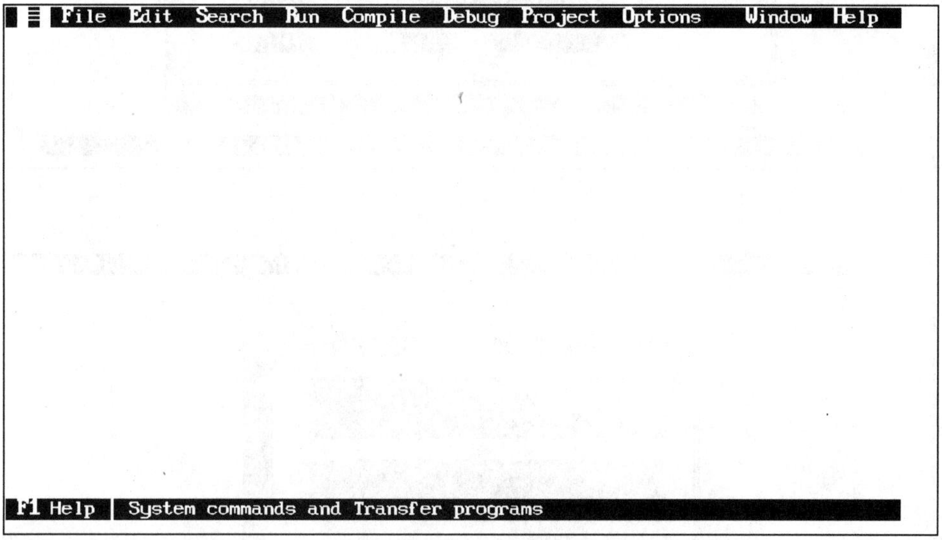

Figure 2-2: Clean desktop

3. Select the *Options|Compiler|Code Generation* menu item to pull up the Code Generation dialog as seen in Figure 2-3. Change the memory model to Large.

4. Select the *Options|Compiler|Entry/Exit* menu item and turn on "Test stack overflow" as seen in Figure 2-4.

5. Select the *Options|Compiler|Messages|Display* menu item to bring up the Compiler Messages dialog as seen in Figure 2-5. Select All to display all the warning messages.

6. Select the *Options|Save* menu item to save all the options we've used so far.

7. Select the *Project|Open* menu item to select a project file. In this case, our project file is called *HELLO.PRJ*. The screen should look like Figure 2-6 when you're done.

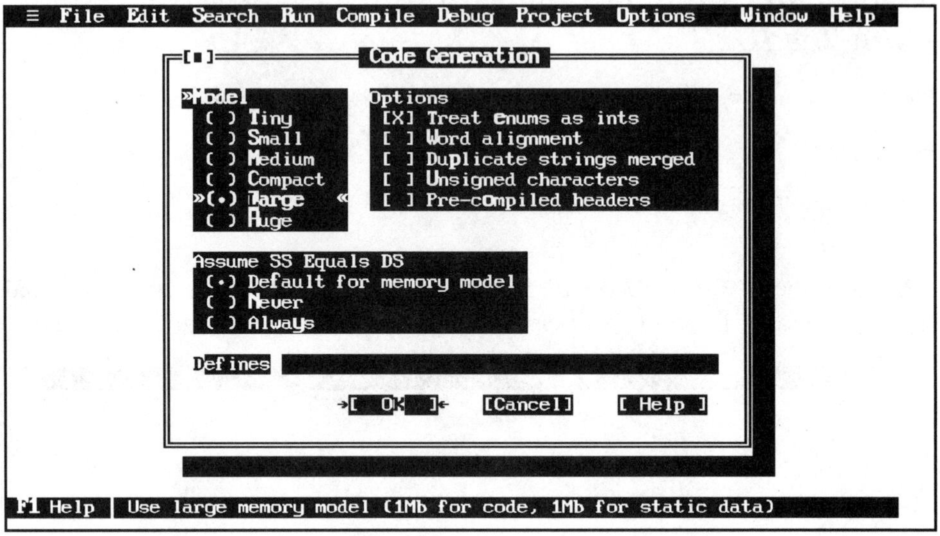

Figure 2-3: Code Generation dialog

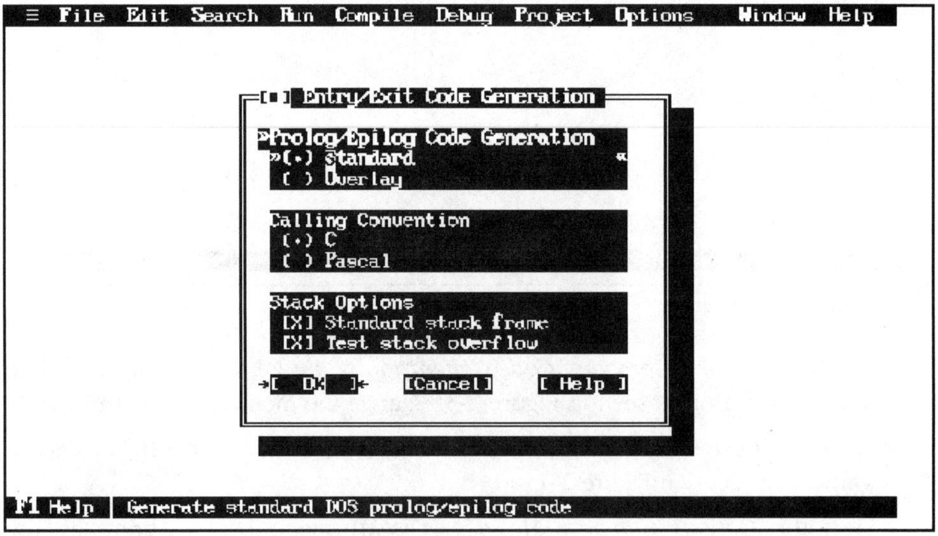

Figure 2-4: Entry/Exit Code Generation dialog

8. Press the INSERT key to add a file to the project. The file we want to add is *HELLO.C* as seen in Figure 2-7.

9. Press ESC to get out of the add-file cycle.

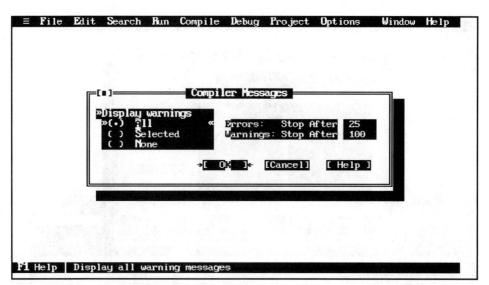

Figure 2-5: Compiler Messages dialog

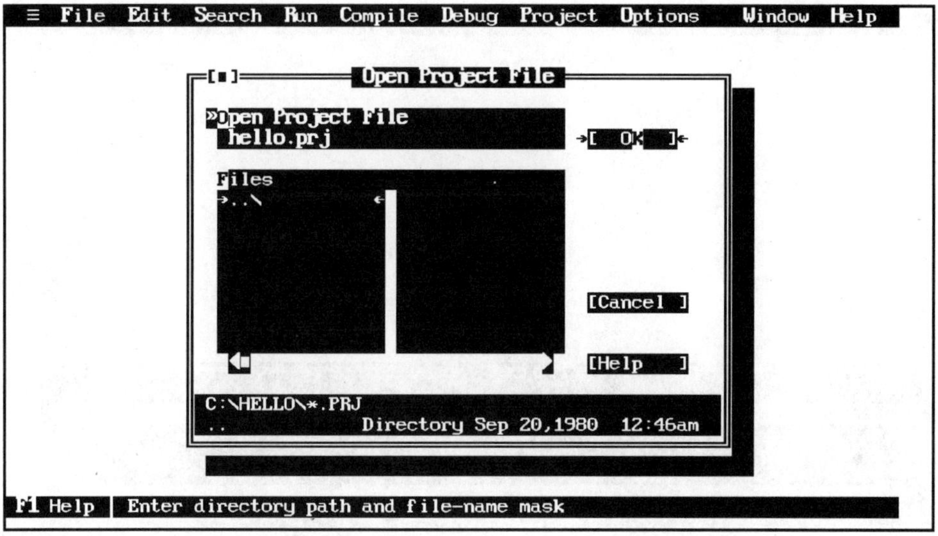

Figure 2-6: Open Project File dialog

10. Press UP-ARROW to go up one line. The line with *HELLO.C* should now be highlighted as seen in Figure 2-8.

11. Press ENTER to edit this file.

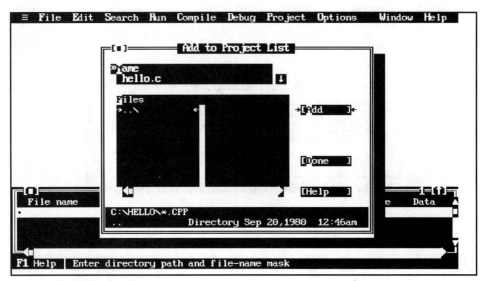

Figure 2-7: Add to Project List dialog

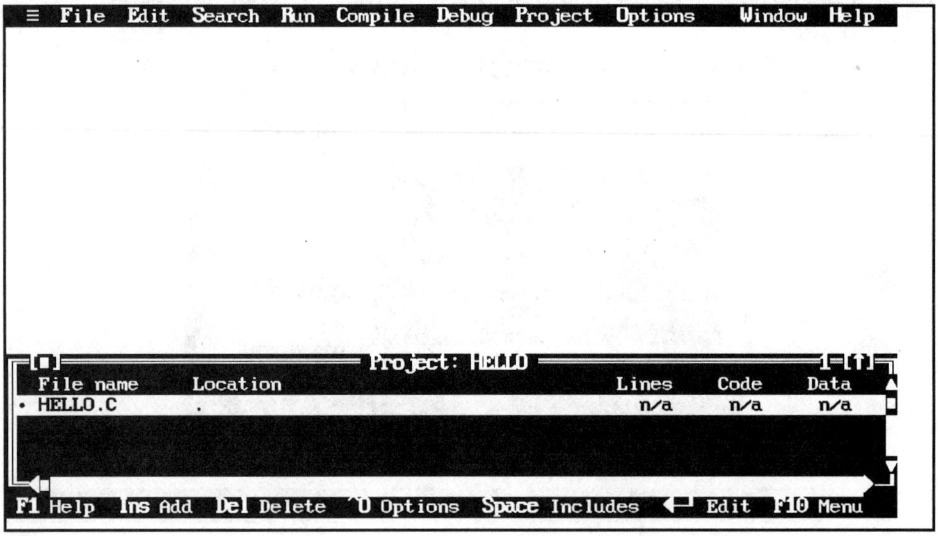

≡ File Edit Search Run Compile Debug Project Options   Window Help

```
┌[■]═══════════════════Project: HELLO════════════════1=[↑]═┐
  File name    Location                      Lines   Code   Data  ▲
• HELLO.C        .                            n/a    n/a    n/a   □
                                                                   ▼
F1 Help  Ins Add  Del Delete  ^O Options  Space Includes  ← Edit  F10 Menu
```

Figure 2-8: Hello project

12. Enter Example 2-2.

Example 2-2: hello/hello.c

```
[File: hello/hello.c]
#include <stdio.h>
int main()
{
```

Example 2-2: hello/hello.c (continued)

```
    printf("Hello World\n");
    return (0);
}
```

The results should look like Figure 2-9.

```
 ≡  File  Edit  Search  Run  Compile  Debug  Project  Options    Window  Help
┌─[■]─────────────────────── HELLO.C ──────────────────────── 2─[↑]─┐
│#include <stdio.h>                                                  ▲
│int main()                                                         ■
│{
│    printf("Hello World\n");
│    return (0);
│}


    ──── 6:2 ────◄█────────────────────────────────────────────►▼
 ─────────────────────── Project: HELLO ──────────────────── 1──
     File name      Location                     Lines    Code    Data
   • HELLO.C          .                            n/a     n/a     n/a


 F1 Help  F2 Save  F3 Open  Alt-F9 Compile  F9 Make  F10 Menu
```

Figure 2-9: Finished project

13. Select the *Run|Run* menu item to execute the program.

14. After the program runs, control returns to the IDE. This control change means that you can't see what your program output. To see the results of the program you must switch to the user screen by selecting the *Window|User* menu item.

    To return to the IDE, press any key. Figure 2-10 shows the output of the program.

15. When you are finished, you can save your program by selecting the *File|Save* menu item.

16. To exit the IDE, select the *File|Quit* menu item.

Borland C++

1. Create a directory called *\HELLO* to hold the files for our Hello World program. You can create a directory using the Windows' File Manager program or by typing the following command at the MS-DOS prompt:

    ```
    C:> mkdir \HELLO
    ```

2. From Windows, double-click on the "Borland C++" icon to start the IDE. Select the *Window|Close all* menu item to clean out any old junk. The program begins execution and displays a blank workspace as seen in Figure 2-11.

```
C:\HELLO>tc
Hello World
```

Figure 2-10: User screen

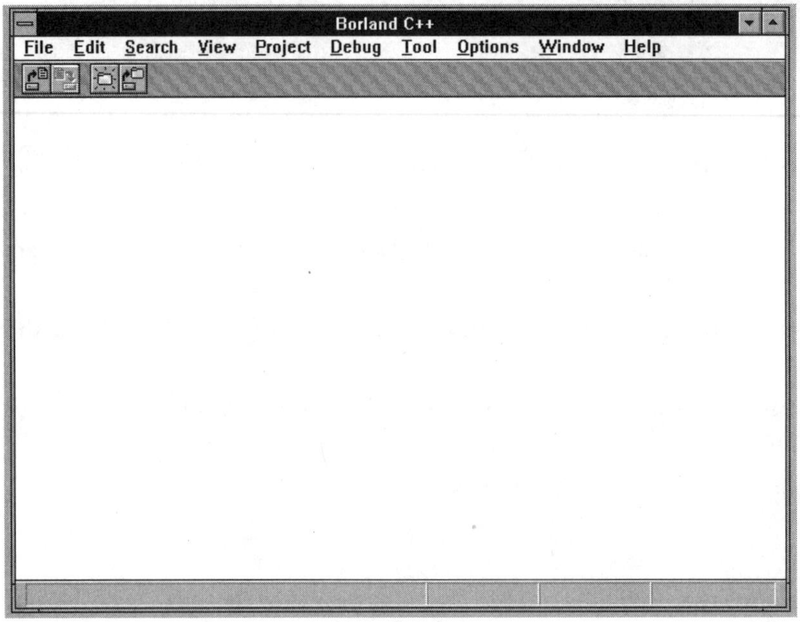

Figure 2-11: Borland C++ initial screen

3. Select the *Project|New Project* menu item to create a project for our program.
   Fill in the "Project Path and Name:" blank with **c:\hello\hello.ide**. For the

Target Type, select *EasyWin(.exe).* The *Target Model* is set to *Large.* The results are shown in Figure 2-12.

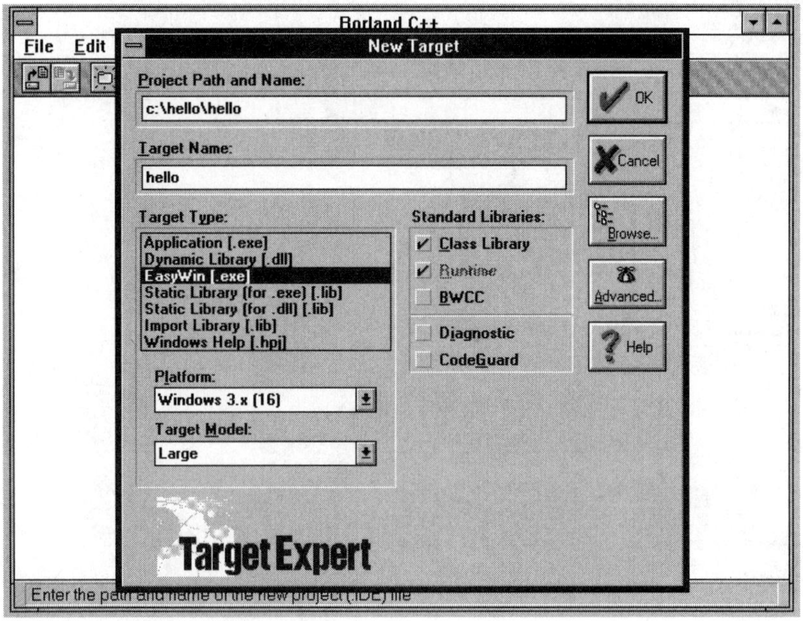

Figure 2-12: New Target dialog

4. Click on the *Advanced* button to bring up the Advanced Options dialog. Clear the *.rc* and *.def* items and set the *.c Node* items as shown in Figure 2-13.

5. Click on *OK* to return to the New Target dialog. Click on *OK* again to return to the main window.

6. Press **ALT-F10** to bring up the node submenu shown in Figure 2-14.

7. Select the *Edit node attributes* menu item to bring up the dialog shown in Figure 2-15. In the *Style Sheet* blank, select the item *Debug Info and Diagnostics.* Click on *OK* to return to the main window.

8. Go to the Project Options dialog by selecting the *Options|Project Options* menu item. Go down to the Compiler item and click on the + to expand the options.

   Turn on the *Test stack overflow* option as seen in Figure 2-16. Click on *OK* to save these options.

9. Click on *OK* to return to the main window. Press **DOWN-ARROW** to select the *hello[.C]* item in the project as seen in Figure 2-17.

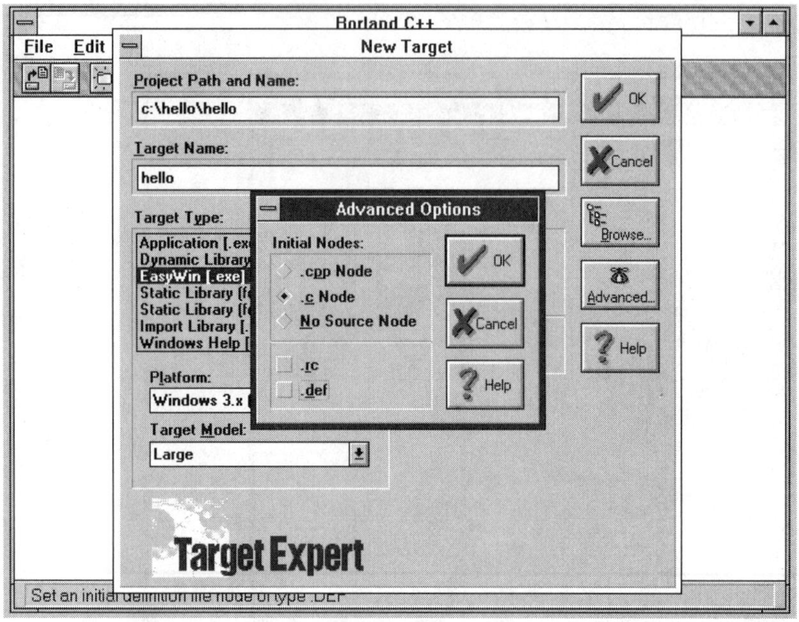

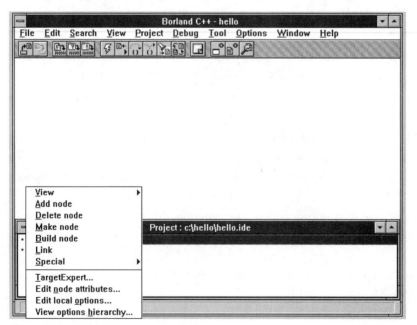

Figure 2-13: Advanced Options dialog

Figure 2-14: Target Options submenu

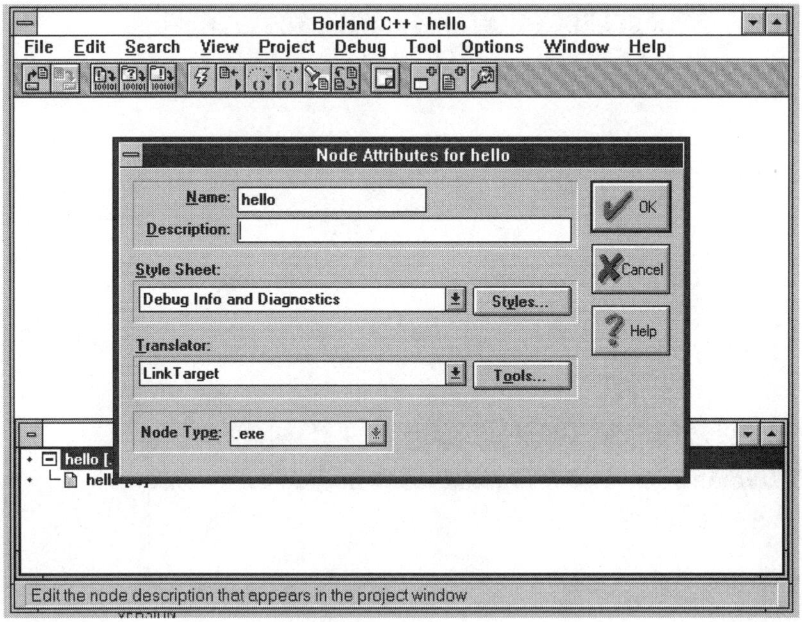

Figure 2-15: Node Attributes dialog

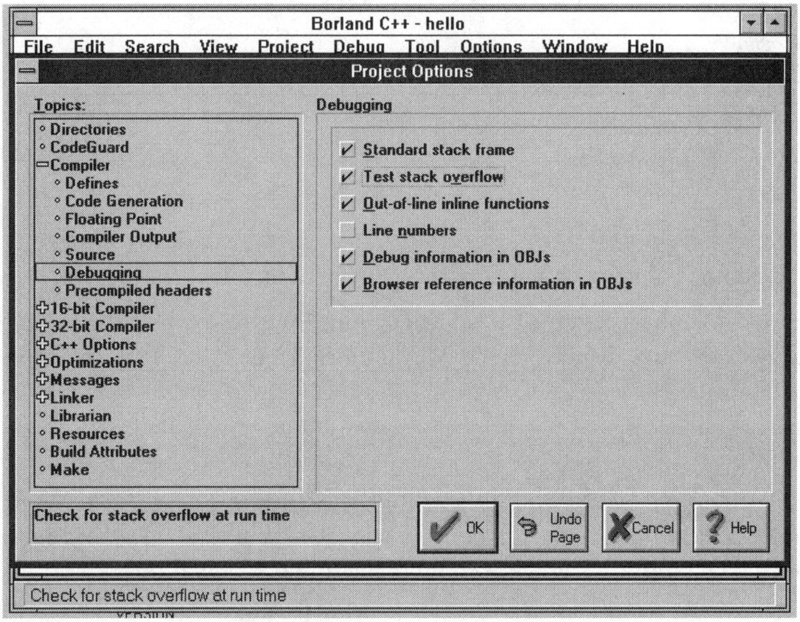

Figure 2-16: Project Options dialog

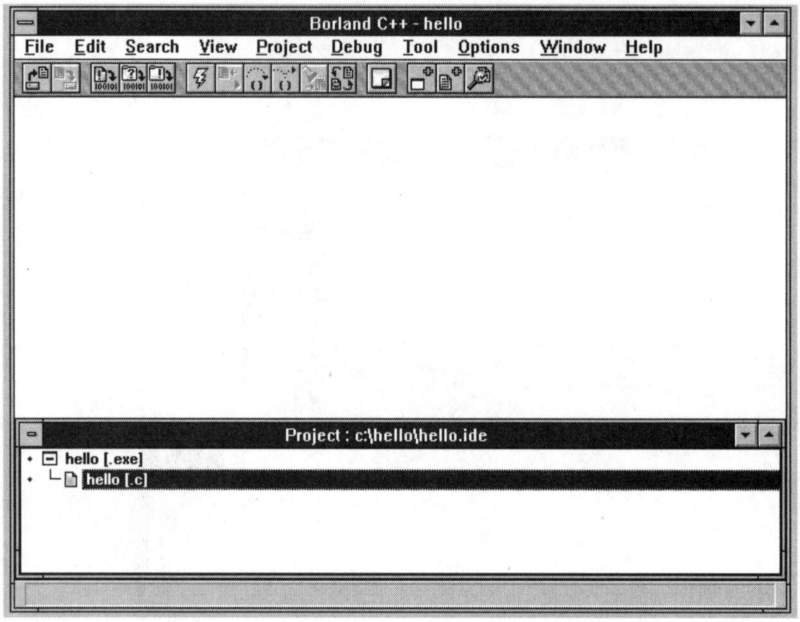

Figure 2-17: Hello project

10. Press RETURN to start editing the file *hello.c*. Type in Example 2-3.

Example 2-3: hello/hello.c

```
#include <stdio.h>
int main()
{
    printf("Hello World\n");
    return (0);
}
```

When you finish, your screen will look like Figure 2-18.

11. Compile and run the program by selecting the *Debug|Run* menu item. The program will run and display "Hello World" in a window as seen in Figure 2-19.

Microsoft Visual C++

1. Create a directory called *\HELLO* to hold the files for our *Hello World* program. You can create a directory using the Windows' *File Manager* program or by typing the following command at the MS-DOS prompt:

```
C:> mkdir \HELLO
```

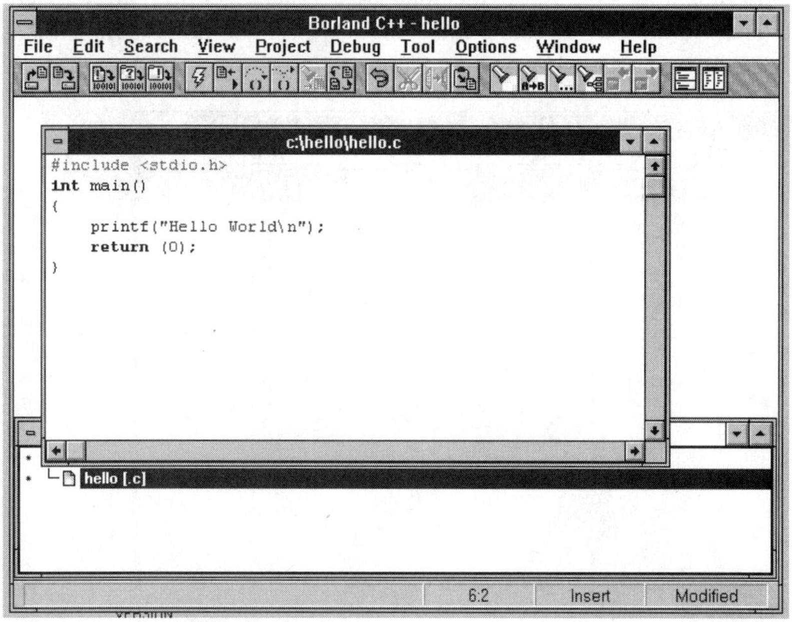

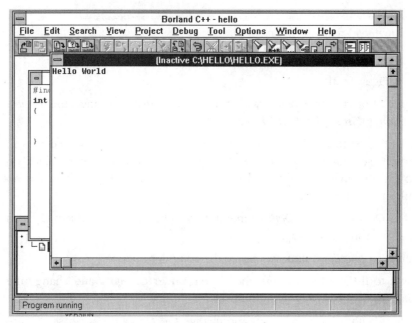

Figure 2-18: Hello World program

Figure 2-19: Hello World program after execution

2. From Windows, double-click on the Microsoft Visual C++ to start the IDE. Clear out any old junk by selecting the *Window | Close All* menu item. A blank workspace will be displayed as seen in Figure 2-20.

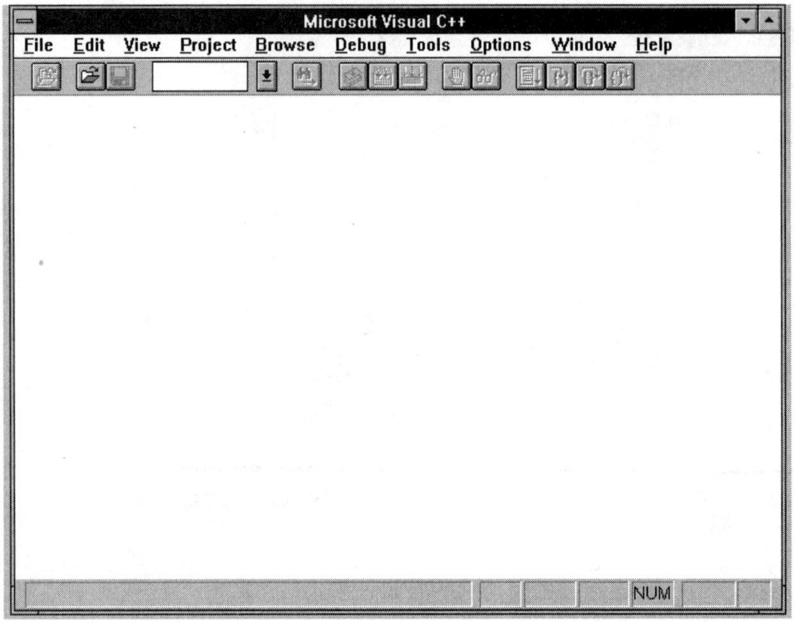

Figure 2-20: Microsoft Visual C++ initial screen

3. Click on the *Project | New* menu item to bring up the New Project dialog as shown in Figure 2-21.

   Fill in the Project Name blank with "\hello\hello.mak". Change the *Project Type* to *QuickWin application (.EXE)*.

4. Visual C++ goes to the Edit dialog to allow you to name the source files in this project (see Figure 2-22). In this case, we have only file *hello.c*. Click on *Add* to put this in the project and *Close* to tell Visual C++ that there are no more files in the program.

5. Select the *Options | Project Options* menu item to bring up the Project Options dialog as seen in Figure 2-23.

   Click on the *Compiler* button to change the compiler options.

6. Go down to the *Custom Options* menu item under *Category* and change the *Warning Level* to 4 as seen in Figure 2-24.

7. Select the *Memory Model* category and change the *Model* to *Large* (see Figure 2-25).

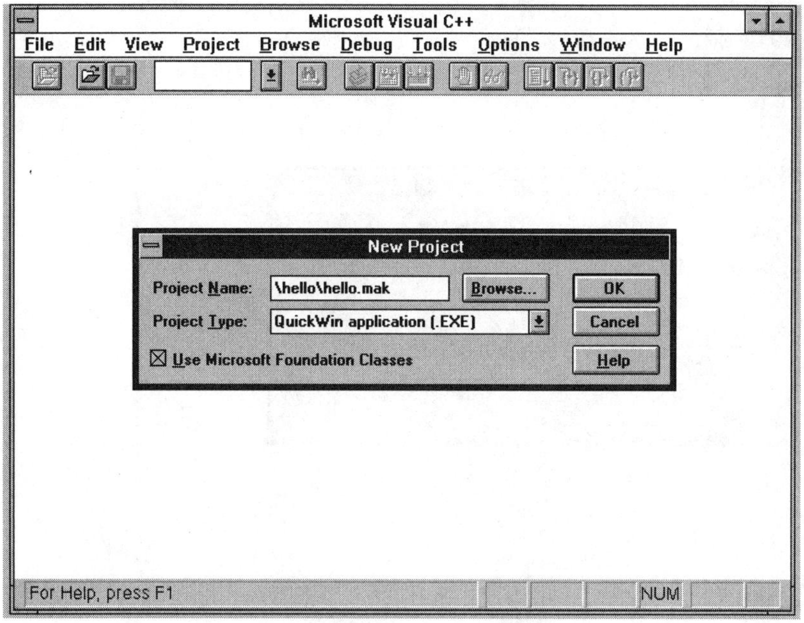

Figure 2-21: New Project dialog

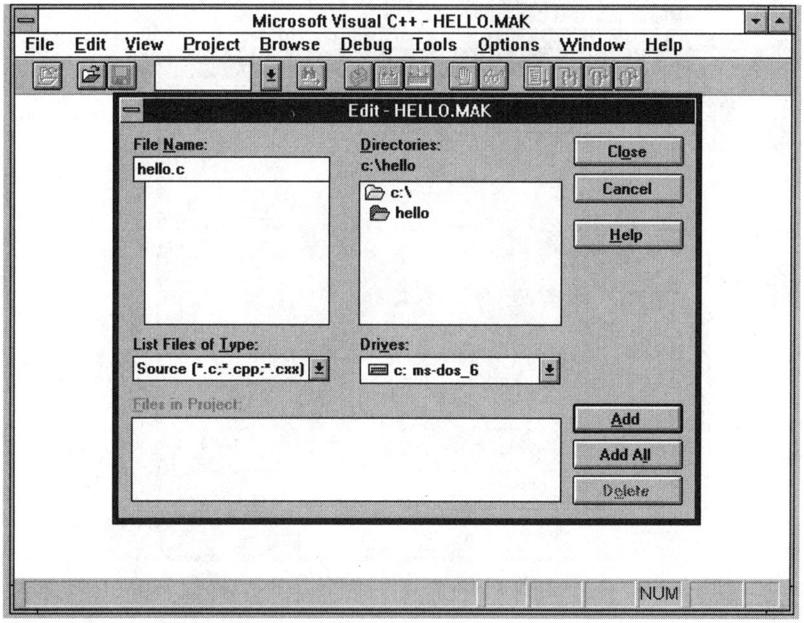

Figure 2-22: Edit Project dialog

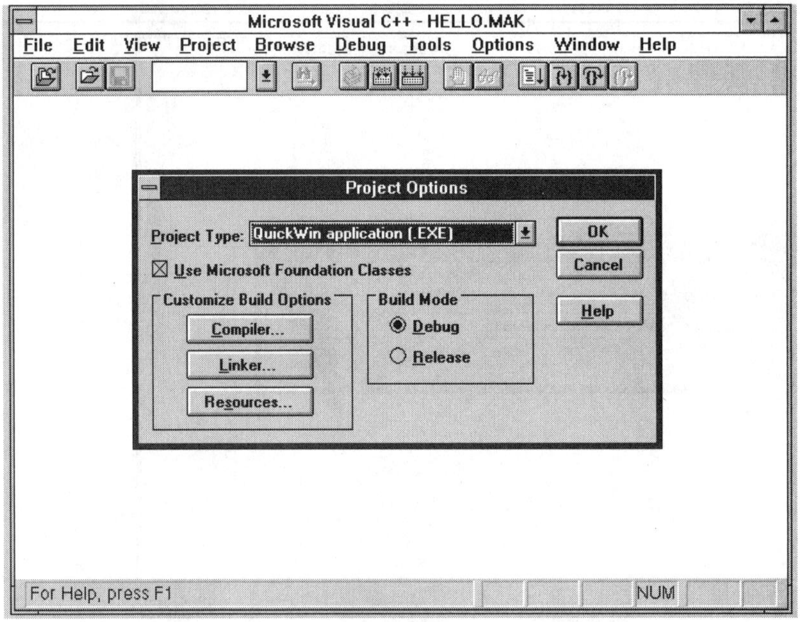

Figure 2-23: Project Options dialog

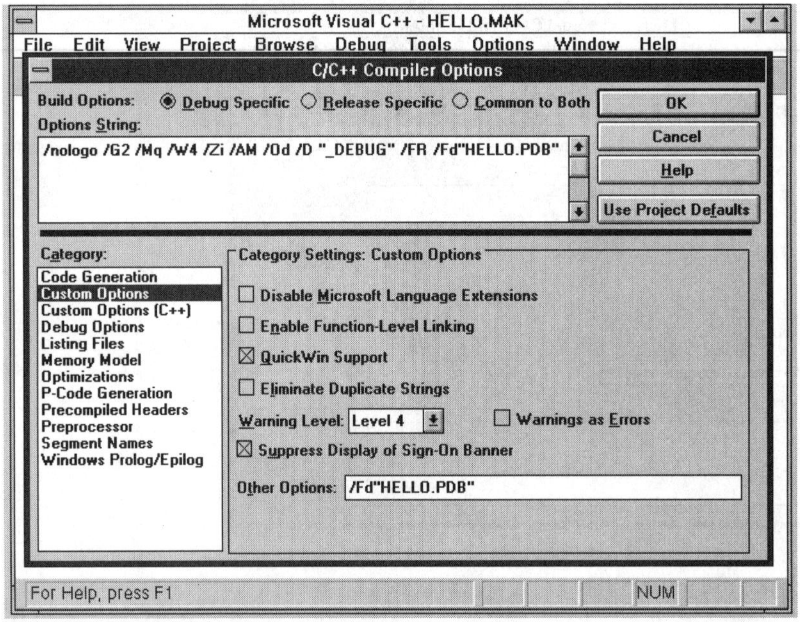

Figure 2-24: C/C++ Compiler Options dialog

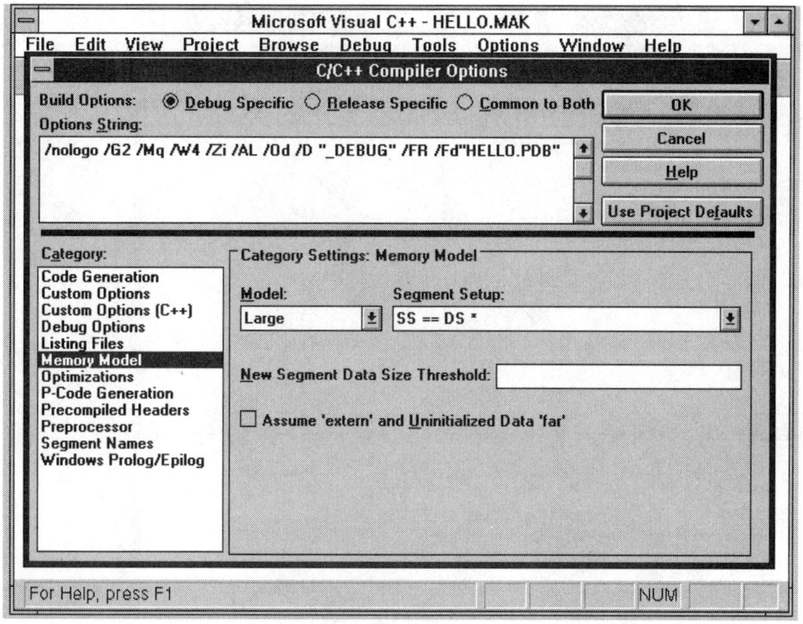

Figure 2-25: Memory Model options

8. Close the dialog by clicking on the *OK* button. You return to the Project Options dialog. Click on *OK* to dismiss this dialog as well.

9. Select the *File|New* menu item to start a new program file. Type in Example 2-4.

Example 2-4: hello/hello.c

```
[File: hello/hello.c]
#include <stdio.h>
int main()
{
    printf("Hello World\n");
    return (0);
}
```

Your results should look Figure 2-26.

10. Use the *File|Save As* menu item to save the file under the name *hello.c*.

11. Use the *Project|Build* menu item to compile the program. The compiler will output messages as it builds. When the compiler is finished, your screen should look like Figure 2-27.

12. The program can now be started with the *Debug|Go* menu item. The results appear in Figure 2-28.

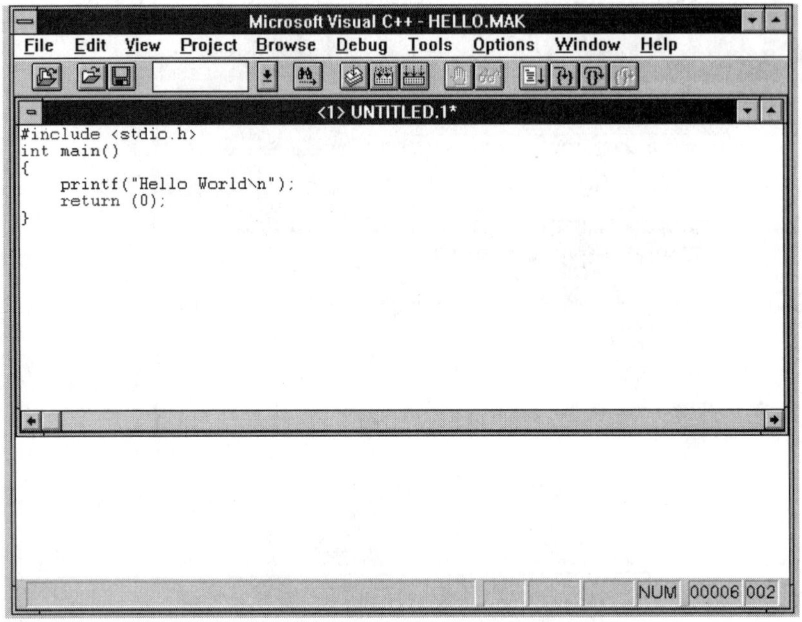

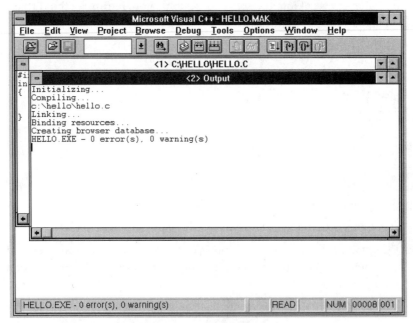

Figure 2-26: Microsoft Visual C++ with Hello World entered

Figure 2-27: Microsoft Visual C++ project build screen

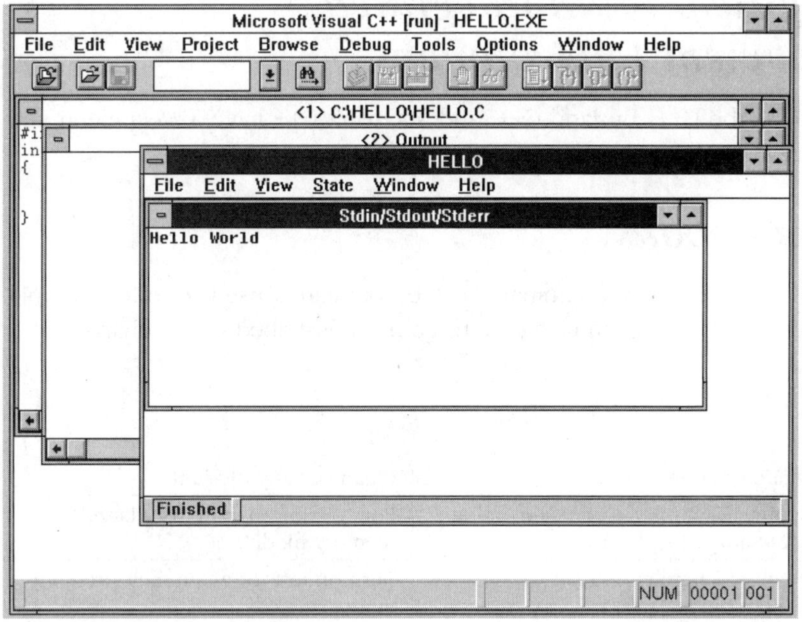

Figure 2-28: Hello World results

Getting Help on UNIX

Most UNIX systems have an online documentation system called the *manpages*. These manpages can be read with the *man* command. (UNIX uses *man* as an abbreviation for *manual*.) To get information about a particular subject, use the following command:

    man *subject*

For example, to find out about the classes defined in the `printf` function, you would type:

    man printf

The command also has a keyword search mode:

    man -k *keyword*

To determine the name of manpage with the word "output" in its title, use the command:

    man -k output

Getting Help in an Integrated Development Environment

IDEs such as Turbo C++, Borland C++, and Microsoft C++ have a *Help* menu item. This item activates a hypertext-based help system.

IDE Cookbooks

This section contains a brief summary of the commands used to enter, compile, and execute a simple program using the three IDEs described in this chapter.

Turbo C++

1.	Window | Close All	Clean out any old junk.
2.	Options | Compiler | Code Generation Memory Model = Large	For simple program, use large memory model.
3.	Options | Compiler | Entry/Exit Test stack overflow = On	Turn on test for a common programming error.
4.	Options | Compiler | Messages | Display Display warnings = All	Tell compiler that you want all diagnostics that it can give you.
5.	Options | Save	Save options.
6.	Project | Open Project file = *program*.PRJ	Create a new project.
7.	Insert Add file *program*.c	Add program file to project.
8.	ESC	Get out of "add-file" cycle.
9.	UP-ARROW	Move to *program*.c line.
10.	RETURN	Edit program file.
11.	Type in the program	Enter text of program.
12.	Run | Run	Execute program.
13.	Window | User	Display results of the program.
14.	File | Save	Save the program.
15.	File | Quit	Exit Turbo C++ IDE.

Borland C++

1.	Window | Close All	Clean out any old junk.

2.	Project | New Project
	    Project Path and Name = c.\
	 program\program.ide
	    Target Type = EasyWin(.exe)
	    Target Model = Large
		Create new project.

3.	Click on Advanced button Set .c Node Clear .rc and .def	Setup a simple C program.
4.	Click on OK	Return to New Target window.
5.	Click on OK	Return to main window.
6.	ALT-F10	Select node submenu.

7.	Edit | Node Attributes
	    Style Sheet = Debug Info and
	    Diagnostics
		Turn on debugging.

8.	Click on OK button	Return to main menu.

9.	Options | Project Options
	    Click on + under Compiler
	    Test stack overflow = On
		Turn on valuable run-time test.

10.	Click on OK button	Save options.
11.	Click on OK button	Return to main window.
12.	DOWN-ARROW	Move to *program*[.c] line.
13.	RETURN	Edit program file.
14.	Type in the program	Enter text of program.
15.	Debug | Run	Run program.

Microsoft Visual C++

1.	Window | Close All	Clean out any old junk.

2.	Project | New
	    Project Name =
	    *program**program*.mak
	    Project Type =
	        QuickWin application (.EXE)
		Start project.
		Set up project.
		Click on OK button.
		Go to Edit dialog.

3.	File name = *program*.c	Enter program name.
4.	Click on Add button	Add program to project.
5.	Click on Close button	Tell Visual C++ that there are no more files.
6.	Options | Project Options	Get to Project Options dialog.
7.	Click on Compiler button	Go to C | C++ Compiler Options dialog.
8.	Select Custom Options category Warning Level = 4	Turn on all warnings.
9.	Select the Memory Model category Memory Model = Large	For simple program, use large-memory model.
10.	Click on OK button	Return to Project Options dialog.
11.	Click on OK button	Return to main window.
12.	File | New	Open program file.
13.	Type in the program	Edit program file.
14.	File | Save As -- File name = *program.c*	Save file.
15.	Project | Build	Compile program.
16.	Debug | Go	Execute program.

NOTE   These instructions are for version 4.0 of Microsoft Visual C++. Microsoft frequently changes the user interface from version to version, so these instructions may require some slight modification.

Programming Exercises

Exercise 2-1: On your computer, type in the *hello* program and execute it.

Exercise 2-2: Take several programming examples from any source, enter them into the computer, and run them.

3

Style

There is no programming language, no matter how structured, that will prevent programmers from writing bad programs.

—L. Flon

It is the nobility of their style which will make our writers of 1840 unreadable forty years from now.

—Stendhal

This chapter discusses how to use good programming style to create a simple, easy-to-read program. Discussing style before we know how to program might seem backward, but style is the most important part of programming. Style is what separates the gems from the junk. It is what separates the programming artist from the butcher. You must learn good programming style first, before typing in your first line of code, so that everything you write will be of the highest quality.

Contrary to popular belief, programmers do not spend most of their time writing programs. Far more time is spent maintaining, upgrading, and debugging existing code than is ever spent on creating new works. According to Datamation, the amount of time spent on maintenance is skyrocketing. From 1980 to 1990, the average number of lines in a typical application went from 23,000 to 1,200,000. The average system age went from 4.75 to 9.4 years.

What's worse, 74% of the managers surveyed at the 1990 Annual Meeting and Conference of the Software Maintenance Association reported that they "have systems in their department, that have to be maintained by specific individuals because no one else understands them."

Most software is built on existing software. I recently completed the code for 12 new programs. Only one of these was created from scratch; the other 11 are adaptations of existing programs.

Some programmers believe that the purpose of a program is only to present the computer with a compact set of instructions. This concept is not true. Programs written only for the machine have two problems:

- They are difficult to correct because sometimes even the author does not understand them.

- Modifications and upgrades are difficult to make because the maintenance programmer must spend a considerable amount of time figuring out what the program does from its code. Ideally, a program serves two purposes: first, it presents the computer with a set of instructions, and second, it provides the programmer with a clear, easy-to-read description of what the program does.

Example 2-1 contains a glaring error that many programmers still make, and that causes more trouble than any other problem. *The program contains no comments.*

A working but uncommented program is a time bomb waiting to explode. Sooner or later, someone will have to fix a bug in the program, modify it, or upgrade it, and the lack of comments will make the job much more difficult. A well-commented, simple program is a work of art. Learning how to comment is as important as learning how to code properly.

Comments in C start with a slash asterisk (/*) and end with an asterisk slash (*/). Example 3-1 is an improved version of Example 2-1.

Example 3-1: hello2/hello2.c

```
[File: hello2/hello2.c]
/**********************************************************
 * hello -- program to print out "Hello World".          *
 *      Not an especially earth-shattering program.       *
 *                                                        *
 * Author:  Steve Oualline.                               *
 *                                                        *
 * Purpose:  Demonstration of a simple program.           *
 *                                                        *
 * Usage:                                                 *
 *      Runs the program and the message appears.         *
 **********************************************************/
#include <stdio.h>

int main()
{
    /* Tell the world hello */
    printf("Hello World\n");
    return (0);
}
```

In this example, we put the beginning comments in a box of asterisks (*) called a *comment box*. This formatting is done to emphasize the more important comments, much as we use bold characters for the headings in this book. Less important comments are not boxed. For example:

```
/* Tell the world hello */
printf("Hello World\n");
```

In order to write a program, you must have a clear idea of what you are going to do. One of the best ways to organize your thoughts is to write them down in a language that is clear and easy to understand. After the process has been clearly stated, it can be translated into a computer program.

Understanding what you are doing is the most important part of programming. I once wrote two pages of comments describing a complex graphics algorithm. The comments were revised twice before I even started coding. The actual instructions took only half a page. Because I had organized my thoughts well (and was lucky), the program worked the first time.

Your program should read like an essay. It should be as clear and easy to understand as possible. Good programming style comes from experience and practice. The style described in the following pages is the result of many years of programming experience. It can be used as a starting point for developing your own style. These are not rules, only suggestions. Only one rule exists: make your program as *clear, concise,* and *simple* as possible.

At the beginning of the program is a comment block that contains information about the program. Boxing the comments makes them stand out. The list that follows contains some of the sections that should be included at the beginning of your program. Not all programs will need all sections, so use only those that apply:

- *Heading*. The first comment should contain the name of the program. Also include a short description of what the program does. You may have the most amazing program, one that slices, dices, and solves all the world's problems, but the program is useless if no one knows what it is.

- *Author*. You've gone to a lot of trouble to create this program. Take credit for it. Also, anyone who has to modify the program can come to you for information and help.

- *Purpose*. Why did you write this program? What does it do?

- *Usage*. In this section, give a short explanation of how to run the program. In an ideal world, every program would come with a set of documents describing how to use it. The world is not ideal. Oualline's law of documentation states: 90% of the time the documentation is lost. Of the remaining 10%, 9% of the time the revision of the documentation is different from the revision of the program and therefore completely useless. The 1% of the time you actu-

Poor Man's Typesetting

In typesetting, you can use letter size, **bold**, and *italic* to make different parts of your text stand out. In programming, you are limited to a single, monospaced font. However, people have come up with ingenious ways to get around the limitations of the typeface.

Some of the various commenting tricks are:

```
/***********************************************************
 ***********************************************************
 ******** WARNING:  This is an example of a     ******
 ********    warning message that grabs the     ******
 ********    attention of the programmer.        ******
 ***********************************************************
 **********************************************************/

/*------------> Another, less important warning <--------*/

/*>>>>>>>>>>>>  Major section header  <<<<<<<<<<<<<< */

/***********************************************************
 * We use boxed comments in this book to denote the     *
 * beginning of a section or program.                   *
 **********************************************************/

/*------------------------------------------------------*\
 * This is another way of drawing boxes.                *
\*------------------------------------------------------*/

/*
 * This is the beginning of a section.
 * ^^^^ ^^ ^^^ ^^^^^^^^^ ^^ ^ ^^^^^^^
 *
 * In the paragraph that follows, we explain what
 * the section does and how it works.
 */

/*
 * A medium-level comment explaining the next
 * dozen (or so) lines of code.  Even though we don't have
 * the bold typeface, we can **emphasize** words.
 */

/* A simple comment explaining the next line */
```

ally have documentation and the correct revision of the documentation, the information will be written in Chinese*.

---

* My wife comes from Hong Kong and has a talking electronic translator. It is a very expensive and complex device, and comes with a 150-page manual, written entirely in Chinese.

To avoid Oualline's law of documentation, put the documentation in the program.

- *References.* Creative copying is a legitimate form of programming (if you don't break the copyright laws in the process). In the real world, you needn't worry about how you get a working program, as long as you get it, but give credit where credit is due. In this section, you should reference the original author of any work you copied.

- *File formats.* List the files that your program reads or writes and a short description of their formats.

- *Restrictions.* List any limits or restrictions that apply to the program, such as "The data file must be correctly formatted" or "The program does not check for input errors."

- *Revision history.* This section contains a list indicating who modified the program, and when and what changes were made. Many computers have a source control system (RCS and SCCS on UNIX; PCVS and MKS-RCS on MS-DOS/Windows) that will keep track of this information for you.

- *Error handling.* If the program detects an error, describe what the program does with it.

- *Notes.* Include special comments or other information that has not already been covered.

The format of your beginning comments will depend on what is needed for the environment in which you are programming. For example, if you are a student, the instructor may ask you to include in the program heading the assignment number, your name and student identification number, and other information. In industry, a project number or part number might be included.

Comments should explain everything the programmer needs to know about the program, but no more. You can overcomment a program. (This case is rare, but it does occur.) When deciding on the format for your heading comments, make sure there is a reason for everything you include.

The actual code for your program consists of two parts: variables and executable instructions. Variables are used to hold the data used by your program. Executable instructions tell the computer what to do with the data.

Common Coding Practices

A *variable* is a place in the computer's memory for storing a value. C identifies that place by the variable name. Names can be of any length and should be chosen so their meanings are clear. (Actually, a length limit exists, but it is so large that you probably will never encounter it.) Every variable in C must be

Inserting Comments—The Easy Way

If you are using the UNIX editor *vi*, put the following in your *.exrc* file to make constructing boxes easier:

```
:abbr #b /********************************************
:abbr #e ********************************************/
```

These two lines define `vi` abbreviations `#b` and `#e`, so that typing:

```
#b
```

at the beginning of a block will cause the string:

```
/**********************************************
```

to appear (for beginning a comment box). Typing:

```
#e
```

will end a box. The number of stars was carefully selected so that the end of the box is aligned on a tab stop.

Similar macros or related tools are available in most other editors. For instance, GNU Emacs lets you achieve the a similar effect by putting the following LISP code in a file named *.emacs* in your home directory:

```
(defun c-begin-comment-box ()
  "Insert the beginning of a comment, followed by a string of asterisks."
  (interactive)
  (insert "/**********************************************\n")
  )
(defun c-end-comment-box ()
  "Insert a string of asterisks, followed by the end of a comment."
  (interactive)
  (insert "**********************************************/\n")
  )
(add-hook 'c-mode-hook
  '(lambda ()
     (define-key c-mode-map "\C-cb" 'c-begin-comment-box)
     (define-key c-mode-map "\C-ce" 'c-end-comment-box)
   )
)
```

declared. Variable declarations will be discussed in Chapter 9. The following declaration tells C that we're going to use three integer (**int**) variables: p, q, and r:

```
int p,q,r;
```

But what are these variables for? The reader has no idea. They could represent the number of angels on the head of a pin or the location and acceleration of a plasma bolt in a game of Space Invaders. Avoid abbreviations. Exs. abb. are diff. to rd. and hd. to ustnd. (Excess abbreviations are difficult to read and hard to understand.)

Now consider another declaration:

```
int account_number;
int balance_owed;
```

Now we know that we're dealing with an accounting program, but we could still use some more information. For example, is the `balance_owed` in dollars or cents? We should have added a comment after each declaration to explain what we were doing. For example:

```
int account_number;       /* Index for account table */
int balance_owed;         /* Total owed us (in pennies)*/
```

By putting a comment after each declaration, we, in effect, create a mini-dictionary where we define the meaning of each variable name. Because the definition of each variable is in a known place, it's easy to look up the meaning of a name. (Programming tools like editors, cross-referencers, and searching tools such as `grep` can also help you quickly find a variable's definition.)

Units are very important. I was once asked to modify a program that converted plot data files from one format to another. Many different units of length were used throughout the program, and none of the variable declarations were commented. I tried very hard to figure out what was going on, but I could not determine what units were being used in the program. Finally, I gave up and put the following comment in the program:

```
/*********************************************************
 * Note:  I have no idea what the input units are, nor   *
 *     do I have any idea what the output units are,     *
 *     but I have discovered that if I divide by 3       *
 *     the plot sizes look about right.                  *
 *********************************************************/
```

You should take every opportunity to make sure that your program is clear and easy to understand. Do not be clever. Clever kills. Clever makes for unreadable and unmaintainable programs. Programs, by their nature, are extremely complex. Anything that you can to do to cut down on this complexity will make your programs better. Consider the following code, written by a very clever programmer:[*]

```
while ('\n' != (*p++ = *q++));
```

---

[*] Note that the first version of this code:

```
while ('\n' != *p++ = *q++);
```

contained a syntax error and would not compile. No one noticed this error for the first five years that this book was in publication.

It is almost impossible for the reader to tell at a glance what this mess does. Properly written this should be:

```
while (1) {
    *destination_ptr = *source_ptr;
    if (*destination_ptr == '\n')
        break;    /* Exit the loop if at end of line */
    destination_ptr++;
    source_ptr++;
}
```

Although the second version is longer, it is much clearer and easier to understand.* Even a novice programmer who does not know C well can tell that this program has something to do with moving data from a source to a destination.

The computer doesn't care which version is used. A good compiler will generate the same machine code for both versions. The programmer is the beneficiary of the verbose code.

Coding Religion

Computer scientists have devised many programming styles. These include structured programming, top-down programming, goto-less programming, and object-oriented design (OOD). Each of these styles has its own following or cult. I use the term "religion" because people are taught to follow the rules blindly without knowing the reasons behind them. For example, followers of the goto-less cult will never use a **goto** statement, even when it is natural to do so.

The rules presented in this book result from years of programming experience. I have discovered that by following these rules, I can create better programs. You do not have to follow them blindly. If you find a better system, by all means use it. (If your solution really works, drop me a line. I'd like to use it too.)

Indentation and Code Format

In order to make programs easier to understand, most programmers indent their programs. The general rule for a C program is to indent one level for each new block or conditional. In our previous example, there are three levels of logic, each with its own indentation level. The **while** statement is outermost. The statements inside the **while** are at the next level. Finally, the statement inside the **if** (**break**) is at the innermost level.

There are two styles of indentation, and a vast religious war is being raged in the programming community as to which style is better. The first is the short form:

```
while (! done) {
    printf("Processing\n");
```

---

* Expert C programmers can spot a slight difference between the two versions, but both do the required job.

```
        next_entry();
    }
    if (total <= 0) {
        printf("You owe nothing\n");
        total = 0;
    } else {
        printf("You owe %d dollars\n", total);
        all_totals = all_totals + total;
    }
```

In this case, curly braces ({}) are put on the same line as the statements. The other style puts the {} on lines by themselves:

```
    while (! done)
    {
        printf("Processing\n");
        next_entry();
    }
    if (total <= 0)
    {
        printf("You owe nothing\n");
        total = 0;
    }
    else
    {
        printf("You owe %d dollars\n", total);
        all_totals = all_totals + total;
    }
```

Both formats are frequently used. You should use the format you feel most comfortable with. This book uses the short format because it's more compact and therefore saves book space.

The amount of indentation is left to the programmer. Two, four, and eight spaces are common. Studies have shown that a four-space indent makes the code most readable. However, being consistent in your indentation is far more important than the indention size you use.

Some editors, like the UNIX Emacs editor, the Turbo C++, Borland C++, and Microsoft Visual C++ internal editors, contain code that automatically indents your programs as you create them. Although these editor-based indentation systems are not perfect, they do go a long way to helping you create properly formatted code.

Clarity

A program should read like a technical paper. It should be organized into sections and paragraphs. Procedures form a natural section boundary. (We'll learn about function in Chapter 9.) You must organize your code into paragraphs. You should begin a paragraph with a topic-sentence comment and separate the comment from other paragraphs with a blank line. For example:

```
/* poor programming practice */
temp = box_x1;
box_x1 = box_x2;
box_x2 = temp;
temp = box_y1;
box_y1 = box_y2;
box_y2 = temp;
```

A better version would be:

```
/*
 * Swap the two corners
 */

/* Swap X coordinate */
temp = box_x1;
box_x1 = box_x2;
box_x2 = temp;

/* Swap Y coordinate */
temp = box_y1;
box_y1 = box_y2;
box_y2 = temp;
```

Simplicity

Your program should be simple. Some general rules of thumb are:

- A single function should not be longer than two or three pages. (See Chapter 9.) If the function gets longer, it can probably be split into two simpler functions. This rule comes about because the human mind can only hold so much in short-term memory. Three pages are about the most that the human mind can wrap itself around in one sitting.

  Also if your function goes beyond the three-page limit, it probably doesn't define a single operation, or probably contains too much detail.

- Avoid complex logic like multiply nested ifs. The more complex your code, the more indentation levels you will need. When you start running into the right margin, you should consider splitting your code into multiple procedures, to decrease the level of complexity.

- Did you ever read a sentence, like this one, in which the author went on and on, stringing together sentence after sentence with the word "and," and didn't seem to understand the fact that several shorter sentences would do the job much better, and didn't it bother you? C statements should not go on forever. Long statements should be avoided. If it looks like an equation or formula is going to be longer than one or two lines, you should split it into two shorter equations.

- Finally, the most important rule: make your program as simple and easy to understand as possible, even if you must break some of the rules. The goal is clarity, and the rules given in this chapter are designed to help you accomplish that goal. If they get in the way, get rid of them. I have seen one program with a single statement that spanned over 20 pages; however, because of the specialized nature of the program, this statement was simple and easy to understand.

Summary

A program should be concise and easy to read. It must serve as a set of computer instructions, but also as a reference work describing the algorithms and data used inside it. Everything should be documented with comments. Comments serve two purposes. First, they tell the programmer to follow the code, and second, they help the programmer remember what he did.

Class discussion: Create a style sheet for class assignments. Discuss what comments should go into the programs and why.

4

Basic Declarations and Expressions

A journey of a thousand miles must begin with a single step.

—Lao-zi

If carpenters made buildings the way programmers make programs, the first woodpecker to come along would destroy all of civilization.

—Weinberg's Second Law

Elements of a Program

If you are going to construct a building, you need two things: the bricks and a blueprint that tells you how to put them together. In computer programming, you need two things: data (variables) and instructions (code or functions). Variables are the basic building blocks of a program. Instructions tell the computer what to do with the variables.

Comments are used to describe the variables and instructions. They are notes by the author documenting the program so that the program is clear and easy to read. Comments are ignored by the computer.

In construction, before we can start, we must order our materials: "We need 500 large bricks, 80 half-size bricks, and 4 flagstones." Similarly, in C, we must declare our variables before we can use them. We must name each one of our "bricks" and tell C what type of brick to use.

After our variables are defined, we can begin to use them. In construction, the basic structure is a room. By combining many rooms, we form a building. In C, the basic structure is a function. Functions can be combined to form a program.

An apprentice builder does not start out building the Empire State Building, but rather starts on a one-room house. In this chapter, we will concentrate on constructing simple one-function programs.

Basic Program Structure

The basic elements of a program are the data declarations, functions, and comments. Let's see how these can be organized into a simple C program.

The basic structure of a one-function program is:

```
/*****************************************************
 *  ...Heading comments...                          *
 *****************************************************/
...Data declarations...
int main()
{
    ...Executable statements...
    return (0);
}
```

Heading comments tell the programmer about the program, and *data declarations* describe the data that the program is going to use.

Our single function is named **main**. The name **main** is special, because it is the first function called. Other functions are called directly or indirectly from **main**. The function **main** begins with:

```
int main()
{
```

and ends with:

```
    return (0);
}
```

The line **return(0);** is used to tell the operating system (UNIX or MS-DOS/ Windows) that the program exited normally (Status=0). A nonzero status indicates an error—the bigger the return value, the more severe the error. Typically, a status of 1 is used for the most simple errors, like a missing file or bad command-line syntax.

Now, let's take a look at our *Hello World* program (Example 3-1).

At the beginning of the program is a comment box enclosed in /* and */. Following this box is the line:

```
#include <stdio.h>
```

This statement signals C that we are going to use the standard I/O package. The statement is a type of data declaration.* Later we use the function **printf** from this package.

---

* Technically, the statement causes a set of data declarations to be taken from an include file. Chapter 10, *C Preprocessor*, discusses include files.

Our main routine contains the instruction:

```
printf("Hello World\n");
```

This line is an executable statement instructing C to print the message "Hello World" on the screen. C uses a semicolon (;) to end a statement in much the same way we use a period to end a sentence. Unlike line-oriented languages such as BASIC, an end-of-line does not end a statement. The sentences in this book can span several lines—the end of a line is treated just like space between words. C works the same way. A single statement can span several lines. Similarly, you can put several sentences on the same line, just as you can put several C statements on the same line. However, most of the time your program is more readable if each statement starts on a separate line.

The standard function `printf` is used to output our message. A library routine is a C procedure or function that has been written and put into a library or collection of useful functions. Such routines perform sorting, input, output, mathematical functions, and file manipulation. See your C reference manual for a complete list of library functions.

Hello World is one of the simplest C programs. It contains no computations; it merely sends a single message to the screen. It is a starting point. After you have mastered this simple program, you have done a number of things correctly.

Simple Expressions

Computers can do more than just print strings—they can also perform calculations. Expressions are used to specify simple computations. The five simple operators in C are listed in Table 4-1.

Table 4-1: Simple Operators

Operator	Meaning
*	Multiply
/	Divide
+	Add
-	Subtract
%	Modulus (return the remainder after division)

Multiply (*), divide (/), and modulus (%) have precedence over add (+) and subtract (-). Parentheses, (), may be used to group terms. Thus:

```
(1 + 2) * 4
```

yields 12, while:

```
    1 + 2 * 4
```

yields 9.

Example 4-1 computes the value of the expression (1 + 2) * 4.

Example 4-1: simple/simple.c
```
int main()
{
    (1 + 2) * 4;
    return (0);
}
```

Although we calculate the answer, we don't do anything with it. (This program will generate a "null effect" warning to indicate that there is a correctly written, but useless, statement in the program.)

Think about how confused a workman would be if we were constructing a building and said,

> "Take your wheelbarrow and go back and forth between the truck and the building site."

> "Do you want me to carry bricks in it?"

> "No. Just go back and forth."

We need to store the results of our calculations.

Variables and Storage

C allows us to store values in *variables*. Each variable is identified by a *variable name*.

In addition, each variable has a *variable type*. The type tells C how the variable is going to be used and what kind of numbers (real, integer) it can hold. Names start with a letter or underscore (_), followed by any number of letters, digits, or underscores. Uppercase is different from lowercase, so the names **sam**, **Sam**, and **SAM** specify three different variables. However, to avoid confusion, you should use different names for variables and not depend on case differences.

Nothing prevents you from creating a name beginning with an underscore; however, such names are usually reserved for internal and system names.

Most C programmers use all-lowercase variable names. Some names like **int**, **while**, **for**, and **float** have a special meaning to C and are considered *reserved words*. They cannot be used for variable names.

The following is an example of some variable names:

```
average             /* average of all grades */
pi                  /* pi to 6 decimal places */
number_of_students  /* number students in this class */
```

The following are *not* variable names:

```
3rd_entry   /* Begins with a number */
all$done    /* Contains a "$" */
the end     /* Contains a space */
int         /* Reserved word */
```

Avoid variable names that are similar. For example, the following illustrates a poor choice of variable names:

```
total    /* total number of items in current entry */
totals   /* total of all entries */
```

A much better set of names is:

```
entry_total /* total number of items in current entry */
all_total   /* total of all entries */
```

Variable Declarations

Before you can use a variable in C, it must be defined in a *declaration statement.*

A variable declaration serves three purposes:

1. It defines the name of the variable.

2. It defines the type of the variable (integer, real, character, etc.).

3. It gives the programmer a description of the variable. The declaration of a variable **answer** can be:

```
int answer;    /* the result of our expression */
```

The keyword **int** tells C that this variable contains an integer value. (Integers are defined below.) The variable name is **answer**. The semicolon (;) marks the end of the statement, and the comment is used to define this variable for the programmer. (The requirement that every C variable declaration be commented is a style rule. C will allow you to omit the comment. Any experienced teacher, manager, or lead engineer will not.)

The general form of a variable declaration is:

```
type  name;   /* comment */
```

where *type* is one of the C variable types (**int**, **float**, etc.) and *name* is any valid variable name. This declaration explains what the variable is and what it will be used for. (In Chapter 9, *Variable Scope and Functions*, we will see how local variables can be declared elsewhere.)

Variable declarations appear just before the **main()** line at the top of a program.

Integers

One variable type is integer. Integer numbers have no fractional part or decimal point. Numbers such as 1, 87, and -222 are integers. The number 8.3 is not an integer because it contains a decimal point. The general form of an integer declaration is:

```
int   name;   /* comment */
```

A calculator with an 8-digit display can only handle numbers between 99999999 and -99999999. If you try to add 1 to 99999999, you will get an overflow error. Computers have similar limits. The limits on integers are implementation dependent, meaning they change from computer to computer.

Calculators use decimal digits (0–9). Computers use binary digits (0–1) called bits. Eight bits make a byte. The number of bits used to hold an integer varies from machine to machine. Numbers are converted from binary to decimal for printing.

On most UNIX machines, integers are 32 bits (4 bytes), providing a range of 2147483647 (2^{31}-1) to -2147483648. On the PC, most compilers use only 16 bits (2 bytes), so the range is 32767 (2^{15}-1) to -32768. These sizes are typical. The standard header file *limits.h* defines constants for the various numerical limits. (See Chapter 18, *Modular Programming*, for more information on header files.)

The C standard does not specify the actual size of numbers. Programs that depend on an integer being a specific size (say 32 bits) frequently fail when moved to another machine.

Question 4-1: *The following will work on a UNIX machine, but will fail on a PC:*

```
int zip;        /* zip code for current address */
.........
zip = 92126;
```

Why does this fail? What will be the result when it is run on a PC?

Assignment Statements

Variables are given a value through the use of *assignment statements*. For example:

```
answer = (1 + 2) * 4;
```

is an assignment. The variable **answer** on the left side of the equal sign (=) is assigned the value of the expression (1 + 2) * 4 on the right side. The semi-colon (;) ends the statement.

Declarations create space for variables. Figure 4-1A illustrates a variable declaration for the variable **answer**. We have not yet assigned it a value so it is known as an *uninitialized variable*. The question mark indicates that the value of this variable is unknown.

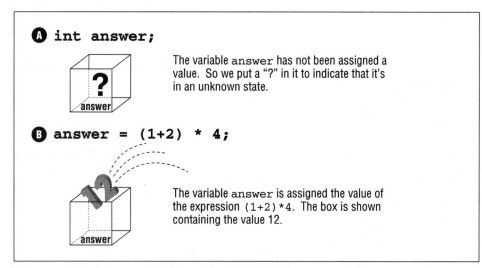

Figure 4-1: Declaration of answer and assigning it a value

Assignment statements are used to give a variable a value. For example:

```
answer = (1 + 2) * 4;
```

is an assignment. The variable **answer** on the left side of the equals operator (=) is assigned the value of the expression (1 + 2) * 4. So the variable **answer** gets the value 12 as illustrated in Figure 4-1B.

The general form of the assignment statement is:

```
variable = expression;
```

The = is used for assignment. It literally means: Compute the expression and assign the value of that expression to the variable. (In some other languages, such as PASCAL, the = operator is used to test for equality. In C, the operator is used for assignment.)

In Example 4-2, we use the variable **term** to store an integer value that is used in two later expressions.

Example 4-2: term/term.c

```
[File: term/term.c]
int term;       /* term used in two expressions */
int term_2;     /* twice term */
int term_3;     /* three times term */
int main()
{
```

Example 4-2: term/term.c (continued)

```
    term = 3 * 5;
    term_2 = 2 * term;
    term_3 = 3 * term;
    return (0);
}
```

A problem exists with this program. How can we tell if it is working or not? We need some way of printing the answers.

printf Function

The library function `printf` can be used to print the results. If we add the statement:

```
    printf("Twice %d is %d\n", term, 2 * term);
```

the program will print:

```
    Twice 15 is 30
```

The special characters `%d` are called the *integer conversion specification*. When `printf` encounters a `%d`, it prints the value of the next expression in the list following the format string. This is called the *parameter list*.

The general form of the `printf` statement is:

```
    printf(format, expression-1, expression-2, ...);
```

where *format* is the string describing what to print. Everything inside this string is printed verbatim except for the `%d` conversions. The value of *expression-1* is printed in place of the first `%d`, *expression-2* is printed in place of the second, and so on.

Figure 4-2 shows how the elements of the `printf` statement work together to generate the final result.

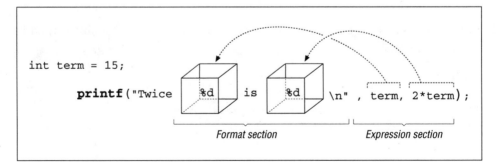

Figure 4-2: printf structure

The format string `"Twice %d is %d\n"` tells `printf` to display `Twice` followed by a space, the value of the first expression, then a space followed by `is` and a space, the value of the second expression, finishing with an end-of-line (indicated by `\n`).

Example 4-3 shows a program that computes `term` and prints it via two `printf` functions.

Example 4-3: twice/twice.c

```
[File: twice/twice.c]
#include <stdio.h>

int term;       /* term used in two expressions */
int main()
{
    term = 3 * 5;
    printf("Twice %d is %d\n", term, 2*term);
    printf("Three times %d is %d\n", term, 3*term);
    return (0);
}
```

The number of `%d` conversions in the format should exactly match the number of expressions in the `printf`. C will not verify this. (Actually, the GNU *gcc* compiler will check `printf` arguments, if you turn on the proper warnings.) If too many expressions are supplied, the extra ones will be ignored. If there are not enough expressions, C will generate strange numbers for the missing expressions.

Floating Point

Because of the way they are stored internally, real numbers are also known as floating-point numbers. The numbers 5.5, 8.3, and -12.6 are all floating-point numbers. C uses the decimal point to distinguish between floating-point numbers and integers. So 5.0 is a floating-point number, while 5 is an integer. Floating-point numbers must contain a decimal point. Floating-point numbers include: 3.14159, 0.5, 1.0, and 8.88.

Although you could omit digits before the decimal point and specify a number as .5 instead of 0.5, the extra 0 clearly indicates that you are using a floating-point number. A similar rule applies to 12. versus 12.0. A floating-point zero should be written as 0.0.

Additionally, the number may include an exponent specification of the form:

e ± exp

For example, 1.2e34 is a shorthand version of 1.2×10^{34}.

The form of a floating-point declaration is:

```
float    variable;   /* comment */
```

Again, there is a limit on the range of floating-point numbers that the computer can handle. This limit varies widely from computer to computer. Floating-point accuracy will be discussed further in Chapter 16, *Floating Point*.

When a floating-point number using `printf` is written, the `%f` conversion is used. To print the expression `1.0/3.0`, we use this statement:

```
printf("The answer is %f\n", 1.0/3.0);
```

Floating Point Versus Integer Divide

The division operator is special. There is a vast difference between an integer divide and a floating-point divide. In an integer divide, the result is truncated (any fractional part is discarded). So the value of 19/10 is 1.

If either the divisor or the dividend is a floating-point number, a floating-point divide is executed. So 19.0/10.0 is 1.9. (19/10.0 and 19.0/10 are also floating-point divides; however, 19.0/10.0 is preferred for clarity.) Several examples appear in Table 4-2.

Table 4-2: Expression Examples

Expression	Result	Result type
1 + 2	3	Integer
1.0 + 2.0	3.0	Floating Point
19 / 10	1	Integer
19.0 / 10.0	1.9	Floating Point

C allows the assignment of an integer expression to a floating-point variable. C will automatically perform the conversion from integer to floating point. A similar conversion is performed when a floating-point number is assigned to an integer. For example:

```
int   integer;  /* an integer */
float floating; /* a floating-point number */

int main()
{
    floating = 1.0 / 2.0;        /* assign "floating" 0.5 */
    integer = 1 / 3;             /* assign integer 0 */
    floating = (1 / 2) + (1 / 2); /* assign floating 0.0 */
    floating = 3.0 / 2.0;        /* assign floating 1.5 */
    integer = floating;          /* assign integer 1 */
    return (0);
}
```

Notice that the expression 1 / 2 is an integer expression resulting in an integer divide and an integer result of 0.

Question 4-2: *Why is the result of Example 4-4 "0.0"? What must be done to this program to fix it?*

Example 4-4: q_zero/q_zero.c

```
#include <stdio.h>

float answer;    /* The result of our calculation */

int main()
{
    answer = 1/3;
    printf("The value of 1/3 is %f\n", answer);
    return (0);
}
```

Question 4-3: *Why does 2 + 2 = 5928? (Your results may vary. See Example 4-5.)*

Example 4-5: two/two.c

```
[File: two/two.c]
#include <stdio.h>

/* Variable for computation results */
int answer;

int main()
{
    answer = 2 + 2;

    printf("The answer is %d\n");
    return (0);
}
```

Question 4-4: *Why is an incorrect result printed? (See Example 4-6.)*

Example 4-6: div/div.c

```
[File: div/div.c]
#include <stdio.h>

float result;    /* Result of the divide */

int main()
{
    result = 7.0 / 22.0;

    printf("The result is %d\n", result);
    return (0);
}
```

Characters

The type **char** represents single characters. The form of a character declaration is:

```
char    variable;   /* comment */
```

Characters are enclosed in single quotes (`'`). `'A'`, `'a'`, and `'!'` are character constants. The backslash character (\) is called the *escape character*. It is used to signal that a special character follows. For example, the characters \" can be used to put a double quote inside a string. A single quote is represented by \'. \n is the newline character. It causes the output device to go to the beginning of the next line (similar to a return key on a typewriter). The characters \\ are the backslash itself. Finally, characters can be specified by *nnn*, where *nnn* is the octal code for the character. Table 4-3 summarizes these special characters. Appendix A, *ASCII Table*, contains a table of ASCII character codes.

Table 4-3: Special Characters

Character	Name	Meaning
\b	Backspace	Move the cursor to the left by one character
\f	Form Feed	Go to top of new page
\n	Newline	Go to next line
\r	Return	Go to beginning of current line
\t	Tab	Advance to next tab stop (eight column boundary)
\'	Apostrophe	Character '
\"	Double quote	Character ".
\\	Backslash	Character \.
nnn		Character number *nnn* (octal)

NOTE   While characters are enclosed in single quotes (`'`), a different data type, the string, is enclosed in double quotes (`"`). A good way to remember the difference between these two types of quotes is to remember that single characters are enclosed in single quotes. Strings can have any number of characters (including one), and they are enclosed in double quotes.

Characters use the `printf` conversion `%c`. Example 4-7 reverses three characters.

Example 4-7: rev/rev.c

```
[File: rev/rev.c]
#include <stdio.h>
```

Example 4-7: rev/rev.c (continued)

```
char char1;      /* first character */
char char2;      /* second character */
char char3;      /* third character */

int main()
{
    char1 = 'A';
    char2 = 'B';
    char3 = 'C';
    printf("%c%c%c reversed is %c%c%c\n",
        char1, char2, char3,
        char3, char2, char1);
    return (0);
}
```

When executed, this program prints:

```
ABC reversed is CBA
```

Answers

Answer 4-1: The largest number that can be stored in an **int** on most UNIX machines is 2147483647. When using Turbo C++, the limit is 32767. The zip code 92126 is larger than 32767, so it is mangled, and the result is 26590.

This problem can be fixed by using a **long int** instead of just an **int**. The various types of integers will be discussed in Chapter 5, *Arrays, Qualifiers, and Reading Numbers*.

Answer 4-2: The problem concerns the division: 1/3. The number 1 and the number 3 are both integers, so this question is an integer divide. Fractions are truncated in an integer divide. The expression should be written as:

```
answer = 1.0 / 3.0
```

Answer 4-3: The `printf` statement:

```
printf("The answer is %d\n");
```

tells the program to print a decimal number, but there is no variable specified. C does not check to make sure `printf` is given the right number of parameters. Because no value was specified, C makes one up. The proper `printf` statement should be:

```
printf("The answer is %d\n", answer);
```

Answer 4-4: The problem is that in the `printf` statement, we used a `%d` to specify that an integer was to be printed, but the parameter for this conversion was a floating-point number. The `printf` function has no way of checking its parameters for type. So if you give the function a floating-point number, but the format specifies an integer, the function will treat the number as an integer and print unexpected results.

Programming Exercises

Exercise 4-1: Write a program to print your name, social security number, and date of birth.

Exercise 4-2: Write a program to print a block E using asterisks (*), where the E has a height of seven characters and a width of five characters.

Exercise 4-3: Write a program to compute the area and perimeter of a rectangle with a width of three inches and a height of five inches. What changes must be made to the program so that it works for a rectangle with a width of 6.8 inches and a length of 2.3 inches?

Exercise 4-4: Write a program to print "HELLO" in big block letters; each letter should have a height of seven characters and width of five characters.

Exercise 4-5: Write a program that deliberately makes the following mistakes:

* Prints a floating-point number using the **%d** conversion.

* Prints an integer using the **%f** conversion.

* Prints a character using the **%d** conversion.

5

Arrays, Qualifiers, and Reading Numbers

That mysterious independent variable of political calculations, Public Opinion.

—Thomas Henry Huxley

Arrays

In constructing our building, we have identified each brick (variable) by name. That process is fine for a small number of bricks, but what happens when we want to construct something larger? We would like to point to a stack of bricks and say, "That's for the left wall. That's brick 1, brick 2, brick 3..."

Arrays allow us to do something similar with variables. An array is a set of consecutive memory locations used to store data. Each item in the array is called an element. The number of elements in an array is called the dimension of the array. A typical array declaration is:

```
/* List of data to be sorted and averaged */
int    data_list[3];
```

The above example declares **data_list** to be an array of three elements. **data_list[0]**, **data_list[1]**, and **data_list[2]** are separate variables. To reference an element of an array, you use a number called the index—the number inside the square brackets ([]). C is a funny language that likes to start counting at 0. So, our three elements are numbered 0 to 2.

NOTE   Common sense tells you that when you declare `data_list` to be three elements long, `data_list[3]` would be valid. Common sense is wrong and `data_list[3]` is illegal.

Example 5-1 computes the total and average of five numbers.

Example 5-1: array/array.c

```
[File: array/array.c]
#include <stdio.h>

float data[5];   /* data to average and total */
float total;     /* the total of the data items */
float average;   /* average of the items */

int main()
{
    data[0] = 34.0;
    data[1] = 27.0;
    data[2] = 45.0;
    data[3] = 82.0;
    data[4] = 22.0;

    total = data[0] + data[1] + data[2] + data[3] + data[4];
    average =  total / 5.0;
    printf("Total %f Average %f\n", total, average);
    return (0);
}
```

This program outputs:

```
Total 210.000000 Average 42.000000
```

Strings

Strings are sequences of characters. C does not have a built-in string type; instead, strings are created out of character arrays. In fact, strings are just character arrays with a few restrictions. One of these restrictions is that the special character `'\0'` (NUL) is used to indicate the end of a string.

For example:

```
char    name[4];

int main()
{
```

```
        name[0] = 'S';
        name[1] = 'a';
        name[2] = 'm';
        name[3] = '\0';
        return (0);
    }
```

This code creates a character array of four elements. Note that we had to allocate one character for the end-of-string marker.

String constants consist of text enclosed in double quotes (`""`). You may have noticed that the first parameter to `printf` is a string constant. C does not allow one array to be assigned to another, so we can't write an assignment of the form:

```
name = "Sam";    /* Illegal */
```

Instead we must use the standard library function `strcpy` to copy the string constant into the variable. (`strcpy` copies the whole string, including the end-of-string character.) To initialize the variable **name** to **Sam**, we would write:

```
#include <string.h>
char    name[4];
int main()
{
    strcpy(name, "Sam");    /* Legal */
    return (0);
}
```

C uses variable-length strings. For example, the declaration:

```
#include <string.h>
char string[50];
int main()
{
    strcpy(string,"Sam");
}
```

creates an array (`string`) that can contain up to 50 characters. The size of the array is 50, but the length of the string is 3. Any string up to 49 characters long can be stored in `string`. (One character is reserved for the NUL that indicates end-of-string.)

NOTE   String and character constants are very different. Strings are surrounded by double quotes (") and characters by single quotes ('). So `"X"` is a one-character string, while `'Y'` is just a single character. (The string `"X"` takes up two bytes, one for the X and one for the end-of-string (\0). The character `'Y'` takes up one byte.)

There are several standard routines that work on string variables, as shown in Table 5-1.

Table 5-1: Partial List of String Functions

Function	Description
strcpy(*string1*, *string2*)	Copy *string2* into *string1*
strcat(*string1*, *string2*)	Concatenate *string2* onto the end of *string1*
length = strlen(*string*)	Get the length of a *string*
strcmp(*string1*, *string2*)	0 if *string1* equals *string2*, otherwise nonzero

The `printf` function uses the conversion `%s` for printing string variables, as shown in Example 5-2.

Example 5-2: str/str.c

```
#include <string.h>
#include <stdio.h>
char name[30];     /* First name of someone */
int main()
{
    strcpy(name, "Sam");     /* Initialize the name */
    printf("The name is %s\n", name);
    return (0);
}
```

Example 5-3 takes a first name and a last name and combines the two strings.

The program works by initializing the variable `first` to the first name (Steve). The last name (Oualline) is put in the variable `last`. To construct the full name, the first name is copied into `full_name`. Then `strcat` is used to add a space. We call `strcat` again to tack on the last name.

The dimension of the string variable is 100 because we know that no one we are going to encounter has a name more than 99 characters long. (If we get a name more than 99 characters long, our program will mess up. What actually happens is that you write into memory that you shouldn't access. This access can cause your program to crash, run normally and give incorrect results, or behave in other unexpected ways.)

Example 5-3: full/full.c

```
#include <string.h>
#include <stdio.h>

char first[100];       /* first name */
char last[100];        /* last name */
```

Example 5-3: full/full.c (continued)

```
char full_name[200];    /* full version of first and last name */

int main()
{
    strcpy(first, "Steve");        /* Initialize first name */
    strcpy(last, "Oualline");      /* Initialize last name */

    strcpy(full_name, first);      /* full = "Steve" */
    /* Note: strcat not strcpy */
    strcat(full_name, " ");        /* full = "Steve " */
    strcat(full_name, last);       /* full = "Steve Oualline" */

    printf("The full name is %s\n", full_name);
    return (0);
}
```

The output of this program is:

```
The full name is Steve Oualline
```

Reading Strings

The standard function **fgets** can be used to read a string from the keyboard. The general form of an **fgets** call is:

```
fgets(name, sizeof(name), stdin);
```

where *name* identifies a string variable. (**fgets** will be explained in detail in Chapter 14, *File Input/Output*.)

The arguments are:

name

is the name of a character array. The line (including the end-of-line character) is read into this array.

sizeof(name)

indicates the maximum number of characters to read (plus one for the end-of-string character). The **sizeof** function provides a convenient way of limiting the number of characters read to the maximum numbers that the variable can hold. This function will be discussed in more detail in Chapter 14.

stdin

is the file to read. In this case, the file is the standard input or keyboard. Other files are discussed in Chapter 14.

Example 5-4 reads a line from the keyboard and reports its length.

Example 5-4: length/length.c

```
#include <string.h>
#include <stdio.h>

char line[100]; /* Line we are looking at */

int main()
{
    printf("Enter a line: ");
    fgets(line, sizeof(line), stdin);

    printf("The length of the line is: %d\n", strlen(line));
    return (0);
}
```

When we run this program, we get:

```
Enter a line: test
The length of the line is: 5
```

But the string test is only four characters. Where's the extra character coming from? fgets includes the end-of-line in the string. So the fifth character is newline (\n).

Suppose we wanted to change our name program to ask the user for his first and last name. Example 5-5 shows how we could write the program.

Example 5-5: full1/full1.c

```
#include <stdio.h>
#include <string.h>

char first[100];        /* First name of person we are working with */
char last[100];         /* His last name */

/* First and last name of the person (computed) */
char full[200];

int main() {
    printf("Enter first name: ");
    fgets(first, sizeof(first), stdin);

    printf("Enter last name: ");
    fgets(last, sizeof(last), stdin);

    strcpy(full, first);
    strcat(full, " ");
    strcat(full, last);

    printf("The name is %s\n", full);
```

Example 5-5: full1/full1.c (continued)

```
    return (0);
}
```

However, when we run this program we get the results:

```
% name2
Enter first name: John
Enter last name: Doe
The name is John
 Doe
%
```

What we wanted was "John Doe" on the same line. What happened? The **fgets** function gets the entire line, *including the end-of-line*. We must get rid of this character before printing.

For example, the name "John" would be stored as:

```
first[0] = 'J'
first[1] = 'o'
first[2] = 'h'
first[3] = 'n'
first[4] = '\n'
first[5] = '\0'    /* end of string */
```

By setting **first[4]** to NUL (**'\0'**), we can shorten the string by one character and get rid of the unwanted newline. This change can be done with the statement:

```
first[4] = '\0';
```

The problem is that this method will work only for four-character names. We need a general algorithm to solve this problem. The length of this string is the index of the end-of-string null character. The character before it is the one we want to get rid of. So, to trim the string, we use the statement:

```
first[strlen(first)-1] = '\0';
```

Our new program is shown in Example 5-6.

Example 5-6: full2/full2.c

```
#include <stdio.h>
#include <string.h>

char first[100];        /* First name of person we are working with */
char last[100];         /* His last name */

/* First and last name of the person (computed) */
char full[200];

int main() {
    printf("Enter first name: ");
    fgets(first, sizeof(first), stdin);
```

Example 5-6: full2/full2.c (continued)

```
    /* trim off last character */
    first[strlen(first)-1] = '\0';

    printf("Enter last name: ");
    fgets(last, sizeof(last), stdin);
    /* trim off last character */
    last[strlen(last)-1] = '\0';

    strcpy(full, first);
    strcat(full, " ");
    strcat(full, last);

    printf("The name is %s\n", full);
    return (0);
}
```

Running this program gives us the following results:

```
    Enter first name:  John
    Enter last name:  Smith
    The name is John Smith
```

Multidimensional Arrays

Arrays can have more than one dimension. The declaration for a two-dimensional array is:

```
    type variable[size1][size2];   /* Comment */
```

For example:

```
    int matrix[2][4]; /* a typical matrix */
```

Notice that C does *not* follow the notation used in other languages of `matrix[10,12]`.

To access an element of the **matrix**, we use the notation:

```
    matrix[1][2] = 10;
```

C allows the programmer to use as many dimensions as needed (limited only by the amount of memory available). Additional dimensions can be tacked on:

```
    four_dimensions[10][12][9][5];
```

Question 5-1: *Why does Example 5-7 print the wrong answer?*

Example 5-7: p_array/p_array.c

```c
#include <stdio.h>

int array[3][2];          /* Array of numbers */

int main()
{
    int x,y;     /* Loop indicies */

    array[0][0] = 0 * 10 + 0;
    array[0][1] = 0 * 10 + 1;
    array[1][0] = 1 * 10 + 0;
    array[1][1] = 1 * 10 + 1;
    array[2][0] = 2 * 10 + 0;
    array[2][1] = 2 * 10 + 1;

    printf("array[%d] ", 0);
    printf("%d ", array[0,0]);
    printf("%d ", array[0,1]);
    printf("\n");

    printf("array[%d] ", 1);
    printf("%d ", array[1,0]);
    printf("%d ", array[1,1]);
    printf("\n");

    printf("array[%d] ", 2);
    printf("%d ", array[2,0]);
    printf("%d ", array[2,1]);
    printf("\n");

    return (0);
}
```

Reading Numbers

So far, we have only read simple strings, but we want more. We want to read numbers as well. The function scanf works like printf, except that scanf reads numbers instead of writing them. scanf provides a simple and easy way of reading numbers *that almost never works*. The function scanf is notorious for its poor end-of-line handling, which makes scanf useless for all but an expert.

However, we've found a simple way to get around the deficiencies of scanf— we don't use it. Instead, we use fgets to read a line of input and sscanf to convert the text into numbers. (The name sscanf stands for "string scanf". sscanf is like scanf, but works on strings instead of the standard input.)

Normally, we use the variable `line` for lines read from the keyboard:

```
char line[100];    /* Line of keyboard input */
```

When we want to process input, we use the statements:

```
fgets(line, sizeof(line), stdin);
sscanf(line, format, &variable1, &variable2 . . .;
```

Here `fgets` reads a line and `sscanf` processes it. *format* is a string similar to the `printf` format string. Note the ampersand (`&`) in front of the variable names. This symbol is used to indicate that `sscanf` will change the value of the associated variables. (For information on why we need the ampersand, see Chapter 13, *Simple Pointers.*)

NOTE   If you forget to put `&` in front of each variable for `sscanf`, the result could be a "Segmentation violation core dumped" or "Illegal memory access" error. In some cases a random variable or instruction will be changed. On UNIX, damage is limited to the current program; however, on MS-DOS/Windows, with its lack of memory protection, this error can easily cause more damage. On MS-DOS/Windows, omitting `&` can cause a program or system crash.

In Example 5-8, we use `sscanf` to get and then double a number from the user.

Example 5-8: double/double.c

```
[File: double/double.c]
#include <stdio.h>
char   line[100];   /* input line from console */
int    value;       /* a value to double */

int main()
{
    printf("Enter a value: ");

    fgets(line, sizeof(line), stdin);
    sscanf(line, "%d", &value);

    printf("Twice %d is %d\n", value, value * 2);
    return (0);
}
```

This program reads in a single number and then doubles it. Notice that there is no `\n` at the end of `Enter a value:`. This omission is intentional because we do not want the computer to print a newline after the prompt. For example, a sample run of the program might look like:

```
Enter a value: 12
Twice 12 is 24
```

If we replaced `Enter a value:` with `Enter a value:\n`, the result would be:

```
Enter a value:
12
Twice 12 is 24
```

Question 5-2: *Example 5-9 computes the area of a triangle, given the triangle's width and height. For some strange reason, the compiler refuses to believe that we declared the variable* `width`. *The declaration is right there on line 2, just after the definition of height. Why isn't the compiler seeing it?*

Example 5-9: tri/tri.c

```
#include <stdio.h>
char line[100];/* line of input data */
int  height;   /* the height of the triangle */
int  width;    /* the width of the triangle */
int  area;     /* area of the triangle (computed) */

int main()
{
    printf("Enter width height? ");

    fgets(line, sizeof(line), stdin);
    sscanf(line, "%d %d", &width, &height);

    area = (width * height) / 2;
    printf("The area is %d\n", area);
    return (0);
}
```

Initializing Variables

C allows variables to be initialized in the declaration statement. For example, the following statement declares the integer `counter` and initializes it to 0:

```
int counter = 0;    /* number cases counted so far */
```

Arrays can also be initialized in this manner. The element list must be enclosed in curly braces ({}). For example:

```
/* Product numbers for the parts we are making */
int product_codes[3] = {10, 972, 45};
```

The previous initialization is equivalent to:

```
product_codes[0] = 10;
product_codes[1] = 972;
product_codes[2] = 45;
```

The number of elements in {} does not have to match the array size. If too many numbers are present, a warning will be issued. If an insufficient amount of numbers are present, C will initialize the extra elements to 0.

If no dimension is given, C will determine the dimension from the number of elements in the initialization list. For example, we could have initialized our variable `product_codes` with the statement:

```
/* Product numbers for the parts we are making */
int product_codes[] = {10, 972, 45};
```

Initializing multidimensional arrays is similar to initializing single-dimension arrays. A set of brackets ([]) encloses each dimension. The declaration:

```
int matrix[2][4]; /* a typical matrix */
```

can be thought of as a declaration of an array of dimension 2 with elements that are arrays of dimension 4. This array is initialized as follows:

```
/* a typical matrix */
int matrix[2][4] =
    {
        {1, 2, 3, 4},
        {10, 20, 30, 40}
    };
```

Strings can be initialized in a similar manner. For example, to initialize the variable **name** to the string "Sam", we use the statement:

```
char    name[] = {'S', 'a', 'm', '\0'};
```

C has a special shorthand for initializing strings: Surround the string with double quotes (`""`) to simplify initialization. The previous example could have been written:

```
char name[] = "Sam";
```

The dimension of **name** is 4, because C allocates a place for the `'\0'` character that ends the string.

The following declaration:

```
char string[50] = "Sam";
```

is equivalent to:

```
char string[50];
    .
    .
    .
strcpy(string, "Sam");
```

An array of 50 characters is allocated but the length of the string is 3.

Types of Integers

C is considered a medium-level language because it allows you to get very close to the actual hardware of the machine. Some languages, like BASIC*, go to great lengths to completely isolate the user from the details of how the processor works. This simplification comes at a great loss of efficiency. C lets you give detailed information about how the hardware is to be used.

For example, most machines let you use different length numbers. BASIC provides the programmer with only one numeric type. Though this restriction simplifies the programming, BASIC programs are extremely inefficient. C allows the programmer to specify many different flavors of integers, so that the programmer can make best use of hardware.

The type specifier **int** tells C to use the most efficient size (for the machine you are using) for the integer. This can be two to four bytes depending on the machine. (Some less common machines use strange integer sizes such as 9 or 40 bits.)

Sometimes you need extra digits to store numbers larger than those allowed in a normal **int**. The declaration:

```
long int answer;    /* the result of our calculations */
```

is used to allocate a long integer. The **long** qualifier informs C that we wish to allocate extra storage for the integer. If we are going to use small numbers and wish to reduce storage, we use the qualifier **short**. For example:

```
short int year;           /* Year including the 19xx part */
```

C guarantees that the size of storage for **short** <= **int** <= **long**. In actual practice, **short** almost always allocates two bytes, **long** four bytes, and **int** two or four bytes. (See Appendix B, *Ranges and Parameter Passing Conversions*, for numeric ranges.)

The type **short int** usually uses 2 bytes, or 16 bits. 15 bits are used normally for the number and 1 bit for the sign. This format gives the type a range of −32768 (-2^{15}) to 32767 ($2^{15} - 1$). An **unsigned short int** uses all 16 bits for the number, giving it the range of 0 to 65535 (2^{16}). All **int** declarations default to **signed**, so that the declaration:

```
signed long int answer;    /* final result */
```

is the same as:

```
long int answer;           /* final result */
```

---

* Some more advanced versions of BASIC do have number types. However, for this example, we are talking about basic BASIC.

Finally, we consider the very short integer of type **char**. Character variables use 1 byte. They can also be used for numbers in the range of −128 to 127 (**signed char**) or 0 to 255 (**unsigned char**). Unlike integers, they do not default to **signed**; the default is compiler dependent.* Very short integers may be printed using the integer conversion (**%d**).

You cannot read a very short integer directly. You must read the number into an integer and then use an assignment statement. For example:

```
#include <stdio.h>
signed char ver_short;    /* A very short integer */
char line[100];           /* Input buffer */
int temp;                 /* A temporary number */

int main()
{
    /* Read a very short integer */
    fgets(line, sizeof(line), stdin);
    sscanf(line, "%d", &temp);
    very_short = temp;
}
```

Table 5-2 contains the **printf** and **sscanf** conversions for integers.

Table 5-2: Integer printf/sscanf Conversions

%Conversion	Uses
%hd	(signed) short int
%d	(signed) int
%ld	(signed) long int
%hu	unsigned short int
%u	unsigned int
%lu	unsigned long int

The range of the various flavors of integers is listed in Appendix B.

long int declarations allow the program to explicitly specify extra precision where it is needed (at the expense of memory). **short int** numbers save space but have a more limited range. The most compact integers have type **char**. They also have the most limited range.

unsigned numbers provide a way of doubling the positive range at the expense of eliminating negative numbers. They are also useful for things that can never be negative, like counters and indices.

---

* Turbo C++ and GNU's *gcc* even have a command-line switch to make the default for type **char** either **signed** or **unsigned**.

The flavor of number you use will depend on your program and storage requirements.

Types of Floats

The **float** type also comes in various flavors. **float** denotes normal precision (usually 4 bytes). **double** indicates double precision (usually 8 bytes). Double-precision variables give the programmer many times the range and precision of single-precision (**float**) variables.

The qualifier **long double** denotes extended precision. On some systems, this is the same as **double**; on others, it offers additional precision. All types of floating-point numbers are always signed.

Table 5-3 contains the `printf` and `sscanf` conversions for floating-point numbers.

Table 5-3: Float printf/sscanf Conversions

% Conversion	Uses	Notes
`%f`	`float`	printf only.[a]
`%lf`	`double`	scanf only.
`%Lf`	`long double`	Not available on all compilers.

[a] The %f format works for printing *double* and *float* because of an automatic conversion built into C's parameter passing.

On some machines, single-precision, floating-point instructions execute faster (but less accurately) than double-precision instructions. Double-precision instructions gain accuracy at the expense of time and storage. In most cases, **float** is adequate; however, if accuracy is a problem, switch to **double**. (See Chapter 16, *Floating Point*.)

Constant Declarations

Sometimes you want to use a value that does not change, such as π. The keyword **const** indicates a variable that never changes. For example, to declare a value for PI, we use the statement:

```
const float PI = 3.1415927;    /* The classic circle constant */
```

NOTE   By convention, variable names use only lowercase and constant names use only uppercase. However, the language does not require this case structure, and some exotic coding styles use a different convention.

Constants must be initialized at declaration time and can never be changed. For example, if we tried to reset the value of PI to 3.0, we would generate an error message:

```
PI = 3.0;      /* Illegal */
```

Integer constants can be used as a size parameter when declaring an array:

```
/* Max. number of elements in the total list.*/
const int TOTAL_MAX = 50;
float total_list[TOTAL_MAX]; /* Total values for each category */
```

NOTE   This way of specifying the use of integer constants is a relatively new innovation in the C language and is not yet fully supported by all compilers.

Hexadecimal and Octal Constants

Integer numbers are specified as a string of digits, such as 1234, 88, −123, etc. These strings are decimal (base 10) numbers: 174 or 174_{10}. Computers deal with binary (base 2) numbers: 10101110. The octal (base 8) system easily converts to and from binary. Each group of three digits ($2^3 = 8$) can be transformed into a single octal digit. Thus, 10101110 can be written as 10   101   110 and changed to the octal 256. Hexadecimal (base 16) numbers have a similar conversion; only 4 bits are used at a time.

The C language has conventions for representing octal and hexadecimal values. Leading zeros are used to signal an octal constant. For example, 0123 is 123 (octal) or 83 (decimal). Starting a number with "0x" indicates a hexadecimal (base 16) constant. So, 0x15 is 21 (decimal). Table 5-4 shows several numbers in all three bases.

Table 5-4: Integer Examples

Base 10	Base 8	Base 16
6	06	0x6
9	011	0x9
15	017	0xF

Operators for Performing Shortcuts

C not only provides you with a rich set of declarations, but also gives you a large number of special-purpose operators.

Frequently, the programmer wants to increment (increase by 1) a variable. Using a normal assignment statement, this operation would look like:

```
total_entries = total_entries + 1;
```

C provides us with a shorthand for performing this common task. The **++** operator is used for incrementing:

```
++total_entries;
```

A similar operator, **--**, can be used for decrementing (decreasing by 1) a variable:

```
--number_left;
/* is the same as */
number_left = number_left - 1;
```

But suppose that we want to add 2 instead of 1. Then we can use the following notation:

```
total_entries += 2;
```

This notation is equivalent to:

```
total_entries = total_entries + 2;
```

Each of the simple operators, as shown in Table 5-5, can be used in this manner.

Table 5-5: Shorthand Operators

Operator	Shorthand	Equivalent Statement
+=	x += 2;	x = x + 2;
-=	x -= 2;	x = x - 2;
*=	x *= 2;	x = x * 2;
/=	x /= 2;	x = x / 2;
%=	x %= 2;	x = x % 2;

Side Effects

Unfortunately, C allows the programmer to use *side effects*. A side effect is an operation that is performed in addition to the main operation executed by the statement. For example, the following is legal C code:

```
size = 5;
result = ++size;
```

The first statement assigns to **size** the value of 5. The second statement assigns to **result** the value of **size** (main operation) and increments **size** (side effect).

But in what order are these processes performed? There are four possible answers.

1. `result` is assigned the value of `size` (5), and then `size` is incremented. `result` is 5 and `size` is 6.

2. `size` is incremented, and then `result` is assigned the value of `size` (6). `result` is 6 and `size` is 6.

3. The answer is compiler-dependent and varies from computer to computer.

4. If we don't write code like this, then we don't have to worry about such questions.

The correct answer is number 2: the increment occurs before the assignment. However, number 4 is a much better answer. The main effects of C are confusing enough without having to worry about side effects.

NOTE   Some programmers value compact code very highly. This attitude is a holdover from the early days of computing when storage cost a significant amount of money. I believe that the art of programming has evolved to the point where clarity is much more valuable than compactness. (Great novels, which a lot of people enjoy reading, are *not* written in shorthand.)

C actually provides two flavors of the ++ operator. One is *variable*++ and the other is ++*variable*. The first:

```
number = 5;
result = number++;
```

evaluates the expressions, and then increments the number; `result` is 5. The second:

```
number = 5;
result = ++number;
```

increments the number first, and then evaluates the expression; `result` is 6. However, using ++ or -- in this way can lead to some surprising code:

```
o = --o - o--;
```

The problem with this line is that it looks as if someone wrote Morse code. The programmer doesn't read this statement, but rather decodes it. If we never use ++ or -- as part of any other statement, and instead always put them on lines by themselves, the difference between the two flavors of these operators will not be noticeable.

++x or x++

The two forms of the increment operator are called the prefix form (++x) and the postfix form (x++). Which form should you use? Actually in C your choice doesn't matter. However, if you use C++ with its overloadable operators, the prefix version (++x) is more efficient.* So, to develop good habits for learning C++, use the prefix form.†

More Side-Effect Problems

More complex side effects can confuse even the C compiler. Consider the following code fragment:

```
value = 1;
result = (value++ * 5) + (value++ * 3);
```

This expression tells C to perform the following steps:

1. Multiply `value` by 5, and add 1 to `value`.

2. Multiply `value` by 3, and add 1 to `value`.

3. Add the results of the two multiplications together.

Steps 1 and 2 are of equal priority (unlike in the previous example) so the compiler can choose the order of execution. Suppose the compiler executes step 1 first, as shown in Figure 5-1.

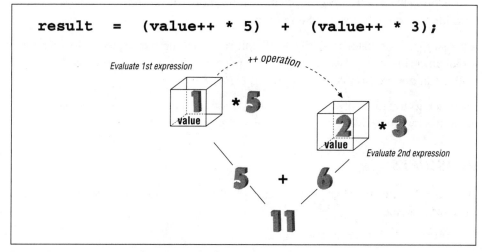

Figure 5-1: Expression evaluation method 1

Or suppose the compiler executes step 2 first, as shown in Figure 5-2.

---

* For details, see the book *Practical C++ Programming* (O'Reilly & Associates).

† Consider the irony of a language with its name in postfix form (C++) working more efficiently with prefix forms of the increment and decrement operators. Maybe the name should be ++C.

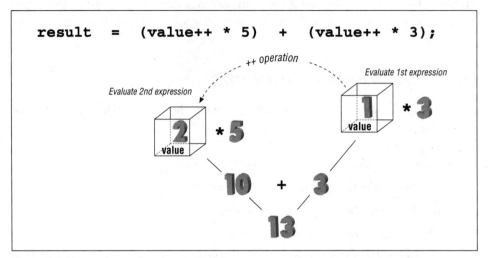

Figure 5-2: Expression evaluation method 2

By using the first method, we get a result of 11. By using the second method, we get a result of 13. The result of this expression is ambiguous. Depending on how the compiler was implemented, the result may be 11 or 13. Even worse, some compilers change the behavior if optimization is turned on. So what was "working" code may break when optimized.

By using the operator ++ in the middle of a larger expression, we created a problem. (This problem is not the only problem that ++ and -- can cause. We will get into more trouble in Chapter 10, *C Preprocessor*.)

In order to avoid trouble and keep the program simple, always put ++ and -- on a line by themselves.

Answers

Answer 5-1: The problem is the use of the expression `array[x,y]` in the `printf` statement:

```
printf("%d ", array[x,y]);
```

Each index to a multidimension array must be placed inside its own set of square brackets ([]). The statement should read:

```
printf("%d ", array[x][y]);
```

For those of you who want to read ahead a little, the comma operator can be used to string multiple expressions together. The value of this operator is the value of the last expressions. As a result `x,y` is equivalent to `y`; and `array[y]` is actually a pointer to row y of the array. Because pointers have strange values, the `printf` outputs strange results. (See Chapter 17, *Advanced Pointers*, and Chapter 21, *C's Dustier Corners*.)

Answer 5-2: The programmer accidentally omitted the end comment (`*/`) after the comment for height. The comment continues onto the next line and engulfs the declaration, as shown in Example 5-10.

Example 5-10: Comment Answer

```
#include <stdio.h>
char line[100];/* line of input data */
int  height;    /* the height of the triangle
int  width;     /* the width of the triangle */
int  area;      /* area of the triangle (computed) */

int main()
{
    printf("Enter width height? ");

    fgets(line, sizeof(line), stdin);
    sscanf(line, "%d %d", &width, &height);

    area = (width * height) / 2;
    printf("The area is %d\n", area);
    return (0);
}
```

Consider another minor problem with this program. If `width` and `height` are both odd, we get an answer that's slightly wrong. (How would you correct this error?)

Programming Exercises

Exercise 5-1: Write a program that converts Centigrade to Fahrenheit. $F = \frac{9}{5}C + 32$

Exercise 5-2: Write a program to calculate the volume of a sphere. $\frac{4}{3}\pi r^3$

Exercise 5-3: Write a program that prints the perimeter of a rectangle given its height and width. $perimeter = 2 \cdot (width + height)$

Exercise 5-4: Write a program that converts kilometers per hour to miles per hour. $miles = (kilometer \cdot 0.6213712)$

Exercise 5-5: Write a program that takes hours and minutes as input, and then outputs the total number of minutes. (1 hour 30 minutes = 90 minutes).

Exercise 5-6: Write a program that takes an integer as the number of minutes, and outputs the total hours and minutes (90 minutes = 1 hour 30 minutes).

6

Decision and Control Statements

> *Once a decision was made, I did not worry about it afterward.*
> —Harry Truman

Calculations and expressions are only a small part of computer programming. Decision and control statements are needed. They specify the order in which statements are to be executed.

So far, we have constructed *linear programs*, that is, programs that execute in a straight line, one statement after another. In this chapter, we will see how to change the *control flow* of a program with *branching statements* and *looping statements*. Branching statements cause one section of code to be executed or not executed, depending on a *conditional clause*. Looping statements are used to repeat a section of code a number of times or until some condition occurs.

if Statement

The **if** statement allows us to put some decision-making into our programs. The general form of the **if** statement is:

```
if (condition)
    statement;
```

If the condition is true (nonzero), the statement will be executed. If the condition is false (0), the statement will not be executed. For example, suppose we are writing a billing program. At the end, if the customer owes us nothing or has a credit (owes us a negative amount), we want to print a message. In C, this program is written:

```
if (total_owed <= 0)
    printf("You owe nothing.\n");
```

The operator `<=` is a relational operator that represents *less than or equal to*. This statement reads "if the `total_owed` is less than or equal to zero, print the message." The complete list of relational operators is found in Table 6-1.

Table 6-1: Relational Operators

Operator	Meaning
<=	Less than or equal to
<	Less than
>	Greater than
>=	Greater than or equal to
==	Equal[a]
!=	Not equal

[a] The equal test (==) is different from the assignment operator (=). One of the most common problems the C programmer faces is mixing them up.

Multiple statements may be grouped by putting them inside curly braces ({}). For example:

```
if (total_owed <= 0) {
    ++zero_count;
    printf("You owe nothing.\n");
}
```

For readability, the statements enclosed in {} are usually indented. This allows the programmer to quickly tell which statements are to be conditionally executed. As we will see later, mistakes in indentation can result in programs that are misleading and hard to read.

else Statement

An alternate form of the **if** statement is:

```
if (condition)
    statement;
else
    statement;
```

If the condition is true (nonzero), the first statement is executed. If it is false (0), the second statement is executed. In our accounting example, we wrote out a message only if nothing was owed. In real life, we probably would want to tell the customer how much is owed if there is a balance due:

```
if (total_owed <= 0)
    printf("You owe nothing.\n");
```

```
    else
        printf("You owe %d dollars\n", total_owed);
```

Now, consider this program fragment (with incorrect indentation):

```
if (count < 10)      /* if #1 */
    if ((count % 4) == 2)    /* if #2 */
        printf("Condition:White\n");
  else
      printf("Condition:Tan\n");
```

NOTE   Note to PASCAL programmers: unlike PASCAL, C requires you to put
              a semicolon at the end of the statement preceding **else**.

There are two **if** statements and one **else**. Which **if** does the **else** belong to?

a. It belongs to **if** #1.

b. It belongs to **if** #2.

c. If you never write code like this, don't worry about this situation.

The correct answer is "c." According to the C syntax rules, the **else** goes with the nearest **if**, so "b" is syntactically correct. But writing code like this violates the KISS principle (Keep It Simple, Stupid). We should write code as clearly and simply as possible. This code fragment should be written as:

```
if (count < 10) {       /* if #1 */
    if ((count % 4) == 2)    /* if #2 */
        printf("Condition:White\n");
    else
        printf("Condition:Tan\n");
}
```

In our original example, we could not clearly determine which **if** statement had the **else** clause; however, by adding an extra set of braces, we improve readability, understanding, and clarity.

How Not to Use strcmp

The function `strcmp` compares two strings, and then returns zero if they are equal or nonzero if they are different. To check if two strings are equal, we use the code:

```
/* Check to see if string1 == string2 */
if (strcmp(string1, string2) == 0)
    printf("Strings equal\n");
else
    printf("Strings not equal\n");
```

Some programmers omit the comment and the == 0 clause. These omissions lead to the following confusing code:

```
if (strcmp(string1, string2))
    printf("......");
```

At first glance, this program obviously compares two strings and executes the `printf` statement if they are equal. Unfortunately, the obvious is wrong. If the strings are equal, `strcmp` returns 0, and the `printf` is not executed. Because of this backward behavior of `strcmp`, you should be very careful in your use of `strcmp` and always comment its use. (It also helps to put in a comment explaining what you're doing.)

Looping Statements

Looping statements allow the program to repeat a section of code any number of times or until some condition occurs. For example, loops are used to count the number of words in a document or to count the number of accounts that have past-due balances.

while Statement

The **while** statement is used when the program needs to perform repetitive tasks. The general form of a **while** statement is:

```
while (condition)
    statement;
```

The program will repeatedly execute the statement inside the **while** until the condition becomes false (0). (If the condition is initially false, the statement will not be executed.)

For example, Example 6-1 later in this chapter will compute all the Fibonacci numbers that are less than 100. The Fibonacci sequence is:

```
1 1 2 3 5 8
```

The terms are computed from the equations:

```
1
1
2 = 1 + 1
3 = 1 + 2
5 = 2 + 3
etc.
```

In general terms this is:

$$f_n = f_{n-1} + f_{n-2}$$

This is a mathematical equation using mathematical variable names (f_n). Mathematicians use this very terse style of naming variables. In programming, terse is dangerous, so we translate these names into something verbose for C. Table 6-2 shows this translation.

Table 6-2: Math to C Name Translation

Math-style name	C-style name
f_n	next_number
f_{n-1}	current_number
f_{n-2}	old_number

In C code, the equation is expressed as:

```
next_number = current_number + old_number;
```

We want to loop until our current term is 100 or larger. The **while** loop:

```
while (current_number < 100)
```

will repeat our computation and printing until we reach this limit.

Figure 6-1 shows what happens to the variable during the execution of the program. At the beginning, current_number and old_number are 1. We print the value of the current term. Then the variable next_number is computed (value 2). Next we advance one term by putting next_number into current_number and current_number into old_number. This process is repeated until we compute the last term and the **while** loop exits.

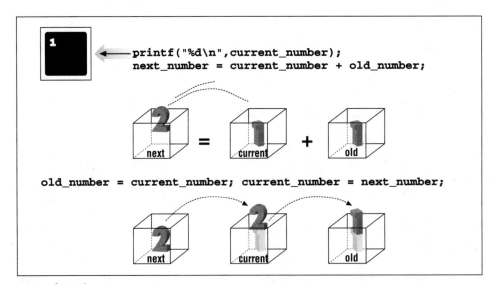

Figure 6-1: Fibonacci execution

This completes the body of the loop. The first two terms of the Fibonacci sequence are 1 and 1. We initialize our first two terms to these values. Putting it all together, we get the code in Example 6-1.

Example 6-1: fib/fib.c

```
#include <stdio.h>
int    old_number;      /* previous Fibonacci number */
int    current_number;  /* current Fibonacci number */
int    next_number;     /* next number in the series */

int main()
{
    /* start things out */
    old_number = 1;
    current_number = 1;

    printf("1\n");      /* Print first number */

    while (current_number < 100) {

        printf("%d\n", current_number);
        next_number = current_number + old_number;

        old_number = current_number;
        current_number = next_number;
    }
    return (0);
}
```

break Statement

We have used a **while** statement to compute the Fibonacci numbers less than 100. The loop exits when the condition after the **while** becomes false (0). Loops can be exited at any point through the use of a **break** statement.

Suppose we want to add a series of numbers, but we don't know how many numbers are to be added together. We need some way of letting the program know that we have reached the end of our list. In Example 6-2, we use the number zero (0) to signal the end-of-list.

Note that the **while** statement begins with:

```
while (1) {
```

Left to its own devices, the program will loop forever because the **while** will exit only when the expression 1 is 0. The only way to exit this loop is through a **break** statement.

When we see the end of the list indicator (0), we use the statement:

```
if (item == 0)
    break;
```

to exit the loop.

Example 6-2: total/total.c

```
#include <stdio.h>
char  line[100];/* line of data for input */
int   total;    /* Running total of all numbers so far */
int   item;     /* next item to add to the list */

int main()
{
    total = 0;
    while (1) {
        printf("Enter # to add \n");
        printf("  or 0 to stop:");

        fgets(line, sizeof(line), stdin);
        sscanf(line, "%d", &item);

        if (item == 0)
            break;

        total += item;
        printf("Total: %d\n", total);
    }
    printf("Final total %d\n", total);
    return (0);
}
```

continue Statement

The **continue** statement is very similar to the **break** statement, except that instead of terminating the loop, **continue** starts reexecuting the body of the loop from the top. For example, if we want to modify the previous program to total only numbers larger than 0, we could write a program such as Example 6-3.

Example 6-3: totalb/totalb.c

```
[File: totalb/totalb.c]
#include <stdio.h>
char  line[100];    /* line from input */
int   total;        /* Running total of all numbers so far */
int   item;         /* next item to add to the list */
int   minus_items;  /* number of negative items */

int main()
{
    total = 0;
    minus_items = 0;
```

Example 6-3: totalb/totalb.c (continued)

```
    while (1) {
        printf("Enter # to add\n");
        printf("  or 0 to stop:");

        fgets(line, sizeof(line), stdin);
        sscanf(line, "%d", &item);

        if (item == 0)
            break;

        if (item < 0) {
            ++minus_items;
            continue;
        }
        total += item;
        printf("Total: %d\n", total);
    }

    printf("Final total %d\n", total);
    printf("with %d negative items omitted\n",
                minus_items);
    return (0);
}
```

Assignment Anywhere Side Effect

C allows the use of assignment statements almost anywhere. For example, you can put assignment statements inside assignment statements:

```
/* don't program like this */
average = total_value / (number_of_entries = last - first);
```

This is the equivalent of saying:

```
/* program like this */
number_of_entries = last - first;
average = total_value / number_of_entries;
```

The first version buries the assignment of **number_of_entries** inside the expression. Programs should be clear and simple and should not hide anything. The most important rule of programming is *keep it simple.*

C also allows the programmer to put assignment statements in the **while** conditional. For example:

```
/* do not program like this */
while ((current_number = last_number + old_number) < 100)
    printf("Term %d\n", current_number);
```

Avoid this type of programming. Notice how much clearer the logic is in the version below:

```
/* program like this */
while (1) {
```

```
    current_number = last_number + old_number;
    if (current_number >= 100)
        break;
    printf("Term %d\n", current_number);
}
```

Question 6-1: *For some strange reason, Example 6-4 thinks that everyone owes a balance of 0 dollars. Why?*

Example 6-4: owe0/owe0.c

```
#include <stdio.h>
char  line[80];        /* input line */
int   balance_owed;    /* amount owed */

int main()
{
    printf("Enter number of dollars owed:");
    fgets(line, sizeof(line), stdin);
    sscanf(line, "%d", &balance_owed);

    if (balance_owed = 0)
        printf("You owe nothing.\n");
    else
        printf("You owe %d dollars.\n", balance_owed);

    return (0);
}
```

Sample output:

```
Enter number of dollars owed: 12
You owe 0 dollars.
```

Answer

Answer 6-1: This program illustrates one of the most common and frustrating of C errors. The problem is that C allows assignment statements inside **if** conditionals. The statement:

```
    if (balance_owed = 0)
```

uses a single equal sign (=) instead of the double equal sign (==). C will assign `balance_owed` the value 0 and test the result (which is 0). If the result was nonzero (true), the **if** clause would be executed. Because the result is 0 (false), the **else** clause is executed and the program prints the wrong answer.

The statement:

```
    if (balance_owed = 0)
```

is equivalent to:

```
    balance_owed = 0;
    if (balanced_owed != 0)
```

The statement should be written:

```
    if (balance_owed == 0)
```

This error is the most common error that beginning C programmers make.

Programming Exercises

Exercise 6-1: Write a program to find the square of the distance between two points. (For a more advanced problem, find the actual distance. This problem involves using the standard function `sqrt`. Use your help system to find out more about how to use this function.)

Exercise 6-2: A professor generates letter grades using Table 6-3.

Table 6-3: Grade Values

% Right	Grade
0–60	F
61–70	D
71–80	C
81–90	B
91–100	A

Given a numeric grade, print the letter.

NOTE   Programmers frequently have to modify code that someone else wrote. A good exercise is to take someone else's code, such as the program that someone wrote for Example 6-4, and then modify it.

Exercise 6-3: Modify the previous program to print a + or – after the letter grade, based on the last digit of the score. The modifiers are listed in Table 6-4.

Table 6-4: Grade Modification Values

Last digit	Modifier
1–3	–
4–7	<blank>
8–0	+

For example, 81=B-, 94=A, and 68=D+. Note: An F is only an F. There is no F+ or F-.

Exercise 6-4: Given an amount of money (less than $1.00), compute the number of quarters, dimes, nickels, and pennies needed.

Exercise 6-5: A leap year is any year divisible by 4, unless the year is divisible by 100, but not 400. Write a program to tell if a year is a leap year.

Exercise 6-6: Write a program that, given the number of hours an employee worked and the hourly wage, computes the employee's weekly pay. Count any hours over 40 as overtime at time and a half.

7

Programming Process

It's just a simple matter of programming.
—Any boss who has never written a program

Programming is more than just writing code. Software has a life cycle. It is born, grows up, becomes mature, and finally dies, only to be replaced by a newer, younger product. Figure 7-1 illustrates the life cycle of a program. Understanding this cycle is important because, as a programmer, you will spend only a small amount of time writing new code. Most programming time is spent modifying and debugging existing code. Software does not exist in a vacuum; it must be documented, maintained, enhanced, and sold. In this chapter, we will take a look at a small programming project using one programmer. Larger projects that involve many people will be discussed in Chapter 18, *Modular Programming*. Although our final code is less than 100 lines, the principles used in its construction can be applied to programs with thousands of lines of code.

The major steps in making a program are:

- *Requirements*. Programs start when someone gets an idea and starts to implement it. The requirement document describes, in very general terms, what is wanted.

- *Program specification*. The specification is a description of what the program does. In the beginning, a *preliminary specification* is used to describe what the program is going to do. Later, as the program becomes more refined, so

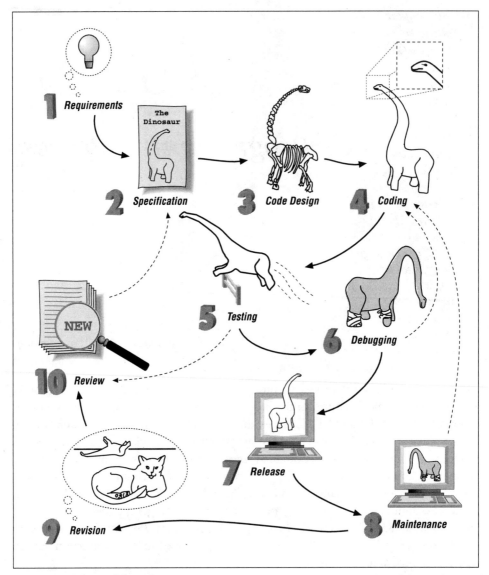

Figure 7-1: Software life cycle

does the specification. Finally, when the program is finished, the specification serves as a complete description of what the program does.

- *Code design.* The programmer does an overall design of the program. The design should include major algorithms, module definitions, file formats, and data structures.

- *Coding.* The next step is writing the program. This step involves first writing a prototype and then filling it in to create the full program.

- *Testing.* The programmer should design a test plan and then use it to test his program. When possible, the programmer should have someone else test the program.

- *Debugging.* Unfortunately, very few programs work the first time. They must be corrected and tested again.

- *Release.* The program is packaged, documented, and sent out into the world to be used.

- *Maintenance.* Programs are never perfect. Bugs will be found and will need correction. This step is the maintenance phase of programming.

- *Revision and updating.* After a program has been working for a while, the users will want changes, such as more features or more intelligent algorithms. At this point, a new specification is created and the process starts again.

Setting Up

The operating system allows you to group files in directories. Just as file folders serve as a way of keeping papers together in a filing cabinet, directories serve as a way of keeping files together. (Windows 95 goes so far as to call its directories "folders.") In this chapter, we create a simple calculator program. All the files for this program are stored in a directory named *calc*. In UNIX, we create a new directory under our home directory and then move to it, as shown in the following example:

```
% cd ~
% mkdir calc
% cd ~/calc
```

On MS-DOS type:

```
C:\> cd \
C:\> mkdir calc
C:\> cd \calc
C:\CALC>
```

This directory setup is extremely simple. As you generate more and more programs, you will probably want a more elaborate directory structure. More information on how to organize directories or folders can be found in your operating system manual.

Specification

For this chapter, we assume that we have the requirement to "write a program that acts like a four-function calculator." Typically, the requirements that you are given is vague and incomplete. The programmer refines it into something that exactly defines the program that he is going to produce. So the first step is to write a preliminary users' specification document that describes what your program is going to do and how to use it. The document does not describe the internal structure of the program or the algorithm you plan on using. A sample specification for our four-function calculator appears below in the sidebar entitled "Calc: A Four-Function Calculator."

The preliminary specification serves two purposes. First, you should give it to your boss (or customer) to make sure that you agree on what each of you said. Second, you can circulate it among your colleagues and see if they have any suggestions or corrections.

This preliminary specification was circulated and received the comments:

* How are you going to get out of the program?

* What happens when you try to divide by 0?

So, we add a new operator, q for quit, and we add the statement:

> "Dividing by 0 results in an error message and the result register is left unchanged."

Code Design

After the preliminary specification has been approved, we can start designing code. In the code design phase, the programmer plans his work. In large programming projects involving many people, the code would be broken up into modules, to be assigned to the programmers. At this stage, file formats are planned, data structures are designed, and major algorithms are decided upon.

Our simple calculator uses no files and requires no fancy data structures. What's left for this phase is to design the major algorithm. Outlined in pseudo code, a shorthand halfway between English and real code, the major algorithm is:

```
Loop
  Read an operator and number
  Do the calculation
  Display the result
End-Loop
```

Calc: A Four-Function Calculator

Preliminary Specification

Dec. 10, 1989

Steve Oualline

Warning: This document is a preliminary specification. Any resemblance to any software living or dead is purely coincidental.

Calc is a program that allows the user to turn a $2,000 computer into a $1.98 four-function calculator. The program will add, subtract, multiply, and divide simple integers.

When the program is run, it will zero the result register and display the register's contents. The user can then type in an operator and number. The result will be updated and displayed. The following operators are valid:

Operator	Meaning
+	Addition
−	Subtraction
*	Multiplication
/	Division

For example (user input is in boldface):

```
calc
Result:  0
Enter operator and number:  + 123
Result:  123
Enter operator and number:  - 23
Result:  100
Enter operator and number:  / 25
Result:  4
Enter operator and number:  * 4
Result:  16
0
```

Prototype

After the code design is completed, we can begin writing the program. But rather than try to write the entire program at once and then debug it, we will use a method called *fast prototyping*. We implement the smallest portion of the specification that will still do something. In our case, we will cut our four functions down to a one-function calculator. After we get this small part working, we can build the rest of the functions onto this stable foundation. Also, the

---

IV + IX = XIII?

A college instructor once gave his students an assignment to "write a four-function calculator." One of his students noticed that this assignment was a very loose specification and decided to have a little fun. The professor didn't say what sort of numbers had to be used, so the student created a program that worked only with Roman numerals (V+ III = VIII). The program came with a complete user manual—written in Latin.

---

prototype gives the boss something to look at and play with, giving him a good idea of the project's direction. Good communication is the key to good programming, and the more you can show someone the better. The code for the first version of our four-function calculator is found in Example 7-1.

Example 7-1: calc1/calc1.c

```
#include <stdio.h>
char  line[100];/* line of data from the input */
int   result;   /* the result of the calculations */
char  operator; /* operator the user specified */
int   value;    /* value specified after the operator */

int main()
{
    result = 0; /* initialize the result */

    /* Loop forever (or till we hit the break statement) */
    while (1) {
        printf("Result: %d\n", result);

        printf("Enter operator and number: ");
        fgets(line, sizeof(line), stdin);
        sscanf(line, "%c %d", &operator, &value);

        if (operator = '+') {
            result += value;
        } else {
            printf("Unknown operator %c\n", operator);
        }
    }
}
```

The program begins by initializing the variable `result` to 0. The main body of the program is a loop starting with:

```
while (1) {
```

This loop will repeat until a **break** statement is reached. The code:

```
        printf("Enter operator and number: ");
        fgets(line, sizeof(line), stdin);
        sscanf(line,"%c %d", &operator, &value);
```

asks the user for an operator and number. These are scanned and stored in the variables `operator` and `value`. Next, we start checking the operators. If the operator is a plus sign (+), we perform an addition using the line:

```
    if (operator = '+') {
        result += value;
```

So far, we only recognize the plus (+) operator. As soon as this operator works correctly, we will add more operators by adding more **if** statements.

Finally, if an illegal operator is entered, the line:

```
    } else {
        printf("Unknown operator %c\n", operator);
    }
```

writes an error message telling the user that he made a mistake.

Makefile

After the source has been entered, it needs to be compiled and linked. Up until now we have been running the compiler manually. This process is somewhat tedious and prone to error. Also, larger programs consist of many modules and are extremely difficult to compile by hand. Fortunately, both UNIX and MS-DOS/ Windows have a utility called *make** that will handle the details of compilation. For now, use this example as a template and substitute the name of your program in place of "calc." *make* will be discussed in detail in Chapter 18. The program looks at the file called *Makefile* for a description of how to compile your program and runs the compiler for you.

Because the Makefile contains the rules for compilation, it is customized for the compiler. The following is a set of *Makefiles* for all of the compilers described in this book.

Generic UNIX

```
File: calc1/makefile.unx
#-----------------------------------------------#
#       Makefile for Unix systems               #
#    using a GNU C compiler                      #
#-----------------------------------------------#
CC=gcc
CFLAGS=-g
#
```

---

* Microsoft's Visual C++ calls this utility **nmake**.

```
# Compiler flags:
#        -g       -- Enable debugging

calc1: calc1.c
        $(CC) $(CFLAGS) -o calc1 calc1.c

clean:
        rm -f calc1
```

WARNING   The *make* utility is responsible for one of the nastiest surprises for
unsuspecting users. The line:

```
$(CC) $(CFLAGS) -o calc1 calc1.c
```

must begin with a tab. Eight spaces won't work. A space and a tab
won't work. The line must start with a tab. Check your editor and
make sure that you can tell the difference between a tab and bunch
of spaces.

UNIX *with the Free Software Foundation's gcc Compiler*

```
File: calc1/makefile.gcc
#--------------------------------------------#
#       Makefile for UNIX systems            #
#    using a GNU C compiler                  #
#--------------------------------------------#
CC=gcc
CFLAGS=-g -D__USE_FIXED_PROTOTYPES__ -ansi
#
# Compiler flags:
#        -g       -- Enable debugging
#        -Wall    -- Turn on all warnings (not used since it gives away
#                       the bug in this program)
#        -D__USE_FIXED_PROTOTYPES__
#                 -- Force the compiler to use the correct headers
#        -ansi    -- Don't use GNU extensions.  Stick to ANSI C.

calc1: calc1.c
        $(CC) $(CFLAGS) -o calc1 calc1.c

clean:
        rm -f calc1
```

Borland C++

```
[File: calc1/makefile.bcc]
#
# Makefile for Borland's Borland-C++ compiler
#
CC=bcc
#
```

```
# Flags
#        -N  -- Check for stack overflow
#        -v  -- Enable debugging
#        -w  -- Turn on all warnings
#        -ml -- Large model
#
CFLAGS=-N -v -w -ml

calc1.exe: calc1.c
         $(CC) $(CFLAGS) -ecalc1 calc1.c

clean:
         erase calc1.exe
```

Turbo C++

```
File: calc1/makefile.tcc
#----------------------------------------------#
#       Makefile for DOS systems               #
#    using a Turbo C compiler.                 #
#----------------------------------------------#
CC=tcc
CFLAGS=-v -w -ml

calc1.exe: calc1.c
         $(CC) $(CFLAGS) -ecalc1.exe calc1.c

clean:
         del calc1.exe
```

Visual C++

```
[File: calc1/makefile.msc]
#----------------------------------------------#
#       Makefile for DOS systems               #
#    using a Microsoft Visual C++ compiler.    #
#----------------------------------------------#
CC=cl
#
# Flags
#        AL -- Compile for large model
#        Zi -- Enable debugging
#        W1 -- Turn on warnings
#
CFLAGS=/AL /Zi /W1

calc1.exe: calc1.c
         $(CC) $(CFLAGS) calc1.c

clean:
         erase calc1.exe
```

To compile the program, just execute the *make* command. *make* will determine which compilation commands are needed and then execute them.

make uses the modification dates of the files to determine whether or not a compile is necessary. Compilation creates an object file. The modification date of the object file is later than the modification date of its source. If the source is edited, the source's modification date is updated, and the object file is then out of date. *make* checks these dates, and if the source was modified after the object, *make* recompiles the object.

Testing

After the program is compiled without errors, we can move on to the testing phase. Now is the time to start writing a test plan. This document is simply a list of the steps we perform to make sure the program works. It is written for two reasons:

- If a bug is found, we want to be able to reproduce it.

- If we change the program, we will want to retest it to make sure new code did not break any of the sections of the program that were previously working.

Our test plan starts out as:

```
Try the following operations:
    + 123   Result should be 123
    + 52    Result should be 175
    x 37    Error message should be output
```

After we run the program, we get:

```
    Result: 0
    Enter operator and number: + 123
    Result: 123
    Enter operator and number: + 52
    Result: 175
    Enter operator and number: x 37
    Result: 212
```

Something is clearly wrong. The entry **x** 37 should have generated an error message, but it didn't. A bug is in the program. So we begin the debugging phase. One of the advantages of making a small working prototype is that we can isolate errors early.

Debugging

First we inspect the program to see if we can detect the error. In such a small program we can easily spot the mistake. However, let's assume that instead of a 21-line program, we have a much larger program containing 5,000 lines. Such a program would make inspection more difficult, so we need to proceed to the next step.

Most systems have C debugging programs; however, each system is different. Some systems have no debugger. In such a case, we must resort to a diagnostic print statement. The technique is simple: put a `printf` at the points at which you know the data is good (just to make sure the data is *really* good). Then put a `printf` at points at which the data is bad. Run the program and keep putting in `printf` statements until you isolate the area in the program that contains the mistake. Our program, with diagnostic `printf` statements added, looks like:

```
printf("Enter operator and number: ");
fgets(line, sizeof(line), stdin);
sscanf("%d %c", &value, &operator);
printf("## after scanf %c\n", operator);
if (operator = '+') {
    printf("## after if %c\n", operator);
    result += value;
```

NOTE   The ## at the beginning of each `printf` is used to indicate a temporary debugging `printf`. When the debugging is complete, the ## makes the associated statements easy to identify and remove.

Running our program again results in:

```
Result: 0
Enter operator and number: + 123
Result: 123
Enter operator and number: + 52
## after scanf +
## after if +
Result: 175
Enter operator and number: x 37
## after scanf x
## after if +
Result: 212
```

From this example we see that something is going wrong with the if statement. Somehow, the variable operator is an "x" going in and a "+" coming out. Closer inspection reveals that we have made the old mistake of using = instead of ==. After we fix this bug, the program runs correctly. Building on this working foundation, we add code for the other operators: dash (–), asterisk (*), and slash (/). The result is shown in Example 7-2.

Example 7-2: calc2/calc2.c

```
#include <stdio.h>
char  line[100];/* line of text from input */

int    result;   /* the result of the calculations */
char   operator; /* operator the user specified */
int    value;    /* value specified after the operator */

int main()
```

Example 7-2: calc2/calc2.c (continued)

```c
{
    result = 0; /* initialize the result */

    /* loop forever (or until break reached) */
    while (1) {
        printf("Result: %d\n", result);
        printf("Enter operator and number: ");

        fgets(line, sizeof(line), stdin);
        sscanf(line, "%c %d", &operator, &value);

        if ((operator == 'q') || (operator == 'Q'))
            break;

        if (operator == '+') {
            result += value;
        } else if (operator == '-') {
            result -= value;
        } else if (operator == '*') {
            result *= value;
        } else if (operator == '/') {
            if (value == 0) {
                printf("Error:Divide by zero\n");
                printf("   operation ignored\n");
            } else
                result /= value;
        } else {
            printf("Unknown operator %c\n", operator);
        }
    }
    return (0);
}
```

We expand our test plan to include the new operators and try it again:

```
+ 123      Result should be 123
+ 52       Result should be 175
x 37       Error message should be output
- 175      Result should be zero
+ 10       Result should be 10
/ 5        Result should be 2
/ 0        Divide by zero error
* 8        Result should be 16
q          Program should exit
```

While testing the program, we find that, much to our surprise, the program works. The word "Preliminary" is removed from the specification, and the program, test plan, and specification are released.

Maintenance

Good programmers put each program through a long and rigorous testing process before releasing it to the outside world. Then the first user tries the program and almost immediately finds a bug. This step is the maintenance phase. Bugs are fixed, the program is tested (to make sure that the fixes didn't break anything), and the program is released again.

Revisions

Although the program is officially finished, we are not done with it. After the program is in use for a few months, someone will come to us and ask, "Can you add a modulus operator?" So we revise the specifications, add the change to the program, update the test plan, test the program, and then release the program again.

As time passes, more people will come to us with additional requests for changes. Soon our program has trig functions, linear regressions, statistics, binary arithmetic, and financial calculations. Our design is based on the concept of one-character operators. Soon we find ourselves running out of characters to use. At this point, our program is doing work far in excess of what it was initially designed to do. Sooner or later we reach the point where the program needs to be scrapped and a new one written from scratch. At that point, we write a preliminary specification and start the process again.

Electronic Archaeology

Electronic archeology is the art of digging through old code to discover amazing things (like how and why the code works).

Unfortunately, most programmers don't start a project at the design step. Instead, they are immediately thrust into the maintenance or revision stage and must face the worst possible job: understanding and modifying someone else's code.

Your computer can aid greatly in your search to discover the true meaning of someone else's code. Many tools are available for examining and formatting code. Some of these tools include:

- *Cross references*. These programs have names like `xref`, `cxref`, and `cross`. System V Unix has the utility `cscope`. A cross reference prints out a list of variables and indicates where each variable is used.

- *Program indenters.* Programs like `cb` and `indent` will take a program and indent it *correctly* (correct indentation is something defined by the tool maker).

- *Pretty printers.* A pretty printer such as `vgrind` or `cprint` will take the source and typeset it for printing on a laser printer.

- *Call graphs.* On System V Unix the program `cflow` can be used to analyze the program. On other systems there is a public-domain utility, `calls`, which produces call graphs. The call graphs show who calls whom and who is called by whom.

Which tools should you use? Whichever work for you. Different programmers work in different ways. Some of the techniques for examining code are listed in the sections below. Choose the ones that work for you and use them.

Marking Up the Program

Take a printout of the program and make notes all over it. Use red or blue ink so that you can tell the difference between the printout and the notes. Use a highlighter to emphasize important sections. These notes are useful; put them in the program as comments, then make a new printout and start the process again.

Using the Debugger

The debugger is a great tool for understanding how something works. Most debuggers allow the user to step through the program one line at a time, examining variables and discovering how things really work. After you find out what the code does, make notes and put them in the program as comments.

Text Editor as a Browser

One of the best tools for going through someone else's code is your text editor. Suppose you want to find out what the variable `sc` is used for. Use the search command to find the first place `sc` is used. Search again and find the second time it is used. Continue searching until you know what the variable does.

Suppose you find out that `sc` is used as a sequence counter. Because you're already in the editor, you can easily do a global search and replace to change `sc` to `sequence_counter`. (Disaster warning: *Before* you make the change, make sure that `sequence_counter` is not already defined as a variable. Also, watch out for unwanted replacements, such as changing the `sc` in "escape.") Comment the declaration and you're on your way to creating an understandable program.

Add Comments

Don't be afraid of putting any information you have, no matter how little, into the comments. Some of the comments I've used include:

```
int state;   /* Controls some sort of state machine */
int rmxy;    /* Something to do with color correction ? */
```

Finally, there is a catch-all comment:

```
int idn;     /* ??? */
```

which means "I have no idea what this variable does." Even though the variable's purpose is unknown, it is now marked as something that needs more work.

As you go through someone else's code adding comments and improving style, the structure will become clearer to you. By inserting notes (comments), you make the code better and easier to understand for future programmers.

For example, suppose we are confronted with the following program written by someone from "The-Terser-the-Better" school of programming. Our assignment is to figure out what this code does. First, we pencil in some comments, as shown in Figure 7-2.

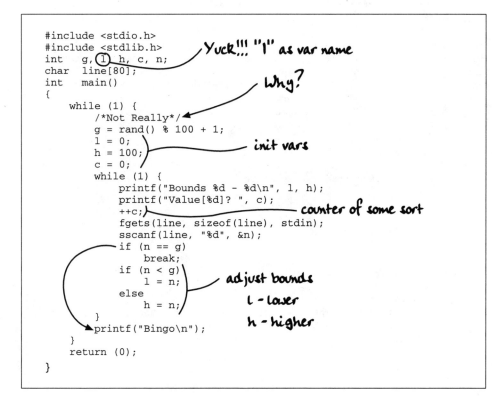

Figure 7-2: A terse program

Our mystery program requires some work. After going through it and applying the principles described in this section, we get a well-commented, easy-to-understand program, such as Example 7-3.

Example 7-3: good/good.c

```
/************************************************************
 * guess -- A simple guessing game.                        *
 *                                                          *
 * Usage:                                                   *
 *      guess                                               *
 *                                                          *
 *      A random number is chosen between 1 and 100.        *
 *      The player is given a set of bounds and             *
 *      must choose a number between them.                  *
 *      If the player chooses the correct number, he wins.  *
 *      Otherwise, the bounds are adjusted to reflect       *
 *      the player's guess and the game continues.          *
 *                                                          *
 *                                                          *
 * Restrictions:                                            *
 *      The random number is generated by the statement     *
 *      rand() % 100.  Because rand() returns a number      *
 *      0 <= rand() <= maxint  this slightly favors         *
 *      the lower numbers.                                  *
 ************************************************************/
#include <stdio.h>
#include <stdlib.h>
int    number_to_guess;  /* random number to be guessed */
int    low_limit;        /* current lower limit of player's range */
int    high_limit;       /* current upper limit of player's range */
int    guess_count;      /* number of times player guessed */
int    player_number;    /* number gotten from the player */
char   line[80];         /* input buffer for a single line */
int main()
{
    while (1) {
        /*
         * Not a pure random number, see restrictions
         */
        number_to_guess = rand() % 100 + 1;

        /* Initialize variables for loop */
        low_limit = 0;
        high_limit = 100;
        guess_count = 0;

        while (1) {
            /* tell user what the bounds are and get his guess */
            printf("Bounds %d - %d\n", low_limit, high_limit);
            printf("Value[%d]? ", guess_count);

            ++guess_count;
```

Example 7-3: good/good.c (continued)

```
        fgets(line, sizeof(line), stdin);
        sscanf(line, "%d", &player_number);

        /* did he guess right? */
        if (player_number == number_to_guess)
            break;

        /* adjust bounds for next guess */
        if (player_number < number_to_guess)
            low_limit = player_number;
        else
            high_limit = player_number;

    }
    printf("Bingo\n");
}
}
```

Programming Exercises

For each of these assignments, follow the software life cycle from specification through release.

Exercise 7-1: Write a program to convert English units to metric (i.e., miles to kilometers, gallons to liters, etc.). Include a specification and a code design.

Exercise 7-2: Write a program to perform date arithmetic such as how many days there are between 6/6/90 and 4/3/92. Include a specification and a code design.

Exercise 7-3: A serial transmission line can transmit 960 characters each second. Write a program that will calculate the time required to send a file, given the file's size. Try the program on a 400MB (419,430,400-byte) file. Use appropriate units. (A 400MB file takes days.)

Exercise 7-4: Write a program to add an 8% sales tax to a given amount and round the result to the nearest penny.

Exercise 7-5: Write a program to tell if a number is prime.

Exercise 7-6: Write a program that takes a series of numbers and counts the number of positive and negative values.

II

Simple Programming

This part builds on the basics to round out our description of simple C programming. In this part, we learn the rest of the control statements as well as some more advanced operations such as bit operations. Finally, we get an introduction to some more sophisticated programming tasks such as file I/O and debugging.

- Chapter 8, *More Control Statements,* describes additional control statements. Included are **for, break,** and **continue**. The **switch** statement is discussed in detail.

- Chapter 9, *Variable Scope and Functions,* introduces local variables, functions, and parameters.

- Chapter 10, *C Preprocessor,* describes the C preprocessor, which gives the programmer tremendous flexibility in writing code. The chapter also provides the programmer with a tremendous number of ways to mess up. Simple rules that help keep the preprocessor from becoming a problem are described.

- Chapter 11, *Bit Operations,* discusses the logical C operators that work on bits.

- Chapter 12, *Advanced Types,* explains structures and other advanced types. The **sizeof** operator and the **enum** type are included.

- Chapter 13, *Simple Pointers,* introduces C pointer variables and shows some of their uses.

- Chapter 14, *File Input/Output,* describes both buffered and unbuffered input/output. ASCII versus binary files are discussed, and you are shown how to construct a simple file.

- Chapter 15, *Debugging and Optimization,* describes how to debug a program, as well as how to use an interactive debugger. You are shown not only how to debug a program, but also how to write a program so that it is easy to debug.

This chapter also describes many optimization techniques for making your program run faster and more efficiently.

* Chapter 16, *Floating Point*, uses a simple decimal floating-point format to introduce you to the problems inherent in floating point, such as roundoff error, precision loss, overflow, and underflow.

In this chapter:
• *for Statement*
• *switch Statement*
• *switch, break, and continue*
• *Answers*
• *Programming Exercises*

8

More Control Statements

Grammar, which knows how to control even kings...
—Molière

for Statement

The **for** statement allows the programmer to execute a block of code for a specified number of times. The general form of the **for** statement is:

```
for (initial-statement; condition; iteration-statement)
    body-statement;
```

This statement is equivalent to:

```
initial-statement;
while (condition) {
    body-statement;
    iteration-statement;
}
```

For example, Example 8-1 uses a **while** loop to add five numbers.

Example 8-1: total5w/totalw.c

```
#include <stdio.h>

int total;      /* total of all the numbers */
int current;    /* current value from the user */
int counter;    /* while loop counter */

char line[80];  /* Line from keyboard */

int main() {
    total = 0;
```

Example 8-1: total5w/totalw.c (continued)

```
    counter = 0;
    while (counter < 5) {
        printf("Number? ");

        fgets(line, sizeof(line), stdin);
        sscanf(line, "%d", &current);
        total += current;

        ++counter;
    }
    printf("The grand total is %d\n", total);
    return (0);
}
```

The same program can be rewritten using a **for** statement as shown in Example 8-2.

Example 8-2: total5f/total5f.c

```
#include <stdio.h>

int total;      /* total of all the numbers */
int current;    /* current value from the user */
int counter;    /* for loop counter */

char line[80];  /* Input from keyboard */

int main() {
    total = 0;
    for (counter = 0; counter < 5; ++counter) {
        printf("Number? ");

        fgets(line, sizeof(line), stdin);
        sscanf(line, "%d", &current);
        total += current;
    }
    printf("The grand total is %d\n", total);
    return (0);
}
```

Note that `counter` goes from 0 to 4. Ordinarily, you count five items as 1, 2, 3, 4, 5; but you will perform much better in C if you change your thinking to zero-based counting and then count five items as 0, 1, 2, 3, 4. (One-based counting is one of the main causes of array overflow errors. See Chapter 5, *Arrays, Qualifiers, and Reading Numbers.*)

Careful examination of the two flavors of our program reveals the similarities between the two versions as seen in Figure 8-1.

Many other programming languages do not allow you to change the control variable (in this case, `counter`) inside the loop. C is not so picky. You can change

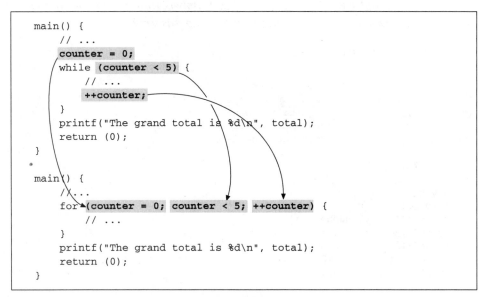

```
main() {
    // ...
    counter = 0;
    while (counter < 5) {
        // ...
        ++counter;
    }
    printf("The grand total is %d\n", total);
    return (0);
}

main() {
    // ...
    for (counter = 0; counter < 5; ++counter) {
        // ...
    }
    printf("The grand total is %d\n", total);
    return (0);
}
```

Figure 8-1: Similarities between "while" and "for"

the control variable at any time—you can jump into and out of the loop and generally do things that would make a PASCAL or FORTRAN programmer cringe. (Although C gives you the freedom to do such insane things, that doesn't mean you should do them.)

Question 8-1: *When Example 8-3 runs, it prints:*

```
Celsius:101 Fahrenheit:213
```

and nothing more. Why?

Example 8-3: cent/cent.c

```
#include <stdio.h>
/*
 * This program produces a Celsius to Fahrenheit conversion
 *    chart for the numbers 0 to 100.
 */

/* The current Celsius temperature we are working with */
int celsius;
int main() {
    for (celsius = 0; celsius <= 100; ++celsius);
        printf("Celsius:%d Fahrenheit:%d\n",
            celsius, (celsius * 9) / 5 + 32);
    return (0);
}
```

Question 8-2: *Example 8-4 reads a list of five numbers and counts the number of 3s and 7s in the data. Why does it give us the wrong answers?*

Example 8-4: seven/seven.c

```
#include <stdio.h>
char line[100];        /* line of input */
int seven_count;       /* number of 7s in the data */
int data[5];           /* the data to count 3 and 7 in */
int three_count;       /* the number of 3s in the data */
int index;             /* index into the data */

int main() {

    seven_count = 0;
    three_count = 0;
    printf("Enter 5 numbers\n");
    fgets(line, sizeof(line), stdin);
    sscanf(line, "%d %d %d %d %d",
        &data[1], &data[2], &data[3],
        &data[4], &data[5]);

    for (index = 1; index <= 5; ++index) {

        if (data[index] == 3)
            ++three_count;

        if (data[index] == 7)
            ++seven_count;
    }
    printf("Threes %d Sevens %d\n",
            three_count, seven_count);
    return (0);
}
```

When we run this program with the data 3 7 3 0 2, the results are:

```
Threes 4 Sevens 1
```

(Your results may vary.)

switch Statement

The **switch** statement is similar to a chain of **if/else** statements. The general form of a **switch** statement is:

```
switch ( expression ) {
    case constant1:
        statement
        . . . .
        break;

    case constant2:
```

```
        statement
        . . . .
        /* Fall through */

'default:
        statement
        . . . .
        break;

case constant3:
        statement
        . . . .
        break;
}
```

The **switch** statement evaluates the value of an expression and branches to one of the case labels. Duplicate labels are not allowed, so only one case will be selected. The expression must evaluate an integer, character, or enumeration.

The **case** labels can be in any order and must be constants. The **default** label can be put anywhere in the **switch**. No two **case** labels can have the same value.

When C sees a **switch** statement, it evaluates the expression and then looks for a matching **case** label. If none is found, the **default** label is used. If no **default** is found, the statement does nothing.

NOTES   The **switch** statement is very similar to the PASCAL **case** statement. The main difference is that while PASCAL allows only one statement after the label, C allows many. C will keep executing until it hits a **break** statement. In PASCAL, you can't fall through from one **case** to another, but in C you can.

Another difference between the C Switch and PASCAL **case** statements is that PASCAL requires that the **default** statement (otherwise statement) appear at the end. C allows the **default** statement to appear anywhere.

Example 8-5 contains a series of **if** and **else** statements:

Example 8-5: Syntax for if and else

```
if (operator == '+') {
    result += value;
} else if (operator == '-') {
    result -= value;
} else if (operator == '*') {
    result *= value;
} else if (operator == '/') {
    if (value == 0) {
        printf("Error:Divide by zero\n");
```

Example 8-5: Syntax for if and else (continued)

```
        printf("   operation ignored\n");
    } else
        result /= value;
    } else {
        printf("Unknown operator %c\n", operator);
    }
```

This section of code can easily be rewritten as a **switch** statement. In this **switch**, we use a different **case** for each operation. The **default** clause takes care of all the illegal operators.

Rewriting our program using a **switch** statement makes it not only simpler, but easier to read. Our revised **calc** program is shown as Example 8-6.

Example 8-6: calc3/calc3.c

```
#include <stdio.h>
char   line[100];    /* line of text from input */

int    result;       /* the result of the calculations */
char   operator;     /* operator the user specified */
int    value;        /* value specified after the operator */
int main()
{
    result = 0;     /* initialize the result */

    /* loop forever (or until break reached) */
    while (1) {
        printf("Result: %d\n", result);
        printf("Enter operator and number: ");

        fgets(line, sizeof(line), stdin);
        sscanf(line, "%c %d", &operator, &value);

        if ((operator == 'q') || (operator == 'Q'))
            break;
        switch (operator) {
        case '+':
            result += value;
            break;
        case '-':
            result -= value;
            break;
        case '*':
            result *= value;
            break;
        case '/':
            if (value == 0) {
                printf("Error:Divide by zero\n");
                printf("   operation ignored\n");
            } else
                result /= value;
```

Example 8-6: calc3/calc3.c (continued)

```
            break;
        default:
            printf("Unknown operator %c\n", operator);
            break;
        }
    }
    return (0);
}
```

A **break** statement inside a **switch** tells the computer to continue execution after the **switch**. If a **break** statement is not there, execution will continue with the next statement.

For example:

```
control = 0;
/* a not so good example of programming */
switch (control) {
        case 0:
                printf("Reset\n");
        case 1:
                printf("Initializing\n");
                break;
        case 2:
                printf("Working\n");
    }
```

In this case, when `control == 0`, the program will print:

```
Reset
Initializing
```

case 0 does not end with a **break** statement. After printing `Reset`, the program falls through to the next statement (**case** 1) and prints `Initializing`.

A problem exists with this syntax. You cannot determine if the program is supposed to fall through from **case** 0 to **case** 1, or if the programmer forgot to put in a **break** statement. In order to clear up this confusion, a **case** section should always end with a **break** statement or the comment /* Fall through */, as shown in the following example:

```
/* a better example of programming */
switch (control) {
        case 0:
                printf("Reset\n");
                /* Fall through */
        case 1:
                printf("Initializing\n");
                break;
        case 2:
                printf("Working\n");
    }
```

Because `case` 2 is last, it doesn't need a **break** statement. A **break** would cause the program to skip to the end of the **switch**, and we're already there.

Suppose we modify the program slightly and add another **case** to the **switch**:

```
/* We have a little problem */
switch (control) {
        case 0:
                printf("Reset\n");
                /* Fall through */
        case 1:
                printf("Initializing\n");
                break;
        case 2:
                printf("Working\n");
        case 3:
                printf("Closing down\n");
}
```

Now when `control == 2`, the program prints:

```
Working
Closing down
```

This result is an unpleasant surprise. The problem is caused by the fact that `case` 2 is no longer the last **case**. We fall through. (Unintentionally—otherwise, we would have included a `/* Fall through */` comment.) A **break** is now necessary. If we always put in a **break** statement, we don't have to worry about whether or not it is really needed.

```
/* Almost there */
switch (control) {
        case 0:
                printf("Reset\n");
                /* Fall through */
        case 1:
                printf("Initializing\n");
                break;
        case 2:
                printf("Working\n");
                break;
}
```

Finally, we ask the question: what happens when `control == 5`? In this case, because no matching **case** or **default** clause exists, the entire **switch** statement is skipped.

In this example, the programmer did not include a **default** statement because `control` will never be anything but 0, 1, or 2. However, variables can get assigned strange values, so we need a little more defensive programming, as shown in the following example:

```
/* The final version */
switch (control) {
    case 0:
        printf("Reset\n");
        /* Fall through */
    case 1:
        printf("Initializing\n");
        break;
    case 2:
        printf("Working\n");
        break;
    default:
        printf(
            "Internal error, control value (%d) impossible\n",
                control);
        break;
}
```

Although a **default** is not required, it should be put in every **switch**. Even though the **default** may be:

```
default:
        /* Do nothing */
        break;
```

it should be included. This method indicates, at the very least, that you want to ignore out-of-range data.

switch, break, and continue

The **break** statement has two uses. Used inside a **switch**, **break** causes the program to go to the end of the **switch**. Inside a **for** or **while** loop, **break** causes a loop exit. The **continue** statement is valid only inside a loop. **Continue** will cause the program to go to the top of the loop. Figure 8-2 illustrates both **continue** and **break** inside a **switch** statement.

The program in Figure 8-2 is designed to convert an integer with a number of different formats into different bases. If you want to know the value of an octal number, you would enter o (for octal) and the number. The command q is used to quit the program. For example:

```
Enter conversion and number: o 55
Result is 45
Enter conversion and number: q
```

The `help` command is special because we don't want to print a number after the command. After all, the result of `help` is a few lines of text, not a number. So a **continue** is used inside the **switch** to start the loop at the beginning. Inside the **switch**, the **continue** statement works on the loop, while the **break** statement works on the **switch**.

There is one **break** outside the **switch** that is designed to let the user exit the program. The control flow for this program can be seen in Figure 8-2.

```
#include <stdio.h>

int    number;      /* Number we are converting */
char   type;        /* Type of conversion to do */
char   line[80];    /* input line */

int main(void)
{
    while (1) {     ◄ - - - - - - - - - - - - - - - - - - - - - -
        printf("Enter conversion and number: ");

        fgets(line, sizeof(line), stdin);
        sscanf(line, "%c", &type);

        if ((type == 'q') || (type == 'Q'))
            break;

        switch (type) {
            case 'o':
            case 'O':               /* Octal conversion */
                sscanf(line, "%c %o", &type, &number);
                break;
            case 'x':
            case 'X':               /* Hexadecimal conversion */
                sscanf(line, "%c %x", &type, &number);
                break;
            case 'd':
            case 'D':               /* Decimal (For completeness) */
                sscanf(line, "%c %d", &type, &number);
                break;
            case '?':
            case 'h':               /* Help */
                printf("Letter  Conversion\n");
                printf("  o     Octal\n");
                printf("  x     Hexadecimal\n");
                printf("  d     Decimal\n");
                printf("  q     Quit program\n");

                /* Don't print the number */
                continue;
            default:
                printf("Type ? for help\n");
                /* Don't print the number */
                continue;   - - - - - - - - - - - - - - - - - - - -
        }
        printf("Result is %d\n", number);
    }
    return (0);     ◄ - - - - - - - - - - - - - - - - - -
}
```

continue (within the while loop)
break (leave the while loop)
break (leave the switch)

Figure 8-2: switch/continue

Answers

Answer 8-1: The problem lies with the semicolon (;) at the end of the **for** statement. The body of the **for** statement is between the closing parentheses and the

semicolon. In this case, the body does not exist. Even though the `printf` statement is indented, it is not part of the **for** statement. The indentation is misleading.
The C compiler does not look at indentation. The program does nothing until the
expression:

```
celsius <= 100
```

becomes false (`celsius == 101`). Then the `printf` is executed.

Answer 8-2: The problem is that we read the number into `data[1]` through
`data[5]`. In C, the range of legal array indices is 0 to *array-size*–1, or in this case,
0 to 4. `data[5]` is illegal. When we use it, strange things happen; in this case,
the variable `three_count` is changed. The solution is to only use `data[0]` to
`data[4]`.

So, we need to change the `sscanf` line to read:

```
sscanf(line, "%d %d %d %d %d",
    &data[0], &data[1], &data[2], &data[3], &data[4]);
```

Also, the **for** loop must be changed from:

```
for (index = 1; index <= 5; ++index)
```

to:

```
for (index = 0; index < 5; ++index)
```

NOTE   Experienced C programmers could look at our broken **for** loop and
               immediately sense that something was wrong. Two clues that some-
               thing strange is going on are 1) the **for** loop starts at 1, and 2) there
               is a <= operator in the loop. Most C **for** loops start at 0 and use <
               for termination.

Programming Exercises

Exercise 8-1: Print a checker board (8-by-8 grid). Each square should be 5-by-3
characters wide. A 2-by-2 example follows:

```
+-----+-----+
|     |     |
|     |     |
|     |     |
+-----+-----+
|     |     |
|     |     |
|     |     |
+-----+-----+
```

Exercise 8-2: The total resistance of n resistors in parallel is:

$$\frac{1}{R} = \frac{1}{R_1} + \frac{1}{R_2} + \frac{1}{R_3} + \ldots + \frac{1}{R_n}$$

Suppose we have a network of two resistors with the values 400Ω and 200Ω. Then our equation would be:

$$\frac{1}{R} = \frac{1}{R_1} + \frac{1}{R_2}$$

Substituting in the value of the resistors we get:

$$\frac{1}{R} = \frac{1}{400} + \frac{1}{200}$$
$$\frac{1}{R} = \frac{3}{400}$$
$$R = \frac{400}{3}$$

So the total resistance of our two-resistor network is 133.3Ω.

Write a program to compute the total resistance for any number of parallel resistors.

Exercise 8-3: Write a program to average *n* numbers.

Exercise 8-4: Write a program to print out the multiplication table.

Exercise 8-5: Write a program that reads a character and prints out whether or not it is a vowel or a consonant.

Exercise 8-6: Write a program that converts numbers to words. For example, 895 results in "eight nine five."

Exercise 8-7: The number 85 is pronounced "eighty-five," not "eight five." Modify the previous program to handle the numbers 0 through 100 so that all numbers come out as we really say them. For example, 13 would be "thirteen" and 100 would be "one hundred."

9

Variable Scope and Functions

> *But in the gross and scope of my opinion*
> *This bodes some strange eruption to our state.*
> —Shakespeare [*Hamlet*, Act 1, Scene 1]

So far, we have been using only global variables. In this chapter, we will learn about other kinds of variables and how to use them. This chapter also tells you how to divide your code into functions.

Scope and Class

All variables have two attributes: *scope* and *class*. The scope of a variable is the area of the program in which the variable is valid. A *global variable* is valid everywhere (hence the name global), so its scope is the whole program. A *local variable* has a scope that is limited to the *block* in which it is declared and cannot be accessed outside that block. A *block* is a section of code enclosed in curly braces ({}). Figure 9-1 shows the difference between local and global variables.

You can declare a local variable with the same name as a global variable. Normally, the scope of the variable `count` (first declaration) would be the whole program. The declaration of a second local `count` takes precedence over the global declaration inside the small block in which the local `count` is declared. In this block, the global `count` is *hidden*. You can also nest local declarations and hide local variables. Figure 9-2 illustrates a hidden variable.

The variable `count` is declared as both a local variable and a global variable. Normally, the scope of `count` (global) is the entire program; however, when a variable is declared inside a block, that instance of the variable becomes the active one for the length of the block. The global `count` has been hidden by the

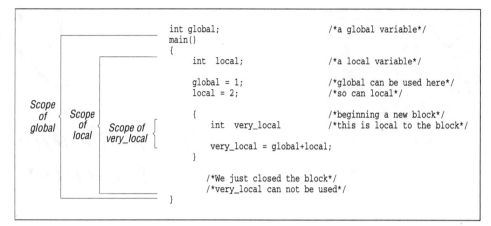

```
                    int global;                /*a global variable*/
                    main()
                    {
                        int  local;            /*a local variable*/

                        global = 1;            /*global can be used here*/
                        local = 2;             /*so can local*/

                        {                      /*beginning a new block*/
                            int  very_local    /*this is local to the block*/

                            very_local = global+local;
                        }
                                               /*We just closed the block*/
                                               /*very_local can not be used*/
                    }
```

Figure 9-1: Local and global variables

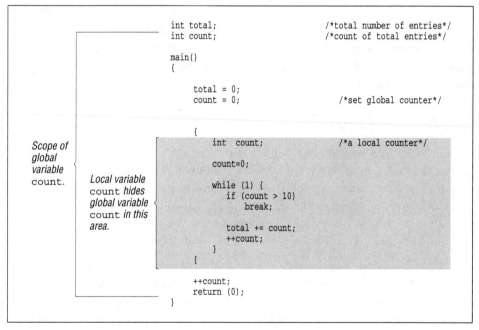

```
                    int total;                 /*total number of entries*/
                    int count;                 /*count of total entries*/

                    main()
                    {
                        total = 0;
                        count = 0;             /*set global counter*/

                        {
                            int  count;        /*a local counter*/

                            count=0;

                            while (1) {
                                if (count > 10)
                                    break;

                                total += count;
                                ++count;
                            }
                        {
                        ++count;
                        return (0);
                    }
```

Figure 9-2: Hidden variables

local `count` for the scope of this block. The shaded block in the figure shows where the scope of `count` (global) is hidden.

A problem exists in that when you have the statement:

```
count = 1;
```

you cannot tell easily to which `count` you are referring. Is it the global count, the one declared at the top of main, or the one in the middle of the **while** loop? You should give these variables different names, like `total_count`, `current_count`, and `item_count`.

The *class* of a variable may be either *permanent* or *temporary*. Global variables are always permanent. They are created and initialized before the program starts and remain until it terminates. Temporary variables are allocated from a section of memory called the *stack* at the beginning of the block. If you try to allocate too many temporary variables, you will get a "Stack overflow" error. The space used by the temporary variables is returned to the stack at the end of the block. Each time the block is entered, the temporary variables are initialized.

The size of the stack depends on the system and compiler you are using. On many UNIX systems, the program is automatically allocated the largest possible stack. On other systems, a default stack size is allocated that can be changed by a compiler switch. On MS-DOS/Windows systems, the stack space must be less than 65,536 bytes. This may seem like a lot of space; however, several large arrays can eat it up quickly. You should consider making all large arrays permanent.

Local variables are temporary unless they are declared **static**.

NOTE static has an entirely different meaning when used with global variables. It indicates that a variable is local to the current file. See Chapter 18, *Modular Programming*.

Example 9-1 illustrates the difference between permanent and temporary variables. We have chosen obvious names: `temporary` is a temporary variable, while `permanent` is permanent. The variable `temporary` is initialized each time it is created (at the beginning of the **for** statement block). The variable **permanent** is initialized only once, at startup time.

In the loop, both variables are incremented. However, at the top of the loop, `temporary` is initialized to one, as shown in Example 9-1.

Example 9-1: vars/vars.c

```
#include <stdio.h>

int main() {
    int counter;    /* loop counter */
    for (counter = 0; counter < 3; ++counter) {
        int temporary = 1;        /* A temporary variable */
        static int permanent = 1; /* A permanent variable */
```

Example 9-1: vars/vars.c (continued)

```
        printf("Temporary %d Permanent %d\n",
            temporary, permanent);
        ++temporary;
        ++permanent;
    }
    return (0);
}
```

The output of this program is:

```
Temporary 1 Permanent 1
Temporary 1 Permanent 2
Temporary 1 Permanent 3
```

NOTE   Temporary variables are sometimes referred to as *automatic* variables because the space for them is allocated automatically. The qualifier **auto** can be used to denote a temporary variable; however, in practice it is almost never used.

Table 9-1 describes the different ways in which a variable can be declared.

Table 9-1: Declaration Modifiers

Declared	Scope	Class	Initialized
Outside all blocks	Global	Permanent	Once
static outside all blocks	Global[a]	Permanent	Once
Inside a block	Local	Temporary	Each time block is entered
static inside a block	Local	Permanent	Once

[a] A **static** declaration made outside blocks indicates the variable is local to the file in which it is declared. (See Chapter 18 for more information on programming with multiple files.)

Functions

Functions allow us to group commonly used code into a compact unit that can be used repeatedly. We have already encountered one function, **main**. It is a special function called at the beginning of the program. All other functions are directly or indirectly called from **main**.

Suppose we want to write a program to compute the area of three triangles. We could write out the formula three times, or we could create a function to do the work. Each function should begin with a comment block containing the following:

Name

    Name of the function

Description

    Description of what the function does

Parameters

    Description of each of the parameters to the function

Returns

    Description of the return value of the function

Additional sections may be added such as file formats, references, or notes. Refer to Chapter 3, *Style*, for other suggestions.

Our function to compute the area of a triangle begins with:

```
/**********************************************
 * triangle -- Computes area of a triangle.  *
 *                                           *
 * Parameters                                *
 *    width -- Width of the triangle.        *
 *    height -- Height of the triangle.      *
 *                                           *
 * Returns                                   *
 *    area of the triangle.                  *
 **********************************************/
```

The function proper begins with the line:

```
float triangle(float width, float height)
```

float is the function type. The two parameters are **width** and **height**. They are of type **float** also.

C uses a form of parameter passing called "Call by value". When our procedure **triangle** is called, with code such as:

```
triangle(1.3, 8.3);
```

C copies the value of the parameters (in this case 1.3 and 8.3) into the function's parameters (**width** and **height**) and then starts executing the function's code. With this form of parameter passing, a function cannot pass data back to the caller using parameters.[*]

> *NOTE*   The function type is not required by C. If no function type is declared, the type defaults to **int**. However, if no type is provided, the maintainer cannot determine if you wanted to use the default (**int**) or if you simply forgot to declare a type. To avoid this confusion, always declare the function type and do not use the default.

---

[*] This statement is not strictly true. We can trick C into passing information back through the use of pointers, as we'll see in Chapter 13.

The function computes the area with the statement:

```
area = width * height / 2.0;
```

What's left is to give the result to the caller. This step is done with the **return** statement:

```
return (area);
```

Example 9-2 shows our full triangle function.

Example 9-2: tri-sub/tri-sub.c

```
#include <stdio.h>
/*********************************************
 * triangle -- Computes area of a triangle. *
 *                                           *
 * Parameters                                *
 *   width -- Width of the triangle.         *
 *   height -- Height of the triangle.       *
 *                                           *
 * Returns                                   *
 *   area of the triangle.                   *
 *********************************************/
float triangle(float width, float height)
{
    float area;      /* Area of the triangle */

    area = width * height / 2.0;
    return (area);
}
```

The line:

```
size = triangle(1.3, 8.3);
```

is a call to the function `triangle`. C assigns `1.3` to the parameter `width` and `8.3` to `height`.

If functions are the rooms of our building, then parameters are the doors between the rooms. In this case, the value `1.3` is going through the door marked `width`. Parameters' doors are one way. Things can go in, but they can't go out. The **return** statement is how we get data out of the function. In our `triangle` example, the function assigns the local variable `area` the value `5.4`, then executes the statement `return (area);`.

The return value of this function is `5.4`, so our statement:

```
size = triangle (1.3, 8.3)
```

assigns `size` the value `5.4`.

Example 9-3 computes the area of three triangles.

Example 9-3: tri-prog/tri-prog.c

```
[File: tri-sub/tri-prog.c]

#include <stdio.h>

/***********************************************
 * triangle -- Computes area of a triangle.    *
 *                                             *
 * Parameters                                  *
 *    width -- Width of the triangle.          *
 *    height -- Height of the triangle.        *
 *                                             *
 * Returns                                     *
 *    area of the triangle.                    *
 ***********************************************/
float triangle(float width, float height)
{
    float area;      /* Area of the triangle */

    area = width * height / 2.0;
    return (area);
}

int main()
{
    printf("Triangle #1 %f\n", triangle(1.3, 8.3));
    printf("Triangle #2 %f\n", triangle(4.8, 9.8));
    printf("Triangle #3 %f\n", triangle(1.2, 2.0));
    return (0);
}
```

If we want to use a function before we define it, we must declare it just like a variable to inform the compiler about the function. We use the declaration:

```
/* Compute a triangle */
float triangle (float width, float height);
```

for the **triangle** function. This declaration is called the *function prototype*.

The variable names are not required when declaring a function prototype. Our prototype could have just as easily been written as:

```
float triangle(float, float);
```

However, we use the longer version because it gives the programmer additional information, and it's easy to create prototypes using the editor's cut and paste functions.

Strictly speaking, the prototypes are optional for some functions. If no prototype is specified, the C compiler assumes the function returns an **int** and takes any number of parameters. Omitting a prototype robs the C compiler of valuable information that it can use to check function calls. Most compilers have a compile-time switch that warns the programmer about function calls without prototypes.

Functions with No Parameters

A function can have any number of parameters, including none. But even when using a function with no parameters, you still need the parentheses:

```
value = next_index();
```

Declaring a prototype for a function without parameters is a little tricky. You can't use the statement:

```
int next_index();
```

because the C compiler will see the empty parentheses and assume that this is a K&R-style function declaration. See Chapter 19, *Ancient Compilers*, for details on this older style. The keyword **void** is used to indicate an empty parameter list. So the prototype for our **next_index** function is:

```
int next_index(void);
```

void is also used to indicate that a function does not return a value. (Void is similar to the FORTRAN subroutine or PASCAL procedure.) For example, this function just prints a result; it does not return a value:

```
void print_answer(int answer)
{
    if (answer < 0) {
        printf("Answer corrupt\n");
        return;
    }
    printf("The answer is %d\n", answer);
}
```

Question 9-1: *Example 9-4 should compute the length of a string.* * *Instead, it insists that all strings are of length 0. Why?*

Example 9-4: len/len.c

```
/************************************************************
 * Question:                                               *
 *      Why does this program always report the length     *
 *      of any string as 0?                                *
 *                                                         *
 * A sample "main" has been provided.  It will ask         *
 * for a string and then print the length.                 *
 ************************************************************/
```

---

* This function performs the same function as the library function strlen.

n/len.c (continued)

```
dio.h>

************************************
Computes the length of a string.          *
                                          *
                                          *
g -- The string whose length we want.     *
                                          *
                                          *
length of the string.                     *
*****************************************/
har string[])

        index;        /* index into the string */

until we reach the end of string character

ex = 0; string[index] != '\0'; ++index)
o nothing */
index);
```

```
ne[100];      /* Input line from user */

1) {
tf("Enter line:");
s(line, sizeof(line), stdin);

tf("Length (including newline) is: %d\n", length(line));
```

red Programming

cientists spend a great deal of time and effort studying how to e result is that they come up with absolutely, positively, the best g methodology—a new one each month. Some of these systems include flow charts, top-down programming, bottom-up programming, structured programming, and object-oriented design (OOD).

Now that we have learned about functions, we can talk about using *structured programming techniques* to design programs. These techniques are ways of dividing up or structuring a program into small, well-defined functions. They make the program easy to write and easy to understand. I don't claim that this method is the absolute best way to program. It happens to be the method that works best for me. If another system works better for you, use it.

The first step in programming is to decide what you are going to do. This has already been described in Chapter 7, *Programming Process*. Next, decide how you are going to structure your data.

Finally, the coding phase begins. When writing a paper, you start with an outline of each section in the paper described by a single sentence. The details will be filled in later. Writing a program is a similar process. You start with an outline, and this becomes your main function. The details can be hidden within other functions. For example, Example 9-5 solves all the world's problems.

Example 9-5: Solve the World's Problems

```
int main()
{
    init();
    solve_problems();
    finish_up();
    return (0);
}
```

Of course, some of the details will have to be filled in later.

Start by writing the main function. It should be less than three pages long. If it grows longer, consider splitting it up into two smaller, simpler functions. After the main function is complete, you can start on the others.

This type of structured programming is called *top-down programming*. You start at the top (`main`) and work your way down.

Another type of coding is called *bottom-up programming*. This method involves writing the lowest-level function first, testing it, and then building on that working set. I tend to use some bottom-up techniques when I'm working with a new standard function that I haven't used before. I write a small function to make sure that I really know how the function works, and then continue from there. This approach is used in Chapter 7 to construct the calculator program.

So, in actual practice, both techniques are useful. A mostly top-down, partially bottom-up technique results. Computer scientists have a term for this methodology: chaos. The one rule you should follow in programming is "Use what works best."

Recursion

Recursion occurs when a function calls itself directly or indirectly. Some programming functions, such as the factorial, lend themselves naturally to recursive algorithms.

A recursive function must follow two basic rules:

- It must have an ending point.

- It must make the problem simpler.

A definition of factorial is:

```
fact(0) = 1

fact(n) = n * fact(n-1)
```

In C, this definition is:

```
int fact(int number)
{
    if (number == 0)
        return (1);
    /* else */
    return (number * fact(number-1));
}
```

This definition satisfies our two rules. First, it has a definite ending point (when number == 0). Second, it simplifies the problem because the calculation of fact(number-1) is simpler than fact(number).

Factorial is legal only for number >= 0. But what happens if we try to compute fact(-3)? The program will abort with a stack overflow or similar message. fact(-3) calls fact(-4), which calls fact(-5), etc. No ending point exists. This error is referred to as an infinite recursion error.

Many things that we do iteratively can be done recursively—for example, summing up the elements of an array. We define a function to add elements *m–n* of an array as follows:

- If we have only one element, then the sum is simple.

- Otherwise, we use the sum of the first element and the sum of the rest.

In C, this function is:

```
int sum(int first, int last, int array[])
{
    if (first == last)
        return (array[first]);
    /* else */
    return (array[first] + sum(first+1, last, array));
}
```

For example:

```
Sum(1 8 3 2) =
    1 + Sum(8 3 2) =
        8 + Sum(3 2) =
            3 + Sum (2) =
                2
            3 + 2 = 5
```

```
        8 + 5 = 13
      1 + 13 = 14
   Answer = 14
```

Answers

Answer 9-1: The programmer went to a lot of trouble to explain that the **for** loop did nothing (except increment the index). However, there is no semicolon (;) at the end of the **for**. C keeps on reading until it sees a statement (in this case `return(index)`), and then puts that statement in the **for** loop. Properly done, this program should look like Example 9-6.

Example 9-6: len2/len2.c

```c
#include <stdio.h>

int  length(char string[])
{
    int              index;        /* index into the string */

    /*
     * Loop until we reach the end-of-string character
     */
    for (index = 0; string[index] != '\0'; ++index)
        continue; /* do nothing */
    return (index);
}

int main()
{
    char line[100];     /* Input line from user */

    while (1) {
        printf("Enter line:");
        fgets(line, sizeof(line), stdin);

        printf("Length (including newline) is: %d\n", length(line));
    }
}
```

Programming Exercises

Exercise 9-1: Write a procedure that counts the number of words in a string. (Your documentation should describe exactly how you define a word.) Write a program to test your new procedure.

Exercise 9-2: Write a function `begins(string1,string2)` that returns true if `string1` begins `string2`. Write a program to test the function.

Exercise 9-3: Write a function count(number, array, length) that counts the number of times **number** appears in **array**. The array has **length** elements. The function should be recursive. Write a test program to go with the function.

Exercise 9-4: Write a function that takes a character array and returns a primitive hash code by adding up the value of each character in the array.

Exercise 9-5: Write a function that returns the maximum value of an array of numbers.

Exercise 9-6: Write a function that scans a character array for the character – and replaces it with _.

10

C Preprocessor

> *The speech of man is like embroidered tapestries,*
> *since like them this has to be extended in order to*
> *display its patterns, but when it is rolled up it*
> *conceals and distorts them.*
> *—Themistocles*

In the early days, when C was still being developed, it soon became apparent that C needed a facility for handling named constants, macros, and include files. The solution was to create a preprocessor that recognized these constructs in the programs before they were passed to the C compiler. The preprocessor is nothing more than a specialized text editor. Its syntax is completely different from that of C, and it has no understanding of C constructs.

The preprocessor was very useful, and soon it was merged into the main C compiler. On some systems, like UNIX, the preprocessor is still a separate program, automatically executed by the compiler wrapper *cc*. Some of the new compilers, like Turbo C++ and Microsoft Visual C++, have the preprocessor built in.

#define Statement

Example 10-1 initializes two arrays (`data` and `twice`). Each array contains 10 elements. Suppose we wanted to change the program to use 20 elements. Then we would have to change the array size (two places) and the index limit (one place). Aside from being a lot of work, multiple changes can lead to errors.

Example 10-1: init2a/init2a.c

```
int data[10];    /* some data */
int twice[10];   /* twice some data */
```

Example 10-1: init2a/init2a.c (continued)

```
int main()
{
    int index;    /* index into the data */

    for (index = 0; index < 10; ++index) {
        data[index] = index;
        twice[index] = index * 2;
    }
    return (0);
}
```

We would like to be able to write a generic program in which we can define a constant for the size of the array, and then let C adjust the dimensions of our two arrays. By using the **#define** statement, we can do just that. Example 10-2 is a new version of Example 10-1.

Example 10-2: init2b/init2b.c

```
#define SIZE 20    /* work on 20 elements */

int data[SIZE];    /* some data */
int twice[SIZE];   /* twice some data */

int main()
{
    int index;    /* index into the data */

    for (index = 0; index < SIZE; ++index) {
        data[index] = index;
        twice[index] = index * 2;
    }
    return (0);
}
```

The line **#define SIZE 20** acts as a command to a special text editor to *globally change* SIZE to 20. This line takes the drudgery and guesswork out of making changes.

All preprocessor commands begin with a hash mark (#) in column one. Although C is free format, the preprocessor is not, and it depends on the hash mark's being in the first column. As we will see, the preprocessor knows nothing about C. It can be (and is) used to edit things other than C programs.

NOTE   You can easily forget that the preprocessor and the C compile use different syntaxes. One of the most common errors new programmers make is to try to use C constructs in a preprocessor directive.

A preprocessor directive terminates at the end-of-line. This format is different from that of C, where a semicolon (;) is used to end a statement. Putting a semi-colon at the end of a preprocessor directive can lead to unexpected results. A line may be continued by putting a backslash (\) at the end.

The simplest use of the preprocessor is to define a replacement macro. For example, the command:

```
#define FOO bar
```

causes the preprocessor to replace the word "FOO" with the word "bar" every-where "FOO" occurs. It is common programming practice to use all uppercase letters for macro names. This practice makes telling the difference between a vari-able (all lowercase) and a macro (all uppercase) very easy.

The general form of a simple define statement is:

```
#define name substitute-text
```

where *name* can be any valid C identifier and *substitute-text* can be anything. You could use the following definition:

```
#define FOR_ALL for(i = 0; i < ARRAY_SIZE; i++)
```

and use it like this:

```
/*
 * Clear the array
 */
FOR_ALL {
    data[i] = 0;
}
```

However, defining macros in this manner is considered bad programming prac-tice. Such definitions tend to obscure the basic control flow of the program. In this example, a programmer who wants to know what the loop does would have to search the beginning of the program for the definition of FOR_ALL.

An even worse practice is to define macros that do large-scale replacement of basic C programming constructs. For example, you can define the following:

```
#define BEGIN {
#define END }
 . . .
    if (index == 0)
    BEGIN
        printf("Starting\n");
    END
```

The problem is that you are no longer programming in C, but in a half-C/half-Pascal mongrel. You can find the extremes to which such mimicry can be taken in the Bourne shell, which uses preprocessor directives to define a language that looks a lot like Algol-68.

Here's a sample section of code:

```
IF (x GREATER_THAN 37) OR (Y LESS_THAN 83) THEN
    CASE value OF
        SELECT 1:
            start();
        SELECT 3:
            backspace();
        OTHERWISE:
            error();
    ESAC
FI
```

Most programmers encountering this program curse at first, and then use the editor to turn the source back into a reasonable version of C.

The preprocessor can cause unexpected problems because it does not check for correct C syntax. For example, Example 10-3 generates an error on line 11.

Example 10-3: big/big.c

```
 1 #define BIG_NUMBER 10 ** 10
 2
 3 main()
 4 {
 5     /* index for our calculations */
 6     int    index;
 7
 8     index = 0;
 9
10     /* syntax error on next line */
11     while (index < BIG_NUMBER) {
12         index = index * 8;
13     }
14     return (0);
15 }
```

The problem is in the **#define** statement on line 1, but the error message points to line 11. The definition in line 1 causes the preprocessor to expand line 11 to look like:

```
while (index < 10 ** 10)
```

Because ** is an illegal operator, this expansion generates a syntax error.

Question 10-1: *Example 10-4 generates the answer 47 instead of the expected answer 144. Why? (See the hint below.)*

Example 10-4: first/first.c

```
#include <stdio.h>

#define FIRST_PART     7
#define LAST_PART      5
```

Example 10-4: first/first.c (continued)

```
#define ALL_PARTS        FIRST_PART + LAST_PART

int main() {
    printf("The square of all the parts is %d\n",
        ALL_PARTS * ALL_PARTS);
    return (0);
}
```

Hint: The answer may not be readily apparent. Luckily, C allows you to run your program through the preprocessor and view the output. In UNIX, the command:

    % cc -E prog.c

will send the output of the preprocessor to the standard output.

In MS-DOS/Windows, the command:

    C:> **cpp prog.c**

will do the same thing.

Running this program through the preprocessor gives us:

```
# 1 "first.c"
# 1 "/usr/include/stdio.h" 1
```

    ... listing of data in include file <stdio.h>

```
# 2 "first.c" 2

main() {
    printf("The square of all the parts is %d\n",
        7 + 5 * 7 + 5);
    return (0);
}
```

Question 10-2: *Example 10-5 generates a warning that* `counter` *is used before it is set. This warning is a surprise to us because the* **for** *loop should set it. We also get a very strange warning, "null effect," for line 11.*

Example 10-5: max/max.c

```
 1 /* warning, spacing is VERY important */
 2
 3 #include <stdio.h>
 4
 5 #define MAX =10
 6
 7 int main()
 8 {
 9     int  counter;
10
11     for (counter =MAX; counter > 0; --counter)
```

Example 10-5: max/max.c (continued)

```
12          printf("Hi there\n");
13
14      return (0);
15 }
```

Hint: Take a look at the preprocessor output.

Question 10-3: *Example 10-6 computes the wrong value for* size. *Why?*

Example 10-6: size/size.c

```
#include <stdio.h>

#define SIZE    10;
#define FUDGE   SIZE -2;
int main()
{
    int size;/* size to really use */

    size = FUDGE;
    printf("Size is %d\n", size);
    return (0);
}
```

Question 10-4: *Example 10-7 is supposed to print the message "Fatal Error: Abort" and exit when it receives bad data. But when it gets good data, it exits. Why?*

Example 10-7: die/die.c

```
 1 #include <stdio.h>
 2 #include <stdlib.h>
 3
 4 #define DIE \
 5    fprintf(stderr, "Fatal Error:Abort\n");exit(8);
 6
 7 int main() {
 8     /* a random value for testing */
 9     int value;
10
11     value = 1;
12     if (value < 0)
13         DIE;
14
15     printf("We did not die\n");
16     return (0);
17 }
```

#define vs. const

The **const** keyword is relatively new. Before **const**, **#define** was the only keyword available to define constants, so most older code uses **#define** directives.

However, the use of **const** is preferred over **#define** for several reasons. First of all, C checks the syntax of **const** statements immediately. The **#define** directive is not checked until the macro is used. Also **const** uses C syntax, while the **#define** has a syntax all its own. Finally, **const** follows normal C scope rules, while constants defined by a **#define** directive continue on forever.

So, in most cases, a **const** statement is preferred over **#define**. Here are two ways of defining the same constant:

```
#define MAX 10 /* Define a value using the preprocessor */
               /* (This definition can easily cause problems) */

const int MAX = 10; /* Define a C constant integer */
                    /* (safer) */
```

NOTE   Some compilers will not allow you to use a constant to define the size of an array. They should, but they have not caught up to the standard yet.

The **#define** directive can only define simple constants. The **const** statement can define almost any type of C constant, including things like structure classes. For example:

```
struct box {
    int width, height;   /* Dimensions of the box in pixels */
};
const box pink_box ={1.0, 4.5};/* Size of a pink box to be used for
input */
```

The **#define** directive is, however, essential for things like conditional compilation and other specialized uses.

Conditional Compilation

One of the problems programmers have is writing code that can work on many different machines. In theory, C code is portable; in actual practice, different operating systems have little quirks that must be accounted for. For example, this book covers both the MS-DOS/Windows compiler and UNIX C. Although they are almost the same, there are differences, especially when you must access the more advanced features of the operating system.

Another portability problem is caused by the fact that the standard leaves some of the features of the language up to the implementers. For example, the size of an integer is implementation dependent.

The preprocessor, through the use of conditional compilation, allows the programmer great flexibility in changing the code generated. Suppose we want to put debugging code in the program while we are working on it, and then remove it in the production version. We could do so by including the code in a **#ifdef/ #endif** section:

```
#ifdef DEBUG
    printf("In compute_hash, value %d hash %d\n", value, hash);
#endif /* DEBUG */
```

NOTE   You do not have to put the /* DEBUG */ after the #endif; however, the entry is very useful as a comment.

If the beginning of the program contains the directive:

```
#define DEBUG       /* Turn debugging on */
```

the `printf` will be included. If the program contains the directive:

```
#undef DEBUG       /* Turn debugging off */
```

the `printf` will be omitted.

Strictly speaking, the **#undef DEBUG** is unnecessary. If there is no **#define DEBUG** statement, then DEBUG is undefined. The **#undef DEBUG** statement is used to indicate explicitly that DEBUG is used for conditional compilation and is now turned off.

The directive **#ifndef** will cause the code to be compiled if the symbol is *not* defined:

```
#ifndef DEBUG
    printf("Production code, no debugging enabled\n");
#endif /* DEBUG */
```

The **#else** directive reverses the sense of the conditional. For example:

```
#ifdef DEBUG
    printf("Test version. Debugging is on\n");
#else DEBUG
    printf("Production version\n");
#endif /* DEBUG */
```

A programmer may wish to remove a section of code temporarily. One common method is to comment out the code by enclosing it in /* */. This method can cause problems, as shown by the following example:

```
1:  /***** Comment out this section
2:      section_report();
3:      /* Handle the end of section stuff */
4:      dump_table();
5:  **** end of commented out section */
```

This code generates a syntax error for the fifth line. Why?

A better method is to use the **#ifdef** construct to remove the code:

```
#ifdef UNDEF
    section_report();
    /* Handle the end of section stuff */
    dump_table();
#endif /* UNDEF */
```

(Of course, the code will be included if anyone defines the symbol UNDEF; however, anyone who does so should be shot.)

The compiler switch -D*symbol* allows symbols to be defined on the command line. For example, the command:

```
% cc -DDEBUG -g -o prog prog.c
```

compiles the program `prog.c` and includes all the code in between `#ifdef DEBUG` and `#endif DEBUG` even though there is no `#define DEBUG` in the program.

The general form of the option is -D*symbol* or -D*symbol*=*value*. For example, the following sets MAX to 10:

```
% cc -DMAX=10 -o prog prog.c
```

Notice that the programmer can override the command-line options with directives in the program. For example, the directive:

```
#undef DEBUG
```

will result in DEBUG being undefined whether or not you use -DDEBUG.

Most C compilers automatically define some system-dependent symbols. For example, Turbo C++ defines the symbols __TURBOC__ and __MSDOS__. The ANSI Standard compiler defines the symbol __STDC__. Most UNIX compilers define a name for the system (i.e., SUN, VAX, Celerity, etc.); however, they are rarely documented. The symbol __unix__ is always defined for all UNIX machines.

include Files

The **#include** directive allows the program to use source code from another file.

For example, we have been using the directive:

```
#include <stdio.h>
```

in our programs. This directive tells the preprocessor to take the file *stdio.h* (Standard I/O) and insert it in the program. Files that are included in other programs are called *header files*. (Most **#include** directives come at the head of the program.) The angle brackets (<>) indicate that the file is a standard header file. On UNIX, these files are located in */usr/include*. On MS-DOS/Windows, they are located in whatever directory was specified at the time the compiler was installed.

Standard include files define data structures and macros used by library routines. For example, `printf` is a library routine that prints data on the standard output. The `FILE` structure used by `printf` and its related routines is defined in *stdio.h*.

Sometimes the programmer may want to write her own set of include files. Local include files are particularly useful for storing constants and data structures when a program spans several files. They are especially useful for information passing when a team of programmers is working on a single project. (See Chapter 18, *Modular Programming*.)

Local include files may be specified by using double quotes (`""`) around the file name, for example:

```
#include "defs.h"
```

The filename `defs.h` can be any valid filename. This specification can be a simple file, `defs.h`; a relative path, `../../data.h`; or an absolute path, `/root/include/const.h`. (On MS-DOS/Windows, you should use backslash (\) instead of slash (/) as a directory separator.)

NOTE   Absolute pathnames should be avoided in **#include** directives be-
              cause they make the program very nonportable.

Include files may be nested, and this feature can cause problems. Suppose you define several useful constants in the file *const.h*. If the files *data.h* and *io.h* both include *const.h* and you put the following in your program:

```
#include "data.h"
#include "io.h"
```

you will generate errors because the preprocessor will set the definitions in *const.h* twice. Defining a constant twice is not a fatal error; however, defining a data structure or union twice is a fatal error and must be avoided.

One way around this problem is to have *const.h* check to see if it has already been included and does not define any symbol that has already been defined. The directive **#ifndef** *symbol* is true if the symbol is *not* defined. The directive is the reverse of **#ifdef**.

Look at the following code:

```
#ifndef _CONST_H_INCLUDED_
/* define constants */
```

```
#define _CONST_H_INCLUDED_
#endif  /* _CONST_H_INCLUDED_ */
```

When *const.h* is included, it defines the symbol _CONST_H_INCLUDED_. If that symbol is already defined (because the file was included earlier), the **#ifndef** conditional hides all defines so they don't cause trouble.

NOTE   Anything can be put in a header file. This includes not only definitions and types, but also code, initialization data, and yesterday's lunch menu. However, good programming practices dictate that you should limit header files to types and definitions only.

Parameterized Macros

So far, we have discussed only simple **#define**s or macros. But macros can take parameters. The following macro will compute the square of a number:

```
#define SQR(x)  ((x) * (x))            /* Square a number */
```

NOTE   No spaces must exist between the macro name (SQR) and the parenthesis.

When used, the macro will replace **x** by the text of the following argument:

```
SQR(5) expands to   ((5) * (5))
```

Always put parentheses, (), around the parameters of a macro. Example 10-8 illustrates the problems that can occur if this rule is not followed.

Example 10-8: sqr/sqr.c

```
#include <stdio.h>
#define SQR(x) (x * x)

int main()
{
    int counter;    /* counter for loop */

    for (counter = 0; counter < 5; ++counter) {
        printf("x %d, x squared %d\n",
            counter+1, SQR(counter+1));
    }
    return (0);
}
```

Question 10-5: *What does Example 10-8 output? Try running it on your machine. Why did it output what it did? Try checking the output of the preprocessor.*

The *keep-it-simple* system of programming tells us to use the increment (++) and decrement (--) operators only on line, by themselves. When used in a macro parameter, they can lead to unexpected results, as illustrated by Example 10-9.

Example 10-9: sqr-i/sqr-i.c

```
#include <stdio.h>
#define SQR(x) ((x) * (x))

int main()
{
    int counter;     /* counter for loop */

    counter = 0;

    while (counter < 5)
        printf("x %d square %d\n", counter, SQR(++counter));

    return (0);
}
```

Question 10-6: *Why will Example 10-9 not produce the expected output? By how much will the counter go up each time?*

Question 10-7: *Example 10-10 tells us that we have an undefined variable* number, *but our only variable name is* counter.

Example 10-10: rec/rec.c

```
#include <stdio.h>
#define RECIPROCAL (number) (1.0 / (number))

int main()
{
    float   counter;     /* Counter for our table */

    for (counter = 1.0; counter < 10.0;
         counter += 1.0) {

        printf("1/%f = %f\n",
                counter, RECIPROCAL(counter));
    }
    return (0);
}
```

Advanced Features

This book does not cover the complete list of C preprocessor directives. Among the more advanced features are an advanced form of the **#if** directive for conditional compilations, and the **#pragma** directive for inserting compiler-dependent commands into a file. See your C reference manual for more information about these features.

Summary

The C preprocessor is a very useful part of the C language. It has a completely different look and feel, though, and it must be treated apart from the main C compiler.

Problems in macro definitions often do not show up where the macro is defined, but result in errors much further down in the program. By following a few simple rules, you can decrease the chances of having problems:

- Put parentheses () around everything. In particular, they should enclose **#define** constants and macro parameters.

- When defining a macro with more than one statement, enclose the code in curly braces ({ }).

- The preprocessor is not C. Don't use = and ; . Finally, if you got this far, be glad that the worst is over.

Answers

Answer 10-1: After the program has been run through the preprocessor, the `printf` statement is expanded to look like:

```
printf("The square of all the parts is %d\n",
        7 + 5 * 7 + 5);
```

The equation 7 + 5 * 7 + 5 evaluates to 47. Put parentheses around all expressions in macros. If you change the definition of **ALL_PARTS** to:

```
#define ALL_PARTS (FIRST_PART + LAST_PART)
```

the program will execute correctly.

Answer 10-2: The preprocessor is a very simple-minded program. When it defines a macro, everything past the identifier is part of the macro. In this case, the definition of **MAX** is literally = 10. When the **for** statement is expanded, the result is:

```
for (counter==10; counter > 0; --counter)
```

C allows you to compute a result and throw it away. (This will generate a null-effect warning in some compilers.) For this statement, the program checks to see if `counter` is 10, and then discards the answer. Removing the = from the definition will correct the problem.

Answer 10-3: As with the previous problem, the preprocessor does not respect C syntax conventions. In this case, the programmer used a semicolon (;) to end the statement, but the preprocessor included it as part of the definition for `SIZE`. The assignment statement for `SIZE`, **when** expanded, is:

```
size = 10; -2;;
```

The two semicolons at the end do not hurt us, but the one in the middle is the killer. This line tells C to do two things:

* Assign 10 to size.

* Compute the value -2 and throw it away (this code results in the null-effect warning). Removing the semicolons will fix the problem.

Answer 10-4: The output of the preprocessor looks like:

```
void exit();
main() {
    int value;

    value = 1;
    if (value < 0)
        printf("Fatal Error:Abort\n");exit(8);
    printf("We did not die\n");
    return (0);
}
```

The problem is that two statements follow the **if** line. Normally, they would be put on two lines. Let's look at this program properly indented:

```
#include <stdio.h>
#include <stdlib.h>

main() {
    int value;   /* a random value for testing */

    value = 1;
    if (value < 0)
        printf("Fatal Error:Abort\n");

    exit(8);

    printf("We did not die\n");
    return (0);
}
```

With this new format, we can easily determine why we always exit. The fact that there were two statements after the **if** was hidden from us by using a single preprocessor macro.

The cure for this problem is to put curly braces ({}) around all multistatement macros; for example:

```
#define DIE {printf("Fatal Error:Abort\n");exit(8);}
```

Answer 10-5: The program prints:

```
x 1 x squared 1
x 2 x squared 3
x 3 x squared 5
x 4 x squared 7
x 5 x squared 9
```

The problem is with the SQR(counter+1) expression. Expanding this expression we get:

```
SQR(counter+1)
(counter + 1 * counter + 1)
```

So our SQR macro does not work. Putting parentheses around the parameters solves this problem:

```
#define SQR(x)   ((x) * (x))
```

Answer 10-6: The answer is that the counter is incremented by two each time through the loop. This incrementation occurs because the macro call:

```
SQR(++counter)
```

is expanded to:

```
((++counter) * (++counter))
```

Answer 10-7: The only difference between a parameterized macro and one without parameters is the parenthesis immediately following the macro name. In this case, a space follows the definition of RECIPROCAL, so the macro is *not* parameterized. Instead, it is a simple text-replacement macro that will replace RECIPROCAL with:

```
(number) (1.0 / number)
```

Removing the space between RECIPROCAL and (number) will correct the problem.

Programming Exercises

Exercise 10-1: Write a macro that returns TRUE if its parameter is divisible by 10 and FALSE otherwise.

Exercise 10-2: Write a macro `is_digit` that returns TRUE if its argument is a decimal digit.

Exercise 10-3: Write a second macro `is_hex` that returns true if its argument is a hex digit (0-9, A-F, a-f).   The second macro should reference the first.

Exercise 10-4: Write a preprocessor macro that swaps two integers. (For the real hacker, write one that does not use a temporary variable declared outside the macro.)

11

Bit Operations

> *To be or not to be, that is the question*
> — Shakespeare, on boolean algebra
> [*Hamlet,* Act 3, Scene 1]

This chapter discusses bit-oriented operations. A bit is the smallest unit of information. Normally, it is represented by the values 1 and 0. (Other representations include on/off, true/false, and yes/no.) Bit manipulations are used to control the machine at the lowest level. They allow the programmer to get under the hood of the machine. Many higher-level programs will never need bit operations. Low-level coding, like writing device drivers or pixel-level graphic programming, requires bit operations.

Eight bits together form a byte, represented by the C data type **char**.*

A byte might contain the following bits:

```
01100100
```

This bit structure can also be written as the hexadecimal number 0x64. (C uses the prefix "0x" to indicate a hexadecimal (base 16) number.) Hexadecimal is

---

* Technically speaking, the C standard does not specify the number of bits in a character. However, on every machine I know of, a C character is 8 bits.

convenient for representing binary data because each hexadecimal digit represents 4 binary bits. Table 11-1 gives the hexadecimal-to-binary conversion:

Table 11-1: Hexadecimal and Binary

Hexadecimal	Binary	Hexadecimal	Binary
0	0000	8	1000
1	0001	9	1001
2	0010	A	1010
3	0011	B	1011
4	0100	C	1100
5	0101	D	1101
6	0110	E	1110
7	0111	F	1111

So the hexadecimal number 0xAF represents the binary number 10101111.

The `printf` format for hexadecimal is `%x`; for octal the format is `%o`. So:

```
int number = 0xAF;
printf("Number is %x %d %o\n", number, number, number);
```

prints:

```
af 175 257
```

Many novice programmers get a number confused with its *representation*. They ask questions like, "How does a number know if it's a hexadecimal number or decimal?"

To illustrate the difference between these two concepts, consider a bag of marbles as illustrated in Figure 11-1.

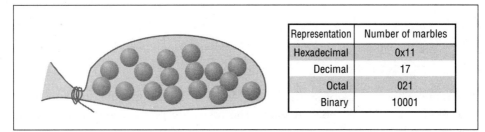

Representation	Number of marbles
Hexadecimal	0x11
Decimal	17
Octal	021
Binary	10001

Figure 11-1: A bag of marbles

This bag contains 17 marbles. But is that hexadecimal 0x11, decimal 17, octal 021, or binary 10001? The answer is that the *number* is 17 no matter what. How we choose to *represent* it (octal, decimal, hex, or binary) is up to us. The marbles don't care how we count them.

Bit Operators

Bit operators allow the programmer to work on individual bits. For example, a short integer holds 16 bits (on most machines). The bit operators treat each bit as independent. By contrast, an add operator treats the 16 bits as a single 16-bit number.

Bit operators allow the programmer to set, clear, test, and perform other operations on bits. The bit operators are listed in Table 11-2.

Table 11-2: Bitwise Operators

Operator	Meaning
&	Bitwise and
|	Bitwise or
^	Bitwise exclusive or
~	Complement
<<	Shift left
>>	Shift right

These operators work on any integer or character data type.

The and Operator (&)

The *and* operator compares two bits. If they both are one, the result is one. The results of the *and* operator are defined according to Table 11-3.

Table 11-3: and Operator

Bit1	Bit2	Bit1 & Bit2
0	0	0
0	1	0
1	0	0
1	1	1

When two eight-bit variables (`char` variables) are "anded" together, the *and* operator works on each bit independently. The following program segment illustrates this operation:

```
int    c1, c2;

c1 = 0x45;
c2 = 0x71;
printf("Result of %x & %x = %x\n", c1, c2, (c1 & c2));
```

The output of this program is:

```
Result of 45 & 71 = 41
```

This is because:

	c1 = 0x45	binary 01000101
&	c2 = 0x71	binary 01110001
=	0x41	binary 01000001

The bitwise *and* (&) is similar to the logical *and* (&&). In the logical *and*, if both operands are true (nonzero), the result is true (1). In the bitwise *and* (&), if the corresponding bits of both the operands are true (ones), then the corresponding bits of the results are true (ones). So, the bitwise *and* (&) works on each bit independently while the logical *and* (&&) works on the operands as a whole.

However & and && are different operators, as Example 11-1 illustrates.

Example 11-1: and/and.c

```c
#include <stdio.h>
int main()
{
    int i1, i2; /* two random integers */

    i1 = 4;
    i2 = 2;

    /* Nice way of writing the conditional */
    if ((i1 != 0) && (i2 != 0))
        printf("Both are not zero\n");

    /* Shorthand way of doing the same thing */
    /* Correct C code, but rotten style */
    if (i1 && i2)
        printf("Both are not zero\n");

    /* Incorrect use of bitwise and resulting in an error */
    if (i1 & i2)
        printf("Both are not zero\n");

    return (0);
}
```

Question: Why does test #3 fail to print **Both are not zero**?

Answer: The operator & is a bitwise *and*. The result of the bitwise *and* is zero.

	i1=4	00000100
	i2=2	00000010
&		00000000

The result of the bitwise *and* is 0, and the conditional is false. If the programmer had used the first form:

```
    if ((i1 != 0) && (i2 != 0))
```

and made the mistake of using & instead of &&:

```
    if ((i1 != 0) & (i2 != 0))
```

the program would still have executed correctly.

    (i1 != 0)   is true (result = 1)
    (i2 != 0)   is true (result = 1)

1 bitwise and 1 is 1 so the expression is true.[*]

You can use the bitwise *and* operator to test if a number is even or odd. In base 2, the last digit of all even numbers is zero and the last digit of all odd numbers is one. The following function uses the bitwise *and* to pick off this last digit. If it is zero (an even number), the result of the function is true.

```
    int even(const int value)
    {
        return ((value & 1) == 0);
    }
```

NOTE   This procedure uses a programming technique known by the technical name "a cute trick." Normally, cute tricks should be avoided whenever possible. Better programming practice would be to use the modulus (%) operator in this case. The only reason we've used the *and* operator (&) is because we are discussing it in this section.

Bitwise or (|)

The *inclusive or* operator (also known as just the *or* operator) compares its two operands and if one or the other bit is a one, the result is a one. Table 11-4 lists the truth table for the *or* operator.

Table 11-4: or Operator

Bit1	Bit2	Bit1 | Bit2
0	0	0
0	1	1

---

[*] Soon after I discovered the bug illustrated by this program, I told my office mate, "I now understand the difference between *and* and *and and*," and he understood me. How we understand language has always fascinated me, and the fact that I could utter such a sentence and have someone understand it without trouble amazed me.

Table 11-4: or Operator (continued)

Bit1	Bit2	Bit1 | Bit2
1	0	1
1	1	1

On a byte, this would be:

```
      i1=0x47     01000111
  |   i2=0x53     01010011
  ─────────────────────────
  =   0x57        01010111
```

The Bitwise Exclusive or (^)

The *exclusive or* (also known as *xor*) operator results in a one when either of its two operands is a one, but not both. The truth table for the exclusive or operator is listed in Table 11-5.

Table 11-5: Exclusive or

Bit1	Bit2	Bit1 ^ Bit2
0	0	0
0	1	1
1	0	1
1	1	0

On a byte this would be:

```
      i1=0x47     01000111
  ^   i2=0x53     01010011
  ─────────────────────────
  =   0x14        00010100
```

The Ones Complement Operator (Not) (~)

The *not* operator (also called the invert operator, or bit flip) is a unary operator that returns the inverse of its operand as shown in Table 11-6.

Table 11-6: not Operator

Bit	~Bit
0	1
1	0

On a byte, this is:

c=	0x45	01000101
~c=	0xBA	10111010

The Left- and Right-Shift Operators (<<, >>)

The left-shift operator moves the data to the left a specified number of bits. Any bits that are shifted out the left side disappear. New bits coming in from the right are zeros. The right shift does the same thing in the other direction. For example:

	c=0x1C	00011100
c << 1	c=0x38	00111000
c >> 2	c=0x07	00000111

Shifting left by one (x << 1) is the same as multiplying by 2 (x * 2). Shifting left by two (x << 2) is the same as multiplying by 4 (x * 4, or x * 2^2). You can see a pattern forming here. Shifting left by n places is the same as multiplying by 2^n. Why shift instead of multiply? Shifting is faster than multiplication, so:

```
i = j << 3;      /* Multiple j by 8 (2**3) */
```

is faster than:

```
i  = j * 8;
```

Or it would be faster if compilers weren't smart enough to turn "multiply by power of two" into "shift."

Many clever programmers use this trick to speed up their programs at the cost of clarity. Don't you do it. The compiler is smart enough to perform the speedup automatically. The result of putting in a shift gains you nothing at the expense of clarity.

The left-shift operator multiplies; the right-shift operator divides. So:

```
q = i >> 2;
```

is the same as:

```
q = i / 4;
```

Again, this trick is clever but should not be used in modern code.

Right-Shift Details

Right shifts are particularly tricky. When a variable is shifted to the right, C needs to fill the space on the left-hand side with something. For signed variables, C uses the value of the sign bit. For unsigned variables, C uses zero. Table 11-7 illustrates some typical shifts.

Table 11-7: Right-Shift Examples

	signed char	signed char	unsigned char
Expression	9 >> 2	-8 >> 2	248 >> 2
Binary Value >> 2	0000 1010 >> 2	1111 1000 >> 2	1111 1000 >> 2
Result	??00 0010	??11 1110	??11 1110
Fill	Sign Bit (0)	Sign Bit (1)[a]	Zero
Final Result (Binary)	0000 0010	1111 1110	0011 1110
Final Result (short int)	2	-2	62

a The ANSI standard specifies that right shifts may be arithmetic (sign bit fill) or logical (zero bit fill). Almost all compilers use the arithmetic right shift.

Setting, Clearing, and Testing Bits

A character (**char**) contains eight bits. Each of these can be treated as a separate flag.

Bit operations can be used to pack eight single-bit values in a single byte. For example, suppose we are writing a low-level communications program. We are going to store the characters in an 8k buffer for later use. With each character we will also store a set of status flags. The flags are listed in Table 11-8.

Table 11-8: Communications Status Values

Name	Description
ERROR	True if any error is set.
FRAMING_ERROR	A framing error occurred for this character.
PARITY_ERROR	Character had the wrong parity.
CARRIER_LOST	The carrier signal went down.
CHANNEL_DOWN	Power was lost on the communication device.

We could store each of these flags in its own character variable. That format would mean that for each character buffered, we would need five bytes of status storage. For a large buffer, that storage adds up. If we instead assign each status flag its own bit within an 8-bit status character, we cut our storage requirements down to one-fifth of our original need.

We assign our flags the bit numbers listed in Table 11-9.

Table 11-9: Bit Assignments

Bit	Name
0	ERROR
1	FRAMING_ERROR
2	PARITY_ERROR
3	CARRIER_LOST
4	CHANNEL_DOWN

Bits are numbered 76543210 by convention, as seen in Table 11-9. In Figure 11-2, we have bits 4 and 1 set.

7	6	5	4	3	2	1	0
0	0	0	1	0	0	1	0

Figure 11-2: Bit numbers

The constants for each bit are defined in Table 11-10.

Table 11-10: Bit Values

Bit	Binary value	Hexadecimal constant
7	10000000	0x80
6	01000000	0x40
5	00100000	0x20
4	00010000	0x10
3	00001000	0x08
2	00000100	0x04
1	00000010	0x02
0	00000001	0x01

The definitions could be:

```
/* True if any error is set */
const int ERROR =       0x01;

/* A framing error occurred for this character */
const int FRAMING_ERROR = 0x02;

/* Character had the wrong parity */
const int PARITY_ERROR = 0x04;

/* The carrier signal went down */
const int CARRIER_LOST =   0x08;
```

```
/* Power was lost on the communication device */
const int CHANNEL_DOWN =   0x10;
```

This method of defining bits is somewhat confusing. Can you tell (without looking at the table) which bit number is represented by the constant 0x10? Table 11-11 shows how we can use the left-shift operator (<<) to define bits.

Table 11-11: Left-Shift Operator and Bit Definition

C Representation	Base 2 Equivalent	Result (Base 2)	Bit Number
1<<0	00000001 << 0	00000001	Bit 0
1<<1	00000001 << 1	00000010	Bit 1
1<<2	00000001 << 2	00000100	Bit 2
1<<3	00000001 << 3	00001000	Bit 3
1<<4	00000001 << 4	00010000	Bit 4
1<<5	00000001 << 5	00100000	Bit 5
1<<6	00000001 << 6	01000000	Bit 6
1<<7	00000001 << 7	10000000	Bit 7

Although you cannot easily tell what bit is represented by 0x10, you can easily tell what bit is meant by 1<<4.

So our flags can be defined as:

```
/* True if any error is set */
const int ERROR =             (1<<0);

/* A framing error occurred for this character  */
const int FRAMING_ERROR =   (1<<1);

/* Character had the wrong parity */
const int PARITY_ERROR =    (1<<2);

/* The carrier signal went down */
const int CARRIER_LOST =    (1<<3);

/* Power was lost on the communication device */
const int CHANNEL_DOWN =    (1<<4);
```

Now that we have defined the bits, we can manipulate them. To set a bit, use the | operator. For example:

```
char    flags = 0;  /* start all flags at 0 */

    flags |= CHANNEL_DOWN; /* Channel just died */
```

To test a bit, we use the & operator to *mask out* the bits:

```
if ((flags & ERROR) != 0)
```

```
        printf("Error flag is set\n");
    else
        printf("No error detected\n");
```

Clearing a bit is a harder task. Suppose we want to clear the bit `PARITY_ERROR`. In binary this bit is 00000100. We want to create a mask that has all bits set *except* for the bit we want to clear (11111011). This step is done with the *not* operator (~). The mask is then *anded* with the number to clear the bit.

PARITY_ERROR	00000100
~PARITY_ERROR	11111011
flags	00000101
flags & ~PARITY_ERROR	00000001

In C, you should use:

```
    flags &= ~PARITY_ERROR; /* Who cares about parity */
```

Question 11-1: *In Example 11-2, the HIGH_SPEED flag works, but the DIRECT_CONNECT flag does not. Why?*

Example 11-2: high/high.c

```
#include <stdio.h>

const int HIGH_SPEED = (1<<7);    /* modem is running fast */

/* we are using a hardwired connection */
const int DIRECT_CONNECT = (1<<8);

char flags = 0;          /* start with nothing */

int main()
{
    flags |= HIGH_SPEED;    /* we are running fast */
    flags |= DIRECT_CONNECT;/* because we are wired together */

    if ((flags & HIGH_SPEED) != 0)
        printf("High speed set\n");

    if ((flags & DIRECT_CONNECT) != 0)
        printf("Direct connect set\n");
    return (0);
}
```

Bitmapped Graphics

More and more computers now have graphics. For the PC, there are graphics devices like EGA and VGA cards. UNIX offers the X windowing system.

In bitmapped graphics, each pixel on the screen is represented by a single bit in memory. For example, Figure 11-3 shows a 14-by-14 bitmap as it appears on the screen, and enlarged so that you can see the bits.

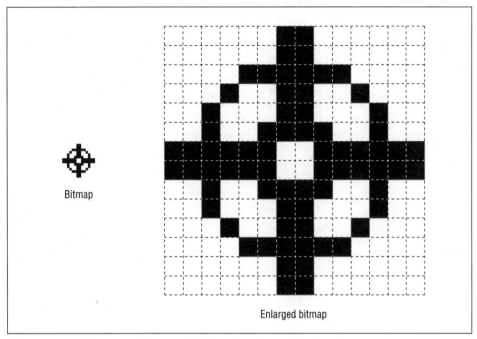

Figure 11-3: Bitmap, actual size and enlarged

Suppose we have a small graphic device—a 16-by-16-pixel black-and-white display. We want to set the bit at 4,7. The bitmap for this device is shown as an array of bits in Figure 11-4.

But we have a problem. No data type exists for an array of bits in C. The closest we can come is an array of bytes. Our 16-by-16 array of bits now becomes a 2-by-16 array of bytes, as shown in Figure 11-5.

Let's see what we need to do to transform our x, y index to a byte_x, byte_y, bit_index, and bit.

The byte_y index is the same as the y index. That transformation is simple:

```
byte_y = y;
```

A byte contains 8 bits. So, in the X direction, our byte index is eight times our bit index. This transformation leaves us with the code:

```
byte_x = x / 8;
```

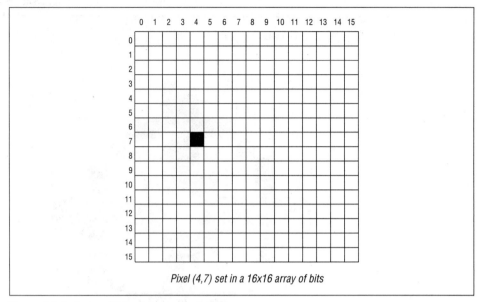

Figure 11-4: Array of bits

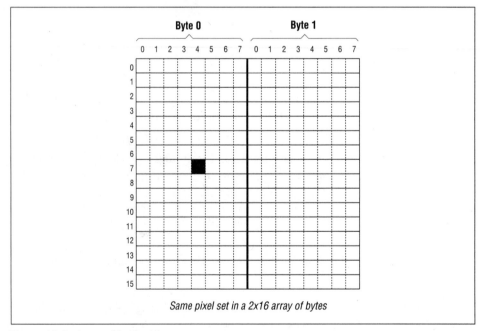

Figure 11-5: Array of bytes

Now we need the bit index. The index starts out at 0, goes to 7, and then goes back to 0. This change gives us the code:

```
bit_index = x % 8;
```

Now to specify the bit itself. A bit index of zero indicates the left-most bit or the bit represented by $1000\ 0000_2$ or `0x80`. A bit index of 1 indicates the next-to-the-left-most bit $0100\ 0000_2$ or `0x80 >> 1`. So the bit we want is given by the expression:

```
bit = 0x80 >> bit_index;
```

The full algorithm looks like:

```
byte_y = y;
byte_x = x / 8;
bit_index = x % 8;
bit = 0x80 >> bit_index;
graphics[byte_x][byte_y] |= bit;
```

This algorithm can be condensed into a single macro:

```
#define set_bit(x, y) graphics[(x)/8][y] |= (0x80 >> ((x)%8))
```

For example, to set the pixel at bit number 4,7, we need to set the fourth bit of byte 0,7. Our macro would generate the statement:

```
bit_array[0][7] |= (0x80 >> (4));
```

Example 11-3 draws a diagonal line across the graphics array and then prints the array on the terminal.

Example 11-3: graph/graph.c

```
#include <stdio.h>

#define X_SIZE 40  /* size of array in X direction */
#define Y_SIZE 60  /* size of array in Y direction */
/*
 * We use X_SIZE/8 because we pack 8 bits per byte
 */
char graphics[X_SIZE / 8][Y_SIZE];   /* the graphics data */

#define SET_BIT(x,y) graphics[(x)/8][y] |= (0x80 >>((x)%8))

int main()
{
    int   loc;         /* current location we are setting */
    void  print_graphics(void); /* print the data */

    for (loc = 0; loc < X_SIZE; ++loc)
        SET_BIT(loc, loc);

    print_graphics();
    return (0);
}
/************************************************************
 * print_graphics -- Prints the graphics bit array         *
 *                   as a set of X and .'s.                *
 ************************************************************/
```

Example 11-3: graph/graph.c (continued)

```
void print_graphics(void)
{
    int x;                 /* current x BYTE */
    int y;                 /* current y location */
    unsigned int bit;      /* bit we are testing in the current byte */

    for (y = 0; y < Y_SIZE; ++y) {
        /* Loop for each byte in the array */
        for (x = 0; x < X_SIZE / 8; ++x) {
            /* Handle each bit */
            for (bit = 0x80; bit > 0; bit = (bit >> 1)) {
                if ((graphics[x][y] & bit) != 0)
                    printf("X");
                else
                    printf(".");
            }
        }
        printf("\n");
    }
}
```

The program defines a bitmapped graphic array:

```
char graphics[X_SIZE / 8][Y_SIZE];   /* the graphics data */
```

The constant **X_SIZE/8** is used because we have **X_SIZE** bits across, which translates to **X_SIZE/8** bytes.

The main **for** loop:

```
for (loc = 0; loc < X_SIZE; ++loc)
        set_bit(loc, loc);
```

draws a diagonal line across the graphics array.

Because we do not have a bitmapped graphics device, we will simulate it with the subroutine **print_graphics**.

The loop:

```
for (y = 0; y < Y_SIZE; ++y) {
    ....
```

prints each row. The loop:

```
for (x = 0; x < X_SIZE / 8; ++x) {
        ...
```

goes through every byte in the row. There are eight bits in each byte handled by the loop:

```
for (bit = 0x80; bit > 0; bit = (bit >> 1))
```

which uses an unusual loop counter. This loop causes the variable `bit` to start with bit 7 (the left-most bit). For each iteration of the loop, the bit is moved to the right one bit by `bit = (bit >> 1)`. When we run out of bits, the loop exits.

The loop counter cycles through:

Binary	Hex
0000 0000 1000 0000	0x80
0000 0000 0100 0000	0x40
0000 0000 0010 0000	0x20
0000 0000 0001 0000	0x10
0000 0000 0000 1000	0x08
0000 0000 0000 0100	0x04
0000 0000 0000 0010	0x02
0000 0000 0000 0001	0x01

Finally, at the heart of the loops is the code:

```
if ((graphics[x][y] & bit) != 0)
    printf("X");
else
    printf(".");
```

This code tests an individual bit and writes an "X" if it is set or a "." if it is not.

Question 11-2: *In Example 11-4 the first loop works, but the second one fails. Why?*

Example 11-4: loop/loop.c

```
#include <stdio.h>
int main()
{
    short int i;        /* Loop counter */
    signed char ch;     /* Loop counter of another kind */

    /* Works */
    for (i = 0x80; i != 0; i = (i >> 1)) {
        printf("i is %x (%d)\n", i, i);
    }

    /* Fails */
    for (ch = 0x80; ch != 0; ch = (ch >> 1)) {
        printf("ch is %x (%d)\n", ch, ch);
    }
    return (0);
}
```

Answers

Answer 11-1: DIRECT_CONNECT is defined to be bit number 8 by the expression (1<<8); however, the eight bits in a character variable are numbered 76543210. Bit number 8 does not exist. A solution to this problem is to make **flags** a short integer with 16 bits.

Answer 11-2: The problem is that **ch** is a character (8 bits). The value 0x80 represented in 8 bits is $1000\ 0000_2$. The first bit, the sign bit, is set. When a right shift is done on this variable, the sign bit is used for fill. So, $1000\ 0000_2 >>1$ is $1100\ 0000_2$.

The variable **i** works even though it is signed because it is 16 bits long. So 0x80 in 16 bits is $0000\ 0000\ 1000\ 0000_2$. Notice that the set bit is not near the sign bit.

The solution to our problem is to declare **ch** as an **unsigned** variable.

Programming Exercises

Exercise 11-1: Write a set of parameterized macros, clear_bit and test_bit, to go with the set_bit operation defined in Example 11-3. Write a main program to test these macros.

Exercise 11-2: Write a program to draw a 10-by-10 bitmapped square. You can borrow the code from Example 11-3 to print the results.

Exercise 11-3: Change Example 11-3 so that it draws a white line across a black background.

Exercise 11-4: Write a program that counts the number of bits set in an integer. For example, the number 5 (decimal), which is 0000000000000101 (binary), has two bits set.

Exercise 11-5: Write a program that takes a 32-bit integer (**long int**) and splits it into eight 4-bit values. (Be careful of the sign bit.)

Exercise 11-6: Write a program that will take the bits in a number and shift them to the left end. For example, 01010110 (binary) would become 11110000 (binary).

12

Advanced Types

> *Total grandeur of a total edifice,*
> *Chosen by an inquisitor of structures.*
> —Wallace Stevens

C provides the programmer with a rich set of data types. Through the use of structures, unions, and enumerated types, the programmer can extend the language with new types.

Structures

Suppose we are writing an inventory program for a warehouse. The warehouse is filled with bins that contain various parts. All the parts in a bin are identical, so we don't have to worry about mixed bins.

For each bin, we need to know:

- The name of the part it holds (string 30 characters long)
- The quantity on hand (integer)
- The price (integer cents)

In previous chapters, we have used arrays for storing a group of similar data types. However, in this example, we have a mixed bag: two integers and a string.

Instead of an array, we will use a new data type called a *structure*. In an array, all the elements are of the same type and are numbered. In a structure, each element or *field* is named and has its own data type.

The general form of a structure definition is:

```
struct structure-name {
    field-type field-name;  /* comment */
```

```
    field-type field-name;   /* comment */
        .  .  .  .
} variable-name;
```

For example, we want to define a bin to hold printer cables. The structure definition is:

```
struct bin {
    char    name[30];    /* name of the part */
    int     quantity;    /* how many are in the bin */
    int     cost;        /* The cost of a single part  (in cents) */
} printer_cable_bin;     /* where we put the print cables */
```

This definition actually tells C two things. The first is what a **struct bin** looks like. This statement defines a new data type that can be used in declaring other variables. The variable **printer_cable_bin** is also declared by this statement. Because the structure of a **bin** has been defined, we can use it to declare additional variables:

```
struct bin terminal_cable_box;   /* Place to put terminal cables */
```

The *structure-name* part of the definition may be omitted:

```
struct {
    char    name[30];    /* name of the part */
    int     quantity;    /* how many are in the bin */
    int     cost;        /* The cost of a single part  (in cents) */
} printer_cable_bin;     /* where we put the print cables */
```

The variable **printer_cable_bin** has been defined, but no data type has been created. In other words, **printer_cable_bin** is the only variable of this structure you want in the program. The data type for this variable is an *anonymous structure*.

The *variable-name* may also be omitted. The following example would define a structure type, but no variables:

```
struct bin {
    char    name[30];    /* name of the part */
    int     quantity;    /* how many are in the bin */
    int     cost;        /* The cost of a single part  (in cents) */
};
```

You can now use the new data type (**struct bin**) to define variables such as **printer_cable_bin**.

In an extreme case, both the *variable-name* and the *structure-name* may be omitted. This syntax creates a section of correct, but totally useless code.

We have defined the variable **printer_cable_bin** containing three named fields: **name**, **quantity**, and **cost**. To access them, we use the syntax:

```
variable.field
```

For example, if we just found out that the price of the cables went up to $12.95, we would do the following:

```
printer_cable_bin.cost = 1295;    /* $12.95 is the new price */
```

To compute the value of everything in the bin, we can use the following:

```
total_cost = printer_cable_bin.cost * printer_cable_bin.quantity;
```

Structures may be initialized at declaration time by putting the list of elements in curly braces ({}):

```
/*
 * Printer cables
 */
struct bin {
    char    name[30];    /* name of the part */
    int     quantity;    /* how many are in the bin */
    int     cost;        /* The cost of a single part  (in cents) */
} printer_cable_bin = {
    "Printer Cables",    /* Name of the item in the bin */
    0,                   /* Start with empty box */
    1295                 /* cost -- $12.95  */
};
```

Unions

A structure is used to define a data type with several fields. Each field takes up a separate storage location. For example, the structure:

```
struct rectangle {
    int width;
    int height;
};
```

appears in memory. A *union* is similar to a structure; however, it defines a single location that can be given many different field names:

```
union value {
    long int i_value;    /* integer version of value */
    float f_value;       /* floating version of value */
};
```

The fields `i_value` and `f_value` share the same space.

You might think of a structure as a large box divided up into several different compartments, each with its own name. A union is a box, not divided at all, with several different labels placed on the single compartment inside.

Figure 12-1 illustrates a structure with two fields. Each field is assigned a different section of the structure. A union contains only one compartment, which is assigned different names.

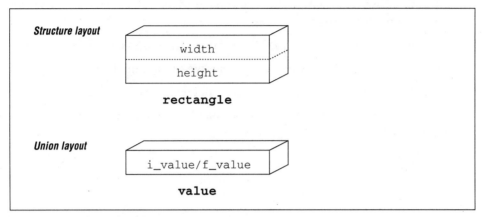

Figure 12-1: Layout of structure and union

In a structure, the fields do not interact. Changing one field does not change any others. In a union, all fields occupy the same space, so only one may be active at a time. In other words, if you put something in `i_value`, assigning something to `f_value` wipes out the old value of `i_value`.

Example 12-1 shows how a union can be used.

Example 12-1: Using a Union

```
/*
 * Define a variable to hold an integer or
 * a real number (but not both)
 */
union value {
    long int i_value;    /* The real number */
    float f_value;       /* The floating-point number */
} data;
int i;                   /* Random integer */
float f;                 /* Random floating-point number */
main()
{
    data.f_value = 5.0;
    data.i_value = 3;    /* data.f_value overwritten */
    i = data.i_value;    /* legal */
    f = data.f_value;    /* not legal, will generate unexpected results */
    data.f_value = 5.5;  /* put something in f_value/clobber i_value */
    i = data.i_value;    /* not legal, will generate unexpected results */
    return(0);
}
```

Unions are frequently used in the area of communications. For example, suppose we have a remote tape and we want to send it four messages: open, close, read, and write. The data contained in these four messages is vastly different depending on the message.

The open message needs to contain the name of the tape; the write message needs to contain the data to write; the read message needs to contain the maximum number of characters to read; and the close message needs no additional information.

```
#define DATA_MAX 1024 /* Maximum amount of data for a read and write */

struct open_msg {
    char name[30];      /* Name of the tape */
};

struct read_msg {
    int length;         /* Max data to tranfer in the read */
};

struct write_msg {
    int length;         /* Number of bytes to write */
    char data[DATA_MAX]; /* Data to write */
};

struct close_msg {
};

const int OPEN_CODE=0;    /* Code indicating an open message */
const int READ_CODE=1;    /* Code indicating a read message */
const int WRITE_CODE=2;   /* Code indicating a write message */
const int CLOSE_CODE=3;   /* Code indicating a close message */

struct msg {
    int msg;/* Message type */
    union {
        struct open_msg open_data;
        struct read_msg read_data;
        struct write_msg write_data;
        struct close_msg close_data;
    } msg_data;
};
```

typedef

C allows the programmer to define her own variable types through the **typedef** statement. This statement provides a way for the program to extend C's basic types. The general form of the **typedef** statement is:

```
typedef type-declaration;
```

where *type-declaration* is the same as a variable declaration except that a type name is used instead of a *variable-name*. For example:

```
typedef int count;
```

defines a new type count that is the same as an integer.

So the declaration:

```
count flag;
```

is the same as:

```
int flag;
```

At first glance, this statement is not much different from:

```
#define count int
count flag;
```

However, **typedef**s can be used to define more complex objects that are beyond the scope of a simple **#define** statement. For example:

```
typedef int group[10];
```

A new type named **group** now exists, denoting an array of ten integers:

```
main()
{
    typedef int group[10];     /* Create a new type "group" */
    group totals;              /* Use the new type for a variable */
    for (i = 0; i < 10; i++)
        totals[i] = 0;
    return (0);
}
```

One frequent use of typedef's is in the definition of a new structure. For example:

```
struct complex_struct {
    double real;
    double imag;
};
typedef struct complex_struct complex;

complex voltag1 = {3.5, 1.2};
```

enum Type

The enumerated data type is designed for variables that contain only a limited set of values. These values are referenced by name (tag). The compiler assigns each tag an integer value internally. Consider an application, for example, in which we want a variable to hold the days of the week. We could use the **const** declaration to create values for the **week_days**, as follows:

```
typedef int week_day;   /* define the type for week_days */
const int SUNDAY    = 0;
const int MONDAY    = 1;
const int TUESDAY   = 2;
const int WEDNESDAY = 3;
const int THURSDAY  = 4;
const int FRIDAY    = 5;
const int SATURDAY  = 6;
```

```
/* now to use it */
week_day today = TUESDAY;
```

This method is cumbersome. A better method is to use the **enum** type:

```
enum week_day {SUNDAY, MONDAY, TUESDAY, WEDNESDAY, THURSDAY,
    FRIDAY, SATURDAY};
/* now use it */
enum week_day today = TUESDAY;
```

The general form of an **enum** statement is:

```
enum enum-name { tag-1, tag-2, . . .} variable-name
```

Like structures, the *enum-name* or the *variable-name* may be omitted. The tags may be any valid C identifier; however, they are usually all uppercase.

C implements the **enum** type as compatible with integer. So in C, it is perfectly legal to say:

```
today = 5;   /* 5 is not a week_day */
```

although some compilers will issue a warning when they see this line. In C++, **enum** is a separate type and is not compatible with integer.

Casting

Sometimes you must convert one type of variable to another type. This is accomplished through the *cast* or *typecast operation*. The general form of a cast is:

```
(type) expression
```

This operation tells C to compute the value of the *expression*, and then convert it to the specified *type*. This operation is particularly useful when you work with integers and floating-point numbers:

```
int won, lost;      /* # games won/lost so far */
float   ratio;      /* win/lose ratio */
won = 5;
lost = 3;
ratio = won / lost; /* ratio will get 1.0 (a wrong value) */
/* The following will compute the correct ratio */
ratio = ((float) won) / ((float) lost);
```

Another common use of this operation is for converting pointers from one type to another.

Bit Fields or Packed Structures

Packed structures allow us to declare structures in a way that takes up a minimum amount of storage. For example, the following structure takes up six bytes (on a 16-bit machine).

```
struct item {
    unsigned int list;      /* true if item is in the list */
    unsigned int seen;      /* true if this item has been seen */
    unsigned int number;    /* item number */
};
```

The storage layout for this structure can be seen in Figure 12-2. Each structure uses six bytes of storage (two bytes for each integer).

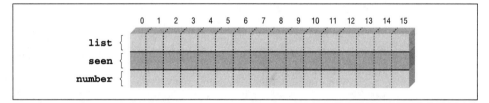

Figure 12-2: Unpacked structure

However, the fields `list` and `seen` can only have two values, 0 and 1, so only one bit is needed to represent them. We never plan on having more than 16383 items (0x3fff or 14 bits). We can redefine this structure using bit fields, so that it takes only two bytes, by following each field with a colon and the number of bits to be used for that field:

```
struct item {
    unsigned int list:1;    /* true if item is in the list */
    unsigned int seen:1;    /* true if this item has been seen */
    unsigned int number:14; /* item number */
};
```

In this example, we tell the compiler to use one bit for `list`, one bit for `seen`, and 14 bits for `number`. Using this method, we can pack our data into only two bytes, as seen in Figure 12-3.

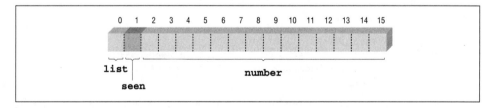

Figure 12-3: Packed structure

Packed structures should be used with care. The code to extract data from bit fields is relatively large and slow. Unless storage is a problem, packed structures should not be used.

In Chapter 10, *C Preprocessor*, we needed to store character data and five status flags for 8,000 characters. In this case, using a different byte for each flag would eat up a lot of storage (five bytes for each incoming character). We used bitwise operations to pack the five flags into a single byte. Alternatively, a packed structure could have accomplished the same thing:

```
struct char_and_status {
    char character;     /* Character from device */
    int error:1;        /* True if any error is set */
    int framing_error:1;/* Framing error occurred */
    int parity_error:1; /* Character had the wrong parity */
    int carrier_lost:1; /* The carrier signal went down */
    int channel_down:1; /* Power was lost on the channel */
};
```

Using packed structures for flags is clearer and less error prone than using bitwise operators. However, bitwise operators give the programmer additional flexibility. You should use the one that is clearest and easiest for you to use.

Arrays of Structures

Structures and arrays can be combined. For example, suppose we want to record the time a runner completes each lap of a four-lap race. We define a structure to store the time:

```
struct time {
    int hour;   /* hour (24 hour clock ) */
    int minute; /* 0-59 */
    int second; /* 0-59 */
};
const int MAX_LAPS = 4; /* we will have only 4 laps */
/* the time of day for each lap*/
struct time lap[MAX_LAPS];
```

We can use this structure as follows:

```
/*
 * Runner just passed the timing point
 */
lap[count].hour = hour;
lap[count].minute = minute;
lap[count].second = second;
++count;
```

This array can also be initialized at run time.

Initialization of an array of structures is similar to the initialization of multi-dimensional arrays:

```
struct time start_stop[2] = {
    {10, 0, 0},
    {12, 0, 0}
};
```

Suppose we want to write a program to handle a mailing list. Mailing labels are 5 lines high and 60 characters wide. We need a structure to store names and addresses. The mailing list will be sorted by name for most printouts, and sorted in zip code order for actual mailings. Our mailing list structure looks like this:

```
struct mailing {
    char name[60];      /* Last name, first name */
    char address1[60];/* Two lines of street address */
    char address2[60];
    char city[40];
    char state[2];      /* Two character abbreviation */
    long int zip;       /* Numeric zip code */
};
```

We can now declare an array to hold our mailing list:

```
/* Our mailing list */
struct mailing list[MAX_ENTRIES];
```

The state field is two elements because it is designed to hold two characters. The field is not a string because we have not allocated enough space for the end of string character ('\0').

Summary

Structures and unions are some of the more powerful features of the C language. No longer are you limited to C's built-in data types—you can create your own. As we will see in later chapters, structures can be combined with pointers to create very complex and powerful data structures.

Programming Exercises

Exercise 12-1: Design a structure to hold the data for a mailing list. Write a function to print out the data.

Exercise 12-2: Design a structure to store time and date. Write a function to find the difference between two times in minutes.

Exercise 12-3: Design an airline reservation data structure that contains the following data:

- Flight number
- Originating airport code (three characters)
- Destination airport code (three characters)
- Starting time
- Arrival time

Exercise 12-4: Write a program that lists all the planes that leave from two airports specified by the user.

13

Simple Pointers

The choice of a point of view is the initial act of culture.

—José Ortega y Gasset

There are things and pointers to things. Knowing the difference between the two is very important. This concept is illustrated in Figure 13-1.

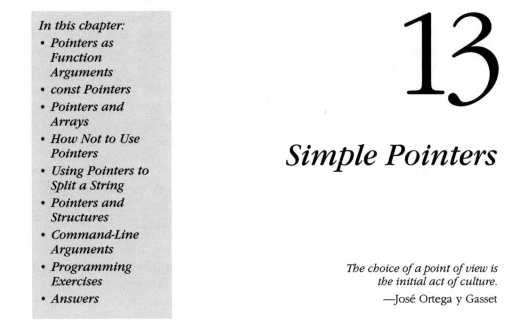

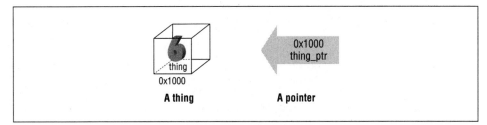

Figure 13-1: A thing and a pointer to a thing

In this book, we use a box to represent a thing. The name of the variable is written on the bottom of the box. In this case, our variable is named `thing`. The value of the variable is 6.

The address of `thing` is `0x1000`. Addresses are automatically assigned by the C compiler to every variable. Normally, you don't have to worry about the addresses of variables, but you should understand that they're there.

Our pointer (`thing_ptr`) points to the variable `thing`. Pointers are also called *address variables* because they contain the addresses of other variables. In this case, our pointer contains the address `0x1000`. Because this is the address of `thing`, we say that `thing_ptr` points to `thing`.

Variables and pointers are much like street addresses and houses. For example, your address might be "214 Green Hill Lane." Houses come in many different shapes and sizes. Addresses are approximately the same size (street, city, state, and zip). So, while "1600 Pennsylvania Ave." might point to a very big white house and "8347 Undersea Street" might be a one-room shack, both addresses are the same size.

The same is true in C. While things may be big and small, pointers come in one size (relatively small).*

Many novice programmers get pointers and their contents confused. In order to limit this problem, all pointer variables in this book end with the extension `_ptr`. You might want to follow this convention in your own programs. Although this notation is not as common as it should be, it is extremely useful.

Many different address variables can point to the same thing. This concept is true for street addresses as well. Table 13-1 lists the location of important services in a small town.

Table 13-1: Directory of Ed's Town USA

Service (variable name)	Address (address value)	Building (thing)
Fire Department	1 Main Street	City Hall
Police Station	1 Main Street	City Hall
Planning office	1 Main Street	City Hall
Gas Station	2 Main Street	Ed's Gas Station

In this case, we have a government building that serves many functions. Although it has one address, three different pointers point to it.

As we will see in this chapter, pointers can be used as a quick and simple way to access arrays. In later chapters, we will discover how pointers can be used to create new variables and complex data structures such as linked lists and trees. As you go through the rest of the book, you will be able to understand these data structures as well as create your own.

A pointer is declared by putting an asterisk (*) in front of the variable name in the declaration statement:

```
int thing;       /* define a thing */
int *thing_ptr;  /* define a pointer to a thing */
```

---

* This statement is not strictly true for MS-DOS/Windows compilers. Because of the strange architecture of the 8086, these compilers are forced to use both *near* pointers (16 bits) and *far* pointers (32 bits). See your C compiler manual for details.

Table 13-2 lists the operators used in conjunction with pointers.

Table 13-2: Pointer Operators

Operator	Meaning
*	*Dereference* (given a pointer, get the thing referenced)
&	*Address of* (given a thing, point to it)

The operator ampersand (&) returns the address of a thing which is a pointer. The operator asterisk (*) returns the object to which a pointer points. These operators can easily cause confusion. Table 13-3 shows the syntax for the various pointer operators.

Table 13-3: Pointer Operator Syntax

C Code	Description
`thing`	Simple thing (variable)
`&thing`	Pointer to variable `thing`
`thing_ptr`	Pointer to an integer (may or may not be specific integer `thing`)
`*thing_ptr`	Integer

Let's look at some typical uses of the various pointer operators:

```
int thing; /* Declare an integer (a thing) */
thing = 4;
```

The variable `thing` is a thing. The declaration `int thing` does *not* contain an *, so `thing` is not a pointer:

```
int *thing_ptr;      /* Declare a pointer to a thing */
```

The variable `thing_ptr` is a pointer. The * in the declaration indicates this is a pointer. Also, we have put the extension `_ptr` onto the name:

```
thing_ptr = &thing;  /* Point to the thing */
```

The expression `&thing` is a pointer to a thing. The variable `thing` is an object. The & (address of operator) gets the address of an object (a pointer), so `&thing` is a pointer. We then assign this to `thing_ptr`, also of type pointer:

```
*thing_ptr = 5;      /* Set "thing" to 5 */
                     /* We may or may not be pointing */
                     /* to the specific integer "thing" */
```

The expression `*thing_ptr` indicates a thing. The variable `thing_ptr` is a pointer. The * (dereference operator) tells C to look at the data pointed to, not the pointer itself. Note that this points to any integer. It may or may not point to the specific variable `thing`.

These pointer operations are summarized in Figure 13-2.

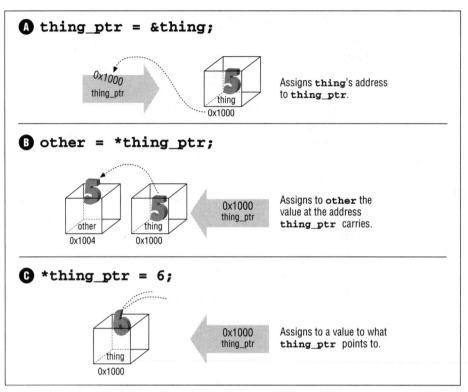

Figure 13-2: Pointer operations

The following examples show how to misuse the pointer operations:

*thing
> is illegal. It asks C to get the object pointed to by the variable *thing*. Because *thing* is not a pointer, this operation is invalid.

&thing_ptr
> is legal, but strange. *thing_ptr* is a pointer. The & (address of operator) gets a pointer to the object (in this case *thing_ptr*). The result is a pointer to a pointer.

Example 13-1 illustrates a simple use of pointers. It declares one object, one thing, and a pointer, thing_ptr. thing is set explicitly by the line:

```
thing = 2;
```

The line:

```
thing_ptr = &thing;
```

causes C to set `thing_ptr` to the address of `thing`. From this point on, `thing` and `*thing_ptr` are the same.

Example 13-1: thing/thing.c

```c
#include <stdio.h>
int main()
{
    int    thing_var;  /* define a variable for thing */
    int    *thing_ptr;  /* define a pointer to thing */

    thing_var = 2;       /* assigning a value to thing */
    printf("Thing %d\n", thing_var);

    thing_ptr = &thing_var; /* make the pointer point to thing */
    *thing_ptr = 3;       /* thing_ptr points to thing_var so */
                          /* thing_var changes to 3 */
    printf("Thing %d\n", thing_var);

    /* another way of doing the printf */
    printf("Thing %d\n", *thing_ptr);
    return (0);
}
```

Several pointers can point to the same thing:

```
1:          int something;
2:
3:          int      *first_ptr;      /* one pointer */
4:          int      *second_ptr;     /* another pointer */
5:
6:          something = 1;              /* give the thing a value */
7:
8:          first_ptr = &something;
9:          second_ptr = first_ptr;
```

In line 8, we use the & operator to change **something**, a thing, into a pointer that can be assigned to `first_ptr`. Because `first_ptr` and `second_ptr` are both pointers, we can do a direct assignment in line 9.

After executing this program fragment, we have the situation shown in Figure 13-3.

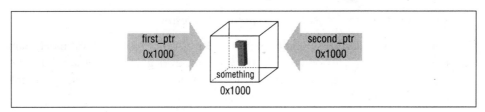

Figure 13-3: Two pointers and a thing

You should note that while we have three variables, there is only one integer (`something`). The following are all equivalent:

```
something = 1;
*first_ptr = 1;
*second_ptr = 1;
```

Pointers as Function Arguments

C passes parameters using "call by value." That is, the parameters go only one way into the function. The only result of a function is a single return value. This concept is illustrated in Figure 13-4.

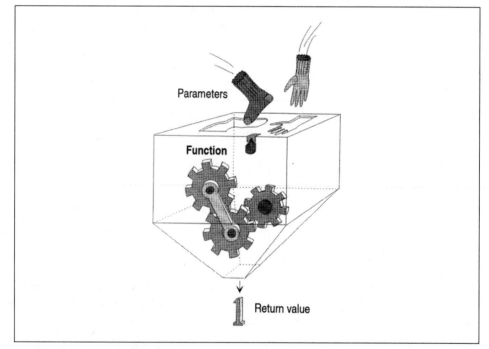

Figure 13-4: Function call

However, pointers can be used to get around this restriction.

Imagine that there are two people, Sam and Joe, and whenever they meet, Sam can only talk and Joe can only listen. How is Sam ever going to get any information from Joe? Simple: all Sam has to do is tell Joe, "I want you to leave the answer in the mailbox at 335 West 5th Street."

C uses a similar trick to pass information from a function to its caller. In Example 13-2, `main` wants the function `inc_count` to increment the variable `count`.

Passing it directly would not work, so a pointer is passed instead ("Here's the address of the variable I want you to increment"). Note that the prototype for `inc_count` contains an `int *`. This format indicates that the single parameter given to this function is a pointer to an integer, not the integer itself.

Example 13-2: call/call.c

```
#include <stdio.h>
void inc_count(int *count_ptr)
{
    (*count_ptr)++;
}

int main()
{
    int   count = 0;      /* number of times through */

    while (count < 10)
        inc_count(&count);

    return (0);
}
```

This code is represented graphically in Figure 13-5. Note that the parameter is not changed, but what it points to is changed.

Finally, there is a special pointer called **NULL**. It points to nothing. (The actual numeric value is 0.) The standard include file, *locale.h*, defines the constant **NULL**. (This file is usually not directly included, but is usually brought in by the include files *stdio.h* or *stdlib.h*.) The **NULL** pointer is represented graphically in Figure 13-6.

const Pointers

Declaring constant pointers is a little tricky. For example, the declaration:

```
const int result = 5;
```

tells C that `result` is a constant so that:

```
result = 10;      /* Illegal */
```

is illegal. The declaration:

```
const char *answer_ptr = "Forty-Two";
```

does *not* tell C that the variable `answer_ptr` is a constant. Instead, it tells C that the data pointed to by `answer_ptr` is a constant. The data cannot be changed, but the pointer can. Again we need to make sure we know the difference between "things" and "pointers to things."

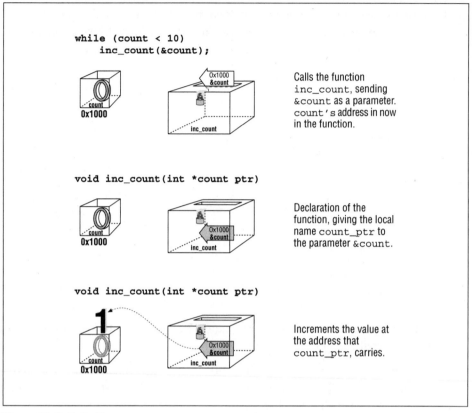

Figure 13-5: Call of inc_count

Figure 13-6: NULL

What's **answer_ptr**? A pointer. Can it be changed? Yes, it's just a pointer. What does it point to? A **const char** array. Can the data pointed to by **answer_ptr** be changed? No, it's constant.

In C this is:

```
answer_ptr = "Fifty-One";     /* Legal (answer_ptr is a variable) */
*answer_ptr = 'X';            /* Illegal (*answer_ptr is a constant) */
```

If we put the **const** after the * we tell C that the pointer is constant.

For example:

```
char *const name_ptr = "Test";
```

What's **name_ptr**? It is a constant pointer. Can it be changed? No. What does it point to? A character. Can the data we pointed to by **name_ptr** be changed? Yes.

```
name_ptr = "New";          /* Illegal (name_ptr is constant) */
*name_ptr = 'B';           /* Legal (*name_ptr is a char) */
```

Finally, we can put **const** in both places, creating a pointer that cannot be changed to a data item that cannot be changed:

```
const char *const title_ptr = "Title";
```

Pointers and Arrays

C allows pointer arithmetic (addition and subtraction). Suppose we have:

```
char array[5];
char *array_ptr = &array[0];
```

In this example, ***array_ptr** is the same as **array[0]**, ***(array_ptr+1)** is the same as **array[1]**, ***(array_ptr+2)** is the same as **array[2]**, and so on. Note the use of parentheses. Pointer arithmetic is represented graphically in Figure 13-7.

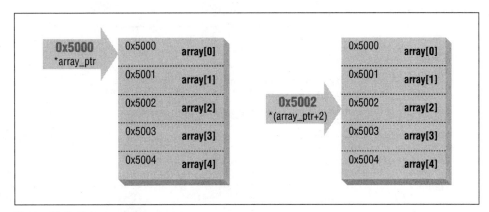

Figure 13-7: Pointers into an array

However, **(*array_ptr)+1** is *not* the same as **array[1]**. The +1 is outside the parentheses, so it is added after the dereference. So **(*array_ptr)+1** is the same as **array[0]+1**.

At first glance, this method may seem like a complex way of representing simple array indices. We are starting with simple pointer arithmetic. In later chapters we will use more complex pointers to handle more difficult functions efficiently.

The elements of an array are assigned to consecutive addresses. For example, `array[0]` may be placed at address `0xff000024`. Then `array[1]` would be placed at address `0xff000025`, and so on. This structure means that a pointer can be used to find each element of the array. Example 13-3 prints out the elements and addresses of a simple character array.

Example 13-3: array-p/array-p.c

```
#include <stdio.h>

#define ARRAY_SIZE 10

char array[ARRAY_SIZE + 1] = "0123456789";

int main()
        {
            int index ;
            printf("&array[index] (array+index) array[index]\n");
            for(index=0;index < ARRAY_SIZE;++index)
                    printf("0x%-10p 0x%-10p 0x%x\n",,
                    &array[index],(array+index),array[index]);

            return 0;
        }
```

NOTE   When printing pointers, the special conversion `%p` should be used.

When run, this program prints:

```
&array[index]  (array+index)  array[index]
0x20a50        0x20a50        0x30
0x20a51        0x20a51        0x31
0x20a52        0x20a52        0x32
0x20a53        0x20a53        0x33
0x20a54        0x20a54        0x34
0x20a55        0x20a55        0x35
0x20a56        0x20a56        0x36
0x20a57        0x20a57        0x37
0x20a58        0x20a58        0x38
0x20a59        0x20a59        0x39
```

Characters use one byte, so the elements in a character array will be assigned consecutive addresses. A `short  int` font uses two bytes, so in an array of `short  int`, the addresses increase by two. Does this mean that `array+1` will not work for anything other than characters? No. C automatically scales pointer arithmetic so that it works correctly. In this case, `array+1` will point to element number 1.

C provides a shorthand for dealing with arrays. Rather than writing:

```
array_ptr = &array[0];
```

we can write:

```
array_ptr = array;
```

C blurs the distinction between pointers and arrays by treating them in the same manner in many cases. Here we use the variable **array** as a pointer, and C automatically does the necessary conversion.

Example 13-4 counts the number of elements that are nonzero and stops when a zero is found. No limit check is provided, so there must be at least one zero in the array.

Example 13-4: ptr2/ptr2.c

```c
#include <stdio.h>

int array[] = {4, 5, 8, 9, 8, 1, 0, 1, 9, 3};
int index;

int main()
{
    index = 0;
    while (array[index] != 0)
        ++index;

    printf("Number of elements before zero %d\n",
                index);
    return (0);
}
```

Example 13-5 is a version of Example 13-4 that uses pointers.

Example 13-5: ptr3/ptr3.c

```c
#include <stdio.h>

int array[] = {4, 5, 8, 9, 8, 1, 0, 1, 9, 3};
int *array_ptr;

int main()
{
    array_ptr = array;

    while ((*array_ptr) != 0)
        ++array_ptr;

    printf("Number of elements before zero %d\n",
                array_ptr - array);
    return (0);
}
```

Notice that when we wish to examine the data in the array, we use the deference operator (*). This operator is used in the statement:

```
while ((*array_ptr) != 0)
```

When we wish to change the pointer itself, no other operator is used. For example, the line:

```
++array_ptr;
```

increments the pointer, not the data.

Example 13-4 uses the expression (`array[index] != 0`). This expression requires the compiler to generate an index operation, which takes longer than a simple pointer dereference, (`(*array_ptr) != 0`).

The expression at the end of this program, `array_ptr - array`, computes how far `array_ptr` is into the array.

When passing an array to a procedure, C will automatically change the array into a pointer. In fact, if you put & before the array, C will issue a warning. Example 13-6 illustrates the various ways in which an array can be passed to a subroutine.

Example 13-6: init-a/init-a.c

```
#define MAX 10   /* Size of the array */
/********************************************************
 * init_array_1 -- Zeroes out an array.                 *
 *                                                      *
 * Parameters                                           *
 *      data -- The array to zero out.                  *
 ********************************************************/
void init_array_1(int data[])
{
    int  index;

    for (index = 0; index < MAX; ++index)
        data[index] = 0;
}


/********************************************************
 * init_array_2 -- Zeroes out an array.                 *
 *                                                      *
 * Parameters                                           *
 *      data_ptr -- Pointer to array to zero.           *
 ********************************************************/
void init_array_2(int *data_ptr)
{
    int index;

    for (index = 0; index < MAX; ++index)
        *(data_ptr + index) = 0;
```

Example 13-6: init-a/init-a.c (continued)

```c
}
int main()
{
    int  array[MAX];

    void init_array_1();
    void init_array_2();

    /* one way of initializing the array */
    init_array_1(array);

    /* another way of initializing the array */
    init_array_1(&array[0]);

    /* works, but the compiler generates a warning */
    init_array_1(&array);

    /* Similar to the first method but  */
    /*    function is different */
    init_array_2(array);

    return (0);
}
```

How Not to Use Pointers

The major goal of this book is to teach you how to create clear, readable, maintainable code. Unfortunately, not everyone has read this book and some people still believe that you should make your code as compact as possible. This belief can result in programmers using the ++ and -- operators inside other statements.

Example 13-7 shows several examples in which pointers and the increment operator are used together.

Example 13-7: Bad Pointer Usage

```c
/* This program shows programming practices that should **NOT** be used */
/* Unfortunately, too many programmers use them */
int array[10];    /* An array for our data */
int main()
{
    int *data_ptr;   /* Pointer to the data */
    int value;       /* A data value */

    data_ptr = &array[0];/* Point to the first element */
    value = *data_ptr++;  /* Get element #0, data_ptr points to element #1 */
    value = *++data_ptr;  /* Get element #2, data_ptr points to element #2 */
    value = ++*data_ptr;  /* Increment element #2, return its value */
                          /* Leave data_ptr alone */
```

To understand each of these statements, you must carefully dissect each expression to discover its hidden meaning. When I do maintenance programming, I don't want to have to worry about hidden meanings, so please don't code like this, and shoot anyone who does.

These statements are dissected in Figure 13-8.

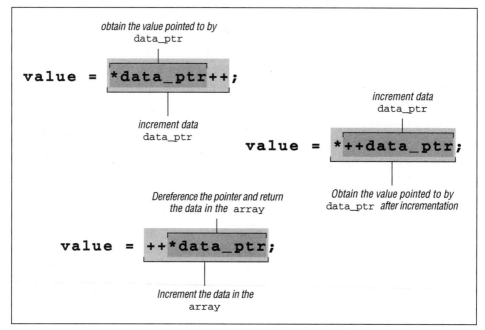

Figure 13-8: Pointer operations dissected

This example is a little extreme, but it illustrates how side effects can easily become confusing.

Example 13-8 is an example of the code you're more likely to run into. The program copies a string from the source (q) to the destination (p).

Example 13-8: Cryptic Use of Pointers

```
void copy_string(char *p, char *q)
{
    while (*p++ = *q++);
}
```

Given time, a good programmer will decode this. However, understanding the program is much easier when we are a bit more verbose, as in Example 13-9.

Example 13-9: Readable Use of Pointers

```
/*******************************************************
 * copy_string -- Copies one string to another.        *
 *                                                      *
```

Example 13-9: Readable Use of Pointers (continued)

```
 * Parameters                                               *
 *      dest -- Where to put the string                     *
 *      source -- Where to get it                           *
 ***********************************************************/
void copy_string(char *dest, char *source)
{
    while (1) {
        *dest = *source;

        /* Exit if we copied the end of string */
        if (*dest == '\0')
            return;

        ++dest;
        ++source;
    }
}
```

Using Pointers to Split a String

Suppose we are given a string of the form "Last/First." We want to split this into two strings, one containing the first name and one containing the last name.

We need a function to find the slash in the name. The standard function `strchr` performs this job for us. In this program, we have chosen to duplicate this function to show you how it works.

This function takes a pointer to a string (`string_ptr`) and a character to find (`find`) as its arguments. It starts with a **while** loop that will continue until we find the character we are looking for (or we are stopped by some other code below).

```
    while (*string_ptr != find) {
```

Next we test to see if we've run out of string. In this case, our pointer (`string_ptr`) points to the end-of-string character. If we have reached the end of string before finding the character, we return NULL:

```
    if (*string_ptr == '\0')
        return (NULL);
```

If we get this far, we have not found what we are looking for, and are not at the end of the string. So we move the pointer to the next character, and return to the top of the loop to try again:

```
    ++string_ptr;
    }
```

Our main program reads in a single line, stripping the newline character from it. The function `my_strchr` is called to find the location of the slash (/).

At this point, `last_ptr` points to the first character of the last name and `first_ptr` points to slash. We then split the string by replacing the slash (/) with an end of string (NUL or \0). Now `last_ptr` points to just the last name and `first_ptr` points to a null string. Moving `first_ptr` to the next character makes it point to the beginning of the first name.

The sequence of steps in splitting the string is illustrated in Figure 13-9.

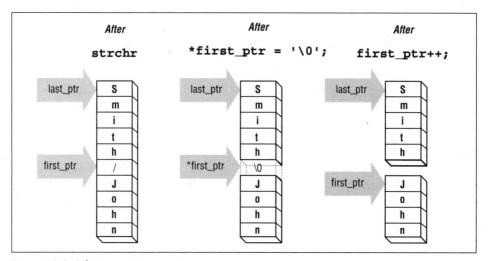

Figure 13-9: Splitting a string

Example 13-10 contains the full program, which demonstrates how pointers and character arrays can be used for simple string processing.

Example 13-10: split/split.c

```c
#include <stdio.h>
#include <string.h>
#include <stdlib.h>

/********************************************************
 * my_strchr -- Finds a character in a string.         *
 *      Duplicate of a standard library function,       *
 *      put here for illustrative purposes              *
 *                                                      *
 * Parameters                                           *
 *      string_ptr -- String to look through.           *
 *      find -- Character to find.                      *
 *                                                      *
 * Returns                                              *
 *      pointer to 1st occurrence of character          *
 *      in string or NULL for error.                    *
 ********************************************************/
char *my_strchr(char * string_ptr, char find)
{
```

Example 13-10: split/split.c (continued)

```
    while (*string_ptr != find) {

        /* Check for end */

        if (*string_ptr == '\0')
            return (NULL);          /* not found */

         ++string_ptr;
    }
    return (string_ptr);        /* Found */
}

int main()
{
    char line[80];        /* The input line */
    char *first_ptr;      /* pointer to the first name */
    char *last_ptr;       /* pointer to the last name */

    fgets(line, sizeof(line), stdin);

    /* Get rid of trailing newline */
    line[strlen(line)-1] = '\0';

    last_ptr = line;      /* last name is at beginning of line */

    first_ptr = my_strchr(line, '/');       /* Find slash */

    /* Check for an error */
    if (first_ptr == NULL) {
        fprintf(stderr,
            "Error: Unable to find slash in %s\n", line);
        exit (8);
    }

    *first_ptr = '\0';  /* Zero out the slash */

    ++first_ptr;          /* Move to first character of name */

    printf("First:%s Last:%s\n", first_ptr, last_ptr);
    return (0);
}
```

Question 13-1: *Example 13-11 is supposed to print out:*

```
    Name: tmp1
```

but instead, we get:

```
    Name: !_@$#ds80
```

(Your results may vary.) Why?

Example 13-11: tmp-name/tmp-name.c

```
#include <stdio.h>
#include <string.h>

/********************************************************
 * tmp_name -- Return a temporary filename.            *
 *                                                      *
 * Each time this function is called, a new name will   *
 * be returned.                                         *
 *                                                      *
 * Returns                                              *
 *      Pointer to the new filename.                    *
 ********************************************************/
char *tmp_name(void)
{
    char name[30];      /* The name we are generating */
    static int sequence = 0;    /* Sequence number for last digit */

    ++sequence; /* Move to the next filename */

    strcpy(name, "tmp");

    /* But in the sequence digit */
    name[3] = sequence + '0';

    /* End the string */
    name[4] = '\0';

    return(name);
}

int main()
{
    char *tmp_name(void);        /* Get name of temporary file */

    printf("Name: %s\n", tmp_name());
    return(0);
}
```

Pointers and Structures

In Chapter 12, *Advanced Types*, we defined a structure for a mailing list:

```
struct mailing {
    char name[60];     /* last name, first name */
    char address1[60];/* two lines of street address */
    char address2[60];
    char city[40];
    char state[2];     /* two-character abbreviation */
    long int zip;      /* numeric zip code */
} list[MAX_ENTRIES];
```

Mailing lists must frequently be sorted by name and zip code. We could sort the entries themselves, but each entry is 226 bytes long. That's a lot of data to move around. One way around this problem is to declare an array of pointers, and then sort the pointers:

```
/* Pointer to the data */
struct mailing *list_ptrs[MAX_ENTRIES];
int current;     /* current mailing list entry */

    for (current = 0; current = number_of_entries; ++current)
        list_ptrs[current] = &list[current];
    /* Sort list_ptrs by zip code */
```

Now, instead of having to move a 226-byte structure around, we are moving 4-byte pointers. Our sorting is much faster. Imagine that you had a warehouse full of big heavy boxes and you needed to locate any box quickly. You could put them in alphabetical order, but that would require a lot of moving. Instead, you assign each location a number, write down the name and number on index cards, and sort the cards by name.

Command-Line Arguments

The procedure **main** actually takes two arguments. They are called **argc** and **argv**[*]:

```
main(int argc, char *argv[])
{
```

(If you realize that the arguments are in alphabetical order, you can easily remember which one comes first.)

The parameter **argc** is the number of arguments on the command line (including the program name). The array **argv** contains the actual arguments. For example, if the program **args** were run with the command line:

```
args this is a test
```

then:

```
    argc =      5
argv[0] =     "args"
argv[1] =     "this"
argv[2] =     "is"
argv[3] =     "a"
argv[4] =     "test"
argv[5] =     NULL
```

---

[*] Actually, they can be named anything. However, in 99.9% of programs, they are named **argc** and **argv**. When most programmers encounter the other 0.1%, they curse loudly, and then change the names to **argc** and **argv**.

NOTE   The UNIX shell expands wildcard characters like *, ?, and [] before
                sending the command line to the program. See your sh or csh man-
                ual for details.

                Turbo C++ and Borland C++ expand wildcard characters if the
                file *WILDARG.OBJ* is linked with your program. See the manual
                for details.

Almost all UNIX commands use a standard command-line format. This standard
has carried over into other environments. A standard UNIX command has the
form:

```
command options file1 file1 file3 ...
```

Options are preceded by a dash (–) and are usually a single letter. For example,
the option –v might turn on verbose mode for a particular command. If the
option takes a parameter, it follows the letter. For example, the option –m1024
sets the maximum number of symbols to 1024 and –ooutfile sets the output
filename to *outfile*.

Let's look at writing a program that can read the command-line arguments and act
accordingly. This program formats and prints files. Part of the documentation for
the program is given here:

```
print_file [-v] [-llength] [-oname] [file1] [file2] ...
```

where:

–v

   specifies verbose options; turns on a lot of progress information messages

–l*length*

   sets the page size to length lines (default = 66)

–o*name*

   sets the output file to name (default = print.out)

file1, file2, ...

   is a list of files to print. If no files are specified, the file *print.in* is printed.

We can use a **while** loop to cycle through the command-line options. The actual
loop is:

```
while ((argc > 1) && (argv[1][0] == '-')) {
```

One argument always exists: the program name. The expression (`argc > 1`)
checks for additional arguments. The first one is numbered 1. The first character
of the first argument is `argv[1][0]`. If this is a dash, we have an option.

At the end of the loop is the code:

```
        --argc;
        ++argv;
    }
```

This consumes an argument. The number of arguments is decremented to indicate one less option, and the pointer to the first option is incremented, shifting the list to the left one place. (Note: after the first increment, `argv[0]` no longer points to the program name.)

The **switch** statement is used to decode the options. Character 0 of the argument is the dash (–). Character 1 is the option character, so we use the expression:

```
    switch (argv[1][1]) {
```

to decode the option.

The option –v has no arguments; it just causes a flag to be set.

The option –o takes a filename. Rather than copy the whole string, we set the character pointer `out_file` to point to the name part of the string. By this time we know the following:

```
    argv[1][0]    ='-'
    argv[1][1]    ='o'
    argv[1][2]    = first character of the filename
```

We set `out_file` to point to the string with the statement:

```
    out_file = &argv[1][2];
```

The address of operator (`&`) is used to get the address of the first character in the output filename. This process is appropriate because we are assigning the address to a character pointer named `out_file`.

The –1 option takes an integer argument. The library function `atoi` is used to convert the string into an integer. From the previous example, we know that `argv[1][2]` is the first character of the string containing the number. This string is passed to `atoi`.

Finally, all the options are parsed and we fall through to the processing loop. This merely executes the function `do_file` for each file argument. Example 13-12 contains the `print` program.

This is one way of parsing the argument list. The use of the **while** loop and **switch** statement is simple and easy to understand. This method does have a limitation. The argument must immediately follow the options. For example, –odata.out will work, but "–o data.out" will not. An improved parser would make the program more friendly, but the techniques described here work for simple programs.

Example 13-12: print/print.c

```
[File: print/print.c]
/*********************************************************
 * Program: Print                                        *
 *                                                       *
 * Purpose:                                              *
 *      Formats files for printing.                      *
 *                                                       *
 * Usage:                                                *
 *      print [options] file(s)                          *
 *                                                       *
 * Options:                                              *
 *      -v              Produces verbose messages.       *
 *      -o<file>        Sends output to a file           *
 *                      (default=print.out).             *
 *      -l<lines>       Sets the number of lines/page    *
 *                      (default=66).                    *
 *********************************************************/
#include <stdio.h>
#include <stdlib.h>

int verbose = 0;          /* verbose mode (default = false) */
char *out_file = "print.out";   /* output filename */
char *program_name;       /* name of the program (for errors) */
int line_max = 66;        /* number of lines per page */

/*********************************************************
 * do_file -- Dummy routine to handle a file.            *
 *                                                       *
 * Parameter                                             *
 *      name -- Name of the file to print.               *
 *********************************************************/
void do_file(char *name)
{
    printf("Verbose %d Lines %d Input %s Output %s\n",
        verbose, line_max, name, out_file);
}
/*********************************************************
 * usage -- Tells the user how to use this program and   *
 *             exit.                                      *
 *********************************************************/
void usage(void)
{
    fprintf(stderr,"Usage is %s [options] [file-list]\n",
                              program_name);
    fprintf(stderr,"Options\n");
    fprintf(stderr,"  -v          verbose\n");
    fprintf(stderr,"  -l<number>  Number of lines\n");
    fprintf(stderr,"  -o<name>    Set output filename\n");
    exit(8);
}
int main(int argc, char *argv[])
{
```

Example 13-12: print/print.c (continued)

```
/* save the program name for future use */
program_name = argv[0];

/*
 * loop for each option
 *   Stop if we run out of arguments
 *   or we get an argument without a dash
 */
while ((argc > 1) && (argv[1][0] == '-')) {
    /*
     * argv[1][1] is the actual option character
     */
    switch (argv[1][1]) {
        /*
         * -v verbose
         */
        case 'v':
            verbose = 1;
            break;
        /*
         * -o<name>  output file
         *     [0] is the dash
         *     [1] is the "o"
         *     [2] starts the name
         */
        case 'o':
            out_file = &argv[1][2];
            break;
        /*
         * -l<number> set max number of lines
         */
        case 'l':
            line_max = atoi(&argv[1][2]);
            break;
        default:
            fprintf(stderr,"Bad option %s\n", argv[1]);
            usage();
    }
    /*
     * move the argument list up one
     * move the count down one
     */
    ++argv;
    --argc;
}

/*
 * At this point, all the options have been processed.
 * Check to see if we have no files in the list.
 * If no files exist, we need to process just standard input stream.
 */
if (argc == 1) {
```

Example 13-12: print/print.c (continued)

```
        do_file("print.in");
    } else {
        while (argc > 1) {
          do_file(argv[1]);
          ++argv;
          --argc;
        }
    }
    return (0);
}
```

Programming Exercises

Exercise 13-1: Write a program that uses pointers to set each element of an array to zero.

Exercise 13-2: Write a function that takes a single string as its argument and returns a pointer to the first nonwhite character in the string.

Answers

Answer 13-1: The problem is that the variable **name** is a temporary variable. The compiler allocates space for the name when the function is entered and reclaims the space when the function exits. The function assigns **name** the correct value and returns a pointer to it. However, the function is over, so **name** disappears and we have a pointer with an illegal value.

The solution is to declare **name static**. In this manner, name is a permanent variable and will not disappear at the end of the function.

Question 13-2: *After fixing the function, we try using it for two filenames. Example 13-13 should print out:*

```
    Name: tmp1
    Name: tmp2
```

but it doesn't. What does it print and why?

Example 13-13: tmp2/tmp2.c

```
#include <stdio.h>
#include <string.h>

/**********************************************************
 * tmp_name -- Returns a temporary filename.              *
 *                                                        *
 * Each time this function is called, a new name will     *
 * be returned.                                           *
 *                                                        *
```

Example 13-13: tmp2/tmp2.c (continued)

```
 * Warning: There should be a warning here, but if we    *
 *      put it in, we would answer the question.         *
 *                                                       *
 * Returns                                               *
 *      Pointer to the new filename.                     *
 ********************************************************/
char *tmp_name(void)
{
    static char name[30];       /* The name we are generating */
    static int sequence = 0;    /* Sequence number for last digit */

    ++sequence; /* Move to the next filename */

    strcpy(name, "tmp");

    /* But in the squence digit */
    name[3] = sequence + '0';

    /* End the string */
    name[4] = '\0';

    return(name);
}

int main()
{
    char *tmp_name(void);       /* get name of temporary file */
    char *name1;                /* name of a temporary file */
    char *name2;                /* name of a temporary file */

    name1 = tmp_name();
    name2 = tmp_name();

    printf("Name1: %s\n", name1);
    printf("Name2: %s\n", name2);
    return(0);
}
```

Answer 13-2: The first call to **tmp_name** returns a pointer to **name**. There is only one **name**. The second call to **tmp_name** changes **name** and returns a pointer to it. So we have two pointers, and they point to the same thing, **name**.

Several library functions return pointers to **static** strings. A second call to one of these routines will overwrite the first value. A solution to this problem is to copy the values as shown below:

```
    char name1[100];
    char name2[100];
    strcpy(name1, tmp_name());
    strcpy(name2, tmp_name());
```

This problem is a good illustration of the basic meaning of a pointer; it doesn't create any new space for data, but just refers to data that is created elsewhere.

This problem is also a good example of a poorly designed function. The problem is that the function is tricky to use. A better design would make the code less risky to use. For example, the function could take an additional parameter: the string in which the filename is to be constructed:

```
void tmp_name(char *name_to_return);
```

14

File Input/Output

> *I the heir of all the ages, in the foremost files of time.*
> —Alfred, Lord Tennyson

A *file* is a collection of related data. C treats a file as a series of bytes. Many files reside on disk; however, devices like terminals, printers, and magnetic tapes are also considered files.

The C library contains a large number of routines for manipulating files. The declarations for the structures and functions used by the file functions are stored in the standard include file `<stdio.h>`. Before doing anything with files, you must put the line:

```
#include <stdio.h>
```

at the beginning of your program.

The declaration for a file variable is:

```
FILE *file-variable;        /* comment */
```

For example:

```
#include <stdio.h>
FILE *in_file;  /* file containing the input data */
```

Before a file can be used, it must be opened using the function `fopen`. `fopen` returns a pointer to the file structure for the file. The format for `fopen` is:

```
file-variable = fopen(name, mode);
```

where:

file-variable
    is a file variable. A value of *NULL* is returned on error.

name

 is the actual name of the file (data.txt, *temp*.dat, etc.).

mode

 indicates if the file is to be read or written. mode is **"w"** for writing and **"r"** for reading. The flag "b" can be added to indicate a binary file. Omitting the binary flag indicates an ASCII (text) file. (See the section "Binary and ASCII Files" for a description of ASCII and binary files.)

 Flags can be combined. So "**wb**" is used to write a binary file.

The function returns a file handle that will be used in subsequent I/O operations. If there is an I/O error, then the value NULL is returned:

```
FILE *in_file; /* File to read */

in_file = fopen("input.txt", "r"); /* Open the input file */
if (in_file == NULL) { /* Test for error */
    fprintf(stderr, "Error: Unable to input file 'input.txt'\n");
    exit (8);
}
```

The function **fclose** will close the file. The format of **fclose** is:

```
status = fclose(file-variable);
```

or:

```
fclose(file-variable);
```

The variable *status* is zero if the **fclose** was successful or nonzero for an error. If you don't care about the status, the second form closes the file and discards the return value.

C provides three pre-opened files. These are listed in Table 14-1.

Table 14-1: Standard Files

File	Description
stdin	Standard input (open for reading)
stdout	Standard output (open for writing)
stderr	Standard error (open for writing)

The function **fgetc** reads a single character from a file. If no more data exists in the file, the function will return the constant EOF (EOF is defined in *stdio.h*). Note that **fgetc** returns an integer, not a character. This return is necessary because the EOF flag must be a noncharacter value.

Example 14-1 counts the number of characters in the file *input.txt*.

Example 14-1: copy/copy.c

```
[File: copy/copy.c]
#include <stdio.h>
const char FILE_NAME[] = "input.txt";
#include <stdlib.h>

int main()
{
    int            count = 0;  /* number of characters seen */
    FILE           *in_file;   /* input file */

    /* character or EOF flag from input */
    int            ch;

    in_file = fopen(FILE_NAME, "r");
    if (in_file == NULL) {
        printf("Cannot open %s\n", FILE_NAME);
        exit(8);
    }

    while (1) {
        ch = fgetc(in_file);
        if (ch == EOF)
            break;
        ++count;
    }
    printf("Number of characters in %s is %d\n",
                FILE_NAME, count);

    fclose(in_file);
    return (0);
}
```

A similar function, **fputc**, exists for writing a single character. Its format is:

```
fputc(character, file);
```

The functions **fgets** and **fputs** work on one line at a time. The format of the **fgets** call is:

```
string_ptr = fgets(string, size, file);
```

where:

string_ptr

is equal to *string* if the read was successful, or *NULL* if end-of-file or an error is detected.

string

is a character array in which the function places the string.

size

is the size of the character array. *fgets* reads until it gets a line (complete with ending \n) or it reads size–1 characters. It then ends the string with a null (\0).

Problems can occur if the size specified is too big. C provides a convenient way of making sure that the size parameter is just right through the use of the sizeof operator.

The sizeof operator returns the size of its argument in bytes. For example:

```
long int array[10];     /* (Each element contains 4 bytes) */
char string[30];
```

Then sizeof(string) is 30. This size is not the same as the length. The length of string can be anywhere from 0 to 29 characters. **The sizeof** function returns the number of bytes in **string** (used or not). A **long int** takes up 4 bytes so sizeof(array) is 40.

The sizeof operator is particularly useful when you use the fgets routine. By using sizeof, you don't have to worry about how big a string is or, worse, what happens if someone changes the dimension of the string.

For example:

```
char    string[100];
. . .
fgets(string, sizeof(string), in_file);
```

fputs is similar to fgets except that it writes a string instead of reading it. The format of the fputs function is:

```
string_ptr = fputs(string, file);
```

The parameters to fputs are similar to the ones for fgets. fputs needs no size because it gets the size of the line to write from the length of the string. (It keeps writing until it hits a null, '\0'.)

Conversion Routines

So far we have just discussed writing characters and strings. In this section, we will discuss some of the more sophisticated I/O operations and conversions.

In order to write a number to a printer or terminal, you must convert it to characters. The printer understands only characters, not numbers. For example, the number 567 must be converted to the three characters 5, 6, and 7 in order to be printed.

The function `fprintf` converts data and writes it to a file. The general form of the `fprintf` function is:

```
count = fprintf(file, format, parameter-1, parameter-2, ...);
```

where:

count

is the number of characters sent or −1 if an error occurred.

format

describes how the arguments are to be printed.

parameter-1, parameter-2, ...

are parameters to be converted and sent.

`fprintf` has two sister functions: `printf` and `sprintf`. `printf()` has been seen often in this book, and is equivalent to `fprintf` with a first argument of `stdout`. `sprintf` is similar to `fprintf`, except that the first argument is a string. For example:

```
char string[40];        /* the filename */
int file_number = 0;    /* current file number for this segment */

sprintf(string, "file.%d", file_number);
++file_number;
out_file = fopen(string, "w");
```

`scanf` has similar sister functions: `fscanf` and `sscanf`. The format for `fscanf` is:

```
number = fscanf(file, format, &parameter-1, ...);
```

where:

number

is the number of parameters successfully converted. If there was input but nothing could be converted, a zero is returned. If no data is present, *EOF* is returned.

file

is a file opened for reading.

format

describes the data to be read.

parameter-1

is the first parameter to be read.

`sscanf` is similar to `fscanf`, except that a string is scanned instead of a file.

`scanf` is very fussy about where the end-of-line characters occur in the input. Frequently, the user has to type extra returns to get `scanf` unstuck.

We have avoided this problem by using `fgets` to read a line from the file and then using `sscanf` to parse it. `fgets` almost always gets a single line without trouble.

Example 14-2 shows a program that attempts to read two parameters from the standard input (the keyboard). It then prints a message based on the number of inputs actually found.

Example 14-2: Using the sscanf Return Value

```
char line[100];      /* Line from the keyboard */
int count, total;    /* Number of entries & total value */
int scan_count;      /* Number of parameters scanned */

fgets(line, sizeof(line), stdin);
scan_count = sscanf(line,"%d %d", &count, &total);

switch (scan_count) {
    case EOF:
    case 0:
        printf("Didn't find any number\n");
        break;
    case 1:
        printf("Found 'count'(%d), but not 'total'\n", count);
        break;
    case 2:
        printf("Found both 'count'(%d) and 'total'(%d)\n", count, total);
        break;
    default:
        printf("This should not be possible\n");
        break;
}
```

Question 14-1: *No matter what filename we give Example 14-3, our program can't find it. Why?*

Example 14-3: fun-file/fun-file.c

```
#include <stdio.h>
#include <stdlib.h>

int main()
{
    char            name[100];  /* name of the file to use  */
    FILE            *in_file;    /* file for input */

    printf("Name? ");
    fgets(name, sizeof(name), stdin);

    in_file = fopen(name, "r");
    if (in_file == NULL) {
        fprintf(stderr, "Could not open file\n");
```

Example 14-3: fun-file/fun-file.c (continued)

```
        exit(8);
    }
    printf("File found\n".);
    fclose(in_file);
    return (0);
}
```

Binary and ASCII Files

We have been working with ASCII files. ASCII stands for *American* *S*tandard *C*ode for *I*nformation *I*nterchange. It is a set of 95 printable characters and 33 control codes. ASCII files are readable text. When you write a program, the *prog*.c file is in ASCII.

Terminals, keyboards, and printers deal with character data. When you want to write a number like 1234 to the screen, it must be converted to four characters ('1', '2', '3', and '4') and written. Similarly, when you read a number from the keyboard, the data must be converted from characters to integers. This is done by the `sscanf` routine.

The ASCII character '0' has the value of 48, '1' has the value of 49, and so on. When you want to convert a single digit from ASCII to integer, you must subtract this number. For example:

```
    int integer;
    char ch;

    ch = '5';
    integer = ch - 48;
    printf("Integer %d\n", integer);
```

Rather than remember that '0' is 48, you can just subtract '0':

```
    integer = ch - '0';
```

Computers work on binary data. When reading numbers from an ASCII file, the program must process the character data through a conversion routine like `sscanf`. This is expensive. Binary files require no conversion. They also generally take up less space than ASCII files. The drawback is that they cannot be directly printed on a terminal or printer. (If you've ever seen a long printout coming out of the printer displaying pages with a few characters at the top that look like "!E#(@$%@^Aa^AA^^JHC%^X," then you know what happens when you try to print a binary file.)

ASCII files are portable (for the most part). They can be moved from machine to machine with very little trouble. Binary files are almost certainly nonportable.

Unless you are an expert programmer, you will find it almost impossible to make a portable binary file.

Which file type should you use? In most cases, ASCII. If you have small-to-medium amounts of data, the conversion time will not seriously affect the performance of your program. (Who cares if it takes 0.5 seconds to start up instead of 0.3?) ASCII files allow you to easily check the data for correctness.

Only when you are using large amounts of data will the space and performance problems force you to use the binary format.

The End-of-Line Puzzle

Back in the dark ages BC (Before Computers), a magical device called a Teletype Model 33 existed. This amazing machine contained a shift register made out of a motor, with a rotor, and a keyboard ROM consisting solely of levers and springs. It contained a keyboard, a printer, and a paper tape reader/punch. It could transmit messages over the phones using a modem at the rate of 10 characters a second.

The Teletype had a problem. It took two-tenths of a second to move the printhead from the right side to the left. Two-tenths of a second is two character times. If a second character came while the printhead was in the middle of a return, that character was lost.

The Teletype people solved this problem by making end-of-line two characters: <RETURN> to position the printhead at the left margin and <LINE FEED> to move the paper up one line.

When the early computers came out, some designers realized that using two characters for end-of-line wasted storage (at this time, storage was very expensive). Some picked <LINE FEED> for their end-of-line, some <RETURN>. Some of the diehards stayed with the two-character sequence.

UNIX uses <LINE FEED> for end-of-line. The newline character, \n, is code 0x0A (LF or <LINE FEED>). MS-DOS/Windows uses the two characters: <LINE FEED> <RETURN>. Apple uses <RETURN>.

MS-DOS/Windows compiler designers had a problem. What do we do about the old C programs that thought that newline was just <LINE FEED>? The solution was to add code to the I/O library that stripped out the <RETURN> characters from ASCII input files and changed <LINE FEED> to <LINE FEED> <RETURN> on output.

In MS-DOS/Windows, it makes a difference whether or not a file is opened as ASCII or binary. The flag **b** is used to indicate a binary file:

```
/* open ASCII file for reading */
ascii_file = fopen("name", "r");

/* open binary file for reading */
binary_file = fopen("name", "rb");
```

If you open a file that contains text as a binary file under MS-DOS/Windows, you have to handle the carriage returns in your program. If you open it as ASCII, the carriage returns are automatically removed by the read routines.

Question 14-2: *The routine* `fputc` *can be used to write out a single byte of a binary file. Example 14-4 writes out numbers 0 to 127 to a file called* test.out. *It works just fine on UNIX, creating a 128-byte-long file; however, on MS-DOS/Windows, the file contains 129 bytes. Why?*

Example 14-4: wbin/wbin.c

```
[File: wbin/wbin.c]
#include <stdio.h>
#include <stdlib.h>
#ifndef __MSDOS__
#include <unistd.h>
#endif __MSDOS__

int main()
{
    int cur_char;   /* current character to write */
    FILE *out_file; /* output file */

    out_file = fopen("test.out", "w");
    if (out_file == NULL) {
        fprintf(stderr,"Cannot open output file\n");
        exit (8);
    }

    for (cur_char = 0; cur_char < 128; ++cur_char) {
        fputc(cur_char, out_file);
    }
    fclose(out_file);
    return (0);
}
```

Hint: Here is a hex dump of the MS-DOS/Windows file:

```
000:0001 0203 0405 0607 0809 0d0a 0b0c 0d0e
010:0f10 1112 1314 1516 1718 191a 1b1c 1d1e
020:1f20 2122 2324 2526 2728 292a 2b2c 2d2e
030:2f30 3132 3334 3536 3738 393a 3b3c 3d3e
040:3f40 4142 4344 4546 4748 494a 4b4c 4d4e
050:4f50 5152 5354 5556 5758 595a 5b5c 5d5e
060:5f60 6162 6364 6566 6768 696a 6b6c 6d6e
070:6f70 7172 7374 7576 7778 797a 7b7c 7d7e
080:7f
```

UNIX programmers don't have to worry about the C library automatically fixing their ASCII files. In UNIX, a file is a file and ASCII is no different from binary. In fact, you can write a half-ASCII, half-binary file if you want to.

Binary I/O

Binary I/O is accomplished through two routines: `fread` and `fwrite`. The syntax for `fread` is:

```
read_size = fread(data_ptr, 1, size, file);
```

where:

read_size

is the size of the data that was read. If this value is less than size, then an end-of-file or error was encountered.

data_ptr

is the pointer to the data to be read. This pointer must be cast to a character point *(char *)* if the data is any type other than a character.

size

is the number of bytes to be read.

file

is the input file.

For example:

```
struct {
        int     width;
        int     height;
} rectangle;
int read_size;

read_size = fread((char *)&rectangle, 1, sizeof(rectangle), in_file);
if (read_size != sizeof(rectangle)) {
        fprintf(stderr,"Unable to read rectangle\n");
        exit (8);
}
```

In this example, we are reading in the structure rectangle. The & operator makes it into a pointer. The `sizeof` operator is used to determine how many bytes to read in, as well as to check that the read was successful.

`fwrite` has a calling sequence similar to `fread`:

```
write_size = fwrite(data_ptr, 1, size, file);
```

NOTE In order to make programming simpler and easier, we always use one as the second parameter to `fread` and `fwrite`. Actually, *fread* and *fwrite* are designed to read an array of objects. The second parameter is the size of the object and the third parameter is the number of objects. For a full description of these functions, see your C reference manual.

Buffering Problems

Buffered I/O does not write immediately to the file. Instead, the data is kept in a buffer until there is enough for a big write, or until it is flushed. The following program is designed to print out a progress message as each section is finished:

```
printf("Starting");

do_step_1();
printf("Step 1 complete");

do_step_2();
printf("Step 2 complete");

do_step_3();
printf("Step 3 complete\n");
```

Instead of writing the messages as each step is completed, the `printf` function puts them in a buffer. Only when the program is finished does the buffer get flushed and all the messages come spilling out at once.

The routine `fflush` will force the flushing of the buffers. Properly written, our example should be:

```
printf("Starting");
fflush(stdout);

do_step_1();
printf("Step 1 complete");
fflush(stdout);

do_step_2();
printf("Step 2 complete");
fflush(stdout);

do_step_3();
printf("Step 3 complete\n");
fflush(stdout);
```

Unbuffered I/O

In buffered I/O, data is buffered and then sent to the file. In unbuffered I/O, the data is immediately sent to the file.

If you drop a number of paper clips on the floor, you can pick them up in buffered or unbuffered mode. In buffered mode, you use your right hand to pick up a paper clip and transfer it to your left hand. The process is repeated until your left hand is full, and then you dump a handful of paper clips into the box on your desk.

In unbuffered mode, you pick up a paper clip and dump it immediately into the box. There is no left-hand buffer.

In most cases, buffered I/O should be used instead of unbuffered. In unbuffered I/O, each read or write requires a system call. Any call to the operating system is expensive. Buffered I/O minimizes these calls.

Unbuffered I/O should be used only when reading or writing large amounts of binary data or when direct control of a device or file is required.

Back to our paper clip example—if we were picking up small items like paper-clips, we would probably use a left-hand buffer. But if we were picking up cannonballs (which are much larger), no buffer would be used.

The **open** system call is used for opening an unbuffered file. The macro definitions used by this call differ from system to system. We are using both UNIX and MS-DOS/Windows, so we have used conditional compilation (**#ifdef/#endif**) to bring in the correct files:

```
#ifndef __MSDOS__       /* if we are not MS-DOS */
#define __UNIX__        /* then we are UNIX */
#endif __MSDOS__

#ifdef __UNIX__
#include <sys/types.h>  /* file defines for UNIX filesystem */
#include <sys/stat.h>
#include <fcntl.h>
#endif __UNIX__

#ifdef __MSDOS__
#include <stdlib.h>
#include <fcntl.h>      /* file defines for DOS filesystem */
#include <sys\stat.h>
#include <io.h>
#endif __MSDOS__

int     file_descriptor;
file_descriptor = open(name, flags);          /* existing file */
file_descriptor = open(name, flags, mode);  /*new file */
```

where:

file_descriptor

>   is an integer that is used to identify the file for the read, write, and close calls. If file descriptor is less than zero, an error occurred.

name

>   is the name of the file.

flags

>   are defined in the *fcntl.h* header file. Flags are described in Table 14-2.

mode

>   is the protection mode for the file. Normally, this is 0644 for most files.

Table 14-2: Open Flags

Flag	Meaning
O_RDONLY	Open for reading only
O_WRONLY	Open for writing only
O_RDWR	Open for reading and writing
O_APPEND	Append new data at the end of the file
O_CREAT	Create file (mode is required when this flag is present)
O_TRUNC	If the file exists, truncate it to zero length
O_EXCL	Fail if file exists
O_BINARY	Open in binary mode (MS-DOS/Windows only)
O_TEXT	Open in text mode (MS-DOS/Windows only)

For example, to open the existing file *data.txt* in text mode for reading, we use the following:

```
data_fd = open("data.txt", O_RDONLY);
```

The next example shows how to create a file called *output.dat* for writing only:

```
out_fd = open("output.dat", O_CREAT|O_WRONLY, 0644);
```

Notice that we combined flags using the *or* operator (|). This is a quick and easy way of merging multiple flags.

When any program is initially run, three files are already opened. These are described in Table 14-3.

Table 14-3: Standard Unbuffered Files

File number	Symbolic name	Description
0	STDIN_FILENO	Standard in
1	STDOUT_FILENO	Standard out
2	STDERR_FILENO	Standard err

The symbolic names are defined in the header file *unistd.h*. These are a relatively new part of the language and are very rarely used. (You really should use the symbolic names, but most people don't.)

The format of the **read** call is:

```
read_size = read(file_descriptor, buffer, size);
```

where:

read_size
:   is the number of bytes read. Zero indicates end-of-file, and a negative number indicates an error.

file_descriptor
:   is the file descriptor of an open file.

buffer
:   is the pointer to the place to read the data.

size
:   is the size of the data to be read.

The format of a **write** call is:

```
write_size = write(file_descriptor, buffer, size);
```

where:

write_size
:   is the number of bytes written. A negative number indicates an error.

file_descriptor
:   is the file descriptor of an open file.

buffer
:   is the pointer to the data to be written.

size
:   is the size of the data to be written.

Finally, the **close** call closes the file:

```
flag = close(file_descriptor)
```

where:

flag
:   is zero for success, negative for error.

file_descriptor
:   is the file descriptor of an open file.

Example 14-5 copies a file. Unbuffered I/O is used because of the large buffer
size. Using buffered I/O to read 1K of data into a buffer and then transfer it into a
16K buffer makes no sense.

Example 14-5: copy2/copy2.c

```
[File: copy2/copy2.c]
/*****************************************
 * copy -- Copies one file to another.   *
 *                                       *
 * Usage                                 *
 *      copy <from> <to>                 *
 *                                       *
 * <from> -- The file to copy from.      *
 * <to>   -- The file to copy into.      *
 *****************************************/
#include <stdio.h>
#ifndef __MSDOS__       /* if we are not MS-DOS */
#define __UNIX__        /* then we are UNIX */
#endif /* __MSDOS__ */

#include <stdlib.h>

#ifdef __UNIX__
#include <sys/types.h>  /* file defines for UNIX filesystem */
#include <sys/stat.h>
#include <fcntl.h>
#include <unistd.h>
#endif /* __UNIX__ */

#ifdef __MSDOS__
#include <fcntl.h>      /* file defines for DOS filesystem */
#include <sys\stat.h>
#include <io.h>
#endif __MSDOS__

#ifndef O_BINARY
#define O_BINARY 0      /* Define the flag if not defined yet */
#endif /* O_BINARY */

#define BUFFER_SIZE (16 * 1024) /* use 16K buffers */

int main(int argc, char *argv[])
{
    char  buffer[BUFFER_SIZE];  /* buffer for data */
    int   in_file;              /* input file descriptor */
    int   out_file;             /* output file descriptor */
    int   read_size;            /* number of bytes on last read */

    if (argc != 3) {
        fprintf(stderr, "Error:Wrong number of arguments\n");
        fprintf(stderr, "Usage is: copy <from> <to>\n");
        exit(8);
    }
```

Example 14-5: copy2/copy2.c (continued)

```
    in_file = open(argv[1], O_RDONLY|O_BINARY);
    if (in_file < 0) {
        fprintf("Error:Unable to open %s\n", argv[1]);
        exit(8);
    }
    out_file = open(argv[2], O_WRONLY|O_TRUNC|O_CREAT|O_BINARY, 0666);
    if (out_file < 0) {
        fprintf("Error:Unable to open %s\n", argv[2]);
        exit(8);
    }
    while (1) {
        read_size = read(in_file, buffer, sizeof(buffer));

        if (read_size == 0)
            break;                    /* end of file */

        if (read_size < 0) {
            fprintf(stderr, "Error:Read error\n");
            exit(8);
        }
        write(out_file, buffer, (unsigned int) read_size);
    }
    close(in_file);
    close(out_file);
    return (0);
}
```

Question 14-3: *Why does Example 14-5 dump core instead of printing an error message, if it can't open the input file?*

Several things should be noted about this program. First of all, the buffer size is defined as a constant, so it is easily modified. Rather than have to remember that 16K is 16384, the programmer used the expression (16 * 1024). This form of the constant is obviously 16K.

If the user improperly uses the program, an error message results. To help get it right, the message tells how to use the program.

We may not read a full buffer for the last read. Consequently, *read_size* is used to determine the number of bytes to write.

Designing File Formats

Suppose you are designing a program to produce a graph. The height, width, limits, and scales are to be defined in a graph configuration file. You are also assigned to write a user-friendly program that asks the operator questions and then writes a configuration file so that he does not have to learn the text editor. How should you design a configuration file?

One way would be as follows:

```
height (in inches)
width (in inches)
x lower limit
x upper limit
y lower limit
y upper limit
x scale
y scale
```

A typical plotter configuration file might look like:

```
10.0
7.0
0
100
30
300
0.5
2.0
```

This file does contain all the data, but in looking at it, you have difficulty telling what, for example, is the value of the y lower limit. A solution is to comment the file. That is, to have the configuration program write out not only the data, but a string describing the data.

```
10.0   height (in inches)
7.0    width (in inches)
0      x lower limit
100    x upper limit
30     y lower limit
300    y upper limit
0.5    x scale
2.0    y scale
```

Now the file is user readable. But suppose that one of the users runs the plot program and types in the wrong filename, and the program gets the lunch menu for today instead of a plot configuration file. The program is probably going to get very upset when it tries to construct a plot whose dimensions are "BLT on white" versus "Meatloaf and gravy."

The result is that you wind up with egg on your face. There should be some way of identifying this file as a plot configuration file. One method of doing so is to put the words "Plot Configuration File" on the first line of the file. Then, when someone tries to give your program the wrong file, the program will print an error message.

This solution takes care of the wrong-file problem, but what happens when you are asked to enhance the programs and add optional logarithmic plotting? You could simply add another line to the configuration file, but what about all those old files? You cannot reasonably ask everyone to throw them away. The best thing to do (from a user's point of view) is to accept old format files. You can make this task easier by putting a version number in the file.

A typical file now looks like:

```
Plot      Configuration File V1.0
log       Logarithmic or Normal plot
10.0      height (in inches)
7.0       width (in inches)
0         x lower limit
100       x upper limit
30        y lower limit
300       y upper limit
0.5       x scale
2.0       y scale
```

In binary files, you usually put an identification number in the first four bytes of the file. This number is called the *magic number*. The magic number should be different for each type of file.

One method for choosing a magic number is to start with the first four letters of the program name (i.e., *list*) and then convert them to hexadecimal: `0x6c607374`. Then, add `0x80808080` to the number, producing a magic number of `0xECE0F3F4`.

This algorithm generates a magic number that is probably unique. The high bit is set on each byte to make the byte non-ASCII and avoid confusion between ASCII and binary files.

When reading and writing a binary file containing many different types of structures, a programmer can easily get lost. For example, you might read a name structure when you expected a size structure. This error is usually not detected until later in the program. In order to locate this problem early, the programmer can put magic numbers at the beginning of each structure.

Now, if the program reads the name structure and the magic number is not correct, it knows something is wrong.

Magic numbers for structures do not need to have the high bit set on each byte. Making the magic number just four ASCII characters allows you to easily pick out the beginning of structures in a file dump.

Answers

Answer 14-1: The problem is that `fgets` gets the entire line including the newline character (`\n`). If you have a file named *sam*, the program will read *sam\n* and try to look for a file by that name. Because there is no such file, the program reports an error.

The fix is to strip the newline character from the name:

```
name[strlen(name)-1] = '\0';     /* get rid of last character */
```

The error message in this case is poorly designed. True, we did not open the file, but the programmer could supply the user with more information. Are we trying to open the file for input or output? What is the name of the file we are trying to open? We don't even know if the message we are getting is an error, a warning, or just part of the normal operation. A better error message is:

```
fprintf(stderr,"Error:Unable to open %s for input\n", name);
```

Notice that this message would also help us detect the programming error. When we typed in **sam**, the error would be:

```
Error:Unable to open sam
for input
```

This message clearly shows us that we are trying to open a file with a newline in its name.

Answer 14-2: The problem is that we are writing an ASCII file, but we wanted a binary file. On UNIX, ASCII is the same as binary, so the program runs fine. On MS-DOS/Windows, the end-of-line problem causes us problems. When we write a newline character (0x0a) to the file, a carriage return (0x0D) is added to it. (Remember that end-of-line on MS-DOS/Windows is <RETURN> <LINE FEED>, or 0x0d, 0x0a.) Because of this editing, we get an extra carriage return (0x0d) in the output file.

In order to write binary data (without output editing), we need to open the file with the binary option:

```
out_file = fopen("test.out", "wb");
```

Answer 14-3: The problem is with the `fprintf` call. The first parameter of an `fprintf` should be a file; instead, it is the format string. Trying to use a format string when the program is expecting a file causes a core dump.

Programming Exercises

Exercise 14-1: Write a program that reads a file and then counts the number of lines in it.

Exercise 14-2: Write a program to copy a file, expanding all tabs to multiple spaces.

Exercise 14-3: Write a program that reads a file containing a list of numbers, and then writes two files, one with all numbers divisible by three and another containing all the other numbers.

Exercise 14-4: Write a program that reads an ASCII file containing a list of numbers and writes a binary file containing the same list.   Write a program that goes the other way so that you can check your work.

Exercise 14-5: Write a program that copies a file and removes all characters with the high bit set (((ch & 0x80) != 0)).

Exercise 14-6: Design a file format to store a person's name, address, and other information. Write a program to read this file and produce a set of mailing labels.

15

*Debugging and
Optimization*

*Bloody instructions which, being learned, return
to plague the inventor.*

—Shakespeare, on debugging
[*Macbeth*, Act 1, Scene 7].

Debugging

The hardest part of creating a program is not its design and writing, but its debugging phase. In this phase, you find out how your program really works (instead of how you think it works).

In order to eradicate a bug, you need two things: a way of reproducing it and information from the program that lets you locate and correct the problem.

In some cases, finding the bug is easy. You discover the bug yourself, the test department produces a clear and easy test plan that displays the bug, or else the output always comes out bad.

In some cases, especially with interactive programs, reproducing the bug may be 90% of the problem. This statement is especially true when you deal with bug reports sent in by users in the field. A typical call from a user might be:

User:

That database program you gave me is broken.

Programmer:

What's wrong?

User:

Sometimes, when I'm doing a sort, it gets things in the wrong order.

Programmer:

What command were you using?

User:

The *sort* command.

Programmer (patiently):

Tell me exactly what you typed, keystroke by keystroke, to get it to fail.

User:

I don't remember it exactly. I was doing a lot of sorts.

Programmer:

If I come over can you show me the bug?

User:

Of course.

Two minutes later, the programmer is in the user's office and utters the fatal words, "Show me." The user types away and the program stubbornly works, no matter what the user does to it.

The programmer gives up and goes back to her office only to find a message from the user: "It failed five minutes after you left."

Example 15-1 is a short database lookup program. It asks the user for input and checks the input against a hardcoded list of names. Although very simple, the program's structure is typical of much larger and more complex interactive programs.

Example 15-1: base/base.c

```
/*********************************************************
 * Database -- A very simple database program to        *
 *             look up names in a hardcoded list.        *
 *                                                       *
 * Usage:                                                *
 *      database                                         *
 *              Program will ask you for a name.         *
 *              Enter the name; it will tell you if      *
 *              the name is in the list.                 *
 *                                                       *
 *              A blank name terminates the program.     *
 *********************************************************/
#define STRING_LENGTH 80        /* Length of typical string */
#include <stdio.h>
#include <string.h>

int main()
{
    char name[STRING_LENGTH];   /* a name to lookup */
```

Example 15-1: base/base.c (continued)

```c
    int lookup(char const *const name); /* lookup a name */

    while (1) {
        printf("Enter name: ");
        fgets(name, sizeof(name), stdin);

        /* Check for blank name  */
        /* (remember 1 character for newline) */
        if (strlen(name) <= 1)
            break;

        /* Get rid of newline */
        name[strlen(name)-1] = '\0';

        if (lookup(name))
            printf("%s is in the list\n", name);
        else
            printf("%s is not in the list\n", name);
    }
    return (0);
}
/*********************************************************
 * lookup -- Looks up a name in a list.                 *
 *                                                      *
 * Parameters                                           *
 *      name -- Name to look up.                        *
 *                                                      *
 * Returns                                              *
 *      1 -- Name in the list.                          *
 *      0 -- Name not in the list.                      *
 *********************************************************/
int lookup(char const *const name)
{
    /* List of people in the database */
    /* Note: Last name is a NULL for end of list */
    static char *list[] = {
        "John",
        "Jim",
        "Jane",
        "Clyde",
        NULL
    };

    int index;              /* index into list */

    for (index = 0; list[index] != NULL; ++index) {
        if (strcmp(list[index], name) == 0)
            return (1);
    }
    return (0);
}
```

A typical execution of this program is:

```
Enter name: Sam
Sam is not in the list
Enter name: John
John is in the list
Enter name:
```

When we release this program, of course, the users immediately start complaining about mysterious problems that go away whenever the programmer is around. Wouldn't it be nice to have a little gremlin that sits on the shoulder, copying down everything the user types? Unfortunately, gremlins are not available; however, we can change this program so that it produces a *save file* that contains every keystroke that the user typed in.

Our program uses the statement:

```
fgets(name, sizeof(name), stdin);
```

to read the user's data.

Let's write a new routine, **extended_fgets**, and use it instead of **fgets**. It not only gets a line, but also saves the user's response in a save file. Example 15-2 is a revision of Example 15-1 that includes **extended_fgets**.

Example 15-2: xgets/xgets.c

```c
#include <stdio.h>
/*
 * The main program opens this file if -S is on
 * the command line.
 */
FILE *save_file = NULL;
/***********************************************************
 * extended_fgets -- Gets a line from the input file      *
 *              and records it in a save file if needed.  *
 *                                                        *
 * Parameters                                             *
 *      line -- The line to read.                         *
 *      size -- sizeof(line) -- maximum number of         *
 *                      characters to read.               *
 *      file -- File to read data from                    *
 *              (normally stdin).                         *
 *                                                        *
 * Returns                                                *
 *      NULL -- error or end-of-file in read              *
 *      otherwise line (just like fgets).                 *
 ***********************************************************/
char *extended_fgets(char *line, int size, FILE *file)
{

    char *result;               /* result of fgets */
```

Example 15-2: xgets/xgets.c (continued)

```
    result = fgets(line, size, file);

    /* Did someone ask for a save file?? */
    if (save_file != NULL)
        fputs(line, save_file); /* Save line in file */

    return (result);
}
```

We also change our main program to handle a new option, *-Sfile*, to specify a *save file*. (Typically, uppercase letters are used for debugging and other less used options.) Our new main program is shown in Example 15-3.

Example 15-3: base2/base2.c

```
[File: base2/base2.c]
/**********************************************************
 * Database -- A very simple database program to          *
 *             look up names in a hardcoded list.         *
 *                                                         *
 * Usage:                                                  *
 *      database [-S<file>]                                *
 *                                                         *
 *      -S<file>        Specifies save file for            *
 *                      debugging purposes                 *
 *                                                         *
 *              Program will ask you for a name.           *
 *              Enter the name; program will tell you if   *
 *              it is in the list.                         *
 *                                                         *
 *              A blank name terminates the program.       *
 **********************************************************/
#include <stdio.h>
#include <stdlib.h>

FILE *save_file = NULL; /* Save file if any */
char *extended_fgets(char *, int, FILE *);

int main(int argc, char *argv[])
{
    char name[80];      /* a name to lookup */
    char *save_file_name; /* Name of the save file */

    int lookup(char const *const name); /* lookup a name */

    while ((argc > 1) && (argv[1][0] == '-')) {
        switch (argv[1][1]) {
            /* -S<file>  Specify a save file */
            case 'S':
                save_file_name = &argv[1][2];
                save_file = fopen(save_file_name, "w");
                if (save_file == NULL)
```

Example 15-3: base2/base2.c (continued)

```
                    fprintf(stderr,
                        "Warning:Unable to open save file %s\n",
                        save_file_name);
                break;
            default:
                fprintf(stderr,"Bad option: %s\n", argv[1]);
                exit (8);
        }
        --argc;
        ++argv;
    }


    while (1) {
        printf("Enter name: ");
        extended_fgets(name, sizeof(name), stdin);

        /* ... Rest of program ... */
    }
}
```

Now we have a complete record of what the user typed. Looking at the input, we see that the user typed:

```
Sam
 John
```

The second name begins with a space and although "John" is in the list, "<space> John" is not. In this case, we found the error by inspecting the input; however, more complex programs have much more complex input. We could type all that in when debugging, or we could add another feature to `extended_fgets` that would add *playback file* to it. When enabled, input will not be taken from the keyboard, but instead will be taken from the file. Example 15-4 contains the revised `extended_fgets`.

Example 15-4: xgets2/xgets2.c

```
#include <stdio.h>
FILE *save_file = NULL;          /* Save input in this file */
FILE *playback_file = NULL;      /* Playback data from this file */
/************************************************************
 * extended_fgets -- Gets a line from the input file       *
 *               and records it in a save file if needed.  *
 *                                                         *
 * Parameters                                              *
 *      line -- The line to read.                          *
 *      size -- sizeof(line) -- maximum number of          *
 *                     characters to read.                 *
 *      file -- File to read data from                     *
 *             (normally stdin).                           *
 *                                                         *
```

Example 15-4: xgets2/xgets2.c (continued)

```
 * Returns                                                   *
 *       NULL -- error or end-of-file in read                *
 *       otherwise line (just like fgets).                   *
 ***********************************************************/
char *extended_fgets(char *line, int size, FILE *file)
{
    extern FILE *save_file;     /* file to save strings in */
    extern FILE *playback_file; /* file for alternate input */

    char *result;               /* result of fgets */

    if (playback_file != NULL) {
        result = fgets(line, size, playback_file);
        /* echo the input to the standard out so the user sees it */
        fputs(line, stdout);
    } else
        /* Get the line normally */
        result = fgets(line, size, file);

    /* Did someone ask for a save file? */
    if (save_file != NULL)
        fputs(line, save_file); /* Save the line in a file */

    return (result);
}
```

We also add a playback option to the command line −P*file*. This option allows us to automatically type the commands that caused the error. Our main program, revised to support the −P option, is Example 15-5.

Example 15-5: base3/base3.c

```
/***********************************************************
 * Database -- A very simple database program to           *
 *             look up names in a hardcoded list.          *
 *                                                         *
 * Usage:                                                  *
 *     database [-S<file>] [-P<file>]                      *
 *                                                         *
 *     -S<file>          Specifies save file for           *
 *                       debugging purposes.               *
 *                                                         *
 *     -P<file>          Specifies playback file for       *
 *                       debugging or demonstration.       *
 *                                                         *
 *                                                         *
 *               Program will ask you for a name.          *
 *               Enter the name; the program will tell     *
 *               you if it is in the list.                 *
 *                                                         *
 *               A blank name terminates the program.      *
 ***********************************************************/
```

Example 15-5: base3/base3.c (continued)

```c
#include <stdio.h>
#include <stdlib.h>

FILE *save_file = NULL; /* Save file if any */
FILE *playback_file = NULL;     /* Playback file if any */
char *extended_fgets(char *, int, FILE *);

int main(int argc, char *argv[])
{
    char name[80];       /* a Name to look up */
    char *save_file_name; /* Name of the save file */
    char *playback_file_name; /* Name of the playback file */

    int lookup(char const *const name); /* lookup a name */

    while ((argc > 1) && (argv[1][0] == '-')) {
        switch (argv[1][1]) {
            /* -S<file>  Specify save file */
            case 'S':
                save_file_name = &argv[1][2];
                save_file = fopen(save_file_name, "w");
                if (save_file == NULL)
                    fprintf(stderr,
                        "Warning:Unable to open save file %s\n",
                        save_file_name);
                break;
            /* -P<file>  Specify playback file */
            case 'P':
                playback_file_name = &argv[1][2];
                playback_file = fopen(playback_file_name, "r");
                if (playback_file == NULL) {
                    fprintf(stderr,
                        "Error:Unable to open playback file %s\n",
                        playback_file_name);
                    exit (8);
                }
                break;
            default:
                fprintf(stderr,"Bad option: %s\n", argv[1]);
                exit (8);
        }
        --argc;
        ++argv;
    }

    /* ... rest of program ... */
    return (0);
}
```

Now, when a user calls up with an error report, we can tell him, "Try it again with the save-file feature enabled, and then send me a copy of your files." The user then runs the program and saves the input into the file *save.txt*:

```
% database -Ssave.txt
Enter name: Sam
Sam is not in the list
Enter name:  John
John is in the list
Enter name:
```

He sends us the file *save.txt*, and we run the program with the playback option enabled:

```
% database -Psave.txt
Enter name: Sam
Sam is not in the list
Enter name:  John
John is in the list
Enter name:
```

We now have a reliable way of reproducing the problem. In many cases, that's half the battle. After we can reproduce the problem, we can proceed to find and fix the bugs.

A Copy Flip-Flop

Once a programmer asked a user to send him a copy of his floppy. A next-day air package arrived at the programmer's desk containing a photocopy of the floppy. The user was not completely computer illiterate. He knew it was a two-sided floppy, so he had photocopied both sides.

Before you start debugging, save the old, "working" copy of your program in a safe place. (If you are using a source control system like SCCS or RCS, your last working version should be checked in.) Many times while you are searching for a problem, you may find it necessary to try out different solutions or to add temporary debugging code. Sometimes you find you've been barking up the wrong tree and need to start over. That's when the last working copy becomes invaluable.

After you have reproduced the problem, you must determine what caused it to happen. There are several methods for doing this, as described in the following sections.

Divide and Conquer

The *divide-and-conquer* method has already been briefly discussed in Chapter 6, *Decision and Control Statements*. This method consists of putting in `printf` statements where you know the data is good (to make sure it is really good), where the data is bad, and at several points in between. In this manner you can start zeroing in on the section of code that contains the error. More `printf` statements can further reduce the scope of the error until the bug is finally located.

Debug-Only Code

The divide-and-conquer method uses temporary `printf` statements. They are put in as needed and taken out after they are used. The preprocessor conditional compilation directives can be used to put in and take out debugging code. For example:

```
#ifdef DEBUG
    printf("Width %f Height %f\n", width, height);
#endif /* DEBUG */
```

The program can be compiled with `DEBUG` undefined for normal use; you can define it when debugging is needed.

Debug Command-Line Switch

Rather than using a compile-time switch to create a special version of the program, you can permanently include the debugging code and add a special program switch that will turn on the debugging output. For example:

```
if (debug)
    printf("Width %f Height %f\n", width, height);
```

In the debug example, `debug` is a variable that is set if −D is present on the command line.

This method has the advantage that only a single version of the program exists. Also, the customer can turn on this switch in the field, save the output, and send it to you for analysis. The method has a disadvantage, though: a larger executable file. The runtime switch should always be used instead of conditional compilation unless there is some reason that you do not want the customer to be able to get at the debugging information.

Some programs use the concept of a debug level. Level 0 outputs only minimal debugging information, level 1 more information, and so on up to level 9, which outputs everything.

The `ghostscript`[*] program by Aladdin Enterprises implements the idea of debugging letters. The command option −Z*xxx* sets the debugging flags for each type of diagnostic output wanted. For example, `f` is the code for the fill algo-

---

[*] `ghostscript` is a PostScript-like interpreter available from the Free Software Foundation for a minimal copying charge. They can be reached at: Free Software Foundation, Inc., 675 Massachusetts Avenue, Cambridge, MA 02139 (617) 876-3296. Their ftp site is *prep.ai.mit.edu:/pub/gnu*.

rithm, while **p** is the code for the path tracer. If I wanted to trace both these sections, I would specify −**Zfp**.

The option is implemented by the following code:

```
/*
 * Even though we only used one zero, C will fill in the
 * rest of the arrays with zeros.
 */
char debug[128] = {0};    /* the debugging flags */
main(int argc, char *argv[])
{
    while ((argc > 1) && (argv[1][0] == '-')) {
        switch (argv[1][1]) {
            /* .... normal switch .... */
            /* Debug switch */
            case 'Z':
                debug_ptr = argv[1][2];
                /* loop for each letter */
                while (*debug_ptr != '\0') {
                    debug[*debug_ptr] = 1;
                    debug_ptr++;
                }
                break;
        }
        argc--;
        argv++;
    }
    /* rest of program */
}
```

This is used inside the program by:

```
if (debug['p'])
    printf("Starting new path\n");
```

ghostscript is a large program (some 25,000 lines) and rather difficult to debug. This form of debugging allows the user to get a great deal of information easily.

Going Through the Output

Enabling the debug printout is a nice way of getting information, but at many times, there is so much data that the information you want can easily get lost.

C allows you to *redirect* to a file what would normally go to the screen. For example:

```
buggy -D9 >tmp.out
```

runs the program **buggy** with a high level of debugging and sends the output to the file *tmp.out*.

The text editor on your system makes a good file browser. You can use its search capabilities to look for the information you want to find.

Interactive Debuggers

Most compiler manufacturers provide you with an interactive debugger. These debuggers give you the ability to stop the program at any point, examine and change variables, and "single step" through the program. Because each debugger is different, a detailed discussion is not possible.

However, we are going to discuss one debugger, dbx. This program is available on many UNIX machines running the BSD versions of UNIX. On LINUX in particular and other UNIX systems, the Free Software Foundations gdb debugger is popular. SYSTEM-V UNIX uses the debugger sdb, while on HP-UX, the utility cdb is used. Each MS-DOS/Windows compiler has its own debugger. Some compilers actually come with multiple debuggers. For example, Borland C++ comes with a integrated debugger that runs under Windows, a stand-alone debugger that runs under MS-DOS, and a remote debugger that runs on another machine.

Although the exact syntax used by your debugger may be different, the principles shown here will work for all debuggers.

The basic list of dbx commands are:

run
> Start execution of a program.

stop at line-number
> Insert a breakpoint at the given line number. When a running program reaches a breakpoint, execution stops and control returns to the debugger.

stop in function-name
> Insert a breakpoint at the first line of the named function. Commonly, the command stop in main is used to stop at the beginning of the program.

cont
> Continue execution after a breakpoint.

print expression
> Display the value of an expression.

step
> Execute a single line in the program. If the current statement calls a function, the function is single-stepped.

next
> Execute a single line in the program, but treat function calls as a single line. This command is used to skip over function calls.

list

List the source program.

where

Print the list of currently active functions.

We have a program that should count the number of threes and sevens in a series of numbers. Unfortunately, it keeps getting the wrong answer for the number of sevens. Our program is shown in Example 15-6. Your results may vary.

Example 15-6: seven/seven.c

```
 1 #include <stdio.h>
 2 char line[100];     /* line of input */
 3 int seven_count;    /* number of sevens in the data */
 4 int data[5];        /* the data to count 3 and 7 in */
 5 int three_count;    /* the number of threes in the data */
 6 int index;          /* index into the data */
 7
 8 int main() {
 9
10     seven_count = 0;
11     three_count = 0;
12     get_data(data);
13
14     for (index = 1; index <= 5; ++index) {
15
16         if (data[index] == 3)
17             ++three_count;
18
19         if (data[index] == 7)
20     ++seven_count;
21     }
22
23     printf("Threes %d Sevens %d\n",
24             three_count, seven_count);
25     return (0);
26 }
27
28 void get_data(int data)
29 {
30
31     printf("Enter 5 numbers\n");
32     fgets(line, sizeof(line), stdin);
33     sscanf(line, "%d %d %d %d %d",
34         &data[1], &data[2], &data[3],
35         &data[4], &data[5]);
36 }
```

When we run this program with the data 7 3 7 0 2, the results are:

```
Threes 1 Sevens 4
```

We start by invoking the debugger (**dbx**) with the name of the program we are going to debug (**seven**). The debugger initializes itself, outputs the prompt (**dbx**), and waits for a command:

```
% dbx seven
Reading symbolic information...
Read 72 symbols
(dbx)
```

We don't know where the variable is getting changed, so we'll start at the beginning and work our way through until we get an error. At every step, we'll display the variable seven_count just to make sure it's OK.

We need to stop the program at the beginning so that we can single-step through it. The command stop in main tells dbx to set a breakpoint at the first instruction of the function main. The command run tells dbx to start the program and run until it hits the first breakpoint:

```
(dbx) stop in main
(2) stop in main
```

The number (2) is used by dbx to identify the breakpoint. Now we need to start the program:

```
(dbx) run
Running: seven
stopped in main at line 10 in file "/usr/sdo/seven/seven.c"
   10          seven_count = 0;
```

The message "stopped in main..." indicates that the program encountered a breakpoint and the debugger now has control.

We have reached the point where seven_count is initialized. The command next will execute a single statement, treating function calls as one statement. (The names of the command for your debugger may be different.) We go past the initialization and check to see if it worked:

```
(dbx) next
stopped in main at line 11 in file "/usr/sdo/seven/seven.c"
   11          three_count = 0;
(dbx) print seven_count
seven_count = 0
```

It did. We try the next few lines, checking all the time:

```
(dbx) next
stopped in main at line 12 in file "/usr/sdo/seven/seven.c"
   12          get_data(data);
(dbx) print seven_count
seven_count = 0
(dbx) next
Enter 5 numbers
3 7 3 0 2
stopped in main at line 14 in file "/usr/sdo/seven/seven.c"
   14          for (index = 1; index <= 5; index++) {
(dbx) print seven_count
seven_count = 2
```

seven_count somehow changed value to 2. The last statement we executed was get_data(data), so something is going on in that function. We add a breakpoint at the beginning of get_data and start the program over with the run command:

```
(dbx) stop in get_data
(4) stop in get_data
(dbx) run
Running: seven
stopped in main at line 10 in file "/usr/sdo/seven/seven.c"
   10        seven_count = 0;
```

We are at the beginning of main. We want to go onto the next breakpoint, so we issue the cont command to continue execution:

```
(dbx) cont
Running: seven
stopped in get_data at line 31 in file "/usr/sdo/seven/seven.c"
   31        printf("Enter 5 numbers\n");
```

We now start single stepping again until we find the error:

```
(dbx) print seven_count
seven_count = 0
(dbx) next
Enter 5 numbers
stopped in get_data at line 32 in file "/usr/sdo/seven/seven.c"
   32        fgets(line, sizeof(line), stdin);
(dbx) print seven_count
seven_count = 0
(dbx) next
1 2 3 4 5
stopped in get_data at line 33 in file "/usr/sdo/seven/seven.c"
   35            &data[4], &data[5]);
(dbx) print seven_count
seven_count = 0
(dbx) next
stopped in get_data at line 36 in file "/usr/sdo/seven/seven.c"
   36    }
(dbx) print seven_count
seven_count = 5
(dbx) list 30,40
   30
   31        printf("Enter 5 numbers\n");
   32        fgets(line, sizeof(line), stdin);
   33        sscanf(line, "%d %d %d %d %d",
   34            &data[1], &data[2], &data[3],
   35            &data[4], &data[5]);
   36    }
(dbx) quit
```

At line 32, the data was good, but when we reached line 36, the data was bad, so the error is located at line 33 of the program, the sscanf. We've narrowed the

problem down to one statement. By inspection we can see that we are using
`data[5]`, an illegal member of the array `data`.

The computer happened to store `seven_count` after the `data` array, so that is
why (confusingly enough) the problem turned up there. It would be nice if we
could get a clear error message whenever we step outside the declared array, but
bounds checking is time consuming and difficult in C. There are some specialized
debugging tools such as Bounds-Checker by Nu-Mega (MS-DOS/ Windows) and
Purify by Pure Software (UNIX).

Debugging a Binary Search

The binary search algorithm is fairly simple. You want to see if a given number is
in an ordered list. Check your number against the one in the middle of the list. If
it is the number, you were lucky—stop. If your number was bigger, then you
might find it in the top half of the list; try the middle of the top half. If it was
smaller, try the bottom half. Keep trying and dividing the list in half until you find
the number or the list gets down to a single number.

Example 15-7 uses a binary search to see if a number can be found in the file
numbers.dat.

Example 15-7: search/search1.c

```
[File: search/search1.c]
/*********************************************************
 * search -- Searches a set of numbers.                  *
 *                                                       *
 * Usage:                                                *
 *       search                                          *
 *                 You will be asked numbers to look up. *
 *                                                       *
 * Files:                                                *
 *       numbers.dat -- Numbers 1 per line to search     *
 *                      (numbers must be ordered).       *
 *********************************************************/
#include <stdio.h>
#define MAX_NUMBERS    1000    /* Max numbers in file */
const char DATA_FILE[] = "numbers.dat"; /* File with numbers */

int data[MAX_NUMBERS];   /* Array of numbers to search */
int max_count;           /* Number of valid elements in data */
int main()
{
    FILE *in_file;       /* Input file */
    int middle;          /* Middle of our search range */
    int low, high;       /* Upper/lower bound */
    int search;          /* Number to search for */
    char line[80];       /* Input line */
```

Example 15-7: search/search1.c (continued)

```c
    in_file = fopen(DATA_FILE, "r");
    if (in_file == NULL) {
        fprintf(stderr,"Error:Unable to open %s\n", DATA_FILE);
        exit (8);
    }

    /*
     * Read in data
     */

    max_count = 0;
    while (1) {
        if (fgets(line, sizeof(line),  in_file) == NULL)
            break;

        /* convert number */
        sscanf(line, "%d", data[max_count]);
        ++max_count;
    }

    while (1) {
        printf("Enter number to search for or -1 to quit:" );
        fgets(line, sizeof(line), stdin);
        sscanf(line, "%d", &search);

        if (search == -1)
            break;

        low = 0;
        high = max_count;

        while (1) {
            middle = (low + high) / 2;

            if (data[middle] == search) {
                printf("Found at index %d\n", middle);
            }

            if (low == high) {
                printf("Not found\n");
                break;
            }

            if (data[middle] < search)
                low = middle;
            else
                high = middle;
        }
    }
    return (0);
}
```

Our data file, *numbers.dat*, contains:

```
 4
 6
14
16
17
```

When we run this program, the results are:

```
% search
Segmentation fault (core dumped)
```

These results are not good. They mean that something went wrong in our program and it tried to read memory that wasn't there. A file called *core* was created when the error occurred. It contains a snapshot of our executing program. The debugger **dbx** can read this file and help us determine what happened:

```
% dbx search
Reading symbolic information...
Read 79 symbols
warning: core file read error: address not in data space
warning: core file read error: address not in data space
warning: core file read error: address not in data space
program terminated by signal SEGV (no mapping at the fault address)
(dbx)
```

The message "warning: core file..." is the debugger's way of telling you that the temporary variable space (the stack) has been trashed and contains bad data. The **where** command tells you which function is calling which function (also known as a stack trace). The current function is printed first, then the function that called it, and so on until we reach the outer function **main**:

```
(dbx) where
number() at 0xdd7d87a
_doscan() at 0xdd7d329
sscanf(0xdfffadc, 0x200e3, 0x0) at 0xdd7ce7f
main(0x1, 0xdfffb58, 0xdfffb60), line 41 in "search.c"
(dbx)
```

The above example tells us that **main** called **sscanf**. The call was made from line 41 of **main**. **sscanf** called **_doscan**. Because **sscanf** is a standard library routine, we cannot get line-number information. The instruction number is **0xdd7ce7f**; however, this information is not very useful to us. The procedure **_doscan** called **number**. **number** was what tried to perform the illegal memory access.

This information does *not* mean that there is a bug in **number**. The problem could be caused by the parameters passed to **number** by **_doscan**, which could have gotten parameters from **sscanf**, which got parameters from **main**. Any one of the functions along this chain could contain an error that caused a bad pointer to be passed to another function.

Usually the standard library has been debugged, so we should probably look for the error in our code. Looking at the stack trace, we see that the last line of our program to be executed was line 41 of **main**.

Using the **list** command, we can examine that line:

```
(dbx) list 41
   41              sscanf(line, "%d", data[max_count]);
(dbx)
```

This line caused the problem.

Another way of finding the problem is to single-step the program until the error occurs. First, we list a section of the program to find a convenient place to put the breakpoint, then start the execution and the single-step process:

```
(dbx) list 26,31
   22          int low, high;      /* Upper/lower bound */
   23          int search;         /* Number to search for */
   24          char line[80];      /* Input line */
   25
   26          in_file = fopen(DATA_FILE, "r");
   27          if (in_file == NULL) {
   28                  fprintf(stderr,"Error:Unable to open %s\n",
                                                  DATA_FILE);
   29              exit (8);
   30          }
   31
(dbx) stop at 26
(1) stop at "search.c":26
(dbx) run
Running: search
stopped in main at line 26 in file "search.c"
   26          in_file = fopen(DATA_FILE, "r");
(dbx) step
stopped in main at line 27 in file "search.c"
   27        if (in_file == NULL) {
(dbx) step
stopped in main at line 35 in file "search.c"
   35        max_count = 0;
(dbx) step
stopped in main at line 37 in file "search.c"
   37            if (fgets(line, sizeof(line),  in_file) == NULL)
(dbx) step
stopped in main at line 41 in file "search.c"
   41              sscanf(line, "%d", data[max_count]);
(dbx) step
signal SEGV (no mapping at the fault address) in number at 0xdd7d87a
number+0x520:          movl    a6@(0x1c),a0
(dbx) quit
```

This method also points at line 41 as the culprit. On inspection, we notice that we forgot to put an ampersand (&) in front of the variable for **sscanf**. So we change line 41 from:

```
sscanf(line, "%d", data[max_count]);
```

to:

```
sscanf(line, "%d", &data[max_count]);
```

and try again. The first number in our list is 4, so we try it. This time our output looks like:

```
Enter number to search for or -1 to quit:4
Found at index 0
Found at index 0
Not found
Enter number to search for or -1 to quit:^C
```

The program should find the number, let us know it's at index 0, and then ask for another number. Instead, we get two "found" messages and one "not found" message. We know that everything is running smoothly up until we get the first "found" message. After that point, things go downhill. So we have at least one more bug in our program.

Getting back into the debugger, we use the **list** command to locate the found message and put a breakpoint there:

```
% dbx search
Reading symbolic information...
Read 79 symbols
(dbx) list 58,60
   58
   59                    if (data[middle] == search) {
   60                        printf("Found at index %d\n", middle);
   61                    }
   62
   63                    if (low == high) {
   64                        printf("Not found\n");
   65                        break;
   66                    }
   67
(dbx) stop at 60
(3) stop at "search.c":60
(dbx) run
stopped in main at line 60 in file "search.c"
   60                        printf("Found at index %d\n", middle);
(dbx)
```

Now we start single-stepping to see what happens:

```
   60                        printf("Found at index %d\n", middle);
(dbx) step
Found at index 0
```

```
    stopped in main at line 63 in file "search.c"
       63                    if (low == high) {
    (dbx) step
    stopped in main at line 68 in file "search.c"
       68                    if (data[middle] < search)
    (dbx) step
    stopped in main at line 71 in file "search.c"
       71                        high = middle;
    (dbx) step
    stopped in main at line 57 in file "search.c"
       57                    middle = (low + high) / 2;
    (dbx) quit
```

The program doesn't exit the loop. Instead, it continues with the search. Because the number has already been found, in strange behavior results. We are missing a **break** after the `printf`.

We need to change:

```
if (data[middle] == search) {
    printf("Found at index %d\n", middle);
}
```

to:

```
if (data[middle] == search) {
    printf("Found at index %d\n", middle);
    break;
}
```

Making this fix, we try our program again:

```
% search
Enter number to search for or -1 to quit:4
Found at index 0
Enter number to search for or -1 to quit:6
Found at index 1
Enter number to search for or -1 to quit:3
Not found
Enter number to search for or -1 to quit:5
...program continues forever or until we abort it...
```

We have a runaway program. This time, instead of setting a breakpoint, we just start running the program. After a few seconds pass and we believe that we are stuck in the infinite loop, we stop the program with a CTRL-C to return to the shell prompt. Because we are running with the debugger, control returns to **dbx**:

```
% dbx search
Reading symbolic information...
Read 80 symbols
(dbx) run
Running: search
Enter number to search for or -1 to quit:5
^C
interrupt in main at line 70 in file "search.c"
       70                        low = middle;
```

Now we can use the single-step command to step through our infinite loop, looking at key values along the way:

```
    70                    low = middle;
(dbx) step
stopped in main at line 57 in file "search.c"
    57                    middle = (low + high) / 2;
(dbx) step
stopped in main at line 59 in file "search.c"
    59                    if (data[middle] == search) {
(dbx) print middle
middle = 0
(dbx) print data[middle]
data[middle] = 4
(dbx) print search
search = 5
(dbx) step
stopped in main at line 64 in file "search.c"
    64                    if (low == high) {
(dbx) step
stopped in main at line 69 in file "search.c"
    69                    if (data[middle] < search)
(dbx) step
stopped in main at line 70 in file "search.c"
    70                    low = middle;
(dbx) step
stopped in main at line 57 in file "search.c"
    57                    middle = (low + high) / 2;
(dbx) step
stopped in main at line 59 in file "search.c"
    59                    if (data[middle] == search) {
(dbx) step
stopped in main at line 64 in file "search.c"
    64                    if (low == high) {
(dbx) step
stopped in main at line 69 in file "search.c"
    69                    if (data[middle] < search)
(dbx) step
stopped in main at line 70 in file "search.c"
    70                     low = middle;
(dbx) step
stopped in main at line 57 in file "search.c"
    57                    middle = (low + high) / 2;
(dbx) step
stopped in main at line 59 in file "search.c"
    59                    if (data[middle] == search) {
(dbx) step
stopped in main at line 64 in file "search.c"
    64                    if (low == high) {
(dbx) step
stopped in main at line 69 in file "search.c"
    69                    if (data[middle] < search)
(dbx) print low,middle,high
low = 0
```

```
    middle = 0
    high = 1
    (dbx) print search
    search = 5
    (dbx) print data[0], data[1]
    data[0] = 4
    data[1] = 6
    (dbx) quit
```

The problem is that we have reached a point where:

```
    low=      0
    middle=   0
    high=     1
```

The item we are seeking (value 5) falls between element 0 (value 4) and element 1 (value 6). Our algorithm has an off-by-one error. This type of error occurs when one variable in a program is just one off the value it should have. In this case, the variable is our index `middle`.

We have narrowed our search to the interval 0 to 1. We then take the middle of this interval. But our algorithm is flawed. Because the interval is so small, the "middle" works out to be element 1. So we "narrow" our search from 0 to 1 to the new interval 0 to 1, and start over. Because this interval is what we started out with, we have an infinite loop.

To solve this problem, we look at the code. If the middle element matches, we print out a "found" message and exit. That fact means that we don't need to search the middle element again. So, we adjust our code from:

```
    if (data[middle] < search)
        low = middle;
    else
        high = middle;
```

to:

```
    if (data[middle] < search)
        low = middle +1;
    else
        high = middle -1;
```

The full version of our corrected program is shown in Example 15-8.

Example 15-8: search/search4.c

```
[File: search/search4.c]
/*************************************************************
 * search -- Searches a set of numbers.                     *
 *                                                          *
 * Usage:                                                   *
 *      search                                              *
 *              You will be asked numbers to look up.       *
 *                                                          *
```

Example 15-8: search/search4.c (continued)

```
 * Files:                                              *
 *       numbers.dat -- Numbers 1 per line to search   *
 *                       (Numbers must be ordered).    *
 *******************************************************/
#include <stdio.h>
#define MAX_NUMBERS     1000            /* Max numbers in file */
const char DATA_FILE[] = "numbers.dat"; /* File with numbers */

int data[MAX_NUMBERS];  /* Array of numbers to search */
int max_count;          /* Number of valid elements in data */
int main()
{
    FILE *in_filc;      /* Input file */
    int middle;         /* Middle of our search range */
    int low, high;      /* Upper/lower bound */
    int search;         /* number to search for */
    char line[80];      /* Input line */

    in_file = fopen(DATA_FILE, "r");
    if (in_file == NULL) {
        fprintf(stderr,"Error:Unable to open %s\n", DATA_FILE);
        exit (8);
    }

    /*
     * Read in data
     */

    max_count = 0;
    while (1) {
        if (fgets(line, sizeof(line),  in_file) == NULL)
            break;

        /* convert number */
        sscanf(line, "%d", &data[max_count]);
        ++max_count;
    }

    while (1) {
        printf("Enter number to search for or -1 to quit:" );
        fgets(line, sizeof(line), stdin);
        sscanf(line, "%d", &search);

        if (search == -1)
            break;

        low = 0;
        high = max_count;

        while (1) {
            if (low >= high) {
                printf("Not found\n");
```

Example 15-8: search/search4.c (continued)

```
            break;
        }

        middle = (low + high) / 2;

        if (data[middle] == search) {
            printf("Found at index %d\n", middle);
            break;
        }

        if (data[middle] < search)
            low = middle +1;
        else
            high = middle -1;
    }
}
    return (0);
}
```

Interactive debuggers work well for most programs. Sometimes they need a little help. Consider Example 15-9. We try to debug it and find it fails when `point_number` is 735. We want to put a breakpoint before the calculation is made. When the debugger inserts a breakpoint into a program, the program will execute normally until it hits the breakpoint, then control will return to the debugger. This allows the user to examine and change variables as well as perform other debugging commands. When a `continue` command is typed, the program will continue execution as if nothing had happened. The problem is that there are 734 points before the one we want, and we don't want to stop for each of them.

Example 15-9: cstop/cstop.c

```
extern float lookup(int index);

float point_color(int point_number)
{
    float correction;  /* color correction factor */
    extern float red,green,blue;/* current colors */

    correction = lookup(point_number);
    return (red*correction * 100.0 +
            blue*correction * 10.0 +
            green*correction);
}
```

How do we force the debugger to stop only when `part_number == 735`? We can do this by adding the following temporary code:

```
48      if (point_number == 735)  /* ### Temp code ### */
49          point_number = point_number;   /* ### Line to stop on ### */
```

Line 49 does nothing useful except serve a line that the debugger can stop on. We can put a breakpoint on that line with the command `stop at 49`. The program will process the first 734 points, then execute line 49, hitting the breakpoint. (Some debuggers have a conditional breakpoint. The advanced **dbx** command `stop at 49 if point_number == 735` would also work; however, your debugger may not have such advanced features.)

Runtime Errors

Runtime errors are usually the easiest to fix. Some types of runtime errors are:

- *Segmentation Violation.* This error indicates that the program tried to dereference a pointer containing a bad value.

- *Stack Overflow.* The program tried to use too many temporary variables. Sometimes, stack overflow happens because the program is too big or is using too many big temporary arrays, but most of the time this is due to infinite recursion problems. Almost all UNIX systems automatically check for this error. Turbo C++ and Borland C++ check for stack overflow only if the compile-time option −N is used.

- *Divide by 0.* Divide by 0 is an obvious error. UNIX masks the problem by reporting an *integer* divide by zero with the error message "Floating exception (core dumped)."

All these errors stop program execution. On UNIX, an image of the running program, called a *core file*, is written out.

One problem with runtime errors is that when they occur, the program execution stops immediately. The buffers for buffered files are not flushed. This can lead to some unexpected surprises. Consider Example 15-10.

Example 15-10: flush/flush.c

```c
#include <stdio.h>
int main()
{
    int i,j;    /* two random integers */

    i = 1;
    j = 0;
    printf("Starting\n");
    printf("Before divide...");
    i = i / j;  /* divide by zero error */
    printf("After\n");
    return(0);
}
```

When run, this program outputs the following:

```
Starting
Floating exception (core dumped)
```

This program might lead you to think the divide had never started, when in fact it had. What happened to the message "Before divide..."? The `printf` statement executed and put the message in a buffer, and then the program died. The buffer never got a chance to be emptied.

By putting explicit flush buffer commands inside the code, we get a truer picture of what is happening. See Example 15-11.

Example 15-11: flush2/flush2.c

```
[File: flush2/flush2.c]
#include <stdio.h>
int main()
{
    int i,j;    /* two random integers */

    i = 1;
    j = 0;

    printf("Starting\n");
    fflush(stdout);

    printf("Before divide...");
    fflush(stdout);

    i = i / j;   /* divide by zero error */

    printf("After\n");
    fflush(stdout);
    return(0);
}
```

The `flush` statement makes the I/O less efficient, but more current.

The Confessional Method of Debugging

The confessional method of debugging is one in which the programmer explains the program to someone: an interested party, an uninterested party, a wall—the actual recipient is not important, as long the programmer talks about the program.

A typical confessional session goes like this: "Hey Bill, could you take a look at this. My program has a bug in it. The output should be 8.0 and I'm getting –8.0. The output is computed using this formula and I've checked out the payment value and rate, and the date must be correct unless there is something wrong with the leap year code, which—Thank you, Bill, you've found my problem." Bill never says a word.

This type of debugging is also called a "walkthrough." Getting other people involved brings a fresh point of view to the process, and frequently, other people can spot problems that you have overlooked.

Optimization

Optimization is the art of going through a program and making the code more efficient so that it runs faster. Most compilers have a command-line switch that causes them to generate optimized code. This efficiency comes at the cost of compile time; the compiler takes a lot longer to generate code when optimization is turned on.

The other type of optimization occurs when a programmer modifies a program to use a more efficient algorithm. This section discusses this second type of optimization.

And now a word on optimization: don't. Most programs do not need to be optimized. They run fast enough. Who cares if an interactive program takes 0.5 seconds to start up instead of 0.2?

The simplest way to get your program to run faster is to get a faster computer. Many times buying a more powerful machine is cheaper than optimizing a program, and possibly introducing new errors into your code. Don't expect miracles from optimization. Usually most programs can be sped up by only 10% to 20%.

Still, to give you an idea what you can accomplish, I'll optimize a sample function. Example 15-12 initializes a matrix (two-dimensional array).

Example 15-12: matrix/matrix1.c

```
[File: matrix/matrix1.c]
#define X_SIZE 60
#define Y_SIZE 30

/* A random matrix */
int matrix[X_SIZE][Y_SIZE];

/********************************************************
 * init_matrix -- Sets every element of matrix to -1.   *
 ********************************************************/
void init_matrix(void)
{
    int x,y;    /* current element to zero */

    for (x = 0; x < X_SIZE; ++x) {
        for (y = 0; y < Y_SIZE; ++y) {
            matrix[x][y] = -1;
        }
    }
}
```

How can this function be optimized? First, we notice that we are using two local variables. By using the qualifier **register** on these variables, we tell the compiler that they are frequently used and should be placed in fast registers instead of relatively slow main memory. The number of registers varies from computer to computer. Slow machines like the PC have two registers, most UNIX systems have about 11, and supercomputers can have as many as 128. You can declare more register variables than you have registers. C will put the extra variables in main memory.

Our program now looks like Example 15-13.

Example 15-13: matrix/matrix2.c

```
[File: matrix/matrix2.c]
#define X_SIZE 60
#define Y_SIZE 30

int matrix[X_SIZE][Y_SIZE];

/***********************************************************
 * init_matrix -- Sets every element of matrix to -1.    *
 ***********************************************************/
void init_matrix(void)
{
    register int x,y;      /* current element to zero */

    for (x = 0; x < X_SIZE; ++x) {
        for (y = 0; y < Y_SIZE; ++y) {
            matrix[x][y] = -1;
        }
    }
}
```

The outer loop is executed 60 times. This means that the overhead associated with starting the inner loop is executed 60 times. If we reverse the order of the loops, we will have to deal with the inner loop only 30 times.

In general, loops should be ordered so that the innermost loop is the most complex and the outermost loop is the simplest, as in Example 15-14.

Example 15-14: matrix/matrix3.c

```
[File: matrix/matrix3.c]
#define X_SIZE 60
#define Y_SIZE 30

int matrix[X_SIZE][Y_SIZE];

/***********************************************************
 * init_matrix -- Sets every element of matrix to -1.    *
 ***********************************************************/
```

Example 15-14: matrix/matrix3.c (continued)

```c
void init_matrix(void)
{
    register int x,y;      /* current element to zero */

    for (y = 0; y < Y_SIZE; ++y) {
        for (x = 0; x < X_SIZE; ++x) {
            matrix[x][y] = -1;
        }
    }
}
```

The Power of Powers of 2

Indexing an array requires a multiply. Look at the following line from the previous example:

```c
matrix[x][y] = -1;
```

To get the location where the −1 will be stored, the program must perform the following steps:

1. Get the address of the matrix.

2. Compute x * Y_SIZE.

3. Compute y.

4. Add up all three parts to form the address.

In C, this code looks like:

```c
*(matrix + (x * Y_SIZE) + y) = -1;
```

However, we typically don't write a matrix access this way because C handles the details. But being aware of the details can help us generate more efficient code.

Almost all C compilers will convert multiples by a power of 2 (2, 4, 8, ...) into shifts, thus taking an expensive operation (multiply) and changing it into an inexpensive operation (shift).

For example:

```c
i = 32 * j;
```

is compiled as:

```c
i = j << 5; /* 2**5 == 32 */
```

Y_SIZE is 30, which is not a power of 2. By increasing it to 32, we waste some memory, but get a faster program, as shown in Example 15-15.

Because we are initializing consecutive memory locations, we can initialize the matrix by starting at the first location and storing a −1 in the next X_SIZE *

Example 15-15: matrix/matrix4.c

```
[File: matrix/matrix4.c]
#define X_SIZE 60
#define Y_SIZE 32

int matrix[X_SIZE][Y_SIZE];

/**********************************************************
 * init_matrix -- Sets every element of matrix to -1.    *
 **********************************************************/
void init_matrix(void)
{
    register int x,y;      /* current element to zero */

    for (y = 0; y < Y_SIZE; ++y) {
        for (x = 0; x < X_SIZE; ++x) {
            matrix[x][y] = -1;
        }
    }
}
```

Y_SIZE elements. (See Example 15-16.) Using this method, we cut the
number of loops down to one. The indexing of the matrix has changed from a
standard index (matrix[x][y]), requiring a shift and add to a pointer dereference (*matrix_ptr), and an increment (matrix_ptr++).

Example 15-16: matrix/matrix5.c

```
[File: matrix/matrix5.c]
#define X_SIZE 60
#define Y_SIZE 30

int matrix[X_SIZE][Y_SIZE];


/**********************************************************
 * init_matrix -- set every element of matrix to -1      *
 **********************************************************/
void init_matrix(void)
{
    register int index;            /* element counter */
    register int *matrix_ptr;

    matrix_ptr = &matrix[0][0];
    for (index = 0; index < X_SIZE * Y_SIZE; ++index) {
        *matrix_ptr = -1;
        ++matrix_ptr;
    }
}
```

But why have both a loop counter and a `matrix_ptr`? Couldn't we combine the two? In fact, we can, as shown in Example 15-17.

Example 15-17: matrix/matrix6.c

```
[File: matrix/matrix6.c]
#define X_SIZE 60
#define Y_SIZE 30

int matrix[X_SIZE][Y_SIZE];

/*********************************************************
 * init_matrix -- Sets every element of matrix to -1.   *
 *********************************************************/
void init_matrix(void)
{
    register int *matrix_ptr;

    for (matrix_ptr = &matrix[0][0];
            matrix_ptr <= &matrix[X_SIZE-1][Y_SIZE-1];
            ++matrix_ptr) {

        *matrix_ptr = -1;
    }
}
```

The function is now well optimized. The only way we could make it better is to hand-code it into assembly language. This change might make the function faster; however, assembly language is highly nonportable and very error-prone.

The library routine `memset` can be used to fill a matrix or an array with a single character value. As shown in Example 15-18, we can use it to initialize the matrix in this program. Frequently used library subroutines like `memset` are often coded into assembly language and may make use of special processor-dependent tricks to do the job faster than could be done in C.

Example 15-18: matrix/matrix7.c

```
[File: matrix/matrix7.c]
#include <memory.h>      /* Gets definition of memset */
#define X_SIZE 60
#define Y_SIZE 30

int matrix[X_SIZE][Y_SIZE];
/*********************************************************
 * init_matrix -- Sets every element of matrix to -1.   *
 *********************************************************/
void init_matrix(void)
{
    memset(matrix, -1, sizeof(matrix));
}
```

Now our function consists of only a single function call. Having to call a function just to call another function seems a shame. We have to pay for the overhead of two function calls. Instead we should call **memset** from the main function. Why don't we tell the user to rewrite his code using **memset** instead of **init_matrix**? Because he has several hundred **init_matrix** calls and doesn't want to do all that editing.

If we redefine our function as a macro, we have an **init_matrix** that looks like a function call. But, because it is a macro, it is expanded inline, avoiding all the extra overhead associated with a function call. Look at Example 15-19.

Example 15-19: matrix/matrix8.c

```
#define X_SIZE 60
#define Y_SIZE 30

int matrix[X_SIZE][Y_SIZE];

/**********************************************************
 * init_matrix -- Sets every element of matrix to -1.    *
 **********************************************************/
#define init_matrix() \
    memset(matrix, -1, sizeof(matrix));
```

Question 15-1: *Why does* **memset** *successfully initialize the matrix to −1, but when we try to use it to set every element to 1 in Example 15-20, we fail?*

Example 15-20: matrix/matrix9.c

```
#define X_SIZE 60
#define Y_SIZE 30

int matrix[X_SIZE][Y_SIZE];

#define init_matrix() \
    memset(matrix, 1, sizeof(matrix));
```

How to Optimize

Our matrix initialization function illustrates several optimizing strategies. These are:

Loop ordering
> Nested loops should be ordered with the simplest loop outermost and the most complex loops innermost.

Reduction in strength

This phrase is a fancy way of saying you should use cheap operations instead of expensive ones. Table 15-1 lists the relative cost of common operations.

Table 15-1: Relative Cost of Operations

Operation	Relative cost
printf and scanf	1000
malloc and free	800
trigonometric functions (sin, cos...)	500
floating point (any operation)	100
integer divide	30
integer multiple	20
function call	10
simple array index	6
shifts	5
add/subtract	5
pointer dereference	2
bitwise and, or, not	1
logical and, or, not	1

NOTE   Formatting functions like printf, scanf, and sscanf are extremely costly because they have to go through the format string one character at a time, looking for a format conversion character (%). Then they have to do a costly conversion between a character string and a number. These functions should be avoided in time-critical sections of code.

Powers of 2

Use a power of 2 when doing integer multiply or divide. Most compilers substitute a shift for the operation.

Pointers

Using pointers is faster than indexing an array. Pointers are, however, more tricky to use.

Macros

Using a macro eliminates the overhead associated with a function call. It also makes the code bigger and a little more difficult to debug.

Case Study: Macros Versus Functions

I once worked on writing a word processing program for a large computer manufacturer. We had a function, `next_char`, that was used to get the next character from the current file. It was used in thousands of places throughout the program. When we first tested the program with `next_char` written as a function, the program was unacceptably slow. Analyzing our program, we found that 90% of our time was spent in `next_char`. So we changed the function to a macro. The speed doubled, but, our code size went up 40% and required a memory expansion card to work. So the speed was all right, but the size was still unacceptable. We finally had to write the routine as a function in hand-optimized assembly language to get both the size and the speed to acceptable levels.

Case Study: Optimizing a Color Rendering Algorithm

I was once asked to optimize a program that did color rendering for a large picture. The problem was that the program took eight hours to process a single picture. This sluggishness limited us to doing one run a day.

The first thing I did was to run the program on a machine with a floating-point accelerator. This brought the time down to about six hours. Next, I got permission to use a high-speed RISC computer that belonged to another project, but was now sitting idle. That reduced the time to two hours.

I saved six hours solely by using faster machines. No code had changed yet.

Two fairly simple functions were being called only once from the innermost loop. Rewriting these functions as macros saved me about 15 minutes.

Next, I changed all applicable floating-point operations to integer operations. The savings amounted to 30 minutes out of an hour and 45 minutes of runtime.

I noticed the program was spending about five minutes reading an ASCII file containing a long list of floating-point numbers used in the conversion process. Knowing that `scanf` is an extremely expensive function, I cut the initialization process down to almost nothing by making the file binary. Total runtime was now down to one hour and ten minutes.

By carefully inspecting the code and using every trick I knew, I saved another five minutes, leaving me five minutes short of my goal of an hour per run.

At this point, my project was refocused and the program put in mothballs for use at some future date.

Answers

Answer 15-1: The problem is that `memset` is a *character* fill routine. An integer consists of 2 or 4 bytes (characters). Each byte is assigned the value 1. So a 2-byte integer will receive the value:

```
integer = 0x0101;
```

The 1-byte hex value for –1 is 0xFF. The two-byte hex value of –1 is 0xFFFF. So we can take two single byte –1 values, put them together, and come out with –1. This method also works for 0. Any other number will produce the wrong answer. For example, 1 is 0x01. Two bytes of this is 0x0101, or 257.

Programming Exercises

Exercise 15-1: Take one of your previous programs and run it using the interactive debugger to examine several intermediate values.

Exercise 15-2: Write a matrix multiply function. Create a test program that not only tests the function, but times it as well. Optimize it using pointers and determine the time savings.

Exercise 15-3: Write a program to sum the elements in an array. Optimize it.

Exercise 15-4: Write a program that counts the number of bits in a character array. Optimize it through the use of register integer variables. Time it on several different arrays of different sizes. How much time do you save?

Exercise 15-5: Write your own version of the library function `memcpy`. Optimize it. Most implementations of `memcpy` are written in assembly language and take advantage of all the quirks and tricks of the processor. How does your `memcpy` compare with others?

16

Floating Point

1 is equal to 2 for sufficiently large values of 1.
—Anonymous

Computers handle integers very well. The arithmetic is simple, exact, and fast. Floating-point arithmetic is the opposite. Computers do floating-point arithmetic only with great difficulty.

This chapter discusses some of the problems that can occur with floating-point. In order to understand the principles involved in floating-point arithmetic, we have defined a simple decimal floating-point format. We suggest you put aside your computer and work through these problems using pencil and paper so that you can see firsthand the problems and pitfalls that occur.

The format used by computers is very similar to the one defined in this chapter, except that instead of using base 10, computers use base 2, 8, or 16. However, all the problems demonstrated here on paper can occur in a computer.

Floating-Point Format

Floating-point numbers consist of three parts: a sign, a fraction, and an exponent. Our fraction is expressed as a 4-digit decimal. The exponent is a single-decimal digit. So, our format is:

$$\pm f.fff \times 10^{\pm e}$$

where:

±

    is the sign (plus or minus).

f.fff
    is the 4 digit fraction.

±*e*

    is the single-digit exponent with sign.

Zero is $+0.000 \times 10^{+0}$. We represent these numbers in "E" format: ±*0.000E±e*.

This format is similar to the floating-point format used in many computers. The IEEE has defined a floating-point standard (#754), but not all machines use it.

Table 16-1 shows some typical floating-point numbers.

Table 16-1: Floating-Point Examples

Notation	Number
+1.000E+0	1.0
+3.300E+4	33000.0
−8.223E-3	−0.008223
+0.000E+0	0.0

The floating-point operations defined in this chapter follow a rigid set of rules. In order to minimize errors, we make use of a *guard digit*. That is an extra digit added to the end of our fraction during computation. Many computers use a guard digit in their floating-point units.

Floating Addition/Subtraction

To add two numbers like 2.0 and 0.3, you must perform the following steps.

1. Start with the numbers:

    +2.000E+0   The number is 2.0.

    +3.000E-1   The number is 0.3.

2. Add guard digits to both numbers:

    +2.0000E+0   The number is 2.0.

    +3.0000E-1   The number is 0.3.

3. Shift the number with the smallest exponent to the right one digit, and then increment its exponent. Continue until the exponents of the two numbers match:

+2.0000E+0   The number is 2.0.

+0.3000E-0   The number is 0.3.

4. Add the two fractions. The result has the same exponent as the two numbers:

+2.0000E+0   The number is 2.0.

+0.3000E-0   The number is 0.3.

───────────────

+2.3000E+0   The result is 2.3.

5. Normalize the number by shifting it left or right until there is just one non-zero digit to the left of the decimal point. Adjust the exponent accordingly. A number like +0.1234E+0 would be normalized to +1.2340E-1. Because the number +2.3000E+0 is already normalized, we do nothing.

6. Finally, if the guard digit is greater than or equal to 5, round the next digit up; otherwise, truncate the number:

+2.3000E+0   Round the last digit.

───────────────

+2.300E+0   The result is 2.3.

For floating-point subtraction, change the sign of the second operand and add.

Multiplication

When we want to multiply two numbers such as 0.12 × 11.0, the following rules apply.

1. Add the guard digit:

+1.2000E-1   The number is 0.12.

+1.1000E+1   The number is 11.0.

2. Multiply the two fractions and add the exponents, (1.2 × 1.1 = 1.32) (-1 + 1 = 0):

+1.2000E-1   The number is 0.12.

+1.1000E+1   The number is 11.0.

───────────────

+1.3200E+0   The result is 1.32.

3. Normalize the result.

If the guard digit is greater than or equal to 5, round the next digit up. Otherwise, truncate the number:

+1.3200E+0   The number is 1.32.

Notice that in multiplying, you didn't have to go through all that shifting. The rules for multiplication are a lot shorter than those for addition. Integer multiplication is a lot slower than integer addition. In floating-point arithmetic, multiplication speed is a lot closer to that of addition.

Division

To divide numbers like 100.0 by 30.0, we must perform the following steps.

1. Add the guard digit:

   +1.0000E+2   The number is 100.0.

   +3.0000E+1   The number is 30.0.

2. Divide the fractions and subtract the exponents:

   +1.0000E+2   The number is 100.0.

   +3.0000E+1   The number is 30.0.
   _____

   +0.3333E+1   The result is 3.333.

3. Normalize the result:

   +3.3330E+0   The result is 3.333.

4. If the guard digit is greater than or equal to 5, round the next digit up. Otherwise, truncate the number:

   +3.333E+0   The result is 3.333.

Overflow and Underflow

There are limits to the size of the number that a computer can handle. What are the results of the following calculation?

```
9.000E+9 × 9.000E+9
```

Multiplying it out, we get:

```
8.1 × 10 +19
```

However, we are limited to a single-digit exponent, too small to hold 19. This example illustrates *overflow* (sometimes called exponent overflow). Some computers generate a trap when this overflow occurs, thus interrupting the program and causing an error message to be printed. Other computers are not so nice and generate a wrong answer (like 8.100E+9). Computers that follow the IEEE floating-point standard generate a special value called +Infinity.

Underflow occurs when the numbers become too small for the computer to handle. For example:

```
1.000E-9 × 1.000E-9
```

The result is:

```
1.0 × 10 -18
```

Because −18 is too small to fit into one digit, we have underflow.

Roundoff Error

Floating-point arithmetic is not exact. Everyone knows that 1+1 is 2, but did you know that 1/3 + 1/3 does not equal 2/3?

This result can be shown by the following floating-point calculations:

2/3 as floating-point is 6.667E-1.

1/3 as floating-point is 3.333-1.

+3.333E-1

+3.333E-1

+6.666E-1 or 0.6666

which is not:

+6.667E-1

Every computer has a similar problem with its floating point. For example, the number 0.2 has no exact representation in binary floating-point.

Floating-point arithmetic should never be used for money. Because we are used to dealing with dollars and cents, you might be tempted to define the amount of $1.98 as:

```
float amount = 1.98;
```

However, the more calculations you do with floating-point arithmetic, the bigger the roundoff error. Banks, credit card companies, and the IRS tend to be very fussy about money. Giving the IRS a check that's almost right is not going to make them happy. Money should be stored as an integer number of pennies.

Accuracy

How many digits of the fraction are accurate? At first glance you might be tempted to say all four digits. Those of you who have read the previous section on roundoff error might be tempted to change your answer to three.

The answer is: the accuracy depends on the calculation. Certain operations, like subtracting two numbers that are close to each other, generate inexact results. For example, consider the following equation:

```
1 - 1/3 - 1/3 - 1/3
```

    1.000E+0

  - 3.333E-1

  - 3.333E-1

  - 3.333E-1

or:

    1.000E+0

  - 0.333E+0

  - 0.333E+0

  - 0.333E+0
  _____

  0.0010E+0 or 1.000E-3

The correct answer is 0.000E+0 and we got 1.000E-3. The very first digit of the fraction is wrong. This error is an example of the problem called "roundoff error" that can occur during floating-point operations.

Minimizing Roundoff Error

There are many techniques for minimizing roundoff error. Guard digits have already been discussed. Another trick is to use **double** instead of **float**. This solution gives you approximately twice the accuracy as well as an enormously greater range. It also pushes away the minimization problem twice as far. But roundoff errors still can creep in.

Advanced techniques for limiting the problems caused by floating point can be found in books on numerical analysis. They are beyond the scope of this text. The purpose of this chapter is to give you some idea of the sort of problems that can be encountered.

Floating-point by its very nature is not exact. People tend to think of computers as very accurate machines. They can be, but they also can give wildly wrong results. You should be aware of the places where errors can slip into your program.

Determining Accuracy

There is a simple way of determining how accurate your floating point is (for simple calculations). The method used in the following program is to add 1.0+0.1, 1.0+0.01, 1.0+0.001, and so on until the second number gets so small that it makes no difference in the result.

The C language specifies that all floating-point numbers are to be done in **double**. This method means that the expression:

```
float number1, number2;

    . . .

while (number1 + number2 != number1)
```

is equivalent to:

```
while (double(number1) + double(number2) != double(number1))
```

When using the 1+0.001 trick, the automatic conversion of **float** to **double** may give a distorted picture of the accuracy of your machine. (In one case, 84 bits of accuracy were reported for a 32-bit format.) Example 16-1 computes both the accuracy of floating-point numbers as used in equations and floating-point numbers as stored in memory. Note the trick used to determine the accuracy of the floating-point numbers in storage.

Example 16-1: float/float.c

```
#include <stdio.h>
int main()
{
    /* two numbers to work with */
    float number1, number2;
    float result;            /* result of calculation */
    int   counter;           /* loop counter and accuracy check */

    number1 = 1.0;
    number2 = 1.0;
    counter = 0;

    while (number1 + number2 != number1) {
        ++counter;
        number2 = number2 / 10.0;
    }
    printf("%2d digits accuracy in calculations\n", counter);

    number2 = 1.0;
    counter = 0;

    while (1) {
        result = number1 + number2;
        if (result == number1)
            break;
        ++counter;
        number2 = number2 / 10.0;
    }
    printf("%2d digits accuracy in storage\n", counter);
    return (0);
}
```

Running this on a Sun-3/50 with a MC68881 floating-point chip, we get:

```
20 digits accuracy in calculations
 8 digits accuracy in storage
```

This program gives only an approximation of the floating-point precision arithmetic. A more precise definition can be found in the standard include file *float.h*.

Precision and Speed

A variable of type **double** has about twice the precision of a normal **float** variable. Most people assume that double-precision arithmetic takes longer than single-precision arithmetic. This statement is not always true. Remember that C requires that all the arithmetic must be done in **double**.

For the equation:

```
float answer, number1, number2;

answer = number1 + number2;
```

C must perform the following steps:

1. Convert number1 from single to double precision.

2. Convert number2 from single to double precision.

3. Double-precision add.

4. Convert result into single-precision arithmetic and store in *answer*.

If the variables were of type **double**, C would only have to perform these steps:

1. Carry out a double-precision add.

2. Store result in *answer*.

As you can see, the second form is a lot simpler, requiring three fewer conversions. In some cases, converting a program from single-precision arithmetic to double- precision arithmetic makes it run *faster*.

Many computers, including the PC and Sun series machines, have a floating-point processor that does all the floating-point arithmetic. Actual tests using the Motorola 68881 floating-point chip (which is used in the Sun/3) as well as the floating-point on the PC show that single-precision and double-precision run at the same speed.

Power Series

Many trigonometry functions are computed using a power series. For example, the series for sine is:

$$\sin(x) = x - \frac{x^3}{3!} + \frac{x^5}{5!} - \frac{x^7}{7!} + \ldots$$

The question is: how many terms do we need to get 4-digit accuracy? Table 16-2 contains the terms for the $\sin(\pi/2)$.

Table 16-2: Terms for the $\sin(\pi/2)$

	Term	Value	Total
1	x	1.571E+0	
2	$\frac{x^3}{3!}$	6.462E-1	9.248E-1
3	$\frac{x^5}{5!}$	7.974E-2	1.005E+0
4	$\frac{x^7}{7!}$	4.686E-3	9.998E-1
5	$\frac{x^9}{9!}$	1.606E-4	1.000E+0
6	$\frac{x^{11}}{11!}$	3.604E-6	1.000E+0

From this, we conclude that five terms are needed. However, if we try to compute the $\sin(\pi)$, we get the values in Table 16-3.

Table 16-3: Terms for the $\sin(\pi)$

	Term	Value	Total
1	x	3.142E+0	
2	$\frac{x^3}{3!}$	5.170E+0	-2.028E+0
3	$\frac{x^5}{5!}$	2.552E-0	5.241E-1
4	$\frac{x^7}{7!}$	5.998E-1	-7.570E-2
5	$\frac{x^9}{9!}$	8.224E-2	6.542E-3
6	$\frac{x^{11}}{11!}$	7.381E-3	-8.388E-4
7	$\frac{x^{13}}{13!}$	4.671E-4	-3.717E-4

Table 16-3: Terms for the sin(π) (continued)

	Term	Value	Total
8	$\dfrac{x^{15}}{15!}$	2.196E-5	-3.937E-4
9	$\dfrac{x^{17}}{17!}$	7.970E-7	-3.929E-4
10	$\dfrac{x^{19}}{19!}$	2.300E-8	-3.929E-4

π needs nine terms. So different angles require a different number of terms. (A program for computing the sine to four-digit accuracy showing intermediate terms is included in Appendix D, *A Program to Compute a Sine Using a Power Series.*)

Compiler designers face a dilemma when it comes to designing a sine function. If they know ahead of time the number of terms to use, they can optimize their algorithms for that number of terms. However, they lose accuracy for some angles. So a compromise must be struck between speed and accuracy.

Don't assume that because the number came from the computer, it is accurate. The library functions can generate bad answers—especially when you work with excessively large or small values. Most of the time, you will not have any problems with these functions, but you should be aware of their limitations.

Finally there is the question of what is sin(1000000)? Our floating-point format is good for only four digits. The sine function is cyclical. That is, sin(0) = sin(2π) = sin(4π). ... So sin(1000000) is the same as sin(1000000 mod 2π).

Note that our floating-point format is good to only four digits, so sin(1000000) is actually sin(1000000 ± 1000). Because 1000 is bigger than 2π, the error renders meaningless the result of the sine.

How Hot Is It?

I attended a physics class at Caltech that was taught by two professors. One was giving a lecture on the sun when he said, "... and the mean temperature of the inside of the sun is 13,000,000 to 25,000,000 degrees." At this point, the other instructor broke in and asked "Is that Celsius or Kelvin (absolute zero or Celsius–273)?"

The lecturer turned to the board for a minute, then said, "What's the difference?" The moral of the story is that when your calculations have a possible error of 12,000,000, a difference of 273 doesn't mean very much.

Programming Exercises

Exercise 16-1: Write a program that uses strings to represent floating-point numbers in the format used in this chapter. A typical string might look like `"+1.333E+2"`. The program should have functions to read, write, add, subtract, multiply, and divide floating-point numbers.

Exercise 16-2: Create a set of functions to handle fixed-point numbers. A fixed-point number has a constant (fixed) number of digits to the right of the decimal point.

III

Advanced Programming Concepts

In this part we explore the advanced features of C as well as advanced programming tasks such as modular programming and program porting. Finally we explore little-used features such as the ancient K&R C syntax and some of C's darker corners.

- Chapter 17, *Advanced Pointers*, describes advanced uses of pointers for constructing dynamic structures such as linked lists and trees.

- Chapter 18, *Modular Programming*, shows how to split a program into several files and use modular programming techniques. The *make* utility is explained in more detail.

- Chapter 19, *Ancient Compilers*, describes the old, pre-ANSI C language. Although such compilers are rare today, a lot of code was written for them and there are still a large number of programs out there that use the old syntax.

- Chapter 20, *Portability Problems*, describes the problems that can occur when you *port* a program (move it from one machine to another).

- Chapter 21, *C's Dustier Corners*, describes the **do/while** statement, the comma operator, and the ? and : operators.

- Chapter 22, *Putting It All Together*, details the steps necessary to take a complex program from conception to completion. Information-hiding and modular programming techniques are emphasized.

- Chapter 23, *Programming Adages*, lists some programming adages that will help you construct good C programs.

17

Advanced Pointers

A race that binds
Its body in chains and calls them Liberty,
And calls each fresh link progress.
—Robert Buchanan

One of the more useful and complex features of C is its use of pointers. With pointers, you can create complex data structures like linked lists and trees. Figure 17-1 illustrates some of these data structures.

Up to now, all of our data structures have been allocated by the compiler as either permanent or temporary variables. With pointers, we can create and allocate *dynamic data structures* that can grow or shrink as needed. In this chapter, you will learn how to use some of the more common dynamic data structures.

Pointers and Structures

Structures can contain pointers, even a pointer to another instance of the same structure. In the following example:

```
struct node {
    struct node *next_ptr;   /* Pointer to the next node */
    int value;               /* Data for this node */
}
```

the structure `node` is illustrated in Figure 17-2. This structure contains two fields, one named `value`, shown here as the section containing the number 2. The other is a pointer to another structure. The field `next_ptr` is shown as an arrow.

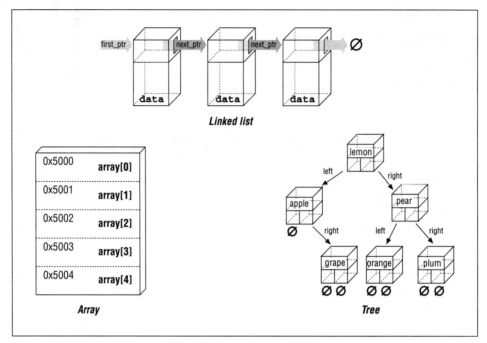

Figure 17-1: How pointers may be used

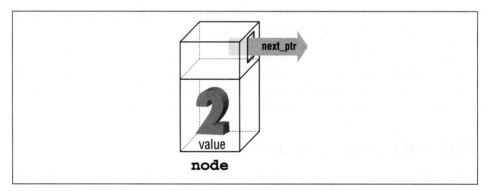

Figure 17-2: Node

The question is: how do we create **nodes**? We could declare them explicitly:

```
struct node *node_1;
struct node *node_2;
```

and so on. The problem with this structure is that we can declare only a limited number of nodes. What we need is a procedure to which we can say, "I want a new node," and then have the procedure create the node for us.

The procedure `malloc` does the job. It allocates storage for a variable and then returns a pointer. It is used to create new things out of thin air (actually out of an area of memory called the *heap*). Up to now, we've used pointers solely to point to named variables. So if we used a statement like:

```
int data;
int *number_ptr;
number_ptr = &data;
```

the thing that we are pointing to has a name (`data`). The function `malloc` creates a new, unnamed variable and returns a pointer to it. The "things" created by `malloc` can be referenced only through pointers, never by name.

The definition of `malloc` is:

```
void *malloc(unsigned int);
```

The function `malloc` takes a single argument: the number of bytes to allocate. If `malloc` runs out of memory, it returns a null pointer.

In the declaration, **void** `*` is used to indicate that `malloc` returns a generic pointer (a pointer that can point to any type of thing). So C uses **void** for two purposes:

- When used as a type in a function declaration, **void** indicates that the function returns no value.

- When used in a pointer declaration, **void** defines a generic pointer.

We will start using `malloc` by allocating space for simple structures. As we go on, we will see how to create bigger structures and link them together to form very complex data structures. Example 17-1 allocates storage for a character string 80 bytes long (`'\0'` included). The variable `string_ptr` points to this storage.

Example 17-1: Allocating Memory for a String

```
[#include <stdlib.h>]
main()
{
    /* Pointer to a string that will be allocated from the heap */
    char *string_ptr;

    string_ptr = malloc(80);
```

Suppose we are working on a complex database that contains (among other things) a mailing list. The structure `person` is used to hold the data for each person:

```
struct person {
    char    name[30];           /* name of the person */
```

```
    char    address[30];        /* where he lives */
    char    city_state_zip[30]; /* Part 2 of address */
    int     age;                /* his age */
    float   height;             /* his height in inches */
}
```

We could use an array to hold our mailing list, but an array is an inefficient use of memory. Every entry takes up space, whether or not it is used. What we need is a way to allocate space for only those entries that are used. We can use `malloc` to allocate space on an as-needed basis.

To create a new person, we use the code:

```
/* Pointer to a person structure to be allocated from the heap */
struct person *new_item_ptr;

new_item_ptr = malloc(sizeof(struct person));
```

We determine the number of bytes to allocate by using the expression `sizeof(struct person)`. Without the `sizeof` operator, we would have to count the number of bytes in our structure, a difficult and error-prone operation.

The size of the heap, although large, is finite. When `malloc` runs out of room, it will return a `NULL` pointer. Good programming practice tells you to check the return value of each `malloc` call to ensure that you really got the memory.

```
new_item_ptr = malloc(sizeof(struct person));
if (new_item_ptr == NULL) {
    fprintf(stderr, "Out of memory\n");
    exit (8);
}
```

Although checking the return value of `malloc` is good programming practice, far too often the check is omitted and the programmer assumes that he got the memory whether on not he really did. The result is that far too many programs crash when they run out of memory.

The problem has gotten so bad that when C++ was designed, it contained a special error handling mechanism for out-of-memory conditions.

free Function

The function `malloc` gets memory from the heap. To free that memory after you are done with it, use the function `free`. The general form of the `free` function is:

```
free(pointer);
pointer = NULL;
```

where *pointer* is a pointer previously allocated by `malloc`. (We don't have to set *pointer* to `NULL`; however, doing so prevents us from trying to used freed memory.)

The following is an example that uses **malloc** to get storage and **free** to dispose of it:

```
const int DATA_SIZE = (16 * 1024); /* Number of bytes in the buffer */
void copy(void)
{
    char *data_ptr;          /* Pointer to large data buffer */
    data_ptr = malloc(DATA_SIZE);       /* Get the buffer */
    /*
     * Use the data buffer to copy a file
     */
    free(data_ptr);
    data_ptr = NULL;
}
```

But what happens if we forget to free our pointer? The buffer becomes dead. That is, the memory management system thinks that the buffer is being used, but no one is using it. If the **free** statement was removed from the function **copy**, then each successive call would eat up another 16K of memory. Do this often enough and your program will run out of memory.

The other problem that can occur is using memory that has been freed. When **free** is called, the memory is returned to the memory pool and can be reused. Using a pointer after a **free** call is similar to an out-of-bounds error for an index to an array. You are using memory that belongs to someone else. This error can cause unexpected results or program crashes.

Linked List

Suppose you are writing a program that displays a series of flash cards as a teaching drill. The problem is that you don't know ahead of time how many cards the user will supply. One solution is to use a linked-list data structure. In that way, the list can grow as more cards are added. Also, as we will see later, linked lists may be combined with other data structures to handle extremely complex data.

A *linked list* is a chain of items in which each item points to the next one in the chain. Think about the treasure hunt games you played when you were a kid. You were given a note that said, "Look in the mailbox." Racing to the mailbox you found your next clue, "Look in the big tree in the back yard," and so on until you found your treasure (or you got lost). In a treasure hunt, each clue points to the next one.[*]

---

[*] A woman was having a treasure hunt at her house for her daughter's Girl Scout troop when the doorbell rang. It was the mailman. "Lady," he said, "I've looked behind the big tree, and I've looked in the birdhouse, and I've even looked under the mat, but I still can't find your letter."

A linked list is shown in Figure 17-3.

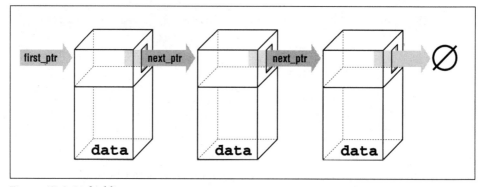

Figure 17-3: Linked list

The structure declarations for a linked list are:

```
struct linked_list {
    char    data[30];              /* data in this element */
    struct linked_list *next_ptr; /* pointer to next element */
};
struct linked_list *first_ptr = NULL;
```

The variable `first_ptr` points to the first element of the list. In the beginning, before we insert any elements into the list (the list is empty), this variable is initialized to NULL.

In Figure 17-4, a new element is created and then inserted at the beginning of an existing list. To insert a new element into a linked list in C, we execute the following steps:

1. Create a structure for the item.

```
new_item_ptr = malloc(sizeof(struct linked_list));
```

2. Store the item in the new element.

```
(*new_item_ptr).data = item;
```

3. Make the first element of the list point to the new element.

```
(*new_item_ptr).next_ptr = first_ptr;
```

4. The new element is now the first element.

```
first_ptr = new_item_ptr;
```

The code for the actual program is:

```
void add_list(char *item)
{
    /* pointer to the next item in the list */
```

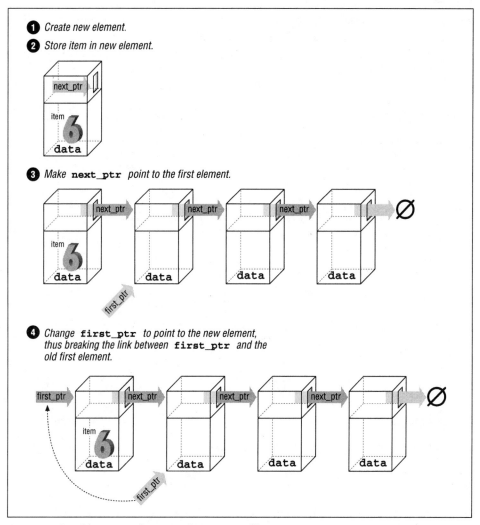

Figure 17-4: Adding new element to beginning of list

```
        struct linked_list *new_item_ptr;

        new_item_ptr = malloc(sizeof(struct linked_list));
        strcpy((*new_item_ptr).data, item);
        (*new_item_ptr).next_ptr = first_ptr;
        first_ptr = new_item_ptr;
}
```

To see if the name is in the list, we must search each element of the list until we either find the name or run out of data. Example 17-2 contains the `find` program, which searches through the items in the list.

Example 17-2: find/find.c

```
[File: find/find.c]
#include <stdio.h>
#include <string.h>

struct linked_list {
    struct linked_list *next_ptr;        /* Next item in the list */
    char *data;                          /* Data for the list */
};

struct linked_list *first_ptr;
/***********************************************************
 * find -- Looks for a data item in the list.            *
 *                                                        *
 * Parameters                                             *
 *      name -- Name to look for in the list.             *
 *                                                        *
 * Returns                                                *
 *      1 if name is found.                               *
 *      0 if name is not found.                           *
 ***********************************************************/
int find(char *name)
{
    /* current structure we are looking at */
    struct linked_list *current_ptr;

    current_ptr = first_ptr;

    while ((strcmp(current_ptr->data, name) != 0) &&
           (current_ptr != NULL))
        current_ptr = (*current_ptr)->next_ptr;

    /*
     * If current_ptr is null, we fell off the end of the list and
     * didn't find the name
     */
    return (current_ptr != NULL);
}
```

Question 17-1: *Why does running this program sometimes result in a bus error? Other times, it will return "1" for an item that is not in the list.*

Structure Pointer Operator

In our `find` program, we had to use the cumbersome notation `(*current_ptr).data` to access the data field of the structure. C provides a shorthand for this construct using the structure pointer (—>) operator. The dot (.) operator indicates the field of a structure. The —> indicates the field of a structure pointer.

The following two expressions are equivalent:

```
(*current_ptr).data = value;
current_ptr->data = value;
```

Ordered Linked Lists

So far, we have added new elements only to the head of a linked list. Suppose we want to add elements in order. Figure 17-5 is an example of an ordered linked list.

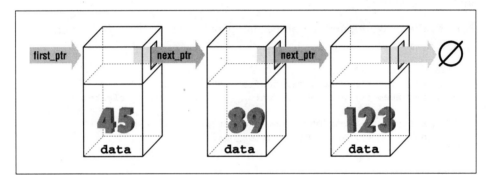

Figure 17-5: Ordered list

The subroutine in Example 17-3 implements this function. The first step is to locate the insert point. **head_ptr** points to the first element of the list. The program moves the variable **before_ptr** along the list until it finds the proper place for the insert. The variable **after_ptr** is set to point to the element that follows the insertion. The new element will be inserted between these elements.

Example 17-3: list/list.p1

```
void enter(struct item *first_ptr, const int value)
{
    struct item *before_ptr;            /* Item before this one */
    struct item *after_ptr;             /* Item after this one */
    struct item *new_item_ptr;          /* Item to add */

    /* Create new item to add to the list */

    before_ptr = first_ptr;             /* Start at the beginning */
    after_ptr =  before_ptr->next_ptr;

    while (1) {
        if (after_ptr == NULL)
```

Example 17-3: list/list.p1 (continued)

```
        break;

    if (after_ptr->value >= value)
        break;

    /* Advance the pointers */
    after_ptr = after_ptr->next_ptr;
    before_ptr = before_ptr->next_ptr;
}
```

In Figure 17-6, we have positioned `before_ptr` so that it points to the element before the insert point. The variable `after_ptr` points to the element after the insert. In other words, we are going to put our new element in between `before_ptr` and `after_ptr`.

Now that we have located the proper insert point, all we have to do is create the new element and link it in:

```
[File: list/list.p2]
    new_item_ptr = malloc(sizeof(struct item));
    new_item_ptr->value = value;        /* Set value of item */

    before_ptr->next_ptr = new_item_ptr;
    new_item_ptr->next_ptr = after_ptr;
}
```

Our new element must now be linked in. The first link we make is between the element pointed to by `before_ptr` (number 45) and our new element, `new_item_ptr` (number 53). This is done with the statement:

```
    before_ptr->next_ptr = new_item_ptr;
```

Next, we must link the new element, `new_item_ptr` (number 53), to the element pointed to by `after_ptr` (number 89). This is accomplished with the code:

```
    new_item_ptr->next_ptr = after_ptr;
```

Double-Linked Lists

A double-linked list contains two links. One link points forward to the next element; the other points backward to the previous element.

The structure for a double-linked list is:

```
struct double_list {
    int data;                           /* data item */
    struct  double_list *next_ptr;      /* forward link */
    struct  double_list *previous_ptr;/* backward link */
};
```

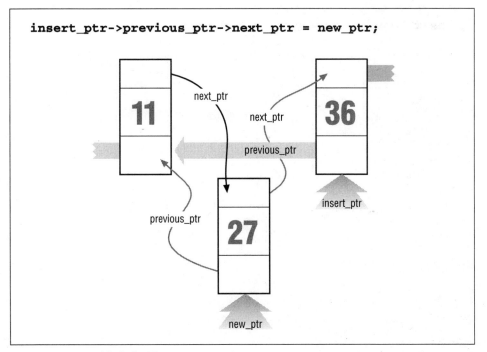

Figure 17-10: Double-linked list insert, part 3

the list alphabetically. The advantage of a tree over a linked list is that searching a tree takes considerably less time.

In this example, each node stores a single word. The left subtree stores all words less than the current word, and the right subtree stores all the words greater than the current word.

For example, Figure 17-13 shows how we descend the tree to look for the word "orange." We would start at the root "lemon." Because "orange" > "lemon," we would descend to the right link and go to "pear." Because "orange" < "pear," we descend to the left link and we have "orange."

Recursion is extremely useful with trees. Our rules for recursion are:

1. The function must make things simpler. This rule is satisfied by trees, because as you descend the hierarchy there is less to search.

2. There must be some endpoint. A tree offers two endpoints, either you find a match, or you reach a null node.

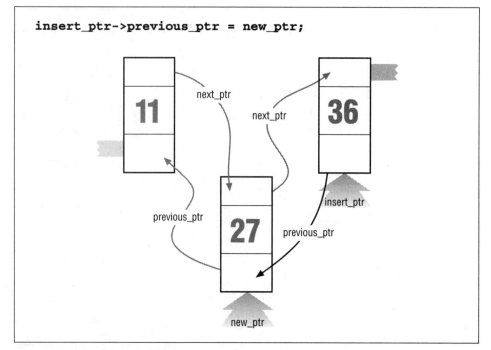

Figure 17-11: Double-linked list insert, part 4

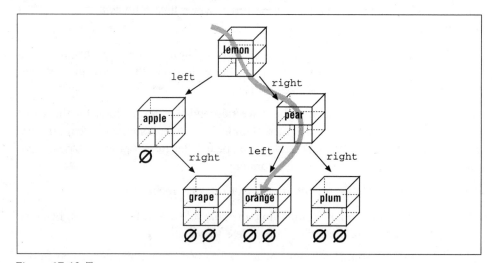

Figure 17-12: Tree

The algorithm for inserting a word in a tree is:

1. If this is a null tree (or subtree), create a one-node tree with this word in it.

2. If the current node contains the word, do nothing.

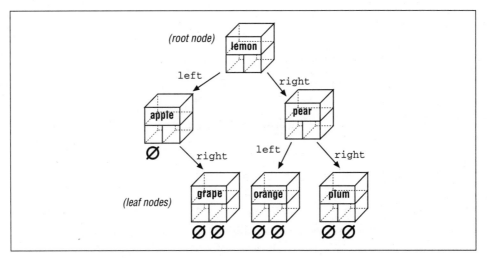

Figure 17-13: Tree search

3. Otherwise, perform a recursive call to "insert word" to insert the word in the left or right subtree, depending on the value of the word.

To see how this algortithm works, consider what happens when we insert the word "fig" into the tree as shown in Figure 17-13. First, we check the word "fig" against "lemon." "Fig" is smaller, so we go to "apple." Because "fig" is bigger, we go to "grape." Because "fig" is smaller than "grape," we try the left link. It is NULL, so we create a new node. The function to enter a value into a tree is:

```
void enter(struct node **node, char *word)
{
    int  result;                /* result of strcmp */
    char *save_string();        /* save a string on the heap */
    void memory_error();        /* tell user no more room */

    /*
     * If the current node is null, then we have reached the bottom
     * of the tree and must create a new node
     */
    if ((*node) == NULL) {

        /* Allocate memory for a new node */
        (*node) = malloc(sizeof(struct node));
        if ((*node) == NULL)
            memory_error();

        /* Initialize the new node */
        (*node)->left = NULL;
        (*node)->right = NULL;
        (*node)->word = save_string(word);
        return;
    }
```

```
          /* Check to see where our word goes */
          result = strcmp((*node)->word, word);

          /* The current node
           * already contains the word,
           * no entry necessary */
          if (result == 0)
              return;

          /* The word must be entered in the left or right subtree */
          if (result < 0)
              enter(&(*node)->right, word);
          else
              enter(&(*node)->left, word);
      }
```

This function is passed a pointer to the root of the tree. If the root is NULL, it creates the node. Because we are changing the value of a pointer, we must pass *a pointer to the pointer*. (We pass one level of pointer because that's the variable type outside the function; we pass the second level because we have to change it.)

Printing a Tree

Despite the complex nature of a tree structure, it is easy to print. Again, we use recursion. The printing algorithm is:

1. For the null tree, print nothing.

2. Print the data that comes before this node (left tree), then print this node and print the data that comes after this node (right tree).

The code for print_tree is:

```
      void print_tree(struct node *top)
      {
          if (top == NULL)
              return;                    /* short tree */
          print_tree(top->left);
          printf("%s\n", top->word);
          print_tree(top->right);
      }
```

Rest of Program

Now that we have defined the data structure, all we need to complete the program is a few more functions.

The main function checks for the correct number of arguments and then calls the scanner and the print_tree routine.

The scan function reads the file and breaks it into words. It uses the standard macro isalpha. This macro, defined in the standard header file *ctype.h*, returns nonzero if its argument is a letter and 0 otherwise. The macro is defined in the standard include file *ctype.b*. After a word is found, the function **enter** is called to put it in the tree.

save_string creates the space for a string on the heap, then returns the pointer to it.

memory_error is called if a **malloc** fails. This program handles the out-of-memory problem by writing an error message and quitting.

Example 17-4 is a listing of *words.c*.

Example 17-4: words/words.c

```
[File: words/words.c]
/************************************************************
 * words -- Scan a file and print out a list of words    *
 *            in ASCII order.                             *
 *                                                        *
 * Usage:                                                 *
 *      words <file>                                      *
 ************************************************************/
#include <stdio.h>
#include <ctype.h>
#include <string.h>
#include <stdlib.h>

struct node {
    struct node    *left;       /* tree to the left */
    struct node    *right;      /* tree to the right */
    char           *word;       /* word for this tree */
};

/* the top of the tree */
static struct node *root = NULL;

/************************************************************
 * memory_error -- Writes error and dies.                *
 ************************************************************/
void memory_error(void)
{
    fprintf(stderr, "Error:Out of memory\n");
    exit(8);
}


/************************************************************
 * save_string -- Saves a string on the heap.            *
 *                                                        *
 * Parameters                                             *
 *      string -- String to save.                        *
 *                                                        *
 * Returns                                                *
 *      pointer to malloc-ed section of memory with       *
 *      the string copied into it.                        *
 ************************************************************/
```

Example 17-4: words/words.c (continued)

```c
char *save_string(char *string)
{
    char *new_string;    /* where we are going to put string */

    new_string = malloc((unsigned) (strlen(string) + 1));

    if (new_string == NULL)
        memory_error();

    strcpy(new_string, string);
    return (new_string);
}
/********************************************************
 * enter -- Enters a word into the tree.                *
 *                                                      *
 * Parameters                                           *
 *      node -- Current node we are looking at.         *
 *      word -- Word to enter.                          *
 ********************************************************/
void enter(struct node **node, char *word)
{
    int   result;         /* result of strcmp */

    char *save_string(char *);   /* save a string on the heap */

    /*
     * If the current node is null, we have reached the bottom
     * of the tree and must create a new node.
     */
    if ((*node) == NULL) {

        /* Allocate memory for a new node */
        (*node) = malloc(sizeof(struct node));
        if ((*node) == NULL)
            memory_error();

        /* Initialize the new node */
        (*node)->left = NULL;
        (*node)->right = NULL;
        (*node)->word = save_string(word);
        return;
    }
    /* Check to see where the word goes */
    result = strcmp((*node)->word, word);

    /* The current node already contains the word, no entry necessary */
    if (result == 0)
        return;

    /* The word must be entered in the left or right subtree */
    if (result < 0)
        enter(&(*node)->right, word);
    else
```

Example 17-4: words/words.c (continued)

```c
        enter(&(*node)->left, word);
}
/***********************************************************
 * scan -- Scans the file for words.                       *
 *                                                         *
 * Parameters                                              *
 *      name -- Name of the file to scan.                  *
 ***********************************************************/
void scan(char *name)
{
    char word[100];      /* word we are working on */
    int  index;          /* index into the word */
    int  ch;             /* current character */
    FILE *in_file;       /* input file */

    in_file = fopen(name, "r");
    if (in_file == NULL) {
        fprintf(stderr, "Error:Unable to open %s\n", name);
        exit(8);
    }
    while (1) {
        /* scan past the whitespace */
        while (1) {
            ch = fgetc(in_file);

            if (isalpha(ch) || (ch == EOF))
                break;
        }

        if (ch == EOF)
            break;

        word[0] = ch;
        for (index = 1; index < sizeof(word); ++index) {
            ch = fgetc(in_file);
            if (!isalpha(ch))
                break;
            word[index] = ch;
        }
        /* put a null on the end */
        word[index] = '\0';

        enter(&root, word);
    }
    fclose(in_file);
}
/***********************************************************
 * print_tree -- Prints out the words in a tree.           *
 *                                                         *
 * Parameters                                              *
 *      top -- The root of the tree to print.              *
 ***********************************************************/
```

Example 17-4: words/words.c (continued)

```
void print_tree(struct node *top)
{
    if (top == NULL)
        return;                      /* short tree */

    print_tree(top->left);
    printf("%s\n", top->word);
    print_tree(top->right);
}

int main(int argc, char *argv[])
{
    if (argc != 2) {
        fprintf(stderr, "Error:Wrong number of parameters\n");
        fprintf(stderr, "       on the command line\n");
        fprintf(stderr, "Usage is:\n");
        fprintf(stderr, "    words 'file'\n");
        exit(8);
    }
    scan(argv[1]);
    print_tree(root);
    return (0);
}
```

Question 17-2: *I once made a program that read the dictionary into memory using a tree structure, and then used the structure in a program that searched for misspelled words. Although trees are supposed to be fast, this program was so slow that you would think I used a linked list. Why?*

Hint: Graphically construct a tree using the words "able," "baker," "cook," "delta," and "easy," and look at the result.

Data Structures for a Chess Program

One of the classic problems in artificial intelligence is the game of chess. As this book goes to press, the Grandmaster who beat the world's best chess-playing computer last year has lost to the computer this year (1997).

We are going to design a data structure for a chess-playing program. In chess, you have several possible moves that you can make. Your opponent has many responses to which you have many answers, and so on, back and forth, for several levels of moves.

Our data structure is beginning to look like a tree. This structure is not a binary tree because we have more than two branches for each node, as shown in Figure 17-14.

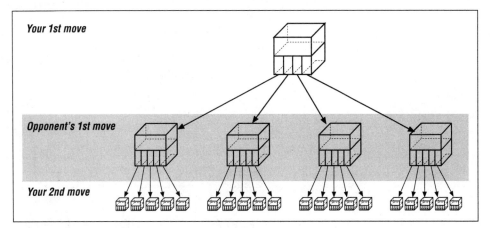

Figure 17-14: Chess tree

We are tempted to use the following data structure:

```
struct chess {
    struct board board;      /* Current board position */
    struct next {
        struct move;         /* Our next move */
        struct *chess_ptr;   /* Pointer to the resulting position */
    } next[MAX_MOVES];
};
```

The problem is that the number of moves from any given position can vary dramatically. For example, in the beginning you have lots of pieces running around.* Things like rooks, queens, and bishops can move any number of squares in a straight line. When you reach the end game (in an evenly matched game), each side probably has only a few pawns and one major piece. The number of possible moves has been greatly reduced.

We want to be as efficient in our storage as possible, because a chess program will stress the limits of our machine. We can reduce our storage requirements by changing the next-move array into a linked list. Our resulting structure is:

```
struct next {
    struct move this_mode;   /* Our next move */
    struct *chess_ptr;       /* Pointer to the resulting position */
};
struct chess {
    struct board board;      /* Current board position */
    struct next *list_ptr;   /* List of moves we can make from here
*/
    struct move this_move;   /* The move we are making */
};
```

---

* Trivia question: What are the 21 moves that you can make in chess from the starting position? You can move each pawn up one (8 moves) or two (8 more), and the knights can move out to the left and right (4 more: 8+8+4=20).   What's the 21st move?

This is shown graphically in Figure 17-15.

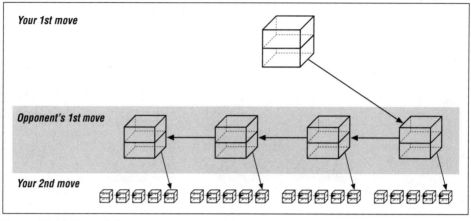

Figure 17-15: Revised chess structure

The new version adds a little complexity, but saves a great deal of storage. In the first version, we must allocate storage for pointers to all possible moves. If we have only a few possible moves, we waste a lot of storage for pointers to unused moves. Using a linked list, we allocate storage on an on-demand basis. So if there are 30 possible moves, our list is 30 long; but if there are only 3 possible moves, our list is 3 long. The list grows only as needed, resulting in a more efficient use of storage.

Answers

Answer 17-1: The problem is with the statement:

```
while ((strcmp(current_ptr->data, name) != 0) &&
       (current_ptr != NULL))
```

current_ptr->data is checked *before* we check to see if current_ptr is a valid pointer (!= NULL). If the pointer is NULL, we can easily check a random memory location that could contain anything. The solution is to check current_ptr before checking what it is pointing to:

```
while (current_ptr != NULL) {
    if (strcmp(current_ptr->data, name) == 0)
        break;
}
```

Answer 17-2: The problem was that because the first word in the dictionary was the smallest, every other word used the right-hand link. In fact, because the entire list was ordered, only the right-hand link was used. Although this structure was defined as a tree structure, the result was a linked list, as shown in Figure 17-16.

Some of the more advanced books on data structures, like Niklaus Wirth's book *Algorithms + Data Structures = Programs*, discuss ways of preventing this error by balancing a binary tree.

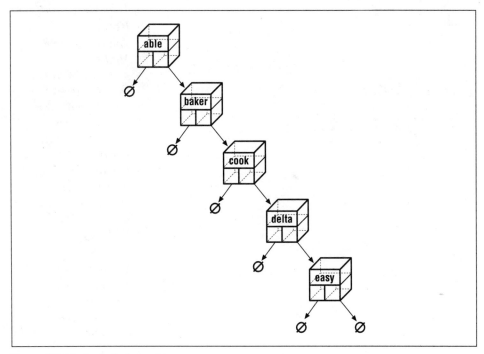

Figure 17-16: An imbalanced tree

Trivia Answer: You give up. That's right; the 21st move is to resign.

Programming Exercises

Exercise 17-1: Write a cross-reference program.

Exercise 17-2: Write a function to delete an element of a linked list.

Exercise 17-3: Write a function to delete an element of a double-linked list.

Exercise 17-4: Write a function to delete an element of a tree.

18

Modular Programming

Many hands make light work.
—John Heywood

All along, we have been dealing with small programs. As programs grow larger and larger, it is more desirable to split them into sections or modules. C allows programs to be split into multiple files, compiled separately, and then combined (linked) to form a single program.

In this chapter, we will go through a programming example, discussing the C techniques needed to create good modules. You will be shown how to use *make* to put these modules together to form a program.

Modules

A module is a collection of functions that perform related tasks. For example, a module could exist to handle database functions such as `lookup`, `enter`, and `sort`. Another module could handle complex numbers, and so on.

Also, as programming problems get bigger, more and more programmers are needed to finish them. An efficient way of splitting up a large project is to assign each programmer a different module. In this manner, each programmer only worries about the internal details of a particular module.

In this chapter, we will discuss a module to handle *infinite arrays*. The functions in this package allow the user to store data into an array without worrying about its size. The infinite array grows as needed (limited only by the amount of memory in the computer). The array will be used to store data for a histogram, but can be used to store things like line numbers from a cross-reference program or other types of data.

Public and Private

Modules are divided into two parts: *public* and *private*. The public part tells the user how to call the functions in the module. It contains the definition of data structures and functions that are to be used outside the module. These definitions are put in a header file, and the file must be included in any program that depends on that module. In our infinite array example, we have put the public declarations in the file *ia.h*, which we will look at shortly. Figure 18-1 illustrates the relationship between the various parts of the infinite array package.

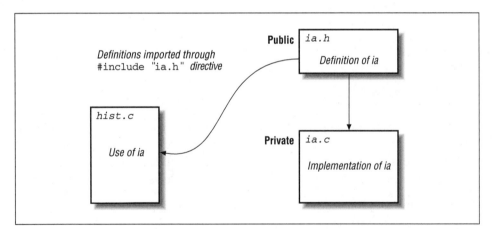

Figure 18-1: Definition, implementation, and use of the infinite array

Anything that is internal to the module is private. Everything that is not directly usable by the outside world should be kept private.

One of the advantages of C++ over C is that you can explicitly declare what is public and what is private, and prevent unauthorized modification of private data.

The extern Modifier

The **extern** modifier is used to indicate that a variable or function is defined outside the current file. For example, look at the contents of two files, *main.c* and *count.c*.

File main.c

```
#include <stdio.h>
/* number of times through the loop */
extern int counter;

/* routine to increment the counter */
extern void inc_counter(void);

main()
{
    int   index; /* loop index */

    for (index = 0; index < 10; index++)
        inc_counter();
    printf("Counter is %d\n", counter);
    return (0);
}
```

File count.c

```
/* number of times through the loop */
int     counter = 0;

/* trivial example */
void    inc_counter(void)
{
    ++counter;
}
```

In this example, the function **main** uses the variable **counter**. The **extern** declaration is used by *main.c* to indicate that **counter** is declared outside the function; in this case, counter is defined in the file *counter.c*. The modifier **extern** is not used in *counter.c* because it contains the "real" declaration of the variable.

There are three modifiers that can be used to indicate where a variable is defined, as shown in Table 18-1.

Table 18-1: Modifiers

Modifier	Meaning
extern	Variable/function is defined in another file.
"none"	Variable/function is defined in this file (public) and can be used in other files.
static	Variable/function is local to this file (private).

Notice that the word **static** has two meanings. For data defined globally, static means "private to this file." For data defined inside a function, it means "variable is allocated from static memory (instead of the temporary stack)."

C is very liberal in its use of the rules for the **static** and **extern** modifiers. You can declare a variable **extern** at the beginning of a program and later define it with no modifier:

```
extern sam;
int sam = 1;    /* this is legal */
```

This method is useful when you have all of your external variables defined in a header file. The program includes the header file (and defines the variables as **extern**), then defines the variable for real.

Another problem concerns declaring a variable in two different files:

File main.c

```
int     flag  = 0;      /* flag is off */
main()
{
    printf("Flag is %d\n", flag);
}
```

File sub.c

```
int     flag = 1;       /* flag is on */
```

What happens in this case?

1. **flag** will be initialized to 0 because **main.c** is loaded first.

2. **flag** will be initialized to 1 because the entry in *sub.c* will overwrite the one in *main.c*.

3. The compiler will very carefully analyze both programs, then pick out the value that is most likely to be wrong.

There is only one global variable **flag**, and it will be initialized to either 1 or 0 depending on the whims of the compiler. Some of the more advanced compilers will issue an error message when a global is declared twice, but most compilers will silently ignore this error. It is entirely possible for the program **main** to print out:

```
flag is 1
```

even though we initialized flag to 0 and did not change it before printing. To avoid the problem of hidden initializations, use the keyword **static** to limit the scope of each variable to the file in which it is declared.

If we had written:

File main.c

```
static int      flag  = 0;       /* flag is off */
main()
{
        printf("Flag is %d\n", flag);
}
```

File sub.c

```
static int      flag = 1;        /* flag is on */
```

then `flag` in *main.c* is an entirely different variable from `flag` in *sub.c*. However, you should still give the variables different names to avoid confusion.

Headers

Information that is shared between modules should be put in a header file. By convention, all header filenames end with *.h*. In our infinite array example, we use the file *ia.h*.

The header should contain all the public information, such as:

*   A comment section describing clearly what the module does and what is available to the user

*   Common constants

*   Common structures

*   Prototypes of all the public functions

*   **extern** declarations for public variables

In our infinite array example, over half of the file *ia.h* is devoted to comments. This level of comment is not excessive; the real guts of the coding are hidden in the program file *ia.c*. The *ia.h* file serves both as a program file and as documentation to the outside world.

Notice there is no mention in the *ia.h* comments about how the infinite array is implemented. At this level, we don't care about how something is done; we just want to know what functions are available. Look through the file *ia.h* (see Example 18-1).

Example 18-1: File ia.h

```
/************************************************************
 * Definitions for the infinite array (ia) package.       *
 *                                                         *
 * An infinite array is an array whose size can grow       *
```

Example 18-1: File ia.h (continued)

```
 * as needed.  Adding more elements to the array         *
 * will just cause it to grow.                           *
 *-------------------------------------------------------*
 * struct infinite_array                                 *
 *       Used to hold the information for an infinite     *
 *       array.                                           *
 *-------------------------------------------------------*
 * Routines                                              *
 *                                                       *
 *       ia_init -- Initializes the array.               *
 *       ia_store -- Stores an element in the array.     *
 *       ia_get -- Gets an element from the array.       *
 ********************************************************/

/* number of elements to store in each cell of the infinite array */
#define BLOCK_SIZE      10

struct infinite_array {
    /* the data for this block */
    float   data[BLOCK_SIZE];

    /* pointer to the next array */
    struct infinite_array *next;
};

/********************************************************
 * ia_init -- Initializes the infinite array.           *
 *                                                       *
 * Parameters                                            *
 *       array_ptr -- The array to initialize.           *
 ********************************************************/
#define ia_init(array_ptr)      {(array_ptr)->next = NULL;}

/********************************************************
 * ia_get -- Gets an element from an infinite array.     *
 *                                                       *
 * Parameters                                            *
 *       array_ptr -- Pointer to the array to use.       *
 *       index    -- Index into the array.               *
 *                                                       *
 * Returns                                               *
 *       The value of the element.                       *
 *                                                       *
 * Note: You can get an element that                     *
 *       has not previously been stored. The value       *
 *       of any uninitialized element is zero.           *
 ********************************************************/
extern int ia_get(struct infinite_array *array_ptr, int index);
```

Example 18-1: File ia.h (continued)

```
/**********************************************************
 * ia_store -- Store an element in an infinite array.    *
 *                                                        *
 * Parameters                                             *
 *      array_ptr -- Pointer to the array to use.         *
 *      index     -- index into the array.                *
 *      store_data -- Data to store.                      *
 **********************************************************/
extern void  ia_store(struct infinite_array * array_ptr,
    int index, int store_data);
```

A few things should be noted about this file. Three functions are documented: `ia_get`, `ia_store`, and `ia_init`. `ia_init` isn't really a function, but is a macro. For the most part, people using this module do not need to know if a function is really a function or only a macro.

The macro is bracketed in curly braces (`{}`), so it will not cause syntax problems when used in something like an **if/else** sequence. The code:

```
if (flag)
   ia_init(&array);
else
   ia_store(&array, 0, 1.23);
```

will work as expected.

Everything in the file is a constant definition, a data structure definition, or an external definition. No code or storage is defined.

The Body of the Module

The body of the module contains all the functions and data for that module. Private functions that will not be called from outside the module should be declared **static**. Variables declared outside of a function that are not used outside the module are declared **static**.

A Program to Use Infinite Arrays

The program uses a simple linked list to store the elements of the array, as shown in Figure 18-2. A linked list can grow longer as needed (until we run out of room). Each list element or bucket can store 10 numbers. To find element 38, the program starts at the beginning, skips past the first three buckets, then extracts element 8 from the data in the current bucket.

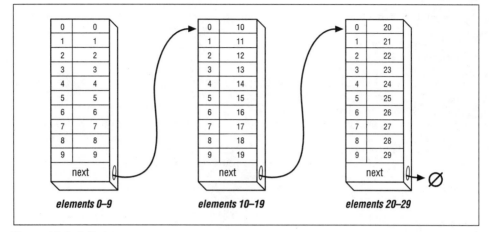

Figure 18-2: Infinite array structure

The code for the module *ia.c* is shown as Example 18-2.

Example 18-2: a/ia.c

```
/********************************************************
 * infinite-array -- routines to handle infinite arrays *
 *                                                       *
 * An infinite array is an array that grows as needed.  *
 * There is no index too large for an infinite array    *
 * (unless we run out of memory).                        *
 ********************************************************/
#include "ia.h"                /* get common definitions */
#include <memory.h>
#include <stdio.h>
#include <stdlib.h>


/********************************************************
 * ia_locate -- Gets the location of an infinite array  *
 *              element.                                 *
 *                                                       *
 * Parameters                                            *
 *      array_ptr -- Pointer to the array to use.        *
 *      index    -- Index into the array.                *
 *      current_index -- Pointer to the index into this  *
 *              bucket (returned).                       *
 *                                                       *
 * Returns                                               *
 *      pointer to the current bucket                    *
 ********************************************************/
static struct infinite_array *ia_locate(
        struct infinite_array *array_ptr, int index,
        int *current_index_ptr)
{
    /* pointer to the current bucket */
```

Example 18-2: a/ia.c (continued)

```
    struct infinite_array *current_ptr;

    current_ptr = array_ptr;
    *current_index_ptr = index;

    while (*current_index_ptr >= BLOCK_SIZE) {
        if (current_ptr->next == NULL) {

            current_ptr->next = malloc(sizeof(struct infinite_array));

            if (current_ptr->next == NULL) {
                fprintf(stderr, "Error:Out of memory\n");
                exit(8);
            }

            memset(current_ptr->next, '\0', sizeof(struct infinite_array));
        }
        current_ptr = current_ptr->next;
        *current_index_ptr -= BLOCK_SIZE;
    }
    return (current_ptr);
}
/********************************************************
 * ia_store -- Stores an element into an infinite array.*
 *                                                      *
 * Parameters                                           *
 *      array_ptr -- Pointer to the array to use.       *
 *      index   -- Index into the array.                *
 *      store_data -- Data to store.                    *
 ********************************************************/
void  ia_store(struct infinite_array * array_ptr,
    int index, int store_data)
{
    /* pointer to the current bucket */
    struct infinite_array *current_ptr;
    int   current_index;         /* index into the current bucket */

    current_ptr = ia_locate(array_ptr, index, &current_index);
    current_ptr->data[current_index] = store_data;
}
/********************************************************
 * ia_get -- Gets an element from an infinite array.    *
 *                                                      *
 * Parameters                                           *
 *      array_ptr -- Pointer to the array to use.       *
 *      index   -- Index into the array.                *
 *                                                      *
 * Returns                                              *
 *      the value of the element                        *
 *                                                      *
 * Note: You can get an element that                    *
 *      has not previously been stored. The value       *
```

Example 18-2: a/ia.c (continued)

```
 *        of any uninitialized element is zero.               *
 ***********************************************************/
int ia_get(struct infinite_array *array_ptr, int index)
{
    /* pointer to the current bucket */
    struct infinite_array *current_ptr;

    int    current_index;        /* index into the current bucket */

    current_ptr = ia_locate(array_ptr, index, &current_index);
    return (current_ptr->data[current_index]);
}
```

This program uses an internal routine, `ia_locate`. Because this routine is not used outside the module, it is defined as **static**. The routine is also not put in the header *ia.h*.

The Makefile for Multiple Files

The program **make** is designed to aid the programmer in compiling and linking programs. Before **make**, the user had to explicitly type in compile commands for every change in the program. For example:

% cc -g -ohello hello.c

As programs grow, the number of commands needed to create them grows. Typing a series of 10 or 20 commands can be tiresome and error prone, so programmers started writing shell scripts (or *.BAT* files on MS-DOS.) All the programmer had to type was a script name such as `do-it`, and the computer would compile everything. This method can be overkill, however, because all the files are recompiled whether or not they need to be.

As the number of files in a project grows, so does the time required for a recompile. Making changes in one small file, starting the compilation, and then having to wait until the next day while the computer executes several hundred compile commands can be frustrating, especially when only one compile was really needed.

The program **make** was created to make compilation dependent upon whether a file has been updated since the last compilation. The program allows you to specify the dependencies of the program file and the source file, and the command that generates the program from its source.

The file *Makefile* (case sensitivity is important in UNIX) contains the rules used by **make** to decide how to build the program.

The *Makefile* contains the following sections:

- Comments
- Macros
- Explicit rules
- Default rules

Any line beginning with a hash mark (#) is a comment.

A macro has the format:

```
name = data
```

where *name* is any valid identifier and *data* is the text that will be substituted whenever make sees $(name).

For example:

```
#
# Very simple Makefile
#
MACRO=Doing All
all:
        echo $(MACRO)
```

Explicit rules tell **make** what commands are needed to create the program. They can take several forms. The most common of these is:

```
target: source [source2] [source3]
        command
        [command]
        [command]         . . .
```

where *target* is the name of a file to create. It is "made" or created out of the source file *source*. If the *target* is created out of several files, they are all listed. This list should include any header files included by the source file. The *command* that generates the target is specified on the next line. Sometimes you need more than one command to create the target. Commands are listed one per line. Each is indented by a tab.

For example, the rule:

```
hello: hello.c
        cc -g -ohello hello.c
```

tells **make** to create the file *hello* from the file *hello.c* using the command:

```
cc -g -ohello hello.c
```

make will create *hello* only if necessary. The files used in the creation of *hello*, arranged in chronological order (by modification times), are shown in Table 18-2.

Table 18-2: Sequence for Building Executable File

UNIX	MS-DOS/Windows	
hello.c	HELLO.C	(oldest)
hello.o	HELLO.OBJ	(old)
hello	HELLO.EXE	(newest)

If the programmer changes the source file *hello.c*, its modification time will be out of date with respect to the other files. **make** will recognize that and re-create the other files.

Another form of the explicit rule is:

```
source:
            command
        [command]
```

In this case, the commands are unconditionally executed each time **make** is run. If the commands are omitted from an explicit rule, **make** will use a set of built-in rules to determine what command to execute. For example, the rule:

```
hist.o: ia.h hist.c
```

tells **make** to create *hist.o* from *hist.c* and *ia.h*, using the standard suffix rule for making *file.o* from *file.c*. This rule is:

```
$(CC) $(CFLAGS) -c file.c
```

(**make** predefines the macros $(CC) and $(CFLAGS).)

We are going to create a main program *hist.c* that calls functions in the module *ia.c*. Both files include the header *ia.h*, so they depend on it. The UNIX *Makefile* that creates the program *hist* from *hist.c* and *ia.c* is:

```
CFLAGS = -g
OBJ=ia.o hist.o

all: hist

hist: $(OBJ)
        $(CC) $(CFLAGS) -o hist $(OBJ)

hist.o:ia.h hist.c

ia.o:ia.h ia.c
```

The macro **OBJ** is a list of all the object (*.o*) files. The lines:

```
hist: $(OBJ)
        $(CC) $(CFLAGS) -o hist $(OBJ)
```

tell **make** to create *hist* from the object files. If any of the object files are out of date, **make** will re-create them.

The line:

```
hist.o:hist.c ia.h
```

tells **make** to create *hist.o* from *ia.h* and *hist.c*. Because no command is specified, the default is used.

The *Makefile* for MS-DOS, using Turbo C++, is:

```
#
SRCS=hist.c ia.c
OBJS=hist.obj ia.obj
CFLAGS=-ml -g -w -A
CC=tcc

ia: $(OBJS)
        $(CC) $(CFLAGS) -ehist.exe $(OBJS)

hist.obj: hist.c ia.h
        $(CC) $(CFLAGS) -c hist.c

ia.obj: ia.c ia.h
        $(CC) $(CFLAGS) -c ia.c
```

This file is similar to the UNIX *Makefile* except that the Turbo C++ **make** does not provide any default rules.

One big drawback exists with **make**. It checks to see only if the files have changed, not the rules. If you have compiled all of your program with **CFLAGS=-g** for debugging and need to produce the production version (**CFLAGS=-O**), **make** will *not* recompile.

The command **touch** changes the modification date of a file. (It doesn't change the file, it just makes the operating system think that it did.) If you **touch** a source file such as *hello.c* and then run **make**, the program will be re-created. This feature is useful if you have changed the compile-time flags and want to force a recompilation.

make provides you with a rich set of commands for creating programs. Only a few have been discussed here.*

Using the Infinite Array

The histogram program, **hist**, is designed to use the infinite array package. (A *histogram* is a graphic representation of the frequency with which data items recur.) It takes one file as its argument. The file contains a list of numbers from 0

---

* If you are going to create programs that require more than 10 or 20 source files, read the Nutshell Handbook *Managing Projects with make*, by Andy Oram and Steve Talbott.

to 99. Any number of entries can be used. The program prints a histogram showing how many times each number appears.

A typical line of output from our program looks like:

```
5 (   6): **************************
```

The first number (5) is the line index. In our sample data, there are six entries with the value 5. The line of asterisks graphically represents our six entries.

Some data fall out of range and are not represented in our histogram. Such data are counted and listed at the end of the printout. Here is a sample printout:

```
 1 (   9): ***********************
 2 (  15): *************************************
 3 (   9): **********************
 4 (  19): **************************************************
 5 (  13): *********************************
 6 (  14): ************************************
 7 (  14): ************************************
 8 (  14): ************************************
 9 (  20): ****************************************************
10 (  13): *********************************
11 (  14): ************************************
12 (   9): **********************
13 (  13): *********************************
14 (  12): ******************************
15 (  14): ************************************
16 (  16): ****************************************
17 (   9): **********************
18 (  13): *********************************
19 (  15): *************************************
20 (  11): ****************************
21 (  22): ********************************************************
22 (  14): ************************************
23 (   9): **********************
24 (  10): ************************
25 (  15): *************************************
26 (  10): ************************
27 (  12): ******************************
28 (  14): ************************************
29 (  15): *************************************
30 (   9): **********************
104 items out of range
```

The program uses the library routine `memset` to initialize the `counters` array. This routine is highly efficient for setting all values of an array to 0. The line:

```
memset(counters, '\0', sizeof(counters));
```

zeroes out the entire array `counters`.

The `sizeof(counters)` makes sure that all of the array is zeroed. Example 18-3 contains the full listing of *hist.c*.

Example 18-3: ia/hist.c

```
/*********************************************************
 * hist -- Generates a histogram of an array of numbers.*
 *                                                      *
 * Usage                                                *
 *      hist <file>                                     *
 *                                                      *
 * Where                                                *
 *      file is the name of the file to work on.        *
 *********************************************************/
#include "ia.h"
#include <stdio.h>
#include <stdlib.h>
#include <memory.h>
/*
 * Define the number of lines in the histogram
 */
#define NUMBER_OF_LINES 30       /* Number of lines in the histogram */
const int DATA_MIN = 1;          /* Number of the smallest item */
const int DATA_MAX = 30;         /* Number of the largest item */
/*
 * WARNING: The number of items from DATA_MIN to DATA_MAX (inclusive)
 * must match the number of lines.
 */

/* number of characters wide to make the histogram */
const int WIDTH = 60;

static struct infinite_array data_array;
static int data_items;

int main(int argc, char *argv[])
{
    /* Function to read data */
    void read_data(const char name[]);

    /* Function to print the histogram */
    void  print_histogram(void);

    if (argc != 2) {
        fprintf(stderr, "Error:Wrong number of arguments\n");
        fprintf(stderr, "Usage is:\n");
        fprintf(stderr, "  hist <data-file>\n");
        exit(8);
    }
    ia_init(&data_array);
    data_items = 0;

    read_data(argv[1]);
    print_histogram();
```

Example 18-3: ia/hist.c (continued)

```
    return (0);
}
/***********************************************************
 * read_data -- Reads data from the input file into        *
 *              the data_array.                             *
 *                                                          *
 * Parameters                                               *
 *      name -- The name of the file to read.               *
 ***********************************************************/
void read_data(const char name[])
{
    char  line[100];     /* line from input file */
    FILE *in_file;       /* input file */
    int data;            /* data from input */

    in_file = fopen(name, "r");
    if (in_file == NULL) {
        fprintf(stderr, "Error:Unable to open %s\n", name);
        exit(8);
    }
    while (1) {
        if (fgets(line, sizeof(line), in_file) == NULL)
            break;

        if (sscanf(line, "%d", &data) != 1) {
            fprintf(stderr,
                "Error: Input data not integer number\n");
            fprintf(stderr, "Line:%s", line);
        }
        ia_store(&data_array, data_items, data);
        ++data_items;
    }
    fclose(in_file);
}
/***********************************************************
 * print_histogram -- Prints the histogram output.         *
 ***********************************************************/
void  print_histogram(void)
{
    /* upper bound for printout */
    int   counters[NUMBER_OF_LINES];

    int   out_of_range = 0;/* number of items out of bounds */
    int   max_count = 0;/* biggest counter */
    float scale;         /* scale for outputting dots */
    int   index;         /* index into the data */

    memset(counters, '\0', sizeof(counters));

    for (index = 0; index < data_items; ++index) {
        int data;/* data for this point */

        data = ia_get(&data_array, index);
```

Example 18-3: ia/hist.c (continued)

```
        if ((data < DATA_MIN) || (data > DATA_MAX))
            ++out_of_range;
        else {
            ++counters[data - DATA_MIN];
            if (counters[data - DATA_MIN] > max_count)
                max_count = counters[data - DATA_MIN];
        }
    }

    scale = ((float) max_count) / ((float) WIDTH);

    for (index = 0; index < NUMBER_OF_LINES; ++index) {
        /* index for outputting the dots */
        int   char_index;
        int   number_of_dots;   /* number of * to output */

        printf("%2d (%4d): ", index + DATA_MIN, counters[index]);

        number_of_dots = (int) (((float) counters[index]) / scale);
        for (char_index = 0;
             char_index < number_of_dots;
             ++char_index) {
            printf("*");
        }
        printf("\n");
    }
    printf("%d items out of range\n", out_of_range);
}
```

Makefile for UNIX Generic C

```
#----------------------------------------------#
#         Makefile for UNIX systems            #
#     using a GNU C compiler.                  #
#----------------------------------------------#
CC=cc
CFLAGS=-g
#
# Compiler flags:
#        -g       -- Enable debugging

ia: ia.c
        $(CC) $(CFLAGS) -o ia ia.c

clean:
        rm -f ia
```

Makefile for Free Software Foundation's gcc

```
[File: ia/makefile.gcc]
#----------------------------------------------#
#         Makefile for UNIX systems            #
```

```
#     using a GNU C compiler.                 #
#---------------------------------------------#
CC=gcc
CFLAGS=-g -Wall -D__USE_FIXED_PROTOTYPES__ -ansi

all:    hist

hist: hist.o ia.o
        $(CC) $(CFLAGS) -o  hist hist.o ia.o

hist.o: hist.c ia.h

ia.o: ia.c ia.h

clean:
        rm -f hist hist.o ia.o
```

Makefile for Turbo C++

```
[File: ia/makefile.tcc]
#---------------------------------------------#
#       Makefile for DOS systems              #
#    using a Turbo C++ compiler.              #
#---------------------------------------------#
CC=tcc
CFLAGS=-v -w -ml

all:    hist.exe

hist.exe: hist.obj ia.obj ia.h
        $(CC) $(CFLAGS) -ehist hist.obj ia.obj

hist.obj: hist.c ia.h
        $(CC) $(CFLAGS) -c hist.c

ia.obj: ia.c ia.h
        $(CC) $(CFLAGS) -c ia.c

clean:
        del hist.exe hist.obj ia.obj
```

Makefile for Borland C++

```
[File: ia/makefile.bcc]
#---------------------------------------------#
#       Makefile for DOS systems              #
#    using a Borland C++ compiler.            #
#---------------------------------------------#
CC=bcc
CFLAGS=-v -w -ml

all:    hist.exe

hist.exe: hist.obj ia.obj ia.h
        $(CC) $(CFLAGS) -ehist hist.obj ia.obj
```

```
hist.obj: hist.c ia.h
        $(CC) $(CFLAGS) -c hist.c

ia.obj: ia.c ia.h
        $(CC) $(CFLAGS) -c ia.c

clean:
        del hist.exe
        del hist.obj
        del ia.obj
```

Makefile for Microsoft Visual C++

```
[File: ia/makefile.msc]
#--------------------------------------------#
#         Makefile for DOS systems           #
#     Microsoft Visual C++ Compiler.         #
#--------------------------------------------#
#
CC=cl
#
# Flags
#       AL -- Compile for large model
#       Zi -- Enable debugging
#       W1 -- Turn on warnings
#
CFLAGS=/AL /Zi /W1
SRC=hist.c ia.cpp
OBJ=hist.obj ia.obj

all: hist.exe

hist.exe: $(OBJ)
        $(CC) $(CFLAGS)  $(OBJ)

hist.obj: ia.h hist.c
        $(CC) $(CFLAGS) -c hist.c

ia.obj: ia.h ia.c
        $(CC) $(CFLAGS) -c ia.c

clean:
        erase hist.exe io.obj hist.obj
```

Dividing a Task into Modules

Unfortunately, computer programming is more of an art than a science. There are no hard and fast rules that tell you how to divide a task into modules. Knowing what makes a good module and what doesn't comes with experience and practice.

This section describes some general rules for module division and how they can be applied to real-world programs. The techniques described here have worked well for me. You should use whatever works for you.

Information is a key part of any program. The key to any program is deciding what information is being used and what processing you want to perform on it. Information flow should be analyzed before the design begins.

Modules should be designed to minimize the amount of information that has to pass between them. If you look at the organization of an army, you'll see that it is divided up into modules. There is the infantry, artillery, tank corps, and so on. The amount of information that passes between these modules is minimized. For example, an infantry sergeant who wants the artillery to bombard an enemy position calls up the artillery command and says, "There's a pillbox at location Y-94. Get rid of it."

The artillery commander handles all the details of deciding which battery is to be used, how much fire power to allocate based on the requirements of other fire missions, keeping the guns supplied, and many more details.*

Programs should be organized in the same way. Information hiding is key to good programming. A module should make public only the minimum number of functions and data needed to do the job. The smaller the interface, the simpler the interface. The simpler the interface, the easier it is to use. Also, a simple interface is less risky and less error prone than a complex one.

Small, simple interfaces are also easier to design, test, and maintain. Data hiding and good interface design are key to making good modules.

Module Division Example: Text Editor

You are already familiar with using a *text editor*. It is a program that allows the user to display and change text files. Most editors are display oriented and continually display about 25 lines of the current file on the screen. The text editor must also interpret commands that are typed in by the user. This information must be parsed so that the computer can understand it and act accordingly. The individual commands are small and perform similar functions ("delete line" is very much like "delete character"). Imposing a standard structure on the command execution modules improves readability and reliability.

The different modules that form a text editor are illustrated in Figure 18-3.

Minimal communication exists between the modules. The display manager needs to know only two things: where the cursor is and what the file currently looks like. All the file handler needs to do is read the file, write the file, and keep track

---

* This is a very general diagram of the chain of command for an ideal army. The system used by the United States Army is more complex and so highly classified that even the army commanders don't know how it works.

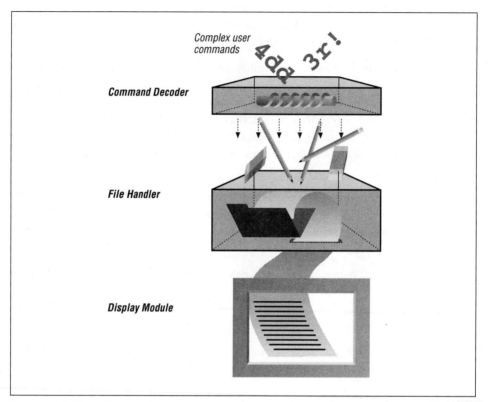

Figure 18-3: Text editor modules

of changes. Even the work involved in making changes can be minimized. All editing commands, no matter how complex, can be broken down into a series of inserts and deletes. The command module must take complex user commands and turn them into simple inserts and deletes that the file handler can process.

The information passing between the modules is minimal. In fact, no information passes between the command decoder and the display manager.

A word processor is just a fancy text editor. Where a simple editor only has to worry about ASCII characters (one font, one size), a word processor must be able to handle many different sizes and shapes.

Compiler

In a compiler, the information being processed is C code. The job of the compiler is to transform that information from C source to machine-dependent object code. Several stages comprise this process. First, the code is run through the preprocessor to expand macros, take care of conditional compilation, and read include files. Next, the processed file is passed to the first stage of the compiler, the lexical analyzer.

The lexical analyzer takes as its input a stream of characters and returns a series of *tokens*. A token is a word or operator. For example, let's look at the English command:

```
Open the door.
```

There are 14 characters in this command. Lexical analysis would recognize three words and a period. These tokens are then passed to the parser, where they are assembled into sentences. At this stage, a symbol table is generated so that the parser can have some idea of what variables are being used by the program.

Now the compiler knows what the program is supposed to do. The optimizer looks at the instructions and tries to figure out how to make them more efficient. This step is optional and is omitted unless the –O flag is specified on the command line.

The code generator turns the high-level statements into machine-specific assembly code. In assembly language, each assembly language statement corresponds to one machine instruction. The assembler turns assembly language into binary code that can be executed by the machine.

The general information flow of a compiler is shown in Figure 18-4.

One of the contributing factors to C popularity is the ease with which a C compiler can be created for a new machine. The Free Software Foundation distributes the source to a C compiler (*gcc*). Because the source is written in modular fashion, you can port it to a new machine by changing the code generator and writing a new assembler. Both of these are relatively simple tasks (see the quote at the beginning of Chapter 7, *Programming Process*).

Lexical analysis and parsing are very common and used in a wide variety of programs. The utility `lex` generates the lexical analyzer module for a program, given a description of the tokens used by the program. Another utility, `yacc`, can be used to generate the parser module.*

Spreadsheet

A simple spreadsheet takes a matrix of numbers and equations and displays the results on the screen. This program manages equations and data.

---

* For descriptions of these programs, see the Nutshell Handbook *lex & yacc*, by John Levine, Tony Mason, and Doug Brown.

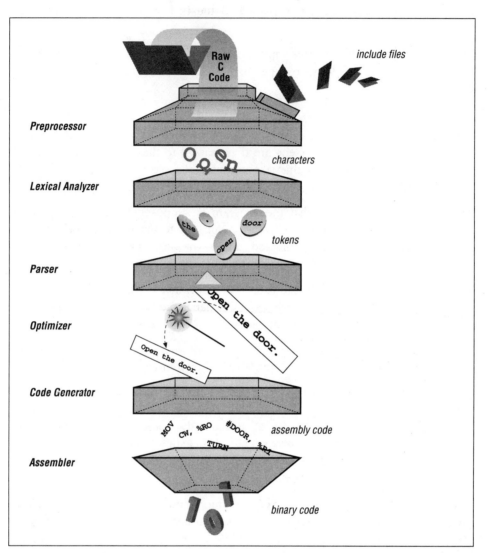

Figure 18-4: Compiler modules

The core of a spreadsheet is its set of equations. To change the equations into numbers, we need to go through lexical analysis and parsing, just like a compiler. But unlike a compiler, we don't generate machine code; instead, we interpret the equations and compute the results.

These results are passed off to the display manager, which puts them on the screen. Add to this an input module that allows the user to edit and change the equations and you have a spreadsheet, as shown in Figure 18-5.

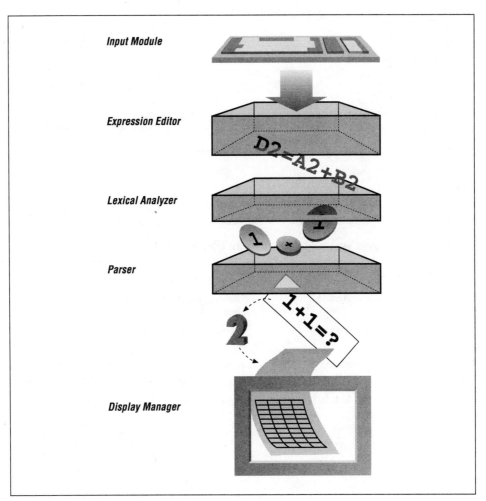

Figure 18-5: Spreadsheet modules

Module Design Guidelines

There are no hard and fast rules when it comes to laying out the modules for a program. Some general guidelines are:

- The number of public functions in a module should be small.

- The information passed between modules should be limited.

- All the functions in a module should perform related jobs.

Programming Exercises

Exercise 18-1: Write a module that will handle page formatting. It should contain the following functions:

`open_file(char *name)`	Open print file.
`define_header(char *heading)`	Define heading text.
`print_line(char *line)`	Send line to file.
`page(void)`	Start new page.
`close_file(void)`	Close printer file.

Exercise 18-2: Write a module called **search_open** that is given an array of file-names, searches until it finds one file that exists, and then opens the file.

Exercise 18-3: Write a symbol table program consisting of the following functions:

`void enter(char *name)`	Enter name into symbol table.
`int lookup(char *name)`	Return 1 if name is in table; return 0 otherwise.
`void delete(char *name)`	Remove name from symbol table.

Exercise 18-4: Take the **words** program from Chapter 17, *Advanced Pointers*, and combine it with the infinite array module to create a cross-reference program. (As an added bonus, teach it about C comments and strings to create a C cross-referencer.)

In this chapter:
• *K&R-Style
  Functions*
• *Library Changes*
• *Missing Features*
• *Free/Malloc
  Changes*
• *lint*
• *Answers*

19

Ancient Compilers

*Almost in every kingdom the most ancient families
have been at first princes' bastards....*
—Robert Burton

C has evolved over the years. In the beginning, it was something thrown together by a couple of hackers (Brian Kernigham and Dennis Ritchie) so that they could use a computer in the basement. Later the C compiler was refined and released as the "Portable C Compiler." The major advantage of this compiler was that you could port it from machine to machine. All you had to do was write a device configuration. True, writing one was extremely difficult, but the task was a lot easier than writing a compiler from scratch.

The Portable C Compiler was widely distributed and soon became the most widely used C compiler around. Because there were no official standards around at the time, whatever the Portable C Compiler could compile became the "official" standard.

This chapter describes that "standard." The Portable C Compiler didn't have many of the features that were later defined in the ANSI standard. Many of these new features were added to make C programs safer and more reliable. Programming in ANSI C is difficult enough. Programing in the old Portable C is like walking a tightrope with no net—blindfolded.

K&R-Style Functions

K&R-style C compilers use an older style of declaring functions. For example, the ANSI C function declaration:

```
int process(int size, float data[], char *how)
```

in K&R C would be:

```
int process(size, data, how)
int size;
float data[];
char *how;
{
    /* Rest of the function */
```

Strictly speaking, we don't need the declaration "`int size`" because all parameter types default to **int** automatically. However, we put it there because declaring everything and not letting things default is a good idea.

Function Prototypes

Functions prototypes are not required in K&R-style C and can be omitted. For example, suppose you use the function **draw** without declaring a prototype:

```
draw(1, 8, 2, 20);
```

C will automatically define this function as a function that returns an **int** and has an unknown number of parameters of an unknown type. Obviously, the type checking of parameters cannot be done. So it is entirely possible to write a program like Example 19-1.

Example 19-1: area/area.c

```
#include <stdio.h>

float area(width, height)
int width;
float height;
{
    return (width * height);
}

int main()
{
    float size = area(3.0, 2);

    printf("Area is %f\n", size);
    return (0);
}
```

Question 19-1: *What will the program in Example 19-1 output when it is run? Why?*

K&R-style C does allow for function prototypes, but only the return type can be declared. The parameter list must be `()`. For example:

```
extern float atof();
```

Again, the () indicates that this function takes an unknown number of parameters of an unknown type.

Question 19-2: *What does Example 19-2 print and why?*

Example 19-2: ret/ret.c

```c
#include <stdio.h>

int main()
{
    /* Get the square of a number */
    int i = square(5);

    printf("i is %d\n", i);
    return (0);
}

float square(s)
int s;
{
    return (s * s);
}
```

Question 19-3: *What does Example 19-3 print and why?*

Example 19-3: sum/sum.c

```c
#include <stdio.h>

int sum(i1, i2, i3)
{
    int i1;
    int i2;
    int i3;

    return (i1 + i2 + i3);
}

int main()
{
    printf("Sum is %d\n", sum(1, 2, 3));
    return (0);
}
```

Question 19-4: *Example 19-4 prints* John' = (3 *instead of* John Doe. *Why? (Your results may vary.)*

Example 19-4: scat/scat.c

```c
#include <stdio.h>
#include <string.h>

char first[100];        /* First name of person */
```

Example 19-4: scat/scat.c (continued)

```
char last[100];        /* Last name of person */

/* First and last name combined */
char full[100];

int main() {
    strcpy(first, "John");
    strcpy(last, "Doe");

    strcpy(full, first);
    strcat(full, ' ');
    strcat(full, last);

    printf("The name is %s\n", full);
    return (0);
}
```

Prototypes are an extremely valuable diagnostic tool for the C compiler. Without them, all sorts of errors can happen without the programmer knowing it. For this reason, prototypes were borrowed from C++ and put in C.

Library Changes

Like the language, the library has evolved as well. The "standard" C library used to be whatever came with the UNIX operating system. Then, the UNIX operating system split into two families: BSD-UNIX and System V UNIX. The standard library split as well.

When ANSI standardized C, it standardized the library as well. However, you will still find code out there with the old library calls. The main differences are:

*   The old K&R C had no *stdlib.h* or *unistd.h* headers.

*   A number of the older functions have been renamed or replaced. Table 19-1 lists the functions that have been updated.

Table 19-1: K&R Versus ANSI Functions

K&R function	ANSI equivalent	Notes
bcopy	memcpy	Copies an array or structure.
bzero	memset	Sets memory to zero.
bcmp	memcmp	Compares two sections of memory.
index	strchr	Finds character in a string.
rindex	strrchr	Finds character starting at end of a string.
char *sprintf	int sprintf	The K&R function returns pointer to string. The ANSI standard one returns number of items converted.

Missing Features

As we've said before, the C language has been evolving for some time. Some of the earlier compilers may not have the latest features. Some of these features include:

- **void** type
- **const** qualifier
- **volatile** qualifier (See Chapter 21, *C's Dustier Corners*)
- The *stdlib.h* header file or *unistd.h* header file
- **enum** types

Free/Malloc Changes

In ANSI C, the `malloc` function is defined as:

```
void *malloc(unsigned long int size);
```

Because **void *** indicates "universal pointer," the return value of `malloc` matches any pointer type:

```
struct person *person_ptr;/* Define a pointer to a person */

/* This is legal in ANSI C */
person_ptr = malloc(sizeof(struct person))
```

Because some K&R C compilers don't have a **void** type, `malloc` is defined as:

```
char *malloc(unsigned long int size)
```

In order to get the compiler to stop complaining about the different pointer types, the output of malloc must be cast to make it the proper type:

```
struct person *person_ptr; /* Define a pointer to a person */

/* This will generate a warning or error in K&R C */
person_ptr = malloc(sizeof(struct person));

/* This will fix that problem */
person_ptr = (struct person *)malloc(sizeof(struct person));
```

The same problem occurs with **free**. While ANSI C defines **free** as:

```
int free(void *);
```

K&R defines it as:

```
int free(char *);
```

So you need to cast the parameter to a character pointer to avoid warnings.

lint

The old C compilers lacked much of the error checking we take for granted now. This deficiency made programming very difficult. To solve this problem, a program called *lint** was written. This program checks for common errors such as calling functions with the wrong parameters, inconsistent function declarations, attempts to use a variable before it is initialized, and so on.

To run *lint* on your program, execute the command:

```
% lint -hpx prog.c
```

Option -h turns on some heuristic checking, option -p checks for possible portability problems, and option -x checks for variables declared **extern** but never used. Note: On System V UNIX systems, the function of the -h option is reversed, so you should omit it on these systems.

Answers

Answer 19-1: The problem is that our area function takes as its arguments an integer and a floating-point number:

```
float area(width, height)
int width;
float height;
```

But we call it with a floating-point number and an integer:

```
float size = area(3.0, 2);
```

We have our types reversed: function(float, int)—call(int, float). But C has no way of identifying this reversal because we are using K&R-style C. The result is that when the program passes the parameters from **main** to **area**, they get mangled and our output is garbled.

Question 19-5: *Example 19-5 contains our "fixed" program. We now use two floating-point parameters, "3.0" and "2.0", but we still get the wrong answer? Why?*

Example 19-5: param2/param2.c

```
#include <stdio.h>

float area(width, height)
float width;
float height;
{
    return (width * height);
```

---

* For more information, see the Nutshell handbook *Checking C Programs with lint,* by Jan F. Darwin.

Example 19-5: param2/param2.c (continued)

```
}

int main()
{
    float size = area(3.0 * 2.0);

    printf("Area is %f\n", size);
    return (0);
}
```

Answer 19-2: The result is garbled. A typical output might look like:

```
i is 1103626240
```

which is a little large for 5^2. The problem is that we have no prototype, even a K&R-style prototype, for **square**. The result is that C assumes the default definition: a function returning an integer that takes any number of parameters.

But the function returns a floating-point number. Because we return a float at a point at which C thinks we are receiving an **int**, we get garbage. The problem can be fixed by putting a K&R-style prototype at the beginning of the program:

```
float square();
```

An even better solution is to turn this program into ANSI C by adding a real prototype and fixing up the function header.

Answer 19-3: This program prints out a random number based on the sum of three uninitialized variables.

The problem is with the function header:

```
int sum(i1, i2, i3)
{
    int i1;
    int i2;
    int i3;
```

Parameter type declaration occurs just before the first curly brace ({) of the function. In this case, we have no braces, so the types i1, i2, and i3 default to integer.

But then we have the declaration of i1, i2, and i3 at the beginning of the function. These declarations define local variables that have nothing to do with the parameters i1, i2, and i3. But, because these variables have the same names as the parameters, they cause the parameters to become hidden variables. These three uninitialized variables are summed and this random result is returned to the caller.

ANSI has outlawed this type of silliness, but many compilers still accept this code.

Answer 19-4: The function `strcat` takes two strings as its arguments. In the statement `strcat(full,  '  ')`, the first argument, `full`, is a string; the second, `'  '`, is a character. Using a character instead of a string is illegal. Old-style C compilers do not type-check parameters, so this error gets by the compiler. The character `'  '` should be replaced by the string `"  "`.

Answer 19-5: The problem is that we wrote:

```
float size = area(3.0 * 2.0);
```

when we should have written:

```
float size = area(3.0, 2.0);
```

The first version passes the expression "3.0 * 2.0" or "6.0" as the first parameter. No second parameter exists. C doesn't check the number of parameters so it made up a random value for the second parameter.

20

Portability Problems

Wherein I spake of most disastrous changes,
Of moving accidents by flood and field,
Of hair-breath 'scapes i' the imminent deadly
breath...

—Shakespeare, on program porting
[*Othello*, Act 1, Scene III]

You've just completed work on your great masterpiece, a ray-tracing program that renders complex three-dimensional shaded graphics on a Cray supercomputer using 300MB of memory and 50GB of disk space. What do you do when someone comes in and asks you to port this program to an IBM PC with 640K of memory and 100MB of disk space? Killing him is out; not only is it illegal, but it is considered unprofessional. Your only choice is to whimper and start the port. During this process, you will find that your nice, working program exhibits all sorts of strange and mysterious problems.

C programs are supposed to be portable; however, C contains many machine-dependent features. Also, because of the vast difference between UNIX and MS-DOS/Windows, system deficiencies can frequently cause portability problems with many programs.

This chapter discusses some of the problems associated with writing truly portable programs as well as some of the traps you might encounter.

Modularity

One of the tricks to writing portable programs is to put all the nonportable code into a separate module. For example, screen handling differs greatly on MS-DOS/

Windows and UNIX. To design a portable program, you'd have to write machine-specific modules that update the screen.

For example, the HP-98752A terminal has a set of function keys labeled F1 to F8. The PC terminal also has a set of function keys. The problem is that they don't send out the same set of codes. The HP terminal sends "<esc>p<return>" for F1 and the PC sends "<NULL>;". In this case, you would want to write a `get_code` routine that gets a character (or function-key string) from the keyboard and translates function keys. Because the translation is different for both machines, a machine-dependent module would be needed for each one. For the HP machine, you would put together the program with *main.c* and *hp-tty.c*, while for the PC you would use *main.c* and *pc-tty.c*.

Word Size

A **long int** is 32 bits, a **short int** is 16 bits, and a normal **int** can be 16 or 32 bits, depending on the machine. This disparity can lead to some unexpected problems. For example, the following code works on a 32-bit UNIX system, but fails when ported to MS-DOS/Windows:

```
int zip;
zip = 92126;
printf("Zip code %d\n", zip);
```

The problem is that on MS-DOS/Windows, `zip` is only 16 bits—too small for 92126. To fix the problem, we declare `zip` as a 32-bit integer:

```
long int zip;
zip = 92126;
printf("Zip code %d\n", zip);
```

Now `zip` is 32 bits and can hold 92126.

Question 20-1: *Why do we still have a problem?* `zip` *does not print correctly on a PC.*

Byte Order Problem

A **short int** consists of 2 bytes. Consider the number 0x1234. The 2 bytes have the values 0x12 and 0x34. Which value is stored in the first byte? The answer is machine dependent.

This uncertainty can cause considerable trouble when you are trying to write portable binary files. The Motorola 68000-series machines use one type of byte order (ABCD), while Intel and Digital Equipment Corporation machines use another (BADC).

One solution to the problem of portable binary files is to avoid them. Put an option in your program to read and write ASCII files. ASCII offers the dual advantages of being far more portable and human readable.

The disadvantage is that text files are larger. Some files may be too big for ASCII. In that case, the magic number at the beginning of a file may be useful. Suppose the magic number is 0x11223344 (a bad magic number, but a good example). When the program reads the magic number, it can check against the correct number as well as the byte-swapped version (0x22114433). The program can automatically fix the file problem:

```
const long int MAGIC     = 0x11223344L /* file identification number*/
const long int SWAP_MAGIC = 0x22114433L /* magic-number byte swapped */

FILE *in_file;                /* file containing binary data */
long int magic;               /* magic number from file */

in_file = fopen("data", "rb");
fread((char *)&magic, sizeof(magic), 1, in_file);
switch (magic) {
    case MAGIC:
        /* No problem */
        break;
    case SWAP_MAGIC:
        printf("Converting file, please wait\n");
        convert_file(in_file);
        break;
    default:
        fprintf(stderr,"Error:Bad magic number %lx\n", magic);
        exit (8);
}
```

Alignment Problem

Some computers limit the address that can be used for integers and other types of data. For example, the 68000 series require that all integers start on a 2-byte boundary. If you attempt to access an integer using an odd address, you will generate an error. Some processors have no alignment rules, while some are even more restrictive—requiring integers to be aligned on a 4-byte boundary.

Alignment restrictions are not limited to integers. Floating-point numbers and pointers must also be aligned correctly.

C hides the alignment restrictions from you. For example, if you declare the following structure on a 68000 series:

```
struct funny {
    char    flag;   /* type of data following */
    long int value; /* value of the parameter*/
};
```

C will allocate storage for this structure as shown on the left in Figure 20-1.

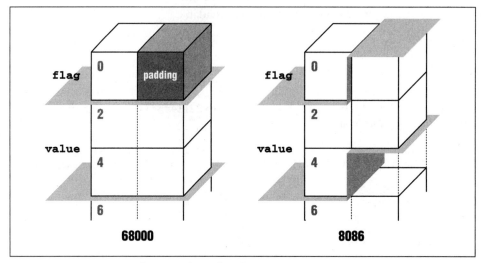

Figure 20-1: Structure on 68000 and 8086 architectures

On an 8086-class machine with no alignment restrictions, this storage will be allocated as shown on the right in Figure 20-1. The problem is that the size of the structure changes from machine to machine. On a 68000, the structure size is 6 bytes, and on the 8086 it is 5 bytes. So if you write a binary file containing 100 records on a 68000, it will be 600 bytes long, while on an 8086, it will be only 500 bytes long. Obviously, the file is not written the same way on both machines.

One way around this problem is to use ASCII files. As we have said before, there are many problems with binary files. Another solution is to explicitly declare a pad byte:

```
struct new_funny {
        char    flag;     /* type of data following */
        char    pad;      /* not used */
        long int value;   /* value of the parameter*/
};
```

The pad character makes the field value align correctly on a 68000 machine while making the structure the correct size on an 8086-class machine.

Using pad characters is difficult and error prone. For example, although **new_ funny** is portable between machines with 1- and 2-byte alignment for 32-bit integers, it is not portable to any machine with a 4-byte integer alignment such as a Sun SPARC system.

NULL Pointer Problem

Many programs and utilities were written using UNIX on VAX computers. On this computer, the first byte of any program is 0. Many programs written on this computer contain a bug—they use the null pointer as a string.

For example:

```
#ifndef NULL
#define NULL ((char *)0)
#endif NULL

char *string;

string = NULL;
printf("String is '%s'\n", string);
```

This code is actually an illegal use of **string**. Null pointers should never be dereferenced. On the VAX, this error causes no problems. Because byte 0 of the program is 0, **string** points to a null string. This result is due to luck, not design.

On a VAX, the following result is produced:

```
String is ''
```

On a Celerity computer, the first byte of the program is a `'Q'`. When this program is run on a C1200, it produces:

```
String is 'Q'
```

On other computers, this type of code can generate unexpected results. Many of the utilities ported from a VAX to a Celerity exhibited the `'Q'` bug.

Many of the newer compilers will now check for **NULL** and print:

```
String is (null)
```

This message does not mean that printing **NULL** is not an error. It means that the error is so common that the compiler makers decided to give the programmer a safety net. The idea is that when the error occurs, the program prints something reasonable instead of crashing.

Filename Problems

UNIX specifies files as */root/sub/file*, while MS-DOS/Windows specifies files as *\root\sub\file*. When porting from UNIX to MS-DOS/Windows, filenames must be changed. For example:

```
#ifndef __MSDOS__
#include <sys/stat.h> /* UNIX version of the file */
#else __MSDOS__
```

```
#include <sys\stat.h> /* DOS version of the file */
#endif __MSDOS__
```

Question 20-2: *The following program works on UNIX, but when we run it on MS-DOS/Windows, we get the following message:*

```
oot
ew       able:   file not found.


FILE *in_file;

#ifndef __MSDOS__
const char NAME[] = "/root/new/table";
#else __MSDOS__
const char NAME[] = "\root\new\table";
#endif __MSDOS__

in_file = fopen(NAME, "r");
if (in_file == NULL) {
    fprintf(stderr,"%s: file not found\n", NAME);
    exit(8);
}
```

File Types

In UNIX there is only one file type. In MS-DOS/Windows there are two: text and binary. The flags O_BINARY and O_TEXT are used in MS-DOS/Windows to indicate file type. These flags are not defined for UNIX.

When you port from MS-DOS/Windows to UNIX, you will need to do something about the flags. One solution is to use the preprocessor to define them if they have not already been defined:

```
#ifndef O_BINARY          /* If we don't have a flag already */
#define O_BINARY 0        /* Define it to be a harmless value */
#define O_TEXT   0        /* Define it to be a harmless value */
#endif /* O_BINARY */
```

This method allows you to use the same opens for both UNIX and MS-DOS/Windows. However, going the other way may present some problems. In UNIX a file is a file. No additional flags are needed. Frequently none are supplied. However, when you get to MS-DOS/Windows, you need the extra flags and will have to put them in.

Summary

You can write portable programs in C. However, because C runs on many different types of machines that use different operating systems; making programs portable is not easy. Still, if you keep portability in mind when creating the code, you can minimize the problems.

Answers

Answer 20-1: The variable `zip` is a **long int**. The `printf` specification `%d` is for a normal **int**, not a **long int**. The correct specification is `%ld` to indicate a **long**:

```
printf("Zip code %ld\n", zip);
```

Answer 20-2: The problem is that C uses the backslash (\) as an escape character. The character \r is a carriage return, \n is newline, and \t is a tab. What we really have for a name is:

```
<return>oot<newline>ew<tab>able
```

The name should be specified as:

```
const char NAME[] = "\\root\\new\\table";
```

NOTE   The **#include** uses a filename, not a C string. While you must use double backslashes (\\) in a C string, in an **#include** file, you use single backslashes (\). The following two lines are both correct:

```
const char NAME[] = "\\root\\new\\table";
#include "\root\new\defs.h"
```

21

In this chapter:
• do/while
• goto
• The ?: Construct
• The , Operator
• volatile Qualifier
• Answer

C's Dustier Corners

> There be of them that have left a name behind
> them.
> —Ecclesiasticus 44:8

This chapter describes the few remaining features of C that have not been described in any of the previous chapters. It is titled *C's Dustier Corners* because these statements are hardly ever used in real programming.

do/while

The **do/while** statement has the following syntax:

```
do {
        statement
        statement
} while (expression);
```

The program will loop, test the expression, and stop if the expression is false (0).

NOTE   This construct will always execute at least once.

---

do/while is not frequently used in C. Most programmers prefer to use a **while/break** combination.

goto

Every sample program in this book was coded without using a single **goto**. In actual practice, I find a **goto** statement useful about once every other year.

For those rare times that a **goto** is necessary, the correct syntax is:

```
goto label;
```

where *label* is a statement label. Statement labels follow the same naming convention as variable names. Labeling a statement is done as follows:

```
label: statement
```

For example:

```
for (x = 0; x < X_LIMIT; x++) {
    for (y = 0; y < Y_LIMIT; y++) {
        if (data[x][y] == 0)
            goto found;
    }
}
printf("Not found\n");
exit(8);
```

found:

```
printf("Found at (%d,%d)\n", x, y);
```

Question 21-1: *Why does Example 21-1 not print an error message when an incorrect command is entered?*

Hint: We put this in the **goto** section.

Example 21-1: def/def.c

```
#include <stdio.h>
#include <stdlib.h>

int main()
{
    char  line[10];

    while (1) {
        printf("Enter add(a), delete(d), quit(q): ");
        fgets(line, sizeof(line), stdin);

        switch (line[0]) {
        case 'a':
            printf("Add\n");
            break;
        case 'd':
            printf("Delete\n");
            break;
        case 'q':
            printf("Quit\n");
            exit(0);
        defualt:
            printf("Error:Bad command %c\n", line[0]);
            break;
        }
    }
}
```

The ?: Construct

The question mark (?) and colon (:) operators work in a manner similar to that of if/then/else. Unlike if/then/else, the ?: construct can be used inside of an expression. The general form of ?: is:

```
(expression) ? value1 : value2
```

For example, the following construct assigns to **amount_owed** the value of the balance or zero, depending on the amount of the balance:

```
amount_owed = (balance < 0) ? 0 : balance;
```

The following macro returns the minimum of its two arguments:

```
#define min(x,y) ((x) < (y) ? (x) : (y))
```

The , Operator

The comma (,) operator can be used to group statements. For example:

```
if (total < 0) {
    printf("You owe nothing\n");
    total = 0;
}
```

can be written as:

```
if (total < 0)
    printf("You owe nothing\n"),total = 0;
```

In most cases, curly braces ({}) should be used instead of a comma. About the only place the comma operator is useful is in a **for** statement. The following **for** loop increments two counters, **two** and **three**, by 2 and 3:

```
for (two = 0, three = 0;
     two < 10;
     two += 2, three += 3)
        printf("%d %d\n", two, three);
```

volatile Qualifier

The **volatile** keyword is used to indicate a variable whose value might change at any moment. The keyword is used for variables such as memory-mapped I/O devices or in real-time control applications where variables can be changed by an interrupt routine.

Things like memory-mapped device drivers, interrupt routines, and real-time control are extremely advanced subjects. You will be programming at a level far beyond the scope of this book before you will need to use the **volatile** keyword.

Answer

Answer 21-1: The compiler didn't see our default line because we misspelled "default" as "defualt." This mistake was not flagged as an error because "defualt:" is a valid **goto** label.

22

Putting It All Together

For there isn't a job on the top of the earth the beggar don't know, nor do.
—Rudyard Kipling

In this chapter, we create a complete program. Every step of the process is covered from setting forth the requirements to testing the result.

Requirements

Before we start, we need to decide what we are going to do. This step is very important and is left out of far too many programming cycles.

This chapter's program must fulfill several requirements. First, it must be long enough to demonstrate modular programming, but at the same time be short enough to fit inside a single chapter. It must be complex enough to demonstrate a wide range of C features, but be simple enough for a novice C programmer to understand.

Finally, the program must be useful. Usefulness is not simple to define. What's useful to one person might not be useful to another. We decided to refine this requirement and restate it as "The program must be useful to C programmers."

The program we have selected reads C source files and generates simple statistics on the nesting of parentheses, and in the ratio of comments to code lines.

Specification

The specification for our statistics program is shown in the following sidebar:

Preliminary Specification for a
C Statistics Gathering Program
Steve Oualline

February 10, 1996

The program stat gathers statistics about C source files and prints them. The command line is:

```
stat <files..>
```

Where <files..> is a list of source files. The following shows the output of the program on a short test file.

```
[File: stat/stat.out]
  1 (0   {0  /*-*/
  2 (0   {0  /********************************************************
  3 (0   {0  * Name: Calculator (Version 2).                        *
  4 (0   {0  *                                                       *
  5 (0   {0  * Purpose:                                              *
  6 (0   {0  *     Act like a simple four-function calculator.       *
  7 (0   {0  *                                                       *
  8 (0   {0  * Usage:                                                *
  9 (0   {0  *     Run the program.                                  *
 10 (0   {0  *     Type in an operator (+ - * /) and a number.       *
 11 (0   {0  *     The operation will be performed on the current    *
 12 (0   {0  *     result, and a new result will be displayed.       *
 13 (0   {0  *                                                       *
 14 (0   {0  *     Type 'Q' to quit.                                 *
 15 (0   {0  *                                                       *
 16 (0   {0  * Notes: Like version 1 but written with a switch       *
 17 (0   {0  *     statement.                                        *
 18 (0   {0  ********************************************************/
 19 (0   {0  /*+*/
 20 (0   {0  #include <stdio.h>
 21 (0   {0  char  line[100];  /* line of text from input */
 22 (0   {0
 23 (0   {0  int   result;    /* the result of the calculations */
 24 (0   {0  char  operator;  /* operator the user specified */
 25 (0   {0  int   value;     /* value specified after the operator */
 26 (0   {0  int main()
 27 (0   {1  {
 28 (0   {1      result = 0;  /* initialize the result */
 29 (0   {1
 30 (0   {1      /* loop forever (or until break reached) */
 31 (0   {2      while (1) {
 32 (0   {2          printf("Result: %d\n", result);
 33 (0   {2          printf("Enter operator and number: ");
 34 (0   {2
 35 (0   {2          fgets(line, sizeof(line), stdin);
 36 (0   {2          sscanf(line, "%c %d", &operator, &value);
 37 (0   {2
 38 (0   {2          if ((operator == 'q') || (operator == 'Q'))
```

(continued)

```
    (continued)
    39  (0   {2                    break;
    40  (0   {3             switch (operator) {
    41  (0   {3             case '+':
    42  (0   {3                 result += value;
    43  (0   {3                 break;
    44  (0   {3             case '-':
    45  (0   {3                 result -= value;
    46  (0   {3                 break;
    47  (0   {3             case '*':
    48  (0   {3      .          result *= value;
    49  (0   {3                 break;
    50  (0   {3             case '/':
    51  (0   {4               if (value == 0) {
    52  (0   {4                   printf("Error:Divide by zero\n");
    53  (0   {4                   printf("   operation ignored\n");
    54  (0   {3               } else
    55  (0   {3                   result /= value;
    56  (0   {3                 break;
    57  (0   {3             default:
    58  (0   {3                 printf("Unknown operator %c\n", operator);
    59  (0   {3                 break;
    60  (0   {2             }
    61  (0   {1         }
    62  (0   {1         return (0);
    63  (0   {0  }
    Total number of lines: 63
    Maximum nesting of () : 2
    Maximum nesting of {} : 4
    Number of blank lines ...............4
    Number of comment only lines .........20
    Number of code only lines ............34
    Number of lines with code and comments 5
    Comment to code ratio 64.1%
```

Code Design

Several schools of code design exist. In structured programming, you divide the code into modules, then divide the modules into submodules, then divide the submodules into subsubmodules, and so on. Other approaches exist, such as state tables and transition diagrams.

All have the same basic principle at heart: "Arrange the program's information in the clearest and simplest way possible, and then try to turn it into C code."

Our program breaks down into several logical modules. First, we have a token scanner, which reads raw C code and turns it into tokens. This subdivides into three smaller modules. The first reads the input file, the second determines what type of character we have, and finally, the third assembles this information into a token. A token is a group of characters that form a single word, number, or symbol.

The main module consumes tokens and output statistics. Again, this module breaks down into smaller submodules: a `do_file` procedure to manage each file and a submodule for each statistic.

Token Module

Our program scans C source code and uses the tokens to generate statistics. For example, the line:

```
answer = (123 + 456) / 89;  /* Compute some sort of result */
```

consists of the tokens:

```
T_ID            The word "answer"
T_OPERATOR      The character "="
T_L_PAREN       Left parenthesis
T_NUMBER        The number 123
T_OPERATOR      The character "+"
T_NUMBER        The number 456
T_R_PAREN       The right parenthesis
T_OPERATOR      The divide operator
T_NUMBER        The number 89
T_OPERATOR      The semicolon
T_COMMENT       The comment
T_NEW_LINE      The end-of-line character
```

So how do we identify a token? Most of the time, we simply have to look at the first character. For example, the * character signals an operator token, while the A character starts an identifier. But some characters are ambiguous. For example, the / character could be the divide operator, or it could be the start of a /* comment. In order to identify this character, we need to look ahead one character. So one of the requirements for our input module is that it allow us to peek ahead one character.

The token module builds tokens from groups of characters. For example, an identifier is defined as a letter or underscore, followed by any number of letters or digits. So our tokenizer needs to contain the pseudo code:

```
if the current character is a letter, then
        scan until we get a character that's not a letter or digit.
```

As you can see from the pseudo code, our tokenizer depends a great deal on character types, so we need a module to help us with the type information.

Input Module

The input module needs to do two things: first, it needs to provide the current and next characters to the token module, and second, it needs to buffer the entire line for display at a later time.

How not to design an input module

Sometimes a software design will undergo several revisions before it is finally coded, as was the case with the input module. I carefully designed the module, reviewed my design, and decided to throw it away.

However, nothing written is completely wasted, so I am including the first design as a example of how things go wrong and what can be done to improve them.

The first design consisted of a public structure:

```
struct input_file {
    FILE *file;          /* File we are reading */
    char line[LINE_MAX];/* Current line */
    char *char_ptr;      /* Current character on the line */

    int cur_char;        /* Current character (can be EOF) */
    int next_char;       /* Next character (can be EOF) */
};
```

and functions that operated on the structure:

```
extern void in_open(struct input_file *in_file, const char name[]);
extern void in_read_char(struct input_file *in_file);
extern void in_flush(struct input_file *in_file);
```

To use this package, the caller needs to call **in_open** to open the file and then check **in_file.file** to see if the file is opened. In C, these operations are done as follows:

```
struct input_file in_file;      /* File for input */
/* ... */
in_open(&in_file, name);
if (in_file.file == NULL) {
    fprintf(stderr,"Error: Could not open input file: %s\n", name);
```

The token module needs to look at the current and next character. For example, when it sees a slash (/) and a star (*), it knows that it's looking at a comment. The current character is stored in **in_file.cur_char** and the next character is in **in_file.next_char**. The C code to check for a comment might look like:

```
if ((in_file.cur_char == '/') && (in_file.next_char == '*')) {
    /* Handle a comment */
```

To move up a character, the user calls **in_read_char** to advance the input by one character.

Finally, when the file is finished, the user closes the file with the statement:

```
fclose(in_file.file);
```

In a good module design:

- The amount of information needed by the people who use the module should be minimized.

- The number rules that the users of the module must follow in order to use the module properly should be small.

- The module should be easily expandable.

The design of the input module requires that the user know an awful lot about how the module is designed. In order to open a file, the user must know to call the `in_open` function, then check the `file` field of the `in_file` structure for errors. Consequently, the user must be aware of the `in_file` structure and, what's worse, the internal workings of the `in_file` structure.

There are other cases for which the user needs to know about the internals of `struct in_file`, such as when accessing the current character (`cur_char`) or next character (`next_char`). Also, the user must manually close the file using yet another member of our data structure.

So this design requires that the user know a great deal about the internal workings of our module and access things properly. A better design would demand much less from the user.

A better input module

Our new module design eliminates the `in_file` structure (as far as the user is concerned) and provides the following functions:

```
extern int in_open(const char name[]);
extern void in_close(void);
extern void in_read_char(void);
extern int in_cur_char(void);
extern int in_next_char(void);
extern void in_flush(void);
```

These functions hide all the bookkeeping necessary to handle the input file. Also, the opening of a file is simpler. We can open the file and check for errors in one function call.

The big win in this design is that the caller does not need to know about the structure of the input file. In fact, the structure has been removed from the header entirely. This design tremendously simplifies the information that the caller needs in order to use the module.

This design has a couple of drawbacks. The module has a lot more functions than our previous design. Also, the module allows us to have only one file open at a time. This restriction exists because the structure we removed from the head is being placed in the module itself. The one-file restriction limits our flexibility. However, we don't need to open multiple files, so we don't need this feature at this time. In this case, we decided that the gain of simplifying the interface was well worth the decrease in flexibility.

Character Type Module

The purpose of the character type module is to read characters and decode their types. Some types overlap. For example, the C_ALPHA_NUMERIC includes the C_NUMERIC character set.

This module stores most of the type information in an array, and requires only a little logic to handle the special types like C_ALPHA_NUMERIC.

The functions in this module are:

```
extern int is_char_type(int ch, enum CHAR_TYPE kind);
extern enum CHAR_TYPE get_char_type(int ch);
```

One question comes up: how do we initialize the character array? We could require the user to initialize it before he calls any of the functions, such as:

```
main() {
    /* .... */
    init_char_type();

    /* ...... */
    type_info = ch_to_type(ch);
```

Another solution is to put a check at the beginning of each function to initialize the array if needed:

```
int is_char_type(int ch, enum CHAR_TYPE kind)
    if (!ch_setup) {
        init_char_type();
        ch_setup = 0;
    }
```

The second method requires a little more code. But it has several advantages. First, it makes life simpler for the user. He doesn't have to remember to initialize the character type module. Also, mistakes are harder to make. If the user doesn't have to do the initialization, he can't forget to do it. Finally, this method hides an internal bookkeeping matter inside the character type module so that the user doesn't have to worry about it.

Statistics Submodules

Each of our statistics submodules looks at the token stream and produces statistics about it. For example, the parentheses counter counts the nesting of parentheses. Some statistics are reported on a line-by-line basis, such as the current parentheses nesting. Others are reported at the end-of-file, such as the maximum nesting of parentheses.

We collect four statistics, a count of the number of lines, the parentheses ()
nesting, the curly-brace {} nesting, and a count of the lines with comments versus
the lines without comments. Because each of our static submodules performs
similar functions, we give the procedures in each of them similar names: (*xx* is
the sub-module identifier listed below).

xx_init

Initializes the statistic. This function is called at the beginning of each file.

xx_take_token

Receives a token and updates the statistic based on it.

xx_line_start

Writes out the value of the statistic that's output at the beginning of each line.
In some cases, this may be nothing.

xx_eof

Writes out the statistical information that goes at the end of the file.

The *xx* part of the identifier is the submodule identifier. It is:

lc

Line counter submodule

pc

Parentheses counter submodule

bc

Brace counter submodule

cc

Comment / not-comment line counter submodule

Coding

The coding process was fairly simple. The only problem that came up was getting
the end-of-line right.

Functional Description

This section describes all modules and major functions in our program. For a
more complete and detailed description, take a look at the listings at the end of
this chapter.

ch_type Module

The `ch_type` module computes the type of a character. For the most part,
this computation is done through a table named **type_info**. Some types like

C_ALPHA_NUMERIC, for example, include two different types of characters, C_ALPHA and C_DIGIT. So, in addition to our table, we need a little code for the special cases.

in_file Module

This modules reads data from the input file one character at a time. It buffers up a line and on demand writes it to the output.

token Module

We want an input stream of tokens. But what we have to start with is an input stream consisting of characters. The main function of this class, next_token, turns characters into tokens. Actually, our tokenizer is rather simple, because we don't have to deal with most of the details that a full C tokenizer must handle.

The coding for this function is fairly straightforward, except for the fact that it breaks up multiline comments into a series of T_COMMENT and T_NEW_LINE tokens.

Line Counter Submodule (lc)

The simplest statistic we collect is a count of the number of lines processed so far. This concept is done through the line_counter submodule. The only token it cares about is T_NEW_LINE. At the beginning of each line, it outputs the line number (the current count of the T_NEW_LINE tokens). At the end-of-file, this submodule outputs nothing. We define a lc_eof function for consistency's sake, but the function does absolutely nothing.

Brace Counter Submodule (bc)

This submodule keeps track of the nesting level of the curly braces {}. We feed the submodule a stream of tokens through the bc_take_token function. This function keeps track of the left and right curly braces and ignores everything else:

```
void bc_take_token(enum TOKEN_TYPE token) {
    switch (token) {
        case T_L_CURLY:
            ++bc_cur_level;
            if (bc_cur_level > bc_max_level)
                bc_max_level = bc_cur_level;
            break;
        case T_R_CURLY:
            --bc_cur_level;
            break;
        default:
            /* Ignore */
```

```
                    break;
            }
    }
```

The results of this statistic are printed in two places. The first is at the beginning of each line. The second is at the end-of-file. We define two functions to print these statistics:

```
static void bc_line_start(void) {
    printf("{%-2d ", bc_cur_level);
}

static void bc_eof(void) {
    printf("Maximum nesting of {} : %d\n", bc_max_level);
}
```

Parentheses Counter Submodule (pc)

This submodule is very similar to the brace counter submodule. As a matter of fact, it was created by copying the brace counter submodule and performing a few simple edits.

We probably should combine the Parentheses Counter submodule and the Brace Counter submodule into one submodule that uses a parameter to tell it what to count. Oh well, something for the next version.

Comment Counter Submodule (cc)

In these functions, we keep track of lines with comments in them, lines with code in them, lines with both, and lines with none. The results are printed at the end-of-file.

do_file Procedure

The `do_file` procedure reads each file one token at a time, and sends each token to the `take_token` routine for every statistic class:

```
while (1) {
cur_token = next_token();

    lc_take_token(cur_token);
    pc_take_token(cur_token);
    bc_take_token(cur_token);
    cc_take_token(cur_token);
```

Expandability

One thing to keep in mind when designing any software is expandability. In other words, what must someone do to add to our program? Suppose someone wants to add a new statistic to our program. What must they do?

Suppose they are adding a Word Count submodule (wc). They need to define four procedures: `wc_init`, `wc_take_token`, `wc_line_start`, and `wc_eof`.

We need to call these procedures at the proper point. But how do they know where to put the procedure calls? The answer is that they can use the editor to look for every place that a Comment Counter submodule procedure is used and clone the Comment Counter calls. This method is not exactly the best way of doing things, especially if the calls are spread across several files. But, the method is the best that we can come up with given the limitations of C.

C++ has no such limitations. In the book *Practical C++ Programming*, we design a similar program using C++ classes. The result is that instead of having multiple lists of procedure classes, we have one class list. The single list makes expandability and maintainability much easier.

Testing

To test this program, we came up with a small C program that contains every different type of possible token. The results are shown in Example 22-1.

Example 22-1: stat/test.out

```
 1 (0   {0  /* This is a single line comment */
 2 (0   {0  /*
 3 (0   {0   * This is a multiline
 4 (0   {0   * comment.
 5 (0   {0   */
 6 (0   {0  int main()
 7 (0   {1  {
 8 (0   {1      /* A procedure */
 9 (0   {1      int i;      /* Comment / code line */
10 (0   {1      char foo[10];
11 (0   {1
12 (0   {1      strcpy(foo, "abc");      /* String */
13 (0   {1      strcpy(foo, "a\"bc");    /* String with special character */
14 (0   {1
15 (0   {1      foo[0] = 'a';      /* Character */
16 (0   {1      foo[1] = '\'';     /* Character with escape */
17 (0   {1
18 (0   {1      i = 3 / 2;         /* Slash that's not a commment */
19 (0   {1      i = 3;             /* Normal number */
20 (0   {1      i = 0x123ABC;      /* Hex number */
21 (0   {1
22 (1   {1      i = ((1 + 2) *     /* Nested () */
23 (0   {1           (3 + 4));
24 (0   {1
25 (0   {2      {
26 (0   {2          int j;         /* Nested {} */
27 (0   {1      }
28 (0   {1      return (0);
```

Example 22-1: stat/test.out (continued)

```
 29 (0  {0   }
 30 (0  {0
Total number of lines: 30
Maximum nesting of () : 2
Maximum nesting of {} : 2
Number of blank lines ................6
Number of comment only lines .........6
Number of code only lines ............8
Number of lines with code and comments 10
Comment to code ratio 88.9%
```

Revisions

Currently, the program collects a very limited set of statistics. You could add things like average identifier size and tracking statistics for each procedure. One thing we kept in mind when we designed our program was the need for expandability.

We stopped our statistics collection at four types of statistics because we had fulfilled our mission to demonstrate a reasonably advanced set of C constructs. We didn't add more because the program would be too complex to fit in the chapter. On the whole, the program does its job well.

A Final Warning

Just because you can generate a statistic doesn't mean that it's useful.

Program Files

The in_file.h File

```
/********************************************************
 * input_file -- Data from the input file.             *
 *                                                     *
 * The current two characters are stored in            *
 *      cur_char and next_char.                        *
 * Lines are buffered so that they can be output to    *
 * the screen after a line is assembled.               *
 *                                                     *
 * Functions:                                          *
 *      in_open -- Opens the input file.               *
 *      in_close -- Closes the input file.             *
 *      read_char   -- Reads the next character.       *
 *      in_char_char -- Returns the current character. *
 *      in_next_char -- Returns the next character.    *
 *      in_flush -- Sends line to the screen.          *
 ********************************************************/
```

```
/**********************************************************
 * in_open -- Opens the input file.                       *
 *                                                        *
 * Parameters                                             *
 *      name -- Name of disk file to use for input.       *
 *                                                        *
 * Returns                                                *
 *      0 -- Open succeeded.                              *
 *      nonzero -- Open failed.                           *
 **********************************************************/
extern int in_open(const char name[]);

/**********************************************************
 * in_close -- Closes the input file.                     *
 **********************************************************/
extern void in_close(void);

/**********************************************************
 * in_read_char -- Read the next character from the       *
 *      input file.                                       *
 **********************************************************/
extern void in_read_char(void);

/**********************************************************
 * in_cur_char -- Gets the current input character.       *
 *                                                        *
 * Returns                                                *
 *      current character.                                *
 **********************************************************/
extern int in_cur_char(void);

/**********************************************************
 * in_next_char -- Peeks ahead one character.             *
 *                                                        *
 * Returns                                                *
 *      next character.                                   *
 **********************************************************/
extern int in_next_char(void);

/**********************************************************
 * in_flush -- Flushes the buffered input line to the     *
 *             screen.                                    *
 **********************************************************/
extern void in_flush(void);
```

The in_file.c File

```
/**********************************************************
 * infile module                                          *
 *      Handles opening, reading, and display of          *
 *      data from the input file.                         *
 *                                                        *
 * Functions:                                             *
 *      in_open -- Opens the input file.                  *
```

```
*       in_close -- Closes the input file.            *
*       read_char   -- Reads the next character.      *
*       in_char_char -- Returns the current character.  *
*       in_next_char -- Returns the next character.   *
*       in_flush -- Sends line to the screen.         *
 ********************************************************/
#include <stdio.h>
#include <errno.h>

#include "in_file.h"

#define LINE_MAX 500     /* Longest possible line */

struct input_file {
    FILE *file;          /* File we are reading */
    char line[LINE_MAX];/* Current line */
    char *char_ptr;      /* Current character on the line */

    int cur_char;        /* Current character (can be EOF)*/
    int next_char;       /* Next character (can be EOF)   */
};

/* Input file that we are reading */
static struct input_file in_file = {
    NULL,                /* file */
    "",                  /* line */
    NULL,                /* char_ptr */
    '\0',                /* cur_char */
    '\0'                 /* next_char */
};


/********************************************************
 * in_open -- Opens the input file.                     *
 *                                                      *
 * Parameters                                           *
 *      name -- Name of disk file to use for input.     *
 *                                                      *
 * Returns                                              *
 *      0 -- Open succeeded.                            *
 *      nonzero -- Open failed.                         *
 ********************************************************/
int in_open(const char name[])
{
    in_file.file = fopen(name, "r");
    if (in_file.file == NULL)
        return (errno);

    /*
     * Initialize the input file and read the first two
     * characters.
     */
    in_file.cur_char = fgetc(in_file.file);
    in_file.next_char = fgetc(in_file.file);
```

```
    in_file.char_ptr = in_file.line;
    return (0);
}

/**********************************************************
 * in_close -- Closes the input file.                     *
 **********************************************************/
void in_close(void)
{
    if (in_file.file != NULL) {
        fclose(in_file.file);
        in_file.file = NULL;
    }
}

/**********************************************************
 * in_cur_char -- Gets the current input character.       *
 *                                                        *
 * Returns                                                *
 *      current character.                                *
 **********************************************************/
int in_cur_char(void)
{
    return (in_file.cur_char);
}

/**********************************************************
 * in_next_char -- Peeks ahead one character.             *
 *                                                        *
 * Returns                                                *
 *      next character.                                   *
 **********************************************************/
int in_next_char(void)
{
    return (in_file.next_char);
}

/**********************************************************
 * in_flush -- Flushes the buffered input line to the     *
 *             screen.                                    *
 **********************************************************/
void in_flush(void)
{
    *in_file.char_ptr = '\0';              /* End the line */
    fputs(in_file.line, stdout);           /* Send the line */
    in_file.char_ptr = in_file.line;       /* Reset the line */
}

/**********************************************************
 * in_read_char -- Reads the next character from the      *
 *      input file.                                       *
 **********************************************************/
void in_read_char(void)
{
```

```
        *in_file.char_ptr = in_file.cur_char;
        ++in_file.char_ptr;

        in_file.cur_char = in_file.next_char;
        in_file.next_char = fgetc(in_file.file);
    };
```

The ch_type.h File

```
/*********************************************************
 * char_type -- Character type module.                   *
 *********************************************************/
enum CHAR_TYPE {
    C_EOF,        /* End of file character */
    C_WHITE,      /* Whitespace or control character */
    C_NEWLINE,    /* A newline character */
    C_ALPHA,      /* A Letter (includes _) */
    C_DIGIT,      /* A Number */
    C_OPERATOR,   /* Random operator */
    C_SLASH,      /* The character '/' */
    C_L_PAREN,    /* The character '(' */
    C_R_PAREN,    /* The character ')' */
    C_L_CURLY,    /* The character '{' */
    C_R_CURLY,    /* The character '}' */
    C_SINGLE,     /* The character '\'' */
    C_DOUBLE,     /* The character '"' */
    /* End of simple types, more complex, derrived types follow */
    C_HEX_DIGIT,/* Hexidecimal digit */
    C_ALPHA_NUMERIC/* Alpha numeric */
};

/*********************************************************
 * is_char_type -- Determines if a character belongs to  *
 *                 a given character type.               *
 *                                                       *
 * Parameters                                            *
 *      ch -- Character to check.                        *
 *      kind -- Type to check it for.                    *
 *                                                       *
 * Returns:                                              *
 *      0 -- Character is not of the specified kind.     *
 *      1 -- Character is of the specified kind.         *
 *********************************************************/
extern int is_char_type(int ch, enum CHAR_TYPE kind);

/*********************************************************
 * get_char_type -- Given a character, returns its type.*
 *                                                       *
 * Note: We return the simple types.  Composite types    *
 * such as C_HEX_DIGIT and C_ALPHA_NUMERIC are not       *
 * returned.                                             *
 *                                                       *
 * Parameters:                                           *
 *      ch -- Character having the type we want.         *
```

```
 *                                                      *
 * Returns                                              *
 *      character type.                                 *
 ********************************************************/
extern enum CHAR_TYPE get_char_type(int ch);
```

The ch_type.c File

```
/********************************************************
 * ch_type package                                     *
 *                                                      *
 * This module is used to determine the type of        *
 * various characters.                                 *
 *                                                      *
 * Public functions:                                   *
 *      init_char_type -- Initializes the table.       *
 *      is_char_type -- Is a character of a given type? *
 *      get_char_type -- Given char, returns type.     *
 ********************************************************/
#include <stdio.h>

#include "ch_type.h"

/* Define the type information array */
static enum CHAR_TYPE type_info[256];
static int ch_setup = 0;          /* True if character type info setup */
/********************************************************
 * fill_range -- Fills in a range of types for the     *
 *      character type class.                          *
 *                                                      *
 * Parameters                                          *
 *      start, end -- Range of items to fill in.       *
 *      type -- Type to use for filling.               *
 ********************************************************/
static void fill_range(int start, int end, enum CHAR_TYPE type)
{
    int cur_ch; /* Character we are handling now */

    for (cur_ch = start; cur_ch <= end; ++cur_ch) {
        type_info[cur_ch] = type;
    }
}


/********************************************************
 * init_char_type -- Initializes the char type table.  *
 ********************************************************/
static void init_char_type(void)
{
    fill_range(0, 255, C_WHITE);

    fill_range('A', 'Z', C_ALPHA);
    fill_range('a', 'z', C_ALPHA);
    type_info['_'] = C_ALPHA;
```

```
        fill_range('0', '9', C_DIGIT);

        type_info['!'] = C_OPERATOR;
        type_info['#'] = C_OPERATOR;
        type_info['$'] = C_OPERATOR;
        type_info['%'] = C_OPERATOR;
        type_info['^'] = C_OPERATOR;
        type_info['&'] = C_OPERATOR;
        type_info['*'] = C_OPERATOR;
        type_info['-'] = C_OPERATOR;
        type_info['+'] = C_OPERATOR;
        type_info['='] = C_OPERATOR;
        type_info['|'] = C_OPERATOR;
        type_info['~'] = C_OPERATOR;
        type_info[','] = C_OPERATOR;
        type_info[':'] = C_OPERATOR;
        type_info['?'] = C_OPERATOR;
        type_info['.'] = C_OPERATOR;
        type_info['<'] = C_OPERATOR;
        type_info['>'] = C_OPERATOR;

        type_info['/'] = C_SLASH;
        type_info['\n'] = C_NEWLINE;

        type_info['('] = C_L_PAREN;
        type_info[')'] = C_R_PAREN;

        type_info['{'] = C_L_CURLY;
        type_info['}'] = C_R_CURLY;

        type_info['"'] = C_DOUBLE;
        type_info['\''] = C_SINGLE;
}


/*******************************************************
 * is_char_type -- Determines if a character belongs to *
 *                 a given character type.              *
 *                                                      *
 * Parameters                                           *
 *      ch -- Character to check.                       *
 *      kind -- Type to check it for.                   *
 *                                                      *
 * Returns:                                             *
 *      0 -- Character is not of the specified kind.    *
 *      1 -- Character is of the specified kind.        *
 *******************************************************/
int is_char_type(int ch, enum CHAR_TYPE kind)
{
    if (!ch_setup) {
        init_char_type();
        ch_setup = 1;
    }

    if (ch == EOF) return (kind == C_EOF);
```

```
    switch (kind) {
        case C_HEX_DIGIT:
            if (type_info[ch] == C_DIGIT)
                return (1);
            if ((ch >= 'A') && (ch <= 'F'))
                return (1);
            if ((ch >= 'a') && (ch <= 'f'))
                return (1);
            return (0);
        case C_ALPHA_NUMERIC:
            return ((type_info[ch] == C_ALPHA) ||
                    (type_info[ch] == C_DIGIT));
        default:
            return (type_info[ch] == kind);
    }
};

/************************************************************
 * get_char_type -- Given a character, returns its type.*
 *                                                      *
 * Note: We return the simple types.  Composite types   *
 * such as C_HEX_DIGIT and C_ALPHA_NUMERIC are not      *
 * returned.                                            *
 *                                                      *
 * Parameters:                                          *
 *      ch -- Character having the type we want.        *
 *                                                      *
 * Returns                                              *
 *      character type.                                 *
 ************************************************************/
enum CHAR_TYPE get_char_type(int ch) {
    if (!ch_setup) {
        init_char_type();
        ch_setup = 1;
    }

    if (ch == EOF) return (C_EOF);

    return (type_info[ch]);
}
```

The token.h File

```
/************************************************************
 * token -- Token handling module.                      *
 *                                                      *
 * Functions:                                           *
 *      next_token -- Gets the next token from the input.*
 ************************************************************/

/*
 * Define the enumerated list of tokens.
 */
enum TOKEN_TYPE {
```

```
    T_NUMBER,              /* Simple number (floating point or integer */
    T_STRING,              /* String or character constant */
    T_COMMENT,    /* Comment */
    T_NEWLINE,    /* Newline character */
    T_OPERATOR,   /* Arithmetic operator */
    T_L_PAREN,    /* Character "(" */
    T_R_PAREN,    /* Character ")" */
    T_L_CURLY,    /* Character "{" */
    T_R_CURLY,    /* Character "}" */
    T_ID,                  /* Identifier */
    T_EOF                  /* End of File */
};

/*
 * We use #define here instead of "const int" because so many old
 * software packages use #define.  We must have picked
 * up a header file that uses #define for TRUE/FALSE.  Consequently,
 * we protect against double defines as well as against using #define
 * ourselves.
 */
#ifndef TRUE
#define TRUE 1          /* Define a simple TRUE/FALSE values */
#define FALSE 0
#endif /* TRUE */

/********************************************************
 * next_token -- Reads the next token in an input stream.*
 *                                                      *
 * Parameters                                           *
 *      in_file -- File to read.                        *
 *                                                      *
 * Returns                                              *
 *      next token.                                     *
 ********************************************************/
extern enum TOKEN_TYPE next_token(void);
```

The token.c File

```
/********************************************************
 * token -- Token handling module.                      *
 *                                                      *
 * Functions:                                           *
 *      next_token -- Gets the next token from the input.*
 ********************************************************/
#include <stdio.h>
#include <stdlib.h>

#include "ch_type.h"
#include "in_file.h"
#include "token.h"

static int in_comment = FALSE;  /* True if we're in a comment */
```

```
/************************************************************
 * read_comment -- Reads in a comment.                     *
 *                                                         *
 * Returns                                                 *
 *      Token read.  Can be a T_COMMENT or T_NEW_LINE,     *
 *      depending on what we read.                         *
 *                                                         *
 *      Multiline comments are split into multiple         *
 *      tokens.                                            *
 ************************************************************/
static enum TOKEN_TYPE read_comment(void)
{
    if (in_cur_char() == '\n') {
        in_read_char();
        return (T_NEWLINE);
    }
    while (1) {
        in_comment = TRUE;
        if (in_cur_char() == EOF) {
            fprintf(stderr, "Error: EOF inside comment\n");
            return (T_EOF);
        }
        if (in_cur_char() == '\n')
            return (T_COMMENT);
        if ((in_cur_char() == '*') &&
            (in_next_char() == '/')) {
            in_comment = FALSE;
            /* Skip past the ending */
            in_read_char();
            in_read_char();
            return (T_COMMENT);
        }
        in_read_char();
    }
}
/************************************************************
 * next_token -- Reads the next token in an input stream.  *
 *                                                         *
 * Returns                                                 *
 *      next token.                                        *
 ************************************************************/
enum TOKEN_TYPE next_token(void)
{
    if (in_comment)
        return (read_comment());

    while (is_char_type(in_cur_char(), C_WHITE)) {
        in_read_char();
    }
    if (in_cur_char() == EOF)
        return (T_EOF);

    switch (get_char_type(in_cur_char())) {
        case C_NEWLINE:
```

```
            in_read_char();
            return (T_NEWLINE);
        case C_ALPHA:
            while (is_char_type(in_cur_char(), C_ALPHA_NUMERIC))
                in_read_char();
            return (T_ID);
        case C_DIGIT:
            in_read_char();
            if ((in_cur_char() == 'X') || (in_cur_char() == 'x')) {
                in_read_char();
                while (is_char_type(in_cur_char(), C_HEX_DIGIT))
                    in_read_char();
                return (T_NUMBER);
            }
            while (is_char_type(in_cur_char(), C_DIGIT))
                in_read_char();
            return (T_NUMBER);
        case C_SLASH:
            /* Check for  '/', '*' characters  */
            if (in_next_char() == '*') {
                return (read_comment());
            }
            /* Fall through */
        case C_OPERATOR:
            in_read_char();
            return (T_OPERATOR);
        case C_L_PAREN:
            in_read_char();
            return (T_L_PAREN);
        case C_R_PAREN:
            in_read_char();
            return (T_R_PAREN);
        case C_L_CURLY:
            in_read_char();
            return (T_L_CURLY);
        case C_R_CURLY:
            in_read_char();
            return (T_R_CURLY);
        case C_DOUBLE:
            while (1) {
                in_read_char();
                /* Check for end of string */
                if (in_cur_char() == '"')
                    break;

                /* Escape character, then skip the next character */
                if (in_cur_char() == '\\')
                    in_read_char();
            }
            in_read_char();
            return (T_STRING);
        case C_SINGLE:
            while (1) {
                in_read_char();
```

```
                      /* Check for end of character */
                      if (in_cur_char() == '\'')
                          break;

                      /* Escape character, then skip the next character */
                      if (in_cur_char() == '\\')
                          in_read_char();
                  }
                  in_read_char();
                  return (T_STRING);
              default:
                  fprintf(stderr, "Internal error: Very strange character\n");
                  abort();
          }
          fprintf(stderr, "Internal error: We should never get here\n");
          abort();
          return (T_EOF);      /* Should never get here either */
                               /* But we put in the return to avoid a compiler */
                               /* warning. */
}
```

The stat.c File

```
/***********************************************************
 * stat                                                    *
 *       Produces statistics about a program.              *
 *                                                         *
 * Usage:                                                  *
 *       stat [options] <file list>                        *
 *                                                         *
 ***********************************************************/
#include <stdio.h>
#include <stdlib.h>
#include <memory.h>

#include "ch_type.h"
#include "in_file.h"
#include "token.h"

/***********************************************************
 ***********************************************************
 ***********************************************************
 * line_counter -- Handles line number / line count        *
 *                 stat.                                    *
 *                                                         *
 * Counts the number of T_NEW_LINE tokens seen and         *
 * outputs the current line number at the beginning        *
 * of the line.                                            *
 *                                                         *
 * At EOF, it will output the total number of lines.       *
 ***********************************************************/
static int cur_line;            /* Current line number */
```

```c
/*********************************************************
 * lc_init -- Initializes the line counter variables.   *
 *********************************************************/
static void lc_init(void)
{
    cur_line = 0;
};

/*********************************************************
 * lc_take_token -- Consumes tokens and looks for       *
 *                  end-of-line tokens.                 *
 *                                                       *
 * Parameters                                            *
 *      token -- The token coming in from the input      *
 *                          stream.                      *
 *********************************************************/
static void lc_take_token(enum TOKEN_TYPE token) {
    if (token == T_NEWLINE)
    ++cur_line;
}

/*********************************************************
 * lc_line_start -- Outputs the per-line statistics,    *
 *                  namely the current line number.     *
 *********************************************************/
static void lc_line_start(void) {
    printf("%4d ", cur_line);
}

/*********************************************************
 * lc_eof -- Outputs the eof statistics.                *
 *           In this case, the number of lines.         *
 *********************************************************/
static void lc_eof(void) {
    printf("Total number of lines: %d\n", cur_line);
}

/*********************************************************
 *********************************************************
 *********************************************************
 * paren_count -- Counts the nesting level of ().       *
 *                                                       *
 * Counts the number of T_L_PAREN vs T_R_PAREN tokens    *
 * and writes the current nesting level at the beginning*
 * of each line.                                         *
 *                                                       *
 * Also keeps track of the maximum nesting level.        *
 *********************************************************/
static int pc_cur_level;
static int pc_max_level;

/*********************************************************
 * pc_init -- Initializes the () counter variables.     *
 *********************************************************/
```

```
void pc_init(void) {
    pc_cur_level = 0;
    pc_max_level = 0;
};

/**********************************************************
 * pc_take_token -- Consumes tokens and looks for        *
 *                  () tokens.                            *
 *                                                        *
 * Parameters                                             *
 *      token -- The token coming in from the input       *
 *                      stream.                           *
 **********************************************************/
void pc_take_token(enum TOKEN_TYPE token) {
    switch (token) {
        case T_L_PAREN:
            ++pc_cur_level;
            if (pc_cur_level > pc_max_level)
                pc_max_level = pc_cur_level;
            break;
        case T_R_PAREN:
            --pc_cur_level;
            break;
        default:
            /* Ignore */
            break;
    }
}

/**********************************************************
 * pc_line_start -- Outputs the per-line statistics,     *
 *                  namely the current () nesting.       *
 **********************************************************/
static void pc_line_start(void) {
    printf("(%-2d ", pc_cur_level);
}

/**********************************************************
 * pc_eof -- Outputs the eof statistics.                 *
 *           In this case, the max nesting of ().        *
 **********************************************************/
void pc_eof(void) {
    printf("Maximum nesting of () : %d\n", pc_max_level);
}

/**********************************************************
 **********************************************************
 **********************************************************
 * brace_counter -- Counts the nesting level of {}.      *
 *                                                        *
 * Counts the number of T_L_CURLY vs T_R_CURLY tokens    *
 * and writes the current nesting level at the beginning *
 * of each line.                                         *
 *                                                        *
```

```
 * Also, keeps track of the maximum nesting level.     *
 *                                                      *
 * Note: brace_counter and paren_counter should         *
 * probably be combined.                                *
 ********************************************************/
static int bc_cur_level;        /* Current nesting level */
static int bc_max_level;        /* Maximum nesting level */

/*********************************************************
 * pc_init -- Initialize the {} counter variables.     *
 ********************************************************/
void bc_init(void) {
    bc_cur_level = 0;
    bc_max_level = 0;
};

/*********************************************************
 * bc_take_token -- Consumes tokens and looks for      *
 *                  {} tokens.                          *
 *                                                      *
 * Parameters                                           *
 *      token -- The token coming in from the input     *
 *                       stream.                        *
 ********************************************************/
void bc_take_token(enum TOKEN_TYPE token) {
    switch (token) {
        case T_L_CURLY:
            ++bc_cur_level;
            if (bc_cur_level > bc_max_level)
                bc_max_level = bc_cur_level;
            break;
        case T_R_CURLY:
            --bc_cur_level;
            break;
        default:
            /* Ignore */
            break;
    }
}

/*********************************************************
 * bc_line_start -- Outputs the per-line statistics,   *
 *                  namely the current {} nesting.     *
 ********************************************************/
static void bc_line_start(void) {
    printf("{%-2d ", bc_cur_level);
}

/*********************************************************
 * bc_eof -- Outputs the eof statistics.               *
 *                  In this case, the max nesting of {}. *
 ********************************************************/
static void bc_eof(void) {
    printf("Maximum nesting of {} : %d\n", bc_max_level);
}
```

```
/***********************************************************
 ***********************************************************
 ***********************************************************
 * comment_counter -- Counts the number of lines          *
 *      with and without comments.                        *
 *                                                        *
 * Outputs nothing at the beginning of each line, but     *
 * will output a ratio at the end of file.                *
 *                                                        *
 * Note: This class makes use of two bits:                *
 *      CF_COMMENT  -- a comment was seen                  *
 *      CF_CODE     -- code was seen                       *
 * to collect statistics.                                 *
 *                                                        *
 * These are combined to form an index into the counter   *
 * array so the value of these two bits is very           *
 * important.                                             *
 ***********************************************************/
static const int CF_COMMENT = (1<<0);   /* Line contains comment */
static const int CF_CODE    = (1<<1);   /* Line contains code */
/* These bits are combined to form the statistics */

/*      0                   -- [0] Blank line */
/*      CF_COMMENT           -- [1] Comment-only line */
/*      CF_CODE              -- [2] Code-only line */
/*      CF_COMMENT|CF_CODE  -- [3] Comments and code on this line */

static int counters[4]; /* Count of various types of stats. */
static int flags;       /* Flags for the current line */

/***********************************************************
 * cc_init -- Initializes the comment counter variables.*
 ***********************************************************/
static void cc_init(void) {
    memset(counters, '\0', sizeof(counters));
    flags = 0;
};

/***********************************************************
 * cc_take_token -- Consumes tokens and looks for         *
 *                  comments tokens.                      *
 *                                                        *
 * Parameters                                             *
 *      token -- The token coming in from the input       *
 *                        stream.                         *
 ***********************************************************/
void cc_take_token(enum TOKEN_TYPE token) {
    switch (token) {
        case T_COMMENT:
            flags |= CF_COMMENT;
            break;
        default:
            flags |= CF_CODE;
            break;
```

```
            case T_NEWLINE:
                ++counters[flags];
                flags = 0;
                break;
        }
}

/**********************************************************
 * cc_line_start -- Outputs the per-line statistics.    *
 **********************************************************/
static void cc_line_start(void)
{
    /* Do nothing */
}

/**********************************************************
 * cc_eof -- Outputs the eof statistics.                *
 *                 In this case, the comment/code ratios.  *
 **********************************************************/
static void cc_eof(void) {
    printf("Number of blank lines ................%d\n",
            counters[0]);
    printf("Number of comment only lines ..........%d\n",
            counters[1]);
    printf("Number of code only lines .............%d\n",
            counters[2]);
    printf("Number of lines with code and comments %d\n",
            counters[3]);
    printf("Comment to code ratio %3.1f%%\n",
        (float)(counters[1] + counters[3]) /
        (float)(counters[2] + counters[3]) * 100.0);
}

/**********************************************************
 * do_file -- Processes a single file.                  *
 *                                                      *
 * Parameters                                           *
 *      name -- The name of the file to process.        *
 **********************************************************/
static void do_file(const char *const name)
{
    enum TOKEN_TYPE cur_token;   /* Current token type */

    /*
     * Initialize the counters
     */
    lc_init();
    pc_init();
    bc_init();
    cc_init();

    if (in_open(name) != 0) {
        printf("Error: Could not open file %s for reading\n", name);
        return;
```

```
        }
    while (1) {
        cur_token = next_token();

        lc_take_token(cur_token);
        pc_take_token(cur_token);
        bc_take_token(cur_token);
        cc_take_token(cur_token);

        switch (cur_token) {
            case T_NEWLINE:
                lc_line_start();
                pc_line_start();
                bc_line_start();
                cc_line_start();
                in_flush();
                break;
            case T_EOF:
                lc_eof();
                pc_eof();
                bc_eof();
                cc_eof();
                in_close();
                return;
            default:
                /* Do nothing */
                break;
        }
    }
}

int main(int argc, char *argv[])
{
    char *prog_name = argv[0];  /* Name of the program */

    if (argc == 1) {
        printf("Usage is %s [options] <file-list>\n", prog_name);
        exit (8);
    }

    for (/* argc set */; argc > 1; --argc) {
        do_file(argv[1]);
        ++argv;
    }
    return (0);
}
```

UNIX Makefile for CC (Generic Unix)

```
# File: stat/makefile.unx

#
```

```
# Makefile for the UNIX standard cc compiler
#
CC=cc
CFLAGS=-g
OBJS= stat.o ch_type.o token.o in_file.o

all: stat.out stat test.out

test.out: test.c stat
        stat test.c >test.out

# This generates a test output based on another example
# in this book.
stat.out: stat
        stat ../calc3/calc3.c >stat.out

stat: $(OBJS)
        $(CC) $(CFLAGS) -o stat $(OBJS)

stat.o: stat.c token.h
        $(CC) $(CFLAGS) -c stat.c

ch_type.o: ch_type.c ch_type.h
        $(CC) $(CFLAGS) -c ch_type.c

token.o: token.c token.h ch_type.h in_file.h
        $(CC) $(CFLAGS) -c token.c

in_file.o: in_file.c in_file.h
        $(CC) $(CFLAGS) -c in_file.c

clean:
        rm -f stat stat.o ch_type.o token.o in_file.o
```

UNIX Makefile for gcc

```
# File: stat/makefile.gcc

#
# Makefile for the Free Software Foundations g++ compiler
#
CC=gcc
CFLAGS=-g -Wall -D__USE_FIXED_PROTOTYPES__
OBJS= stat.o ch_type.o token.o in_file.o

all: stat.out stat test.out

test.out: test.c stat
        stat test.c >test.out

# This generates a test output based on another example
# in this book.
stat.out: stat
        stat ../calc3/calc3.c >stat.out
```

```
stat: $(OBJS)
        $(CC) $(CFLAGS) -o stat $(OBJS)

stat.o: stat.c token.h
        $(CC) $(CFLAGS) -c stat.c

ch_type.o: ch_type.c ch_type.h
        $(CC) $(CFLAGS) -c ch_type.c

token.o: token.c token.h ch_type.h in_file.h
        $(CC) $(CFLAGS) -c token.c

in_file.o: in_file.c in_file.h
        $(CC) $(CFLAGS) -c in_file.c

clean:
        rm -f stat stat.o ch_type.o token.o in_file.o
```

Turbo C++ Makefile

```
# File: stat/makefile.tcc

#
# Makefile for Borland's Borland-C++ compiler
#
CC=tcc
#
# Flags
#       -N  -- Check for stack overflow.
#       -v  -- Enable debugging.
#       -w  -- Turn on all warnings.
#       -ml -- Large model.
#
CFLAGS=-N -v -w -ml
OBJS= stat.obj ch_type.obj token.obj in_file.obj

all: stat.out stat.exe test.out

test.out: test.c stat.exe
        stat test.c >test.out

# This generates a test output based on another example
# in this book.
stat.out: stat.exe
        stat ..\calc3\calc3.c >stat.out

stat.exe: $(OBJS)
        $(CC) $(CFLAGS) -estat $(OBJS)

stat.obj: stat.c token.h
        $(CC) $(CFLAGS) -c stat.c

in_file.obj: in_file.c in_file.h
        $(CC) $(CFLAGS) -c in_file.c
```

```
ch_type.obj: ch_type.c ch_type.h
        $(CC) $(CFLAGS) -c ch_type.c

token.obj: token.c token.h ch_type.h
        $(CC) $(CFLAGS) -c token.c


clean:
        erase stat.exe
        erase stat.obj
        erase ch_type.obj
        erase in_file.obj
        erase token.obj
```

Borland C++ Makefile

```
# File: stat/makefile.bcc

#
# Makefile for Borland's Borland C++ compiler
#
CC=bcc
#
# Flags
#       -N  -- Check for stack overflow.
#       -v  -- Enable debugging.
#       -w  -- Turn on all warnings.
#       -ml -- Large model.
#
CFLAGS=-N -v -w -ml
OBJS= stat.obj ch_type.obj token.obj in_file.obj

all: stat.out stat.exe test.out

test.out: test.c stat.exe
        stat test.c >test.out

# This generates a test output based on another example
# in this book.
stat.out: stat.exe
        stat ..\calc3\calc3.c >stat.out

stat.exe: $(OBJS)
        $(CC) $(CFLAGS) -estat $(OBJS)

stat.obj: stat.c token.h
        $(CC) $(CFLAGS) -c stat.c

in_file.obj: in_file.c in_file.h
        $(CC) $(CFLAGS) -c in_file.c

ch_type.obj: ch_type.c ch_type.h
        $(CC) $(CFLAGS) -c ch_type.c
```

```
token.obj: token.c token.h ch_type.h
        $(CC) $(CFLAGS) -c token.c


clean:
        erase stat.exe
        erase stat.obj
        erase ch_type.obj
        erase in_file.obj
        erase token.obj
```

Microsoft Visual C++ Makefile

```
# File: stat/makefile.msc
#
# Makefile for Microsoft Visual C++
#
CC=cl
#
# Flags
#       AL -- Compile for large model.
#       Zi -- Enable debugging.
#       W1 -- Turn on warnings.
#
CFLAGS=/AL /Zi /W1
OBJS= stat.obj ch_type.obj token.obj in_file.obj

all: stat.out stat.exe test.out

test.out: test.c stat.exe
        stat test.c >test.out

# This generates a test output based on another example
# in this book.
stat.out: stat.exe
        stat ..\calc3\calc3.c >stat.out

stat.exe: $(OBJS)
        $(CC) $(CCFLAGS)  $(OBJS)

stat.obj: stat.c token.h
        $(CC) $(CCFLAGS) -c stat.c

ch_type.obj: ch_type.c ch_type.h
        $(CC) $(CCFLAGS) -c ch_type.c

token.obj: token.c token.h ch_type.h
        $(CC) $(CCFLAGS) -c token.c

in_file.obj: in_file.c
        $(CC) $(CCFLAGS) -c in_file.c
```

```
clean:
        erase stat.exe
        erase stat.obj
        erase ch_type.obj
        erase token.obj
        erase in_file.obj
```

Programming Exercises

Exercise 22-1: Write a program that checks a text file for doubled words (for example, "in the *the* file").

Exercise 22-2: Write a program that removes four-letter words from a file and replaces them with more acceptable equivalents.

Exercise 22-3: Write a mailing list program. This program will read, write, sort, and print mailing labels.

Exercise 22-4: Update the statistics program presented in this chapter, adding a cross-reference capability.

Exercise 22-5: Write a program that takes a text file and splits long lines into two smaller lines. The split point should be at the end of a sentence if possible, or at the end of a word if a sentence is too long.

23

Programming Adages

Second thoughts are ever wiser.
—Euripides

General

- Comment, comment, comment. Put a lot of comments in your program. They tell other programmers what you did. They also tell you what you did.

- Use the "KISS" principle. (Keep It Simple, Stupid.) Clear and simple is better than complex and wonderful.

- Avoid side effects. Use ++ and -- on lines by themselves.

- Use the prefix version of ++ and -- (++x, --x) instead of the postfix version (x++, x--). This adage does nothing for you in C, but will serve you well when you move to C++.

- Never put an assignment inside a conditional.

- Never put an assignment inside any other statement.

- Know the difference between = and ==. Using = for == is a very common mistake and is difficult to find.

- Never do "nothing" silently.

```
/* Don't program like this */
for (index = 0; data[index] < key; ++index);
/* Did you see the semicolon at the end of the last line? */
```

Always put in a comment or statement.

```
for (index = 0; data[index] < key; ++index)
        continue;
```

Design

- When designing your program, keep in mind "The Law of Least Astonishment," which states that your program should behave in a way that least astonishes the user.

- Make the user interface as simple and consistent as possible.

- Give the user as much help as you can.

- Clearly identify all error messages with the word "error," and try to give the user some idea of how to correct his problem.

Declarations

- Put one variable declaration per line, and comment them.

- Make variable-names long enough to be easily understood, but not so long that they are difficult to type in. Two or three words is usually enough.

- Never use default declarations. If a function returns an integer, declare it as type **int**.

- All parameters to a function should be declared and commented. Never use default declarations.

- Always declare **main** as:

```
int main(void)                 /* Correct declaration */
int main(int argc, char *argv[])   /* Also correct */
```

Never declare **main** as:

```
void main()                    /* never program like this */
void main(int ac, char *av[])   /* never use names like this */
```

switch Statement

- Always put a default case in a **switch** statement. Even if the case does nothing, put it in.

```
switch (expression) {
    /* ... */
    default:
            /* do nothing */
}
```

- Every case in a switch should end with a **break** or /* Fall through */ comment.

Preprocessor

- Always put parentheses around each constant expression defined by a preprocessor **#define** directive.

  ```
  #define BOX_SIZE (3*10) /* size of the box in pixels */
  ```
- Use **const** declarations instead of **#define** wherever possible.

- Put () around each argument of a parameterized macro.

  ```
  #define SQUARE(x) ((x) * (x))
  ```
- Surround macros that contain complete statements with curly braces ({}).

  ```
  /* A fatal error has occurred.  Tell user and abort */
  #define DIE(msg) {printf(msg);exit(8);}
  ```
- When using the **#ifdef/#endif** construct for conditional compilation, put the **#define** and **#undef** statements near the top of the program and comment them.

Style

- A single block of code enclosed in {} should not span more than a couple of pages. Anything much bigger than that should probably be split up into several smaller, simpler procedures.

- When your code starts to run into the right margin, you should split the procedure into several smaller, simpler procedures.

Compiling

- Always create a *Makefile* so that others will know how to compile your program.

- Turn on all the warning flags, then make your program warning free.

Final Note

Just when you think you've discovered all of the things that C can do to you—think again. There are still more surprises in store for you.

Question 23-1: *Why does Example 23-1 think everything is two? (This inspired the last adage.)*

Example 23-1: not2/not2.c

```
#include <stdio.h>
int main()
{
```

Example 23-1: not2/not2.c (continued)

```
    char line[80];
    int number;

    printf("Enter a number: ");

    fgets(line, sizeof(line), stdin);
    sscanf(line, "%d", &number);

    if (number =! 2)
        printf("Number is not two\n");
    else
        printf("Number is two\n");

    return (0);
}
```

Answer

Answer 23-1: The statement (`number =! 2`) is not a relational equation, but an assignment statement. It is equivalent to:

```
    number = (!2);
```

Because 2 is nonzero, `!2` is zero.

The programmer accidentally reversed the not equals, `!=`, so it became `=!`. The statement should read:

```
    if (number != 2)
```

IV

Other Language Features

The appendixes fill in some of the more arcane information that this book has referred to, but that is more appropriate to include as reference material.

- Appendix A, *ASCII Table*, lists the octal, hexadecimal, and decimal representations of the ASCII character set that is now in almost universal use.

- Appendix B, *Ranges and Parameter Passing Conversions*, lists the limits you can expect to come up against in handling numbers with various sizes of memory allocation.

- Appendix C, *Operator Precedence Rules*, lists those impossible-to-remember rules, to help you when you encounter code written by rude people who didn't use enough parentheses.

- Appendix D, *Program to Compute a Sine Using a Power Series*, illustrates the manipulation of floating-point (real) numbers, which did not receive complete attention in the rest of the book.

- The *Glossary* defines many of the technical terms used throughout the book.

A

ASCII Table

Table A-1: ASCII Character Chart

Dec	Oct	Hex	Char	Dec	Oct	Hex	Char
0	000	00	NUL	27	033	1B	ESC
1	001	01	SOH	28	034	1C	FS
2	002	02	STX	29	035	1D	GS
3	003	03	ETX	30	036	1E	RS
4	004	04	EOT	31	037	1F	US
5	005	05	ENQ	32	040	20	SP
6	006	06	ACK	33	041	21	!
7	007	07	BEL	34	042	22	"
8	010	08	BS	35	043	23	#
9	011	09	HT	36	044	24	$
10	012	0A	NL	37	045	25	%
11	013	0B	VT	38	046	26	&
12	014	0C	NP	39	047	27	'
13	015	0D	CR	40	050	28	(
14	016	0E	SO	41	051	29	)
15	017	0F	SI	42	052	2A	*
16	020	10	DLE	43	053	2B	+
17	021	11	DC1	44	054	2C	,
18	022	12	DC2	45	055	2D	-
19	023	13	DC3	46	056	2E	.
20	024	14	DC4	47	057	2F	/
21	025	15	NAK	48	060	30	0
22	026	16	SYN	49	061	31	1
23	027	17	ETB	50	062	32	2
24	030	18	CAN	51	063	33	3
25	031	19	EM	52	064	34	4
26	032	1A	SUB	53	065	35	5

Table A-1: ASCII Character Chart (continued)

Dec	Oct	Hex	Char	Dec	Oct	Hex	Char
54	066	36	6	91	133	5B	[
55	067	37	7	92	134	5C	\
56	070	38	8	93	135	5D	]
57	071	39	9	94	136	5E	^
58	072	3A	:	95	137	5F	_
59	073	3B	;	96	140	60	`
60	074	3C	<	97	141	61	a
61	075	3D	=	98	142	62	b
62	076	3E	>	99	143	63	c
63	077	3F	?	100	144	64	d
64	100	40	@	101	145	65	e
65	101	41	A	102	146	66	f
66	102	42	B	103	147	67	g
67	103	43	C	104	150	68	h
68	104	44	D	105	151	69	i
69	105	45	E	106	152	6A	j
70	106	46	F	107	153	6B	k
71	107	47	G	108	154	6C	l
72	110	48	H	109	155	6D	m
73	111	49	I	110	156	6E	n
74	112	4A	J	111	157	6F	o
75	113	4B	K	112	160	70	p
76	114	4C	L	113	161	71	q
77	115	4D	M	114	162	72	r
78	116	4E	N	115	163	73	s
79	117	4F	O	116	164	74	t
80	120	50	P	117	165	75	u
81	121	51	Q	118	166	76	v
82	122	52	R	119	167	77	w
83	123	53	S	120	170	78	x
84	124	54	T	121	171	79	y
85	125	55	U	122	172	7A	z
86	126	56	V	123	173	7B	{
87	127	57	W	124	174	7C		
88	130	58	X	125	175	7D	}
89	131	59	Y	126	176	7E	~
90	132	5A	Z	127	177	7F	DEL

B

Ranges and Parameter Passing Conversions

Ranges

Table B-1 and Table B-2 list the ranges of various variable types.

Table B-1: 32-Bit UNIX Machine

Name	Bits	Low value	High value	Accuracy
int	32	-2147483648	2147483647	
short int	16	-32768	32767	
long int	32	-2147483648	2147483647	
unsigned int	32	0	4294967295	
unsigned short int	16	0	65535	
unsigned long int	32	0	4294967295	
char	8	System Dependent		
unsigned char	8	0	255	
float	32	-3.4E+38	3.4E+38	6 digits
double	64	-1.7E+308	1.7E+308	15 digits
long double	64	-1.7E+308	1.7E+308	15 digits

Table B-2: Turbo C++, Borland C++, and Most Other 16-bit Systems

Name	Bits	Low value	High value	Accuracy
int	16	-32768	32767	
short int	16	-32768	32767	
long int	32	-2147483648	2147483647	
unsigned int	16	0	65535	
unsigned short int	16	0	65535	

Table B-2: Turbo C++, Borland C++, and Most Other 16-bit Systems (continued)

Name	Bits	Low value	High value	Accuracy
unsigned long int	32	0	4294967295	
char	8	-128	127	
unsigned char	8	0	255	
float	32	-3.4E+38	3.4E+38	6 digits
double	64	-1.7E+308	1.7E+308	15 digits
long double	80	-3.4E+4932	3.4E+4932	17 digits

Automatic Type Conversions to Use When Passing Parameters

In order to eliminate some of the problems that may occur when passing parameters to a function, C performs the following automatic conversions to function arguments as shown in Table B-3.

Table B-3: Automatic Conversions

Type	Converted to
char	int
short int	int
int	int
long int	long int
float	double
double	double
long double	long double
array	pointer

C

Operator Precedence Rules

Standard Rules

Operators listed in Table C-1 near the top are evaluated before those below.

Table C-1: C Precedence Rules

Precedence	Operator				
1.	()	[]	->	.	
2.	!	~	++	--	(type)
	- (unary)	* (dereference)			
	& (address of)	sizeof			
3.	* (multiply)	/	%		
4.	+	-			
5.	<<	>>			
6.	<	<=	>	>=	
7.	==	!=			
8.	& (bitwise and)				
9.	^				
10.	|				
11.	&&				
12.	||				
13.	?:				
14.	=	+=	-=	etc.	
15.	,				

Practical Subset

Table C-2: Precedence Rules, Practical Subset

Precedence	Operator		
1.	* (multiply)	/	%
2.	+	-	

Put parentheses around everything else.

D

A Program to Compute a Sine Using a Power Series

This program is designed to compute the *sine* function using a power series. A very limited floating-point format is used to demonstrate some of the problems that can occur when using floating-point.

The program is invoked by:

```
sine value
```

where *value* is an angle in radians.

The program computes each term in the power series and displays the result. It continues computing terms until the last term is so small that it doesn't contribute to the final result.

For comparison purposes, the result of the library function `sin` is displayed as well as the computed sine.

The sine.c Program

Example D-1: sine/sine.c

```
[File: sine/sine.c]
/**********************************************************
 * sine -- Computes sine using very simple floating       *
 *      arithmetic.                                        *
 *                                                         *
 * Usage:                                                  *
 *      sine <value>                                       *
 *                                                         *
 *      <value> is an angle in radians                     *
 *                                                         *
 * Format used in f.fffe+X                                 *
 *                                                         *
```

Example D-1: sine/sine.c (continued)

```
 * f.fff is a 4-digit fraction                              *
 *      + is a sign (+ or -)                                *
 *      X is a single digit exponent                        *
 *                                                          *
 * sine(x) = x  - x**3 + x**5 - x**7                        *
 *               -----   ----   ----  . . .                 *
 *                3!     5!     7!                           *
 *                                                          *
 * Warning: This program is intended to show some of the    *
 *      problems with floating-point. It is not intended    *
 *      to be used to produce exact values for the          *
 *      sine function.                                      *
 *                                                          *
 * Note: Even though we specify only one digit for the      *
 *       exponent, two are used for some calculations.      *
 *       We have to do this because printf has no           *
 *       format for a single digit exponent.                *
 ***********************************************************/
#include <stdlib.h>
#include <math.h>
#include <stdio.h>

/***********************************************************
 * float_2_ascii -- Turns a floating-point string          *
 *      into ascii.                                         *
 *                                                          *
 * Parameters                                               *
 *      number -- Number to turn into ascii.                ^
 *                                                          *
 * Returns                                                  *
 *      Pointer to the string containing the number.        *
 *                                                          *
 * Warning: Uses static storage, so later calls             *
 *              overwrite earlier entries.                  *
 ***********************************************************/
static char *float_2_ascii(float number)
{
    static char result[10]; /*place to put the number */

    sprintf(result,"%8.3E", number);
    return (result);
}
/***********************************************************
 * fix_float -- Turns high-precision numbers into          *
 *              low-precision numbers to simulate a         *
 *              very dumb floating-point structure.         *
 *                                                          *
 * Parameters                                               *
 *      number -- Number to take care of.                   *
 *                                                          *
 * Returns                                                  *
 *      Number accurate to five places only.                *
```

Example D-1: sine/sine.c (continued)

```
 *                                                          *
 * Note: This works by changing a number into ascii and    *
 *       back. Very slow, but it works.                     *
 ***********************************************************/
float fix_float(float number)
{
    float   result; /* result of the conversion */
    char    ascii[10];      /* ascii version of number */

    sprintf(ascii,"%8.4e", number);
    sscanf(ascii, "%e", &result);
    return (result);
}
/***********************************************************
 * factorial -- Computes the factorial of a number.        *
 *                                                          *
 * Parameters                                               *
 *      number -- Number to use for factorial.             *
 *                                                          *
 * Returns                                                  *
 *      Factorial(number) or number!                       *
 *                                                          *
 * Note: Even though this is a floating-point routine,      *
 *       using numbers that are not whole numbers           *
 *       does not make sense.                               *
 ***********************************************************/
float factorial(float number)
{
    if (number <= 1.0)
        return (number);
    else
        return (number *factorial(number - 1.0));
}

int main(int argc, char *argv[])
{
    float   total;  /* total of series so far */
    float   new_total;/* newer version of total */
    float   term_top;/* top part of term */
    float   term_bottom;/* bottom of current term */
    float   term;   /* current term */
    float   exp;    /* exponent of current term */
    float   sign;   /* +1 or -1 (changes on each term) */
    float   value;  /* value of the argument to sin */
    int     index;  /* index for counting terms */

    if (argc != 2) {
        fprintf(stderr,"Usage is:\n");
        fprintf(stderr," sine <value>\n");
        exit (8);
    }
```

Example D-1: sine/sine.c (continued)

```
    value = fix_float(atof(&argv[1][0]));

    total = 0.0;
    exp = 1.0;
    sign = 1.0;

    for (index = 0; /* take care of below */ ; ++index) {
        term_top = fix_float(pow(value, exp));
        term_bottom = fix_float(factorial(exp));
        term = fix_float(term_top / term_bottom);
        printf("x**%d      %s\n", (int)exp,
                       float_2_ascii(term_top));
        printf("%d!       %s\n", (int)exp,
                       float_2_ascii(term_bottom));
        printf("x**%d/%d! %s\n", (int)exp, (int)exp,
                  float_2_ascii(term));
        printf("\n");
        new_total = fix_float(total + sign * term);
        if (new_total == total)
            break;
        total = new_total;
        sign = -sign;
        exp = exp + 2.0;
        printf("  total    %s\n", float_2_ascii(total));
        printf("\n");
    }
    printf("%d term computed\n", index+1);
    printf("sin(%s)=\n", float_2_ascii(value));
    printf("  %s\n", float_2_ascii(total));
    printf("Actual sin(%G)=%G\n",
           atof(&argv[1][0]), sin(atof(&argv[1][0])));
    return (0);
}
```

Glossary

!

The logical NOT operator.

! =

Not-equal relational operator.

"

See *Double quote.*

%

The modulus operator.

&

1) The bitwise AND operator.

2) A symbol used to precede a variable name (as in &x). Means the address of the named variable (address of x). Used to assign a value to a pointer variable.

&&

The logical AND operator (used in comparison operations).

'

See *Single quote.*

*

1) The MULTIPLY operator.

2) A symbol used to precede a pointer variable name that means "get the value stored at the address pointed to by the pointer variable." (***x** means "get the value stored at **x**"). Sometimes known as the dereferencing operator or indirect operator.

+

The ADD operator.

++

The incrementation operator.

,

The comma character is an obscure C operator that can be used to connect two statements together as one.

−

The subtract operator.

− −

The decrementation operator.

->

Used to obtain a member from a class or structure pointer.

/

The divide operator.

<

Less than relational operator.

<<

The left shift operator.

<=

Less than or equal relational operator.

==

Equal relational operator.

>

Greater than relational operator.

>=

Greater than or equal relational operator.

>>

The right shift operator.

?:

C operators to allow a conditional inside an expression. Rarely used.

^

The bitwise exclusive OR operator.

****

Character used in strings to signal a special character.

\b

Backspace character (moves the cursor back one on most output devices).

\f

Form feed character. (On most printers, this character will eject a page. On many terminals, this character will clear the screen.)

\n

New-line character. Moves the cursor to the beginning of the next line.

{}

See *curly braces*.

|

The bitwise OR operator.

||

The logical OR operator.

~

Bitwise complement operator. Inverts all bits.

'\0'

End-of-string character (the NULL character).

#define

A C preprocessor directive that defines a substitute text for a name.

#endif

The closing bracket to a preprocessor macro section that began with an **#ifdef** directive.

#ifdef

Preprocessor directive that checks to see if a macro name is defined. If defined, the code following it is included in the source.

#ifndef

Preprocessor directive that checks to see if a macro name is undefined. If undefined, the code following it is included in the macro expansion.

#include

A preprocessor directive that causes the named file to be inserted in place of the **#include**.

#undef

A preprocessor directive that cancels a **#define**.

_ptr

A convention used in this book. All pointer variables end with the extension _ptr.

Accuracy

A quantitative measurement of the error inherent in the representation of a real number.

Address

A value that identifies a storage location in memory.

and

A Boolean operation that yields 0 if either operand is 0, and 1 if both operands are 1.

ANSI-C

Any version of C that conforms to the specifications of the American National Standards Institute committee X3J.

ANSI-C++

Any version of C++ that conforms to the specification of the American National Standards Institute. At the time of this writing, the standards exist only in draft form and a lot of details must still be worked out.

API

Application Programming Interface. A set of function calls provided by a system to programmers. Frequently used in context with MS-DOS/Windows programming.

Archive

See *library.*

Array

A collection of data elements arranged to be indexed in one or more dimensions. In C, arrays are stored in contiguous memory.

ASCII

American Standard Code for Information Interchange. A code to represent characters.

Assignment statement

An operation that stores a value in a variable.

auto

A C keyword used to create temporary variables. Rarely used because, by default, variables are considered automatic.

Automatic variable

See *temporary variable.*

Base

See *radix.*

Bit

Binary digit; either of the digits 0 or 1.

Bit field

A group of contiguous bits taken together as a unit. A C language feature that allows the access of individual bits.

Bit flip

The inversion of all bits in an operand. See complement.

Bit-mapped graphics

Computer graphics where each pixel in the graphic output device is controlled by a single bit or a group of bits.

Bit operators

See *bitwise operator.*

Bitwise operator

An operator that performs Boolean operations on two operands treating each bit in an operand as individual bits, and performing the operation bit by bit on corresponding bits.

Block

A section of code enclosed in curly braces.

Boolean

An operation or value that can return either a true or false result.

Borland C++

A version of the C++ language for personal computers developed by Borland. This is the high-end version of Borland's Turbo C++ product. This product will handle both C and C++ code.

Boxing (a comment)

The technique of using a combination of asterisks, vertical and horizontal rules, and other typographic characters to draw a box around a comment in order to set it off from the code.

break

A statement that terminates the innermost execution of **for, while, switch,** and **do/while** statements.

Breakpoint

A location in a program where normal execution is suspended and control is turned over to the debugger.

Buffered I/O

Input/Output where intermediate storage (a buffer) is used between the source and destination of an I/O stream.

Byte

A group of eight bits.

C

A general-purpose computer programming language developed in 1974 at Bell Laboratories by Dennis Ritchie. C is considered to be a medium-to-high-level language.

C++

A language based on C invented in 1980 by Bjarne Stroustrup. First called "C with classes," it has evolved into its own language.

C code

Computer instructions written in the C language.

C compiler

Software that translates C source code into machine code.

C syntax.

See *syntax.*

Call by value

A procedure call in which the parameters are passed by passing the values of the parameters.

case

Acts as a label for one of the alternatives in a **switch** statement.

Cast

To convert a variable from one type to another type by explicitly indicating the type conversion.

CGA

Color graphics adaptor. A common color graphics card for the IBM PC.

char

A C keyword used to declare variables that represent characters or small integers.

Class (of a variable)

See *storage class.*

Clear a bit

The operation of setting an individual bit to zero. This operation is not a defined operation in C.

Code design

A document that describes in general terms how the program is to perform its function.

Coding

The act of writing a program in a computer language.

Command-line options

Options to direct the course of a program such as a compiler, entered from the computer console.

Comment

Text included in a computer program for the sole purpose of providing information about the program. Comments are a programmer's notes to himself and future programmers. The text is ignored by the compiler.

Comment block

A group of related comments that convey general information about a program or a section of program.

Compilation

The translation of source code into machine code.

Compiler

A system program that does compilation.

Complement

An arithmetic or logical operation. A logical complement is the same as an INVERT or NOT operation.

Computer language

See *programming language.*

Conditional compilation

The ability to selectively compile parts of a program based on the truth of conditions tested in conditional directives that surround the code.

continue

A flow control statement that causes the next execution of a loop to begin.

Control statements

A statement that determines which statement is to be executed next based on a conditional test.

Control variable

A variable that is systematically changed during the execution of the loop. When the variable reaches a predetermined value, the loop is terminated.

Conversion specification

A C string used by the *printf* family of functions to specify how a variable is to be printed.

Curly braces

One of the characters { or }. They are used in C to delimit groups of elements to treat them as a unit.

Debugging

The process of finding and removing errors from a program.

Decision statement

A statement that tests a condition created by a program and changes the flow of the program based on that decision.

Declaration

A specification of the type and name of a variable to be used in a program.

default

Serves as a case label if no case value match is found within the scope of a **switch**.

Define statement

See **#define**.

Dereferencing operator

The operator that indicates access to the value pointed to by a pointer variable or an addressing expression. See also *****.

Directive

A command to the preprocessor (as opposed to a statement to produce machine code).

double

A C language key word used to declare a variable that contains a real number. The number usually requires twice as much storage as type **float**.

Double linked list

A linked list with both forward and backward pointers. See also *linked list*.

Double quote (")

ASCII character 34. Used in C to delimit character strings.

EGA

Enhanced Graphics Adaptor. A common graphics card for the IBM PC.

else

A clause in an **if** statement specifying the action to take in the event that the statement following the **if** conditional is false.

enum

A C keyword that defines an enumeration data type.

Enumerated data type

A data type consisting of a named set of values. The C compiler assigns an integer to each member of the set.

EOF

End-of-file character defined in *stdio.h*.

Escape character

A special character used to change the meaning of the character(s) that follow. This character is represented in C by the backslash character \.

Exclusive OR

A Boolean operation that yields 0 if both operands are the same and 1 if they are different.

Executable file

A file containing machine code that has been linked and is ready to be run on a computer.

Exponent

The component of a floating-point number that represents the integer power to which the number base is raised.

Exponent overflow

A condition resulting from a floating-point operation in which the result is an exponent too large to fit within the bit field allotted to the exponent.

Exponent underflow

A condition resulting from a floating-point operation in which the result is an exponent too large in negative value to fit within the bit field allotted to the exponent.

extern

C keyword used to indicate that a variable or function is defined outside the current file.

Fast prototyping

A top-down programming technique that consists of writing the smallest portion of a specification that can be implemented and still do something.

fclose

A function that closes a file.

fflush

A routine that forces the flushing of a buffer.

fgetc

A function that reads a single character.

fgets

A stream input library function that reads a single line.

FILE

A macro definition in *stdio.h* that declares a file variable.

File

A group of related records treated as a unit.

float

A C keyword to declare a variable that can hold a real number.

Floating point

A numbering system represented by a fraction and an exponent. The system handles very large and very small numbers.

Floating-point exception (core dumped)

An error caused by a divide by 0 or other illegal arithmetic operation. The exception is a somewhat misleading error because it is caused by integer as well as floating-point errors.

Floating-point hardware

Circuitry that can perform floating-point operations directly without resorting to software. In personal computers, the circuitry is found in the math coprocessor. More advanced processors such as the 80486 have floating-point units built in.

`fopen`

A function that opens a file for stream I/O.

`fprintf`

A function that converts binary data to character data and then writes the data to a file.

`fputc`

A function that writes a single character.

`fputs`

A function that writes a single line.

`fread`

A binary I/O input function.

`free`

A C function that returns data to the memory pool.

Free Software Foundation

A group of programmers who create and distribute high-quality software for free. Among their products are the editor *emacs* and the C compiler *gcc*: Free Software Foundation, Inc., 675 Mass Ave., Cambridge, MA 02139 (617) 876-3296. Their ftp site is *prep.ai.mit.edu:/pub/gnu*. They can be found on the World Wide Web at *http://www.gnu.org*.

`fscanf`

An input routine similar to `scanf` that reads from a file.

function

A procedure that returns a value.

fwrite

A binary I/O output function.

Generic pointer

A pointer that can point to any variable without restriction as to type of variable. A pointer to storage without regard to content.

ghostscript

A PostScript(TM)-like interpreter that is freely available from the Free Software Foundation.

Global variable

A variable known throughout an entire program.

Guard digit

An extra digit of precision used in floating-point calculations to ensure against loss of accuracy.

Header file

See *Include file.*

Heap

A portion of memory used by *malloc* to allocate space to new structures and arrays. Space is returned to this pool by using the *free* function.

Hexadecimal number

A base-16 number.

High-level language

A level of computer language that is between machine language and natural (human) language.

I/O manipulators

Functions that when "output" or "input" cause no I/O, but set various conversion flags or parameters.

IEEE floating-point standard

IEEE standard 754, which standardizes floating-point format, precision, and certain non-numerical values.

if

A statement that allows selective execution of parts of a program based on the truth of a condition.

Implementation dependence

The situation in which the result obtained from the operation of computer or software is not standardized because of variability among computer systems. A particular operation may yield different results when run on another system.

include file

A file that is merged with source code by invocation of the preprocessor directive #**include**. Also called a header file.

Inclusive OR

See *OR*.

Index

A value, variable, or expression that selects a particular element of an array.

Indirect operator

See *dereferencing operator.*

Information hiding

A code design system that tries to minimize the amount of information that is passed between modules. The idea is to keep as much information as possible hidden inside the modules and only make information public if absolutely necessary.

Instruction

A group of bits or characters that defines an operation to be performed by the computer.

int

C keyword for declaring an integer.

Integer

A whole number.

Interactive debugger

A program that aids in the debugging of programs.

Invert operator

A logical operator that performs a not.

Left shift

The operation of moving the bits in a bit field left by a specified amount and filling the vacated positions with 0s.

Library

A collection of files usually containing object code for linking into programs. Also called an archive.

Linked list

A collection of data nodes. Each node consists of a value and a pointer to the next item in the list.

Local include files

Files from a private library that can be inserted by the preprocessor at the directive #**include** `"filename"`.

Local variable

A variable whose scope is limited to the block in which it is declared.

Logical AND

A Boolean operation that returns true if its two arguments are both true.

Logical operator

A C operator that performs a logical operation on its two operands and returns a true or a false value.

Logical OR

A Boolean operation that returns true if any one of its two arguments are true.

long

A qualifier to specify a data type with greater-than-normal range.

Machine code

Machine instructions in a binary format that can be recognized directly by the machine without further translation.

Machine language

See *machine code.*

Macro

A short piece of text, or text template, that can be expanded into a longer text.

Macro processor

A program that generates code by placing values into positions in a defined template.

Magnitude of the number

The value of a number without regard to sign.

Maintenance (of a program)

Modification of a program because of changing conditions external to the computer system.

`make`

A utility in both UNIX and MS-DOS/Windows that manages the compilation of programs.

Makefile

The file that contains the commands for the utility make.

`malloc`

A C procedure that manages a memory heap.

Mask

A pattern of bits for controlling the retention or elimination of another group of bits.

member

> An element of structure. Also called a field.

Module

> One logical part of a program.

MS-DOS

> An operating system for IBM personal computers developed by Microsoft.

Newline character

> A character that causes an output device to go to the beginning of a new line. ('\n').

Nonsignificant digits

> Leading digits that do not affect the value of a number (0s for a positive number, 1s for a negative number in complement form).

Normalization

> The shifting of a floating-point fraction (and adjustment of the exponent) so that there are no leading nonsignificant digits in the fraction.

NOT

> A Boolean operation that yields the logical inverse of the operand. Not 1 yields a 0, not 0 yields a 1.

Not a number

> A special value defined in IEEE 754 to signal an invalid result from a floating-point operation.

NULL

> A constant of value 0 that points to nothing.

Null pointer

> A pointer whose bit pattern is all zeroes. This pattern indicates that the pointer does not point to valid data.

Object-Oriented Design

> A design methodology by which the programmer bases a design on data objects (classes) and the connections between them. Not used much for C programs, but better suited to the C++ language.

Octal number

> A base 8 number.

Ones complement

> An operation that flips all the bits in a integer. Ones become zeroes and zeroes become ones.

Operator

> A symbol that represents an action to be performed.

OR

A Boolean operation that yields a 1 if either of the operands is a 1, or yields a zero if both of the operands are 0.

Overflow error

An arithmetic error caused by the result of an arithmetic operation's being greater than the space the computer provides to store the result.

Packed structure

A data structure technique whereby bit fields are only as large as needed, regardless of word boundaries.

Pad byte

A byte added to a structure whose sole purpose is to ensure memory alignment.

Parameter

A data item to which a value may be assigned. Often means the arguments that are passed between a caller and a called procedure.

Parameterized macro

A macro consisting of a template with insertion points for the introduction of parameters.

Parameters of a macro

The values to be inserted into the parameter positions in the definition of a macro. The insertion occurs during the expansion of the macro.

Permanent variables

A variable that is created and initialized before the program starts, and that retains its memory during the entire execution of the program.

Pixel

The smallest element of a display that can be individually assigned intensity and color. From **Picture Element**.

Pointer

A data type that holds the address of a location in memory.

Pointer arithmetic

C allows three arithmetic operations on pointers. 1) A numeric value can be added to a pointer. 2) A numeric value can be subtracted from a pointer. 3) One pointer can be subtracted from another pointer.

Portable C compiler

A C compiler written by Stephen Johnson that is easily adapted to different computer architectures.

Precision

A measure of the ability to distinguish between nearly equal values.

Preprocessor

A program that performs preliminary processing with the purpose of expanding macro code templates to produce C code.

Preprocessor directive

A command to the preprocessor.

`printf`

A C library routine that produces formatted output.

Procedure

A program segment that can be invoked from different parts of a program or programs. It does not return a value (function of type **void**).

Program

A group of instructions that cause a computer to perform a sequence of operations.

Program header

The comment block at the beginning of the program.

Programmer

An individual who writes programs for a computer.

Programming (a computer)

The process of expressing the solution to a problem in a language that represents instructions for a computer.

Programming language

A scheme of formal notation used to prepare computer programs.

Program specification

A written document that states what a program is to do.

Pseudo code

A coding technique by which precise descriptions of procedures are written in easy-to-read language constructs without the bother of precise attention to syntax rules of a computer language.

Qualifier

A word used to modify the meaning of a data declaration.

Radix

The positive integer by which the weight of the digit place is multiplied to obtain the weight of the next higher digit in the base of the numbering system.

Real number

A number that may be represented by a finite or infinite numeral in a fixed-radix numbering system.

Recursion

Recursion occurs when a function calls itself directly or indirectly. (For a recursive definition, see *Recursion*).

Redirect

The command-line option "*>file*" allows the user to direct the output of a program into a file instead of the screen. A similar option, *<file*, exists for input, taking input from the file instead of the keyboard.

Reduction in strength

The process of substituting cheap (fast) operations for expensive (slow) ones.

Relational operator

An operator that compares two operands and reports either true or false based on whether the relationship is true or false.

Release

The completion of a programming project to the point at which it is ready for general use.

Replay file

A file that is used instead of the standard input for keyboard data.

Return statement

A statement that signals the completion of a function and causes control to return to the caller.

Revision

The addition of significant changes to the program.

Right shift

The operation of moving the bits in a bit field right by a specified amount.

Round

To delete or omit one or more of the least significant digits in a positional representation and adjust the part retained in accordance with some specific rule, e.g., to minimize the error.

Rounding error

An error due to truncation in rounding.

Save file

A debugging tool with which all the keystrokes typed by the user are saved in a file for future use. See also *Replay file*.

scanf

A library input function that reads numbers directly from the keyboard. Hard to use. In most cases a *fgets*/*sscanf* combination is used.

Scope

The portion of a program in which the name of the variable is known.

Segmentation violation

An error caused by a program trying to access memory outside its address space. Caused by dereferencing a bad pointer.

Set a bit

The operation of setting a specified bit to one. This operation is not a defined operation in C.

Shift

The operation of moving the bits in a bit field either left or right.

short

An arithmetic data type that is the same size, or smaller, than an integer.

Side effect

An operation performed in addition to the main operation of a statement such as incrementing a variable in an assignment statement: `result = begin++-end;`.

Significand

The most significant digits of a floating-point number without regard to placement of the radix point.

Significant digits

A digit that must be kept to preserve a given accuracy.

Single quote (')

ASCII character 39. Used in C to delimit a single character.

sizeof

Operator that returns the size, in bytes, of a data type of variable.

Source code

Symbolic coding in its original form before being translated by a computer.

Source file

A file containing source code.

Specification

A document that describes what the program does.

`sprintf`

Similar to `fprintf` except that it uses a string output.

`sscanf`

A library input routine.

Stack

An area of memory used to hold a list of data and instructions on a temporary basis.

Stack variable

See *Temporary variable.*

Stack overflow

An error caused by a program using too much temporary space (stack space) for its variables. Caused by a big program or by infinite recursion.

static

A storage class attribute. Inside a set of curly braces, it indicates a permanent variable. Outside a set of curly braces, it indicates a file-local variable.

stderr

Predefined standard error file.

stdin

Predefined input source.

stdio.h

The C standard I/O package.

stdout

Predefined standard output.

Storage class

An attribute of a variable definition that controls how the variable will be stored in memory.

String

A sequence or array of characters.

struct

A C keyword that identifies a structure data type.

Structure

A hierarchical set of names that refers to an aggregate of data items that may have different attributes.

Style sheet

A document that describes the style of programming used by a particular company or institution.

Sunview

A graphics and windowing system available on SUN workstations.

switch

A multiway branch that transfers control to one of several case statements based on the value of an index expression.

Syntax

Rules that govern the construction of statements.

Syntax error

An error in the proper construction of a C expression.

Temporary variable

A variable whose storage is allocated from the stack. It is initialized each time the block in which it is defined is entered. It exists only during the execution of that block.

Test a bit

The operation of determining if a particular bit is set. This operation is not defined in C.

Test plan

A specification of the tests that a program must undergo.

Text editor

Software used to create or alter text files.

Translation

Creation of a new program in an alternate language logically equivalent to an existing program in a source language.

Tree

A hierarchical data structure.

Truncation

An operation on a real number whereby any fractional part is discarded.

Turbo C++

A version of the C++ language for personal computers developed by Borland.

Typecast

See *Cast*.

typedef

A operator used to create new types from existing types.

typing statement

A statement that establishes the characteristics of a variable.

Unbuffered I/O

Each read or write results in a system call.

union

A data type that allows different data names and data types to be assigned to the same storage location.

UNIX

A popular multiuser operating system first developed by Ken Thompson and Dennis Ritchie of the Bell Telephone Laboratories.

unsigned

A qualifier for specifying **int** and **char** variables that do not contain negative numbers.

Upgrading

Modification of a program to provide improved performance or new features.

value

A quantity assigned to a constant.

Variable

A name that refers to a value. The data represented by the variable name can, at different times during the execution of a program, assume different values.

Variable name

The symbolic name given to a section of memory used to store a variable.

Version

A term used to identify a particular edition of software. A customary practice is to include a version number. Whole numbers indicate major rewrites. Fractions indicate minor rewrites or corrections of problems.

void

A data type in C. When used as a parameter in a function call, it indicates that there is no return value. `void *` indicates that a generic pointer value is returned.

volatile

A C keyword that indicates that the value of a variable or constant can be changed at any time. This attribute is used for memory mapped I/O, shared memory applications, and other advanced programming.

while

An iterative statement that repeats a statement as long as a given condition is true.

Windows

Also knows as MS-Windows. An operating system developed for personal computers by Microsoft Corporation. Also a new operating system with a similar user interface and API such as Windows NT and Windows 95.

X Window System

A graphics and windowing system available from the X Consortium that is currently running on many computing systems.

Zero-based counting

A system of counting by which the first object is given the count zero rather than one.

Index

Symbols and Numbers

& (address of operator), 185
& (and operator), 158, 185
& vs. &&, 159
* operator (dereference), 185
!= operator (not equal), 85
^ (exclusive or), 158, 161
, operator (comma), 85, 346
{} (curly braces), 85
" (double quote), 60
-- operator (decrement), 78
= versus ==, 10, 91
== operator (equal), 85, 105, 382
<< (left shift), 158, 162
> operator (greater than), 85
-> operator (structure pointer), 287
>= operator (greater than or equal to), 85
>> (right shift), 158, 162
++ operator (increment), 78
+= operator (increase), 79
' (single quotes), 60
~ (complement operator), 158, 161
| (or operator), 158, 160

0 character, 64

A

abstract class, 356
accuracy, floating point, 269, 270
addition operator (+), 51
addition, floating point, 266
address of operator (&), 185

alignment restrictions, 339
ambiguous code, 86
and operator (&), 158
and portability, 338
argc, 201
argv, 201
array declarations, 7
arrays, 63, 181
    dimension of, 63
    elements of, 63
    index, 64
    infinite, 310, 313, 316
    initializing, 73
    multi-dimensional, 74
    and pointers, 189, 191
    of structures, 181
ASCII
    characters, 60
    files, 215–216
assembly language, 5
assignment statements, 8, 382
author, 40
auto, 130
automatic parameter changes, 194
automatic variables, 130

B

binary
    files, 215–216, 338
    I/O, 218
    mode for fopen (b), 216
    trees, 292

About the Author

Steve Oualline wrote his first program when he was eleven. It had a bug in it. Since that time he has studied practical ways of writing programs so that the risk of generating a bug is reduced. He currently works as a Software Engineer in Southern California. His spare time is spent on *real* engineering on a steam train at the Poway-Midland Railroad.

Colophon

Our look is the result of reader comments, our own experimentation, and distribution channels. Distinctive covers complement our distinctive approach to technical topics, breathing personality and life into potentially dry subjects. UNIX and its attendant programs can be unruly beasts. Nutshell Handbooks help you tame them.

The animal featured on the cover of Practical C Programming is a Jersey cow. The Jersey, one of the many breeds of modern cows, originated from a now extinct stock of wild cattle that inhabited western Asia, North Africa, and continental Europe. Cows were first introduced into the western hemisphere by Christopher Columbus on his second voyage in 1493.

Jerseys, bred on the British isle of Jersey since 1789, were first introduced to America in the 1850s. Smallest of the modern dairy cows, this fawn-colored beast typically weighs between 1000 and 1500 pounds. As a milk producer, Jerseys are the least prolific of any American dairy cow. However, their milk is creamier than that of any other breed.

Edie Freedman designed the cover of this book, using a 19th-century engraving from the Dover Pictorial Archive. The cover layout was produced with Quark XPress 3.32 using the ITC Garamond font.

The inside layout was designed by Nancy Priest and implemented in FrameMaker 5.0 by Mike Sierra. The text and heading fonts are ITC Garamond Light and Garamond Book. The illustrations that appear in the book were created in Macromedia Freehand 5.0 by Chris Reilley and updated by Robert Romano. This colophon was written by Michael Kalantarian.

Whenever possible, our books use RepKover[TM], a durable and flexible lay-flat binding. If the page count exceeds RepKover's limit, perfect binding is used.

How to stay in touch with O'Reilly

1. Visit Our Award-Winning Web Site
http://www.oreilly.com/

★ "Top 100 Sites on the Web" —*PC Magazine*
★ "Top 5% Web sites" —*Point Communications*
★ "3-Star site" —*The McKinley Group*

Our web site contains a library of comprehensive product information (including book excerpts and tables of contents), downloadable software, background articles, interviews with technology leaders, links to relevant sites, book cover art, and more. File us in your Bookmarks or Hotlist!

2. Join Our Email Mailing Lists
New Product Releases
To receive automatic email with brief descriptions of all new O'Reilly products as they are released, send email to:
ora-news-subscribe@lists.oreilly.com
Put the following information in the first line of your message (*not* in the Subject field):
subscribe ora-news

O'Reilly Events
If you'd also like us to send information about trade show events, special promotions, and other O'Reilly events, send email to:
ora-news-subscribe@lists.oreilly.com
Put the following information in the first line of your message (*not* in the Subject field):
subscribe ora-events

3. Get Examples from Our Books via FTP
There are two ways to access an archive of example files from our books:

Regular FTP
- ftp to:
  ftp.oreilly.com
  (login: anonymous
  password: your email address)
- Point your web browser to:
  ftp://ftp.oreilly.com/

FTPMAIL
- Send an email message to:
  ftpmail@online.oreilly.com
  (Write "help" in the message body)

4. Contact Us via Email
order@oreilly.com
To place a book or software order online. Good for North American and international customers.

subscriptions@oreilly.com
To place an order for any of our newsletters or periodicals.

books@oreilly.com
General questions about any of our books.

software@oreilly.com
For general questions and product information about our software. Check out O'Reilly Software Online at **http://software.oreilly.com/** for software and technical support information. Registered O'Reilly software users send your questions to: **website-support@oreilly.com**

cs@oreilly.com
For answers to problems regarding your order or our products.

booktech@oreilly.com
For book content technical questions or corrections.

proposals@oreilly.com
To submit new book or software proposals to our editors and product managers.

international@oreilly.com
For information about our international distributors or translation queries. For a list of our distributors outside of North America check out:
http://www.oreilly.com/distributors.html

5. Work with Us
Check out our website for current employment opportunites:
http://jobs.oreilly.com/

O'Reilly & Associates, Inc.
101 Morris Street, Sebastopol, CA 95472 USA
TEL   707-829-0515 or 800-998-9938
        (6am to 5pm PST)
FAX   707-829-0104

O'REILLY®
TO ORDER: **800-998-9938** • order@oreilly.com • http://www.oreilly.com/
OUR PRODUCTS ARE AVAILABLE AT A BOOKSTORE OR SOFTWARE STORE NEAR YOU.
FOR INFORMATION: **800-998-9938** • **707-829-0515** • info@oreilly.com

International Distributors

UK, EUROPE, MIDDLE EAST AND AFRICA (EXCEPT FRANCE, GERMANY, AUSTRIA, SWITZERLAND, LUXEMBOURG, AND LIECHTENSTEIN)

INQUIRIES

O'Reilly UK Limited
4 Castle Street
Farnham
Surrey, GU9 7HS
United Kingdom
Telephone: 44-1252-711776
Fax: 44-1252-734211
Email: information@oreilly.co.uk

ORDERS

Wiley Distribution Services Ltd.
1 Oldlands Way
Bognor Regis
West Sussex PO22 9SA
United Kingdom
Telephone: 44-1243-843294
UK Freephone: 0800-243207
Fax: 44-1243-843302 (Europe/EU orders)
or 44-1243-843274 (Middle East/Africa)
Email: cs-books@wiley.co.uk

FRANCE

INQUIRIES & ORDERS

Éditions O'Reilly
18 rue Séguier
75006 Paris, France
Tel: 1-40-51-71-89
Fax: 1-40-51-72-26
Email: france@oreilly.fr

GERMANY, SWITZERLAND, AUSTRIA, LUXEMBOURG, AND LIECHTENSTEIN

INQUIRIES & ORDERS

O'Reilly Verlag
Balthasarstr. 81
D-50670 Köln, Germany
Telephone: 49-221-973160-91
Fax: 49-221-973160-8
Email: anfragen@oreilly.de (inquiries)
Email: order@oreilly.de (orders)

CANADA (FRENCH LANGUAGE BOOKS)

Les Éditions Flammarion ltée
375, Avenue Laurier Ouest
Montréal (Québec) H2V 2K3
Tel: 00-1-514-277-8807
Fax: 00-1-514-278-2085
Email: info@flammarion.qc.ca

HONG KONG

City Discount Subscription Service, Ltd.
Unit A, 6th Floor, Yan's Tower
27 Wong Chuk Hang Road
Aberdeen, Hong Kong
Tel: 852-2580-3539
Fax: 852-2580-6463
Email: citydis@ppn.com.hk

KOREA

Hanbit Media, Inc.
Chungmu Bldg. 210
Yonnam-dong 568-33
Mapo-gu
Seoul, Korea
Tel: 822-325-0397
Fax: 822-325-9697
Email: hant93@chollian.dacom.co.kr

PHILIPPINES

Global Publishing
G/F Benavides Garden
1186 Benavides Street
Manila, Philippines
Tel: 632-254-8949/632-252-2582
Fax: 632-734-5060/632-252-2733
Email: globalp@pacific.net.ph

TAIWAN

O'Reilly Taiwan
1st Floor, No. 21, Lane 295
Section 1, Fu-Shing South Road
Taipei, 106 Taiwan
Tel: 886-2-27099669
Fax: 886-2-27038802
Email: mori@oreilly.com

INDIA

Shroff Publishers & Distributors Pvt. Ltd.
12, "Roseland", 2nd Floor
180, Waterfield Road, Bandra (West)
Mumbai 400 050
Tel: 91-22-641-1800/643-9910
Fax: 91-22-643-2422
Email: spd@vsnl.com

CHINA

O'Reilly Beijing
SIGMA Building, Suite B809
No. 49 Zhichun Road
Haidian District
Beijing, China PR 100080
Tel: 86-10-8809-7475
Fax: 86-10-8809-7463
Email: beijing@oreilly.com

JAPAN

O'Reilly Japan, Inc.
Yotsuya Y's Building
7 Banch 6, Honshio-cho
Shinjuku-ku
Tokyo 160-0003 Japan
Tel: 81-3-3356-5227
Fax: 81-3-3356-5261
Email: japan@oreilly.com

SINGAPORE, INDONESIA, MALAYSIA AND THAILAND

TransQuest Publishers Pte Ltd
30 Old Toh Tuck Road #05-02
Sembawang Kimtrans Logistics Centre
Singapore 597654
Tel: 65-4623112
Fax: 65-4625761
Email: wendiw@transquest.com.sg

ALL OTHER ASIAN COUNTRIES

O'Reilly & Associates, Inc.
101 Morris Street
Sebastopol, CA 95472 USA
Tel: 707-829-0515
Fax: 707-829-0104
Email: order@oreilly.com

AUSTRALIA

Woodslane Pty., Ltd.
7/5 Vuko Place
Warriewood NSW 2102
Australia
Tel: 61-2-9970-5111
Fax: 61-2-9970-5002
Email: info@woodslane.com.au

NEW ZEALAND

Woodslane New Zealand, Ltd.
21 Cooks Street (P.O. Box 575)
Waganui, New Zealand
Tel: 64-6-347-6543
Fax: 64-6-345-4840
Email: info@woodslane.com.au

ARGENTINA

Distribuidora Cuspide
Suipacha 764
1008 Buenos Aires
Argentina
Phone: 5411-4322-8868
Fax: 5411-4322-3456
Email: libros@cuspide.com

O'REILLY®